W9-ADA-962

PSYCHOLOGICAL STRESS
and
PSYCHOPATHOLOGY

Edited by Richard W. J. Neufeld, Ph.D.

Foreword by Hans Selye, M.D.

McGRAW-HILL BOOK COMPANY

New York   St. Louis   San Francisco
Auckland   Bogotá   Hamburg   Johannesburg   London   Madrid
Mexico   Montreal   New Delhi   Panama   Paris   São Paulo
Singapore   Sydney   Tokyo   Toronto

Thomas H. Quinn, Lawrence Apple, Michael Hennelly, and Cheryl Kupper were the editors of this book. Christopher Simon was the designer. Paul Malchow supervised the production. It was set in Times Roman by University Graphics, Inc.
Printed and bound by R. R. Donnelley and Sons, Inc.

Library of Congress Cataloging in Publication Data
Main entry under title:

Psychological stress and psychopathology.

  Bibliography: p.
  Includes index.
  1. Psychology, Pathological.   2. Stress (Psychology)
I. Neufeld, Richard W. J. [DNLM: 1. Stress, Phycholog-
ical—Complications.   2. Mental disorders—Etiology.
3. Mental disorders—Therapy. WM 172 P9743]
RC455.4.S87P79   616.89   81-15556
ISBN 0-07-046309-3   AACR2

ISBN 0-07-046309-3

1 2 3 4 5 6 7 8 9 DODO 8 9 7 6 5 4 3 2

Contents

☐ **Contents**

Part III

THEORY AND RESEARCH ON STRESS BEARING ON PSYCHOPATHOLOGY

Part IV

TREATMENT INTERVENTIONS DIRECTED TOWARD STRESS-RELEVANT PORTIONS OF DISTURBED BEHAVIOR AND EXPERIENCE

Foreword

Dr. Richard W. J. Neufeld has put together a fine anthology on the question of the relations between psychogenic stress and mental disorders, one of the most promising areas of research in medicine today. It may be useful here to discuss some of the connections which have struck me as especially intriguing.

The importance of the adaptive process in nervous and psychic disease is now part of common knowledge. Such expressions as "This work gives me a headache" or "drives me crazy," have their basis in experience. Many types of migraine headaches or mental breakdowns are actually caused by work to which we are ill-adapted. Heredity can doubtless predispose to certain types of mental disease, but there are imperceptible transitions between the healthy, the slightly disturbed, and the insane personality. In people with a defective hereditary structure, it is often the stress of adjustments to life under difficult circumstances that causes a change from healthy to disturbed, or from disturbed to insane. Conversely, a sudden stress (shock therapy) can help a person to snap out of an abnormal behavior pattern.

Though I am not competent to discuss this from the psychiatrist's point of view, as an endocrinologist and a student of stress I have naturally been interested in exploring whether or not there are any demonstrable relationships between abnormal mental reactions and the objectively measurable features of the general adaptation syndrome (G.A.S.).

Here are a few of the more outstanding facts which have come to light:

• *Various species, including man, can be anesthetized with hormones.* Investigators at Ohio State University showed that sleep can be produced in women quite regularly by giving them progesterone. A group of California physicians successfully anesthetized people for surgical operations with hydroxidione. This compound has many advantages over other agents for this purpose. The anesthesia it induces appears to be very similar to natural sleep from which the patients awake mentally alert and fresh, without some of the unpleasant after-effects of other preparations.

• *Adaptive hormones can combat convulsions.* In rats in which I had produced epilepsy-like convulsions with certain stimulants (Metrazol, picrotoxin), Desoxycorticosterone (DOC) and related hormones acted as tranquilizers. Dr. D. M. Woodbury and his associates at the University of Utah discovered that if such convulsions are produced with electric current, their intensity could be diminished by DOC and augmented by Cortisol (COL). This was the first indication of an actual antagonism between anti- and proinflammatory hormones as regards a nervous manifestation. Quite recently a derivative of DOC and of the previously mentioned anesthetic hormones, named Pancuronium, has been synthesized and is currently in clinical use, especially as a muscle relaxant.

• *Under certain conditions an excess of DOC can produce brain lesions such as are often seen in old people.* When blood vessel damage is produced in rats by DOC poisoning, and when the arteries of the brain are involved, the animals can suffer a stroke or even repeated strokes, which eventually destroy large parts of the brain and cause widespread nervous derangements. Interestingly, such rats become extremely irritable and aggressive, a change quite characteristic of certain senile mental derangements among people whose brains often show the same kind of destruction.

• *Adaptive hormones can cause mental changes in man.* Many patients who take Adrenochorticosterone (ACTH) or COL first develop a sense of extraordinary well-being and buoyancy, with excitement and insomnia; this is sometimes followed by a depression which may go so far as to create suicidal tendencies. In hereditarily predisposed people, profound mental derangements may result, although fortunately, these are rare and always disappear when the hormone treatment is interrupted.

Many problems related to this phenomenon remain unsolved. Certain breakdown products of adrenaline can cause hallucinations. Could excessive adrenaline secretion during stress play a part in the production of mental changes, for instance, in patients who become delirious as a result of high fever or after burns?

• *Perhaps adaptive hormones may even be used as tranquilizing agents in mental patients.* In chronic alcoholics, there sometimes develops a delirium characterized by terrifying hallucinations, great excitement, and trembling. This is known as *delirium tremens.* Preliminary observations of the French surgeon H. Laborit suggest that sometimes hydroxydione, the anesthetic DOC derivative, has a strikingly beneficial effect upon this condition. This type of treatment is far from giving reliable results, but it does raise the question of a possible causal relationship between adaptive hormones and certain delirious conditions in mentally deranged people.

The tranquilizing agents chlorpromazine and reserpine, which are now so effectively employed in psychiatry, resemble in many of their actions the tranquilizing DOC derivatives. Could hormones be used in the treatment of confused and disturbed mental patients?

• *DOC-like hormones can cause spells of periodic paralysis.* There is a rare hereditary disease which runs in families and tends to produce sudden spells of paralysis. It is called periodic familial paralysis and—apart from the fact that the predisposition to it is hereditary—very little is known about its cause. Interestingly, very similar spells of paralysis occur in patients in whom an adrenal tumor produces an excess of the DOC-like aldosterone. It is very probable that DOC-like mineralocorticoids have something to do with this condition. Many years ago a group of researchers at

Columbia University in New York had discovered quite similar paralytic spells in dogs treated with DOC. Later Dr. C. E. Hall and I found that, in the DOC-treated animal, attacks can be precipitated and cured at will, merely by giving or withdrawing dietary sodium chloride. In monkeys the paralysis was often accompanied by intense or epilepsy-like attacks of convulsions. Obviously here again we are dealing with nervous derangements produced by DOC, and again these disturbances are aggravated by sodium chloride, just as the changes which the same hormone produces in the kidney and in the cardiovascular system. Is there a causal relationship here?

The many question marks above eloquently show how little we know and how much must still be learned. But they also indicate the ways in which we are using the stress concept as a guide to the study of the intriguing and mysterious borderline between mind and body. Dr. Neufeld's compilation, for all its variety of topic and approach—or perhaps because of it—is a good example of the kind of continuing effort needed to answer such questions.

Hans Selye, M.D.
President
International Institute of Stress
Montreal, Quebec, Canada

INTRODUCTION

RICHARD W. J. NEUFELD

The main purpose of the editor's introduction is not to brief the reader on the content to follow. Such briefing typically aims at stimulating interest. The topics of the present contributions, however, seem sufficiently compelling to make interest-provoking overtures redundant. Instead, this introduction "sets the stage" and alerts the reader to certain issues and distinctions on psychological stress and psychopathology which tend to recur throughout the volume.

The Construct of Stress

With regard to the topic at hand, the "dilemma" of no single consensual definition of stress, lamented in symposia over a decade ago (e.g., Appley & Trumbull, 1967), has not been resolved. Surveys of the "working" definitions in research reports, as well as attempts at formal definition, strongly suggest that *stress* be treated as a "construct" in the following sense. While a satisfactorily comprehensive definition is not forthcoming, recurrent association between the term and certain characteristics of environmental events and organismic effects support its use as a short-hand referent for expediting research and scholarly communication. Lack of precise formal definition invariably risks inaccuracies; the correct inferences and connotations invoked by the term, however, appear to outweigh such "risks." Furthermore, illustrations of now relatively well-defined concepts which emerged as such only after considerable scientific enquiry under interim circumstances (when these concepts were less well defined) are quite plentiful (see Braithwaite, 1961).

Use of any construct implies several properties. Among them are the following (Chronbach & Meehl, 1955): (a) implicitness of definition derived from its characteristic context(s) of usage; (b) tentativeness of indexes of variation in the construct; (c) multiplicity of sources of evidence for the presence-absence of the construct; (d) multiplicity of approaches to quantifying the operation of the construct.

Paralleling somewhat the "formal-single definition versus construct" distinction has been the distinction of "theoretical terms versus chapter-heading terms" (Mandler, 1962):

Chapter-heading terms—and emotion is one of them—do no more than collect under one rubric what are believed to be related phenomena, experiments, and observations. What is the basis of this belief? The collection of these instances has no clearly definable boundaries; it arises historically and empirically, with the structure of the boundaries rarely spelled out and, most frequently, appreciated intuitively. In our common everyday language, we somehow know in general what emotions are, in the same sense that we appreciate words like *morality, the farm problem, bad weather, culture,* and even *animal.* When pressed we can, in the common language, give some boundary conditions for the use of these words, but we cannot find a definition with which we feel quite comfortable. At least we can supply a list of characteristics, relevant behavior, and so forth (pp. 276–277).

In the present instance, the list of characteristics, relevant behaviors, and so forth, takes the form of a list of properties put forth in several formal and ad hoc descriptions of stress:

1. Stress is the state manifested by a specific syndrome which consists of all the nonspecifically induced changes within a biologic system (Selye, 1978);

2. It carries a threat to well being and involves undesirable emotions (Lazarus, 1975; Lazarus & Launier, 1978);

3. It implies environmental demands of a physical or social nature (McGrath, 1970);

4. It occurs under conditions of personal deficit—when environmental demands exceed individual supply—or under personal frustration—when an individual's resources find insufficient environmental outlet (French, Rogers, & Cobb, 1974);

5. It is the variation of an output beyond its normal limits, invoking an unfavorable balance between activation and information-processing capacity with respect to "attentional bandwidth" (Teichner, 1968);

6. It expresses itself in factor-analytically identified ACTH-related response patterns as well as a personality dimension involving mobilization to face the challenge of adaptation stress versus leaving an unsolved problem in withdrawal and retreat (Cattell & Scheier, 1961);

7. It includes multidimensional subjective experiences characterized by "ego threat," "pain," "threat of punishment," "inanimate threat," "guilt," and so on (Ekehammar & Magnusson, 1973; Hodges & Felling, 1970; Magnusson & Ekehammar, 1975; Neufeld, 1978).

In addition to the preceding list, rather specific operations such as inescapable pain stimulation have been put forth in the literature on animal experimentation (see Anisman & Lapierre, pp. 179–217, this volume); "exit" and "entry" types of events have been advanced as rather circumscribed sources of human stress (referred to in Costello, pp. 93–124, this volume); and "stress proneness," at least in the form of "susceptibility to depression," has been associated with a somewhat specific constellation of subjective attributions (see Miller & Seligman, pp. 149–178, this volume).

As compared to the construct approach, narrower orientations such as translating stress into "a psychophysics of environmental demands" (McGrath, 1970) seem to have been far too restrictive for the richness of the concept (e.g., Neufeld, 1972).

Consequences of Stress

Students of consequences of stress have typically placed emphasis on either biological or psychological-behavioral variables. The former emphasis is illustrated by the mapping of biochemical and neurological correlates of stress (e.g., Anisman & Lapierre; Essman, pp. 273–288, this volume; Selyé, 1971); the latter, by the study of behavioral and cognitive events, some of which reflect "disruption" and some of which represent either "automatic-passive" or "controlled-deliberate" counterstress reactions (e.g., most notably the work of Lazarus and his colleagues, see pp. 218–239, this volume). The principal criterion for including material in this work is that whatever other aspects of subject matter are emphasized, some immediate bearing on the expression of stress in the form of psychopathology exists.

A rather vivid example of this criterion appears when we compare biochemical and psychophysiological work on schizophrenia. Recently, there has been considerable interest in "endogenous morphines" (endorphins), anomalies in dopaminergic neural activity, as well as in their interconnections in schizophrenia (see Davis, Buchbaum, & Bunney, 1979; Volavka, Davis, & Ehrlich, 1979; Watson & Akil, 1979). Other work—most notably that of Mednick and his coworkers (e.g., Mednick et al., 1974)—has focused on psychophysiological indices of anomalous autonomic nervous system (ANS) activity. To date, the latter may or may not have received as intensive investigation as the biochemical work; but unlike the biochemical work, certain aspects of schizophrenic symptomatology are expressly seen as the patient's resolution of elevated levels of episodic stress.

With respect to psychopathology, eligible subject matter ranges from "intractable personal distress" to "loss of reality contact." Extreme deviation from "normative behavior," or extreme statistical infrequency, is a relevant concept with the following qualification: to separate out intentional eccentricities, cases where the deviant individual is apparently both cognizant of the anomaly and maintains it voluntarily are excluded.

An important distinction in the types of symptoms consequential to stress include "positive" and "negative" symptoms. Positive symptoms represent the replacement of normal processes and functions with others; for example, some symptoms of paranoid schizophrenia may be viewed as "overcontrol and excessive denial of vulnerability to day-to-day stress" (Shean, pp. 55–66, this volume). Negative symptoms simply reflect some erosion of normal abilities and functions; certain forms of behavioral impoverishment associated with depression fall into this category. Interestingly, negative symptoms at one level of analysis may be associated with either negative or positive symptomatology at another level of analysis. The case of behavioral impoverishment just mentioned has been theoretically linked to loss of certain neurochemical functions on the one hand (see Anisman & Lapierre, this volume) but also to the active involvement of unusual cognitive attributions on the other (Miller & Seligman, this volume).

Degrees of Belief in Relations Among Variables

The advantages of multiple contributions to a given topic include expertise in multiple content areas, availability of different levels of analysis of the topic, and the potential inferences available from one approach with respect to other approaches.

A case of reciprocal implications exists where two avenues of study mutually affect credibility of each other's findings. Consider research directed toward documenting the strength and pattern of association between certain types of stressful events and certain types of psychopathology. Three sources of information come to mind when establishing one's degree of belief in a particular association:

1. Values of numerical coefficients which indicate the size of empirical associations;
2. Methodological rigour in establishing these coefficients;
3. Viability of candidate mechanisms mediating the associations.

For example, the reader might formulate his/her impression of the importance of stress in schizophrenia and in depression according to sources 1 and 2 after consulting the chapters by Spring and Coons, and by Costello; consulting the remaining chapters on these classes of psychopathology would contribute to source 3.

The degree of belief in hypothesized mechanisms mediating stress and psychopathology is subject to similar considerations. These include methodological exactness and strength of results from studies addressed toward mediating mechanisms, as well as the strength of empirical correlations between the stressing agent and the symptomatology which the mechanisms are suspected of mediating.

Interplay of Sources of Information

When considering relations among relevant variables, information available from components of data can increase when the components are placed into a broader context.

In Essman's chapter, the measured effects of pharmacological agents are astutely used to draw inferences about the operation of systemic stress, as well as the opposite. Anisman and Lapierre establish a liaison among symptoms, behaviors, and biochemical correlates of psychopathology among humans, and behaviors and induced biochemical changes among animals, iteratively moving toward their stated position according to agreement among the component data.

A final type of interplay involves the correspondence between correlates of stress and correlates of psychopathology. Among the plethora of constituents of psychopathology and those of stress, the subset of intersecting constituents stimulates the greatest interest in the student of relations between these two domains. This type of intersection is elaborated a bit further at the beginning of my own Chapter 9.

Organization

The first and second sections are arranged into roughly parallel topics on "schizophrenia" and "affective disorders." Chapters by Spring and Coons and by Costello provide evaluative reviews of work on empirical associations between stressing agents and symptomatology. Chapters by Shean, Shaw, and Miller and Seligman examine the cognitive aspects of these disorders; for example, in carrying out their analyses, Shean and Shaw each incorporate the earlier formulations of Richard Lazarus on the functions of "cognitive appraisals." Seligman's "learned helplessness" animal model of depression has by no means stood still; constant efforts at reevaluating the model have led to a productive program of research. To accommodate new findings, the reformulated model presented by Miller and Seligman invokes considerable work on cognitive attributions.

Connections between biochemical effects of stress and the biochemistry of affective disorders are drawn out by Anisman and Lapierre. With respect to biological aspects of schizophrenia, Mednick has earlier suggested that ANS overreaction among these patients leads to responses of cognitive avoidance which are instrumentally reinforced through quickly effected ANS recovery. The chapter by Beuhring et al. extends this work by identifying contextual factors which appear to catalyze the effects of this stress-linked physiological disposition.

The chapters in the third part present promising findings and syntheses which relate to prevalent dimensions rather than to specific syndromes or classes of psychopathology. While several other contributors refer to the work from Richard Lazarus' laboratory in their respective chapters, Lazarus, Coyne, and Folkman present the development of their own ideas on motivation, emotion, and cognition as these constructs relate to selected aspects of psychopathology.

The last section presents prevalent therapeutic strategies directed toward stress-related psychopathology. Psychological (Meichenbaum & Turk) and behavioral-medical (Jessup) techniques are both represented. A reading of Essman's chapter on biological treatments reveals that the effects of stress-directed pharmacological agents are complex. Rather than compromising the data with simplistic interpretations, Essman has carried out a rigorous analysis of the often intricate interactions between these agents and systemic events mediating outward consequences of stress.

The final overview presents some of the more salient issues yet outstanding in this domain of research.

References

Appley, M. H., & Trumbull, R. (Eds.). *Psychological stress.* New York: Appleton-Century-Crofts, 1967.

Braithwaite, R. B. *Scientific explanation.* Cambridge: Cambridge University Press, 1961.

Cattell, R. B., & Scheier, I. H. *The meaning and measurement of neuroticism and anxiety.* New York: Ronald Press, 1961.

Chronbach, L. J., & Meehl, P. E. Construct validity and psychological tests. *Psychological Bulletin,* 1955, *52,* 281–302.

Davis, G. C., Buchsbaum, M. S., & Bunney, W. E. Research in endorphins and schizophrenia. *Schizophrenia Bulletin,* 1979, *5,* 244–250.

Ekehammar, B., & Magnusson, D. A method to study stressful situations. *Journal of Personality and Social Psychology,* 1973, *27,* 176–179.

French, J. R., Rodger, W., & Cobbs, S. Adjustment as person-environment fit. In G. V. Ceolho, D. A. Hamburg, & J. E. Adams (Eds.), *Coping and adaptation.* New York: Basic Books, 1974.

Hodges, W. F., & Felling, J. P. Types of stressful situations and their relation to trait anxiety and sex. *Journal of Consulting and Clinical Psychology,* 1970, *34,* 333–337.

Lazarus, R. S. A cognitively oriented psychologist looks at biofeedback. *American Psychologist,* 1975, *30,* 553–560.

Lazarus, R. S., & Launier, R. Stress-related transactions between person and environment. In L. A. Pervin & M. Lewis (Eds.), *Internal and external determinants of behavior.* New York: Plenum, 1978.

McGrath, J. E. (Ed). *Social and psychological factors in stress.* New York: Holt, 1970.

Magnusson, D., & Ekehammar, B. Perceptions of and reactions to stressful situations. *Journal of Personality and Social Psychology,* 1975, *31,* 1147–1154.

Mandler, G. Emotion. In R. Brown, E. Galanter, E. Hess & G. Mandler (Eds.), *New directions in psychology.* New York: Holt, 1962.

Mednick, S. A., Shulsinger, B. B., Venables, P. H., & Christianses, K. O. *Genetics, environment and psychopathology.* Amsterdam: North Holland Publishing Co., 1974.

Neufeld, R. W. J. Effects of stressors: Multidimensional scaling and discriminant function analyses. Doctoral dissertation, University of Calgary, 1972.

Neufeld, R. W. J. Veridicality of cognitive mapping of stressor effects: Sex differences. *Journal of Personality,* 1978, *46,* 623–644.

Selye, H. *Hormones and resistance.* New York: Springer-Verlag, 1971.

Selye, H. *The stress of life* (2nd ed.). New York: McGraw-Hill, 1978.

Teichner, W. H. Interaction of behavioral and physiological stress reactions. *Psychological Review,* 1968, *75,* 271–291.

Volavka, J., Davis, L. G., & Erlich, Y. H. Endorphins, dopamine, and schizophrenia. *Schizophrenia Bulletin,* 1979, *5,* 227–239.

Watson, S. J., & Akol, H. "Endorphins, dopamine, and schizophrenia": two discussions. *Schizophrenia Bulletin,* 1979, *5,* 240–242.

Part I

Psychopathology of Schizophrenia

Chapter 1

Stress as a Precursor of Schizophrenia*

BONNIE SPRING   HILARY COONS
Harvard University   University of Rochester
Cambridge, Massachusetts   Rochester, New York

Historical Background

Is stress a precursor of schizophrenia? Professional opinions on the question have completed several full cycles over the course of the past century. In the last half of the nineteenth century, the "psychic" school of psychiatry held that emotional shocks have a causal relationship to the onset of schizophrenia. However, during the first half of the twentieth century, the reigning viewpoint was that true schizophrenia arises as a consequence of endogenous factors. Langfeldt (1956) distinguished between typical schizophrenia and schizophreniform illness, an atypical reactive disorder arising acutely in response to exogenous factors. Schneider (1959) and Mayer-

*Preparation of this paper was supported in part by NIMH Grant MH-31154-04 to Dr. Seymour Kety, as well as by NIH Biomedical Sciences Support Grant RR-07046, a William F. Milton Fund Grant, and a Joseph H. Clark Fund Grant to Dr. Spring. The authors express their appreciation to the Biometrics Research Unit, Highland Drive VA Medical Center, Pittsburgh, Pennsylvania, for consultation and financial aid.

Gross, Slater, and Roth (1969) both wrote that schizophreniform illness and other "emotion psychoses" following calamitous stress may mimic schizophrenic symptoms but differ fundamentally from nuclear schizophrenia in etiology, course, and outcome. Further, both authors suggested that differential diagnosis on the basis of symptoms is possible, although very difficult. Thus, a causal role of stress in true schizophrenia was dismissed. Even a possible precipitating or triggering effect of stress was approached with great doubt. Mayer-Gross et al. (1969) stated their position as follows:

> One should, therefore, approach with skeptical reserve the rare cases in which a schizophrenic illness seems to be precipitated by emotional upset, mental conflict or other psychological or social difficulties. On closer enquiry in many of these cases the situations or emotional conflicts to which a precipitating force is assigned prove to be but the earliest social effects of the beginning of the illness itself. . . . Only by a *tour de force* can the primary symptoms on which the diagnosis of schizophrenia is based, be understood as the outcome of an emotional conflict. If these primary symptoms are present, then they are features which refute any purely psychogenic theory. (p. 261).

Jung (1907), E. Bleuler (1911:1950), M. Bleuler (1978), and Arieti (1974) reopened the question of whether stressful life events could exert an important influence on the onset and course of schizophrenia. Each considered that stressful life events could play a precipitating and possibly even a causal role in at least some cases of schizophrenia. From a psychodynamic perspective, Arieti (1974) highlighted the complexity of any theoretical link, suggesting that catastrophes such as war may even inoculate against schizophrenia to the extent that they breed a sense of solidarity with the community. Conversely, he proposed that apparently insignificant events may, by virtue of their symbolism to the individual, have quite calamitous effects because they fit the patient's particular vulnerability. Manfred Bleuler (1978) aptly conveyed the paradox that the impact of life events on the course of schizophrenia may on the one hand be clinically compelling, and on the other hand be empirically undemonstrable:

> If he [the clinician] knows his patients, he could easily construct a psychological novel around the theme of why one and the same event in the life of a patient can cause the eruption or the aggravation of his schizophrenia in one, and the recovery from his schizophrenia in another. But his experience has made him humble, and he would not be so presumptuous as to regard his psychological explanation as infallible. To wit, he would not dare to predict how one patient or another might react in the future to a given unusual event. If he were to succumb to making such "prophecies," he would frequently later on have to admit his error (pp. 275–276).

Despite Bleuler's skepticism, empirical research on stressful life events initially generated considerable support for the role of stress as a precipitant of schizophrenia. In 1968, Brown and Birley concluded that there is sound evidence that events in the three weeks before onset can precipitate a schizophrenic attack. This initial enthusiasm was tempered by later work suggesting that the impact of stress is less impressive for schizophrenia than for depression. By 1973, Brown, Harris, and Peto proposed that, for the majority of schizophrenics, life events merely "trigger" an onset that might have occurred soon in any case. Finding precipitating events in only a minority of cases of functional disorder, Clancy, Crowe, Winokur, and Morrison (1973) even suggested that doctors may persist in seeking precipitants primarily to provide patients and family members with a rational explanation for illness that accords with the lay public's expectations.

In general, stressful life events have been found to account for somewhat less than 10% of the variance in the onset of schizophrenia and depression (Andrews & Tennant, 1978). In fact, no investigator has been able to exceed the 10% mark in predicting illness onset of any kind using life-events checklist measures (Rabkin, 1980). However, it has been suggested that problems of sample size (Rabkin & Struening, 1976) and sample selection (Dohrenwend & Egri, 1979) may have rendered this estimate overconservative. This chapter suggests that current estimates may have also been biased by conceptual difficulties in dating illness onset and in determining the appropriate timing of the maximum stress effect. Consequently, both the magnitude and the importance of the association between stress and schizophrenia appear to warrant reexamination. Because an excellent review of methodological issues in this field has recently appeared (Rabkin, 1980), this chapter touches rather briefly on methodology and focuses instead on conceptual issues in examining stress as a causal factor related to schizophrenia.

The Effect of Environmental Factors
on the Probability that Schizophrenia Will Occur

Formative Versus Triggering Effects of Stress If stress plays a role in bringing about schizophrenia, how might its effects come about? To examine this question, it is important to define and differentiate between two sets of constructs that are often used interchangeably: *recent* versus *remote* life events, and *triggering* versus *formative* effects of stress.

Most studies of life stress and schizophrenia have investigated the period immediately (within two years) before the appearance of schizophrenic disorder. In other words, they investigate the effect of recent events as opposed to more remote events in the individual's developmental history. Further, most researchers of recent events see themselves as investigating a triggering rather than a formative effect of these events on schizophrenia. However, the distinction between the concepts of triggering and formative effects has never been a very clear one conceptually.

In the contemporary empirical literature, a formative role of life events has been defined to mean the following: (1) that life events play *an* etiological role (Rabkin, 1980); (2) that they play a more important role than other causal factors (Brown, Harris, & Peto, 1973); (3) that events substantially advance the onset of a disorder

(Brown et al., 1973). By contrast, a triggering role has been defined to mean: (1) that life events do not fundamentally affect the probability of schizophrenia, although they may affect its timing (Rabkin, 1980); (2) that life events are less important in bringing about schizophrenia than other factors (Brown et al., 1973); (3) that events precipitate an episode of schizophrenia that would probably have occurred before long for other reasons (Brown et al., 1973).

In sum, the formative-triggering distinction is sometimes taken to mean that a factor with a formative effect is a necessary condition for the occurrence of schizophrenia. By contrast, a factor with a triggering effect is not a necessary condition, i.e., not a causal factor. Rather a trigger may influence some ancillary property of the disorder, such as its timing. Alternatively, based on the mathematical assumptions of the "brought-forward time" index, Brown et al. (1973) have argued that the distinction between formative and triggering factors can be made on the basis of which factors are *most* important etiologically. If life events are more important etiologically than predispositional factors (stable properties of the individual and his environment), then they have a formative effect. If they are not, then, by default, a triggering effect cannot be ruled out, although it cannot be directly confirmed either. However, as Dohrenwend and Egri (1979) point out, the inference that the brought-forward index can be used to judge the relative effect of stress versus predisposing factors remains untested because life events and dispositional properties have not generally been measured and directly compared in the same study. Finally, the formative-triggering distinction has been defined with reference to whether life events advance the appearance of schizophrenia a lot or a little in time. Although this latter formulation is again mathematically clever, it is also somewhat teleological and not directly testable.

The Diathesis-Stress, or Vulnerability Model Theoretical differentiation between formative and triggering effects of stress is rooted in the diathesis-stress (Rosenthal, 1970; Meehl, 1962) or vulnerability model (Zubin & Spring, 1977) of schizophrenia. This vulnerability model suggests that stress exerts two types of effects on the probability that schizophrenia will occur. Formative effects come about when stressors contribute to the formation of the *vulnerability,* or diathesis for schizophrenia. It hypothesizes that particularly remote stressors occurring early in life, but also more recent trauma, are able to generate stable deviations within a person that constitute a trait of vulnerability and mediate risk of illness. A second, triggering or precipitating role of stress is also postulated. The precipitating role of stress is qualitatively different from the formative effect that augments vulnerability. Vulnerability is postulated to remain latent until it is elicited by a precipitating, or triggering event. The precipitating event does not add to vulnerability, but rather causes vulnerability to become manifest.

Stated differently, a "trigger" precipitates an episode but does not alter the threshold for future responses to new triggering events. An event with a formative effect changes vulnerability and modifies the response to future stressors. The effects of a trigger are reversible, whereas those of a formative event are relatively irreversible.

In the vulnerability model, precipitants are always necessary for schizophrenia to occur even if vulnerability is very high. Thus, they do not merely influence the timing of an episode of schizophrenia but the very probability that it will occur. It is assumed that even the most vulnerable person may go through life without developing schizophrenia if the appropriate eliciting circumstances are never encountered. The magnitude of event needed to precipitate an episode of schizophrenia is assumed to be greater for a less vulnerable person than for a more vulnerable person. Nonetheless, it is predicted that a precipitating stress of some magnitude is always necessary for schizophrenia to occur.

The Behavioral Model In a strictly behavioral model of schizophrenia (e.g., Ullman & Krasner, 1975; Salzinger, 1973), some type of recent life event is always necessary to produce schizophrenia and is always the preeminent causal factor. Actually, use of the term "life event" distorts this position. Instead, we should state that a series of contingencies arises such that psychotic behavior is reinforced in at least some contexts. The immediate contingency accounts for schizophrenia. This model disputes the need to postulate a construct of vulnerability or to consider formative effects of remote life experiences except as these might influence habitual response patterns. Indeed, according to this position, it is not even necessary to infer that the contingencies evoking schizophrenic behavior are subjectively or objectively stressful. However, this model predicts that, for schizophrenia to occur, it is always necessary for there to be some recent change in the contingencies which relate behavior to external circumstances.

The Medical Model The medical model assigns stress no special role in the etiology of schizophrenia. However, formative effects on vulnerability are compatible with some recent "looser" formulations of this paradigm. Although, as Weiner (1978) points out, various different medical models actually exist, the most general form is the following:

$$\underset{\substack{\text{Causal} \\ \text{factors}}}{} \longrightarrow \underset{\substack{\text{Biological} \\ \text{underpinning}}}{} \longrightarrow \underset{\substack{\text{Clinical} \\ \text{syndrome}}}{}$$

Some causal factor or factors are hypothesized to alter biological functioning in such a way that a defect arises or a biological process is set in motion, which, in turn, gives rise to schizophrenia.

There are two major schools of thought about the domain of causal factors for schizophrenia. One traditional interpretation might be called the "strict form" of the medical model. In this approach, exemplified by Kraepelin and by Mayer-Gross, the domain of causal factors is postulated to include primarily, if not exclusively, biological causes. Genetic inheritance, endocrine changes induced by maturation, degenerative anatomical changes, and other endogenous biological events are all treated as likely causes of schizophrenia. The position that only biological causes can give rise to schizophrenia is illustrated by use of the term "phenocopy," which appears occasionally in the contemporary literature to denote cases that mimic schizophrenia but that do not exemplify it because they arose from nongenetic causes.

Guze (1977) described a second broader interpretation which might be called the "loose form" of the medical model. In this version, the domain of causal factors may include experiential forces which operate to leave an impact on biological functioning. The existence of such effects was demonstrated some time ago at least for depressive disorders, although questions remained about whether they are restricted to early life and whether they involve permanent changes in biological functioning. For example, Harlow and Suomi (1974) demonstrated that early experiences involving prolonged maternal separation, peer separation, or social isolation could induce a behavioral syndrome resembling depression. The effects of isolation seem to be mediated at a biological level, since the behavioral syndrome is responsive to electroconvulsive therapy (ECT) and imipramine (Suomi & Harlow, 1977) as well as to social intervention (Suomi et al., 1976). Paul (1980) has reported an even more direct demonstration that experiential factors can produce structural biological changes. In rats, repeated foot shocks rapidly decrease the number of benzodiazepine receptor sites. (See also Anisman & Lapierre, pp. 179–217, this volume, for documentation of relevant biochemical correlates of uncontrolled aversive events.) The evidence is suggestive, although not entirely conclusive, that biological changes brought about by environmental and experiential factors can be permanent (Young et al., 1973; Seligman & Groves, 1970).

It is difficult to find parallel sources of evidence for human beings because such precise control over environmental and experiential factors is neither feasible nor ethical. However, a bare minimum of evidence indicates that severe trauma might also produce relatively permanent changes in human vulnerability. Suggestive evidence to support this hypothesis comes from the work of Eitinger and Strøm (1973) who demonstrated permanently increased vulnerability in nearly all organ systems of the body following concentration camp internment. Additional support comes from the work of Archibald and Tuddenham (1965) who found persistent symptoms of autonomic nervous system overactivity in 70% of a sample of World War II veterans twenty years after these men developed traumatic neuroses under combat stress.

Concerning the domain of causal factors, then, we might elaborate the original medical model to appear in its looser form as follows:

CAUSAL FACTORS

Biological ⟶
                  Biological   ⟶   *Clinical*
Experiential ⟶   *underpinning*   *syndrome*

We might now begin to incorporate a temporal element into the model to represent the fact that causal factors operate at different times during the life-span:

CAUSAL FACTORS

1. *Inherited at conception*
2. *Acquired over the life cycle* ———→   *Biological*   ———→   *Clinical*
    a. *Experiential* ———→   *underpinning*   *syndrome*
    b. *Biological* ———→

The central tenet of the medical model is that causal factors, whether biological or experiential, exert their effects on the etiology of any disorder by virtue of creating permanent or semipermanent changes in a person's biological functioning. These biological traits provide the underpinnings of the ensuing illness. In traditional medicine, for all forms of disease, measurement of the biological underpinnings of disease by suitable laboratory techniques provides a way of objectively confirming the diagnosis (Feinstein, 1977). In modern medicine, the detection of abnormalities at the biological level may also provide a means of identifying people at risk for disease so that preventive measures can be taken. For example, people with hypertension (high arterial blood pressure) may be treated to reduce the risk of subsequent coronary heart disease (CHD).

It is interesting to note that in contemporary medicine other stable but not strictly biological characteristics of the person have come into widespread use as indicators of nonpsychiatric medical disease. In heart disease, for example, the aspects of personality and life-style described by the Type A personality (Friedman & Rosenman, 1974) are regarded as mediators of risk. The Type A person is characterized by competitiveness and aggressiveness, by intense striving for achievement, and by a life-style involving a sense of time urgency and a high degree of professional commitment. These personality and behavioral characteristics have been found to predispose the person to CHD (Rosenman et al., 1975).

There is some controversy over whether the recognition of nonbiologically defined characteristics as sources of risk for disease represents a real departure from the traditional medical model. To keep strictly within the medical-model framework, it would have to be said that personality patterns and behavioral styles mediate risk for disease only to the extent that they lead to biological changes in the organism. Thus, vulnerability to disease could theoretically be reduced to a strictly biological level even though pragmatically it might be easier to measure risk through nonbiological markers. However, the Western Collaborative Group on coronary heart disease (Rosenman et al., 1975) has found that the Type A personality accounts for a different proportion of variance in predicting CHD than that explained by known physical risk factors. Thus, there is some question whether the mediation of risk even for physical disease can be entirely reduced to biological underpinnings.

At this point, we could introduce a further loosening of the general medical model having to do with the type of effect the causal factors have. Thus far, we have assumed that in explaining disease the only important effect of causal factors is to lead to stable biological changes. These biological changes have heretofore been assumed to be the causal mechanism, or the primary mediators of risk for disease. We have now raised the possibility that risk for disease may be carried not only through genetic or other biological underpinnings, but also through other enduring changes in personality and behavior. It cannot be determined at present whether it might ultimately prove possible to describe the personality and behavioral components of risk in terms of biological underpinnings. However, since the reigning level of science and technology does not presently permit such a reduction, and since nature may never permit it, we may broaden the category of mediating pathways as follows:

Causal ⟶ *Mediating pathways* ⟶ *Clinical*
factors   1. *Brain function*   *syndrome*
            2. *Biochemistry*
            3. *Behavior patterns*
            4. *Personality*

Like the vulnerability model, the loose formulation of the medical model allows at least in principle for formative effects of stress on vulnerability. However, it is probably the case that from a medical perspective this is seen as a relatively rare etiological route to schizophrenia, with most cases deriving their vulnerability solely from genetic and other biological origins. The medical and vulnerability formulations differ most directly in that the medical model postulates no need for precipitants to bring about the onset of illness. In the medical model, the probability that schizophrenia will occur may be seen as solely determined by the level of vulnerability or the pervasiveness of the underpinnings of disorder. When the brim is reached, the cup runneth over and schizophrenia ensues.

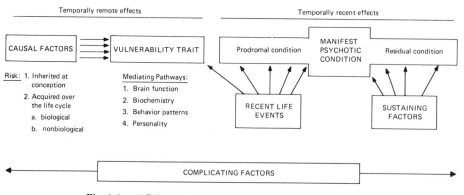

Fig. 1-1. A Schematic Model for the Etiology of Schizophrenia

A Schematic Model for the Etiology of Schizophrenia

Our schematic model, diagrammed in Figure 1-1, represents an extension of the vulnerability model of schizophrenia (Spring & Zubin, 1977; Zubin & Spring, 1977) but focuses on the temporal sequence of etiological events.

Causal Factors A causal factor is one which contributes to the formation of an individual's vulnerability or predisposition to schizophrenia. Inheritance, prenatal conditions, perinatal events, nutrition, physical illness, relationships with peers and caretakers, and various pathogenic life experiences have all been proposed as causal influences on the development of schizophrenia (Zubin & Spring, 1977).

For this chapter, the salient questions about causal factors are two: (1) Can stress help to create a predisposition for schizophrenia? Is it a causal factor? (2) Over what period in the life cycle can such formative effects on vulnerability occur? Can even recent life events have formative effects?

Vulnerability Vulnerability, the predisposition for schizophrenia, is conceptualized as a parameter of individual difference, a stable trait. Our discussion of the controversy over the malleability of vulnerability does not bring into question the description of vulnerability as a trait. Most traits can be modified at least within a certain range, by powerful life experiences, by therapeutic interventions, or by psychotropic drugs.

There is some question whether vulnerability is best conceptualized as a dichotomy, a diathesis that is either present or absent, or as varying along a continuum. If a continuum model is used, there is also a question of whether this scale should be regarded as ranging from the highest possible vulnerability through zero and still further into the domain of immunity or invulnerability as Garmezy (1974a) has proposed. It can hardly be disputed that pathogenic causal factors are only one part of the story in the etiology of schizophrenia. Of equal scientific importance and probably greater clinical importance are those causal factors that convey immunity and invulnerability. Despite this truism, we do not yet know whether invulnerability is best regarded as part of the potential range of vulnerability or as an independent dimension.

In order to test hypotheses about a formative effect of remote life events, it is essential that vulnerability be quantifiable on the basis of empirical referents. A variety of measures has already shown promise as possible indicators of the predisposition to schizophrenia. Many of these techniques fall under the rubric of information processing. Deviant smooth-pursuit eye-tracking, proposed as an index of nonvoluntary attention, has been reported in schizophrenics and their first-degree relatives (Holzman et al., 1974). The span of apprehension task, measuring limits on the amount of information the subject can process in a single glance, has been found to yield comparable deficits in schizophrenic inpatients, in foster-home-reared children of schizophrenics (Asarnow et al., 1978) and in remitted schizophrenics (Asarnow & MacCrimmon, 1978). Slowed reaction time, reflecting impaired alertness to external stimuli, has been found among offspring of schizophrenic mothers (Marcus, 1972). In addition, reaction time crossover, reflecting deficits in sustained attention, has been found in healthy adult relatives of schizophrenics (DeAmicis & Cromwell, 1979). Most consistently, the continuous performance test (CPT), measuring vigilant sustained attention, has provided a promising marker of predisposition. Impaired CPT performance has been demonstrated in children of schizophrenics (Rutschmann, Cornblatt, & Erlenmeyer-Kimling, 1977; Grunebaum et al., 1974), in remitted schizophrenics (Asarnow & MacCrimmon, 1978; Wohlburg & Kornetsky, 1973), and in college students resembling schizophrenics on biochemical measures (Buchsbaum et al., 1978).

Other possible markers of the schizophrenic diathesis include: anhedonia and perceptual aberrations (Chapman, Chapman, & Raulin, 1976); cognitive egocentricity (Strauss, Harder, & Chalder, 1979); unusual word associations (Mednick & Schulsinger, 1968; Rierdon, 1980), alterations in autonomic nervous system responsiveness (Mednick & Schulsinger, 1968); and low levels of monoamine oxidase and dopamine beta hydroxylase (Buchsbaum et al., 1978).

Clearly, a great diversity of measures is under exploration spanning all of the spheres of functioning in which vulnerability might have underpinnings: i.e., brain function, biochemistry, personality, and behavior patterns. However, it must be acknowledged that there is no certainty that any of these techniques *directly* measure the central mediating pathways or underpinnings of vulnerability. Indeed, no evaluation is possible because we do not yet know the nature of the core mediating processes. Consequently, it may be that most of these indices are merely *markers* of vulnerability rather than *measures* of it. An index may be indirectly associated with vulnerability in much the same way that one physical trait can serve as a marker for another if the two are encoded by alleles in proximity on a chromosome. It is to be hoped that as scientific progress enables us to sort the wheat from the chaff, it will be possible to use some of these techniques to quantify vulnerability. When this state of the art has been attained, it may be feasible to make direct tests on whether life stress has a formative effect on vulnerability. In the meanwhile, however, it may be useful to investigate whether any potential vulnerability markers are responsive to stress.

Implications for Research on Formative Effects of Remote Life Events Our schematic model has thus far laid the groundwork for examining the formative effects of *remote* life events on vulnerability. This is an important component of the problem of the role of life events in schizophrenia's etiology, particularly since a formative effect of life events has often been dismissed solely by examining the effect of recent events immediately before the onset of an episode.

One type of research suitable for examining this problem investigates whether there is an excess of stress in the early lives of people who later become schizophrenic. Although this research strategy represents a beginning, its limitations should be appreciated. First, there is serious doubt about whether such a study can yield any meaningful results if a retrospective design is used. Even over the relatively short period of 9 months, Jenkins, Hurst, and Rose, (1979) found that forgetting produced an average drop of 45% in life-change scores. Uhlenhuth, Balter, & Lipman (1977) found forgetting of about 5% of events per month over an 18-month period. Second, unless procedures are used to examine separately stressors that could not have been brought on by the subject, it will be difficult to determine whether any excess of stress might be the consequence of unusual behavior signifying a preschizophrenic condition. Third, it may be difficult to determine whether stress is merely a secondary consequence of other more potent causal factors that are in operation.

For example, a person with a schizophrenic mother who himself later becomes schizophrenic may have had a nightmarish childhood of chronic abuse punctuated by periods of separation during the mother's hospitalizations. However, it may be the inherited genotype rather than the childhood stress that confers most of the vulnerability. Another preschizophrenic child who experienced perinatal anoxia may suffer central nervous system dysfunctions that hinder her ability to learn and to communicate. These defects may have already laid much of the groundwork for a later schizophrenic episode, but they are also certain to provoke considerable stress along the way. These examples illustrate a basic tenet of our model of schizophrenia. We propose that clinically indistinguishable forms of schizophrenia may arise via different etiological routes, much as manifestly similar types of mental retardation can originate in hundreds of ways. In selecting schizophrenia as an end product, one probably automatically selects for heterogeneity of etiology. Particularly because almost any etiological factor is likely to produce stress as a by-product, it is especially difficult to stand at the end of the causal pathway and try to ascertain the prime mover in the etiological sequence.

In the specific examples above, we cannot assume that stress had a less potent formative effect on vulnerability than genetic inheritance or perinatal anoxia. Neither can we assume the converse. Nor can we determine whether the stress was provoked by the child's unusual behavior. The problem is that we cannot safely infer anything without directly measuring whether changes in vulnerability occurred in temporal proximity to stress. A more fruitful design would be one which directly and prospectively monitored the effect of stressful life events on changes in vulnerability. However, it too has a drawback in that we are currently uncertain of whether available techniques can adequately quantify vulnerability.

Recent Life Events We define *recent* to mean the two years immediately preceding onset of schizophrenic disorder because this is the period conventionally used in research on recent life events and schizophrenia. We have chosen to call this term in the model simply "recent life events" in favor of other commonly used names such as "precipitants," "challengers," or "triggering events." This labeling describes the essential property of the events under study (namely their temporal proximity to schizophrenia's onset) but avoids word magic that would imply an understanding of how such events operate (i.e., formatively or as triggers).

The questions for research are: (1) Are recent life events necessary to bring about schizophrenia? (2) Can recent events be a sufficient cause of schizophrenia? (3) What is the nature of the effect of recent life events? (4) Relatively how much variance in schizophrenia's onset is accounted for by recent events as compared to other causal factors?

A behavioral approach predicts that a recent change in life circumstances is both necessary and sufficient for schizophrenia to occur. The nature of the effect is neither formative nor triggering, nor does it necessarily entail stress. Rather, the change involves an alteration in the pattern of contingencies that relate behavior to situational contexts and reinforcements. Contingency changes are as important as habitual response patterns in accounting for the emergence of schizophrenia. For example, according to Salzinger's (1973) immediacy hypothesis, schizophrenics habitually respond to immediately present stimuli in preference to temporally and spatially remote ones. If such an habitual response bias has already been acquired by preschizophrenic people, we would predict an exquisite sensitivity to changes in the immediate response context.

In theory, fairly major differences exist between the loose medical model and the vulnerability model in the role they assign to recent life stress. However, the empirical predictions they generate are quite similar, and few research findings involve recent events which could bear on their differential validity. According to the loose medical model, recent life stressors are not necessary to bring about schizophrenia in all cases; according to the diathesis-stress model, they are always necessary. The loose medical model predicts that schizophrenia ensues when vulnerability has passed a certain threshold. If vulnerability is already at a maximum in the preschizophrenic person, then nothing else is required to explain the emergence of schizophrenia. However, if premorbid vulnerability is low, then the occurrence of some event such as a stress would be predicted to be necessary to create the balance of the vulnerability and initiate the episode.

The vulnerability, or diathesis-stress, model in turn predicts that a stress is always necessary to elicit the expression of vulnerability. If vulnerability provides the lock, life events present the key, and the door to schizophrenia is opened only if circumstances bring the two components together. However, it predicts that the magnitude of the requisite stressor is inversely proportional to the degree of premorbid vulnerability (Zubin & Spring, 1977). It takes a stressor of great intensity to catapult a person of low vulnerability into an episode but a miniscule stress to bring on schizophrenia in a highly vulnerable person. Moreover, a recent version of the vulnerability model (Zubin & Spring, 1977) suggested that the stressors precipitating an episode might be internal biological changes, not necessarily visible as life events.

The postulation of effects of minimal stressors poses a potential problem for the usefulness of the diathesis-stress model. Such stressors are likely to escape detection by measuring instruments. If they cannot be found, can we safely deduce that they did not occur? Strong proponents of the model are likely to reply that the fault lies in inadequate measuring instruments: if we knew more, we would find them. This rebuttal may be true in part, since Lewinsohn and Talkington (1979) have been able to assess life events of small magnitude reliably. However, we should also heed the historical lesson that some scientific constructs, for example, the "unconscious," may owe their longevity in large part to the belief that if we waited long enough, we might learn enough to be able to measure them.

Given the "escape hatch" of unobservable biological stressors and given the difficulties of measuring miniscule life events, for all practical purposes the medical and vulnerability models generate the same prediction about the necessity of recent life events for the onset of schizophrenia. This prediction is shown in Figure 1-2.

Manifest Psychotic Condition In characterizing the nature of the schizophrenic psychotic illness, our three theoretical models come to loggerheads over the natural duration of the manifest illness. Which is in need of explanation: the brevity or the persistence of the schizophrenic psychosis?

The behavioral model finds neither occurrence out of the ordinary. Schizophrenic behaviors appear and persist for as long as the contingencies sustain them. If a patient is reinforced for "crazy talk" in the home but not in the hospital, then disordered speech and bizarre behaviors should gradually extinguish in the hospital and produce a recovery. If, however, hospital staff continue by their attention to reinforce such "interesting" behaviors, then the behaviors will persist. They may become particularly resistent to extinction if reinforcement is intermittent.

According to the medical model, the transience rather than the persistence of the schizophrenic psychosis requires explanation. If schizophrenia is the natural outgrowth of a high level of vulnerability, then it should persist indefinitely once vulnerability has passed the threshold needed to bring the psychosis about in the first place. Elsewhere (Zubin & Spring, 1977), evidence has been reviewed which suggests that in most cases the more flagrant psychotic symptoms of schizophrenia constitute a temporary, episodic state rather than a permanent condition. We cannot determine whether this depiction of schizophrenic illness would have been valid before the advent of psychotropic medications and the open hospital era, but it does seem to correspond to schizophrenia as seen in contemporary society.

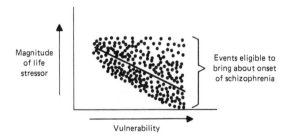

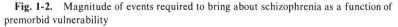

Fig. 1-2. Magnitude of events required to bring about schizophrenia as a function of premorbid vulnerability

How can the medical model account for this occurrence? It must postulate that something reduces vulnerability. One likely candidate for this role is psychotropic medication. Evidence suggests that antipsychotic medications not only reduce schizophrenic symptoms during a frank psychotic episode (Cole, 1964; May, 1968), but also that they lessen the probability of new episodes (Davis, 1975; Goldberg et al., 1977; Hogarty & Ulrich, 1977). Consequently, it does appear likely that antipsychotic drugs lower vulnerability to schizophrenia.

Even so, Manfred Bleuler's (1978) extensive longitudinal data indicate that, among schizophrenics experiencing their first episode requiring hospitalization, the most common course (found in 35–43% of cases) is a single episode or several episodes followed by full recovery. Since the majority of Bleuler's patients were not maintained on drugs but were sufficiently vulnerable to have experienced at least one episode, how can their recoveries be explained? The medical model must seek some other reason for a reduction in vulnerability. Bowers (1974) has presented case material which suggests that for at least some people, the experience of working through and integrating a psychotic episode may convey an invulnerability to future episodes. On the other hand, it seems equally plausible that the experience of a psychotic episode constitutes a traumatic event and might augment acquired vulnerability. We might postulate that therapeutic interventions received as a consequence of the illness produce an enduring reduction in vulnerability to schizophrenic episodes. But it must be acknowledged that none of the suggestions for vulnerability reduction is completely convincing.

The diathesis-stress model takes a very different tack, positing that periods of psychosis are inherently time-limited and episodic. They should subside as soon as the triggering event that elicited them is removed. The problem for the diathesis-stress model is to explain the apparent persistence of the psychosis in the subset of patients who remain continuously ill or hospitalized. This is done in a variety of ways. First, it is acknowledged that some patients may indeed remain continuously psychotic, and such cases are attributed to the persistence of the same stressors that provoked and continue to elicit the expression of the illness. Second, it is posited that for some highly vulnerable people, even relatively mundane events can continually catapult the patient into new episodes. Although the psychotic state may clear briefly between episodes, these periods of remission may escape detection because of the continuous vicious cycling into new episodes.

Another explanation is that, although the schizophrenic's psychosis may clear, he may still not be fully normal, either because he is restored to a premorbid condition that was aberrant or because the psychosis has been succeeded by a nonpsychotic but still pathological residue. These prodromal or residual conditions may be mistaken for the persistence of psychosis. In many cases of schizophrenia, psychotic symptoms are preceded by a period of prodromal symptoms of variable duration. These prodromal symptoms include social withdrawal, eccentric speech or behavior, disturbances of affect, unusual ideation or perceptual experiences, and impairment of personal hygiene or role functioning. After florid psychotic features have dissipated, many patients continue to display residual symptoms similar to the prodromal characteristics described earlier. These may represent the persistence of prodromal features, or they may appear for the first time. Wing (1978) has described this residue as the "clinical poverty syndrome." It consists of emotional apathy, slowness of thought and movement, underactivity, lack of drive, poverty of speech, social withdrawal, and deficient personal hygiene. Although such residual features are not as bizarre or disruptive as psychotic symptoms, they are still troublesome. They seem to preclude the patient's successful return to the community and suggest grounds for continued hospitalization even after the psychotic episode has passed.

Sustaining Factors A final explanation for continued illness or hospitalization may lie in the influence of factors that sustain and prolong psychotic or residual features. According to a behavioral model, the contingencies that sustain illness behavior are the same as those that initiated it. According to a diathesis-stress formulation, the sustaining factors may entail influences somewhat different from those that initially gave rise to an episode of schizophrenia. Some sustaining factors may directly bring about the persistence of psychotic symptoms. For example, the patient's bizarre behavior may be reinforced by the attention of hospital staff or may yield secondary gains in the form of concern and support from relatives. An impending Veterans' Administration compensation exam may encourage an exacerbation of psychosis if the patient believes he will be financially compensated in accord with the severity of his disability. Other sustaining influences appear to act more directly on the persistence of residual features. Wing and Brown (1970) have demonstrated that understimulating conditions in the hospital may directly provoke and sustain the clinical poverty syndrome. Other sustaining factors may more broadly influence the person's role functioning, self-confidence, and level of dependency on the health-care system. The patient may be socially stigmatized: unable to find employment, ostracized by neighbors, and treated gingerly by family members and friends. Progressively, the sphere of role functioning may become constricted so that only the sick role remains viable. Previously held aspirations and drives may need to be relinquished and replaced by a protective withdrawal. As Wing (1978) says, the experiences of illness, hospitalization, and adverse social reactions may assault the patient's self-esteem and confidence, leading to an increased dependence on the hospital.

Together these forces may lower the threshold for seeking care. Before the first hospitalization, there may have been a general reluctance to risk the stigma and admission of "weakness" implied by seeking professional help or hospitalization. After it, the alarmed family members and the increasingly shaken patient may beat a hasty retreat to the hospital at the slightest provocation, fearing a renewed onslaught of the psychosis. Or they may be reluctant to permit the patient to be discharged from the hospital for the same reasons. Indeed, in the wake of a schizophrenic episode there may be renewed alarm over prodromal features that have characterized the patient for years but drew no attention because their implications were not fully appreciated.

Complicating Factors To complete the schematic model of schizophrenia, we need to consider one final category of factors: the complicators. All of the variables discussed thus far may theoretically directly affect the probability or persistence of schizophrenic symptoms. Complicating factors do not have such a direct relationship to mental illness. Rather, at every stage in the model they may interact with and augment the effect of other factors. Poverty may be a complicating factor. It does not directly give rise to mental illness, but it restricts access to resources that might mitigate the effect of noxious causal influences, provide for therapeutic amelioration of vulnerability, or circumvent the social consequences of illness. A lack of social supports complicates the effect of stressful life events and augments their impact (Nuckolls, Cassel, & Kaplan, 1972). Manfred Bleuler's (1978) findings suggest that gender may also be a complicating factor. Females appear to be affected more adversely than males by noxious childhood environments, disturbed parental relationships in adolescence, and life events in adulthood.

Implications for Research on Stressful Life Events as Causes of Schizophrenia

Based on our schematic model, we can now clarify several pitfalls that await the researcher who examines the role of stressful life events in schizophrenia's etiology.

Heterogeneity of Schizophrenia It has frequently been proposed that research will be most fruitful when schizophrenics are subdivided into more homogeneous groups on the basis of symptoms or premorbid social factors. It has even been suggested that patients can be grouped as reactive or process, depending on various factors including the presence of a precipitating stress. Our schematic model suggests that schizophrenic heterogeneity may exist at more fundamental levels than can be observed in symptoms, premorbid adjustment, or even precipitating circumstances. First, there may be considerable heterogeneity at the level of etiological factors that give rise to vulnerability to schizophrenia. Some people may be vulnerable primarily by virtue of inheritance, others primarily by virtue of experience, and others by a combination of both types of causal factors. Second, vulnerability may be mediated differently across individuals. Moreover, it is not safe to assume that the same causal factor always affects the same underpinnings for vulnerability. For example, some people with genetically derived risk, may "carry" and manifest their vulnerability primarily at the level of personality and behavioral functioning; others may manifest their liability exclusively in abnormalities of biochemistry and brain function. Third, and probably most important, even in the weeks or months before an episode of schizophrenia, people may vary considerably in their overall level of vulnerability.

The implication of these observations is that it may not be possible to develop a formulation of the role of stress in schizophrenia that applies with any validity to the majority of schizophrenics. Stress might be a sufficient cause for some schizophrenias, a necessary cause for others, and an irrelevant factor for still others. Progress in explaining the role of stress may come only by way of evaluating subgroups of schizophrenics who are homogeneous with respect to etiology, underpinnings of vulnerability, and premorbid degree of vulnerability. The role of stress may truly be different for each subgroup.

Dating the Onset of Schizophrenia The onset of schizophrenia is most commonly dated by the appearance of psychotic symptoms. An implicit criterion is that the patient must seek care or somehow come to the attention of mental health or medical facilities. When drawing generalizations about factors that influence the onset of schizophrenia, it is important to realize this source of bias because some unknown proportion of cases may escape detection (M. Bleuler, 1978; Dohrenwend & Egri, 1979).

As the revised version of the *Diagnostic and Statistical Manual* (III) points out, prodromal features often antedate psychotic symptoms. This being the case, it is basically an arbitrary decision whether we define *onset* as the appearance of prodromal or psychotic symptoms. Logically, it would be best if we could define onset as the point when there is a veritable certainty that a schizophrenic psychosis will occur. But when has this point been reached? According to the medical model, we might trace onset to the point at which a very high level of vulnerability has developed, because vulnerability beyond a certain threshold will inevitably translate into disorder. Only the timing of this occurrence remains uncertain. However, according to the diathesis-stress model, vulnerability implies no such inevitability. All will depend on *whether*, not just *when*, a triggering event causes vulnerability to germinate into disorder. But what does a trigger initiate—the prodromal syndrome or the psychotic syndrome?

An analogy might be drawn to the following problem: when has an individual lost a job? Is it at the point at which his performance deteriorates to a totally unacceptable level? Some later time when this fact reaches the attention of his supervisor? The point at which the trusted supervisor informs the employer? The employer's memo to the personnel department asking that the employee be discharged? The date of the notification sent to the employee? The time when the employee realizes he is leaving? Or the precise date when he cleans out his desk and goes? By analogy, we conventionally date the onset of schizophrenia to this last, desk-clearing behavior. We could for all practical purposes date it much earlier. Also by analogy, if we looked for the immediate precipitating cause of job loss defined as actually leaving one's post, we would identify the cause as receiving a notification from the personnel department. Actually, this mechanical cause is only the last in a sequence of causal events. The causal factors of greatest importance occurred much earlier.

In psychopathology research, the problem of dating the onset of schizophrenia is often treated as a methodological pitfall to be circumvented by improving interrater agreement. In actuality, it is a conceptual problem. Schizophrenia is a disorder that may develop by gradual accretion. It is difficult to determine when behavioral eccentricities have passed the threshold into a paranoid or schizoid personality, when these have shaded into a prodromal syndrome, and when this in turn has met the criteria for overt psychosis. The issue is further complicated by the fact that not all schizophrenias seem to progress through this sequence of manifestations. Some, often described as "acute schizophrenias," appear to descend suddenly without warning. However, many question whether such an uncomplicated pattern of onset is compatible with a diagnosis of true schizophrenia (Kety et al., 1968; Pope & Lipinski, 1978).

All that can be said with certainty is that present procedures for defining onset are basically arbitrary. If we wish to maintain criteria that apply to acute schizophrenics as well as to other subtypes, then we must use emergence of psychotic symptoms as the benchmark for onset because these are the only features common to all subtypes. If we exclude cases that begin acutely, then it becomes possible to consider earlier markers of onset. However, we are on equally unsure footing when we propose alternative criteria. Can we identify markers that point with absolute certainty to an ensuing schizophrenic psychosis? The appearance of a schizoid personality is clearly unsuitable as a marker because many individuals manifesting such traits will never develop schizophrenia (M. Bleuler, 1978). We do not yet have adequate quantitative ways to assess the level of vulnerability and to test whether high vulnerability is the harbinger of an inevitable episode of schizophrenia. The implications of the appearance of a prodromal syndrome are as yet untested.

Given the complexity of schizophrenia's onset, perhaps the best that could be done is to examine separately those factors immediately preceding the onset of the schizoid or paranoid personality, the schizophrenic prodromal state, and the schizophrenic psychosis. In this way, it may be possible to avoid the pitfall of mechanical and superficial causal inference described earlier in the job-loss analogy and to understand any sequence of causal factors that may bring about schizophrenia.

Independence of Stress from Other Factors Related to Onset of Schizophrenia In order to investigate whether stress is causally related to schizophrenia, it is essential that stress be defined and measured independently of other factors related to the onset of schizophrenia. The problem of disentangling stress from other factors related to the emergence of schizophrenia can only be described as hair-raising. Potential confounding factors exist at many levels: in the implicit or explicit use of information about stress to make a diagnosis of schizophrenia; in the fact that the schizophrenic illness can provoke stress; in the fact that prodromal conditions may also provoke stress; and, finally, in the possibility that aspects of vulnerability present long before the emergence of illness might also influence the occurrence of stress.

When information about stress is used in deciding whether a diagnosis of schizophrenia is warranted, a test of the hypothesis that stress causes schizophrenia can only lead to spurious results. The dominant belief in contemporary medicine is that schizophrenia is a biological disorder that arises endogenously. Hence, it is likely that some proportion of cases presenting typical schizophrenic symptomatology may be diagnosed nonschizophrenic if there is evidence that the illness was preceded by stress. Therefore, to some unknown degree, prevailing contemporary theoretical beliefs about the etiology of schizophrenia may impose a selection bias such that the presence of a stressful event leads diagnosticians to ignore the presence of schizophrenia. It might be argued that diagnostic criteria should legitimately include information other than symptoms (Feighner et al., 1972; Pope & Lipinski, 1978), so that stress might be a justifiable parameter in the diagnostic process. However, if this premise is accepted, it must also be acknowledged that none of the parameters assessed in the diagnostic appraisal can be used to validate the diagnosis etiologically, concurrently or predictively. Only by quintessential circularity can we test whether stress is an etiological factor in schizophrenia when diagnosis is partly based on evidence of recent stress.

It is interesting to speculate on how these forms of bias will be affected by the inclusion of more than one diagnostic group in the experimental design. In contemporary practice, there is probably no researcher who believes that stress is more important etiologically in schizophrenia than in depression, the disorder usually used as the psychiatric control in cross-diagnostic comparisons. Consequently, when attempting to sort cases into these two cells in the design, one might suspect that if there is any confusion about the clinical picture, the presence of an apparent precipitant might tip the scales in favor of a diagnosis of depression.

Research findings have been quite consistent in demonstrating greater stress in the preillness histories of depressed patients than schizophrenics (Clancy et al., 1973; Beck & Worthen, 1972; Jacobs, Prusoff, & Paykel, 1974). Only two studies (Lahniers & White, 1976; Eisler & Polak, 1971) have failed to find significant differences, and as Rabkin (1980) has pointed out, these may have used an overlong retrospective period. However, before these findings are taken as definitive, it should be noted that in no study were diagnoses assigned with clinicians blind to information about stress, nor were those who evaluated stress blind to diagnosis. In the Clancy et al. (1973) study, both variables were rated from hospital charts, and the authors even raise the possibility that psychiatrists who compiled the charts may have been disinclined to search for life events as precipitants of schizophrenia. In the Beck and Worthen (1972) study, both diagnosis and stress were evaluated on the basis of information from a mental status interview. In the Jacobs et al. (1974) study, the psychiatrist who diagnosed the schizophrenics also administered their life-events interviews. For the depressed patients in this study, diagnosis and life events were apparently evaluated at separate times by different researchers, but it does not appear that the life-events interviewer was blind to diagnosis, nor was the diagnostician prevented from learning about stressful precipitants. Consequently, the question of the relative causal role of stress in different psychiatric entities remains problematic because information about precipitants may be used in determining which disorder is present.

The problem of nonindependence adheres primarily in the fact that information about stress may be used implicitly rather than explicitly in determining whether a schizophrenic diagnosis is warranted. Therefore, the confounding is not really eliminated by the usual procedure of deleting stress from the list of explicit criteria for diagnosing schizophrenia or dating its onset. The only real solution may be to assure that diagnosticians are blind to information about recent life events. The counterpart strategy is to keep life-events interviewers blind to diagnosis, but this is rarely feasible. These solutions are clearly undone by the usual research design in which the same clinician administers interviews about life events and symptoms but is then asked to evaluate stress and diagnosis independently.

In addition to separating stress from diagnostic criteria, research on the causal effect of stress in schizophrenia must avoid confounding stressors that are consequences of illness with earlier stressors that might have caused the episode. The strategies generally adopted to achieve this end are twofold: an attempt at carefully dating the onset of the episode, and efforts to eliminate stressors that might have been brought on by *unusual* behavior signifying the onset of disorder (Brown & Birley, 1968). However, the Brown and Birley solution may fall short of the mark of attaining independence for two reasons. One is the conceptual problem of dating onset. The other is that although the patients' pre-episode behavior may not be grossly unusual, it may be influenced by the underlying vulnerability or by prodromal features in such a way that the behavior alters the probable incidence of stress.

Because patients often "slide" toward illness by a very gradual process, it is important to recognize as possibly nonindependent any stressors whose occurrence is influenced by the developing features of the preschizophrenic on this gradual slide. Whether we will perceive such events to be associated with the early symptoms of illness will basically be an arbitrary function of whether we choose early or late criteria for defining onset. It is now apparent that as far back as childhood, there may be certain behavioral features associated with preschizophrenic conditions. Watt, Stolorow, Lubensky, and McClelland (1970) found that a substantial proportion of preschizophrenic boys performed poorly at school and were emotionally unstable and aggressive. Many preschizophrenic girls appeared oversensitive and introverted. These behavior patterns might very well enhance the occurrence of stress.

Leff (1976) reviews evidence that in the few years before a first schizophrenic attack the person often leaves his family in a small town or rural area and moves to a single-person household in the "transitional zone" of a city. Relocations or changes in residence have been found to be significantly more prevalent for first episode preschizophrenics than for controls during a comparable time period (Jacobs & Meyers, 1976). Events involving other people (Schwartz & Myers, 1977) and family related events (Jacobs & Myers, 1976) also appear in significant excess during the period immediately preceding a schizophrenic episode. It is quite true that the preschizophrenic who becomes embroiled in interpersonal conflicts and changes in residence may experience stress and suffer a disruption of social supports. However, it may also be that these events are secondary consequences of the preschizophrenic's tendency to withdraw from close relationships.

The problem of disentangling stress from the schizophrenic diagnosis, from consequences of the illness, and from the effects of precursor conditions of illness is thus a very serious one. In offering any suggestions to contend with this issue, it is best to start at square one: how stress is defined for the purposes of research.

Definitions of Stress

Three major categories of definition appear in the contemporary research literature.

1. Stress as a Response Stress may be defined and measured by a disruption or alteration in biological, physiological, emotional, or behavioral homeostatic functioning. Measures of autonomic nervous system arousal, changes in endocrine function, reports of emotional distress, and disruptions in coping behavior have all been used as indices of stress. The tendency to define stress in terms of disruptions in homeostasis is rooted in biological modes of thinking. The classic response definition of stress is Selyé's (1956): stress is a state manifested by a specific syndrome consisting of all nonspecifically induced changes within a biological system. Response definitions of stress also have some face validity in terms of colloquial usage. We often conclude that we are under stress based on signs of autonomic nervous system activation (e.g., rapid heart rate, perspiration, dizziness, flushing), a feeling of emotional distress, or deterioration of performance.

Unfortunately, response definitions of stress are of limited value for research on stress as a cause of schizophrenia because the measurement of independent and dependent variables is severely confounded. If behavioral disruption or disordered coping is taken as the index of stress, we are likely to encounter confounding with the criteria for diagnosing schizophrenia's onset, as well as with early signs of the disorder. In the DSM-III diagnostic criteria for schizophrenia, one required sign is significant impairment in two or more areas of routine daily functioning, e.g., work, social relations, or self-care. Thus, the diagnosis of schizophrenia of necessity implies behavioral impairment. Moreover, Phillips (1968) has proposed that long-standing inefficiencies in social functioning are prime components of vulnerability to schizophrenia. Thus, the onset of psychotic symptoms often occurs against a backdrop of disordered coping and sometimes provokes even further deterioration of daily functioning. To label either the backdrop or the further plunge "stress" adds no new information and certainly no explanatory power.

If biological responses are used to index stress, similar problems are encountered. Patients in an episode of schizophrenia are characterized by a host of abnormalities in physiological arousal (Venables, 1964; Mednick, 1958; Kornetsky & Eliasson, 1969; Broen & Storms, 1967). If such signs are detected shortly before psychotic symptoms appear, the findings may merely signify that the episode has begun but not yet reached full clinical bloom. Moreover, since there is some evidence (Mednick & Schulsinger, 1968) that individuals at risk for schizophrenia show unusual patterns of arousal, the researcher who calls these signs of stress may be mistakenly examining stable components of the predisposition for schizophrenia.

Indexing stress by anxiety or subjective reports of distress cannot take us much further, particularly because a sense of panic and subjective discomfort is one of the first symptoms of encroaching schizophrenia (Docherty, Vankammen, Siris, & Markir, 1978).

2. Stress as an Interaction Between Stimulus and Moderating Factors An interactionist approach, based in social science modes of thought, defines stress only in relation to the characteristics of the individual and the surrounding life context. A situation or an event is deemed to be a stress if it is perceived as such by the individual, or if in the judgement of a rater it outstrips the available resources for coping. The common theme in the interactionist approach is that it is impossible to define stress objectively, without regard to the person or life context that the stressor befalls. Thus, the effects of any life event are believed to be moderated by the person's idiosyncratic cognitive or perceptual structures and by the general environmental supports available.

Individual theorists tend to place primary emphasis on either the cognitive or the environmental moderators. Among those who stress the cognitive moderators, Mechanic (1967) defines stress as the perception by a person of an inability to meet life demands, and Lazarus (1974) proposes that subjective cognitive appraisals determine which events are stressful. Rahe and Arthur (1978) have also begun to emphasize that events are filtered through a system of perceptual appraisals. Moreover, Rahe (1978) has recently advocated the use of subjective, idiosyncratic perceptions of the magnitude of stress because these afford better predictability of illness than magnitude scores derived from normative samples. Brown (1974) differs from these theorists in emphasizing environmental resources and explicitly attempting to exclude subjective appraisals of stress. In his rating system, the "hazard" of life events is evaluated relative to the target person's idiosyncratic life context. However, the rating is done by a deliberately neutral third party.

As is the case for the response definition of stress, the interactionist definition incorporates conventional wisdom. One person's stressor is another's challenge. A mountain in one life may be a molehill in another. This approach makes excellent common sense and splendid clinical sense. When used in combination with other definitional approaches, it can yield important findings. When used alone, however, no definition of stress is more pernicious to the goal of drawing legitimate causal inferences about schizophrenia.

If stress is defined by the perceptions or cognitive interpretations of the individual, then measurement of stress is hopelessly confounded by phenomena that may be symptoms or predisposing factors for schizophrenia. Cognitive idiosyncracies are the most salient feature of schizophrenia, and the tendency to feel overwhelmed by many events may well be an early symptom of illness. Moreover, eccentricities in cognition or perception may predispose both to schizophrenia (Strauss et al., 1979; Mednick & Schulsinger, 1968) and to the tendency to construe life events in an unusual way. Any real relationship between life events and schizophrenia might be obscured by the preschizophrenic's tendency either to overreact to minor events or to underreact to real danger. The direction of the bias in measurement could not even be specified with certainty.

Brown's (1974) type of interactionist definition represents a more subtle impediment to clear causal inference. Here the hazard of life events is scaled in relation to the person's life context. But to what degree may a person's life context be determined by difficulties in social functioning that predispose to schizophrenia or that are manifestations of an already developing episode of schizophrenia? At least in this case, the direction of bias is clear, since we would expect these predisposing or symptomatic features to lead to a restriction in social resources, and, consequently, to an inflation of stress scores. Nonetheless, within this framework the measurement of predictor and criterion variables is conceptually confounded.

3. Stress as a Stimulus Finally, stress may be defined in terms of stressors, or stimuli whose properties can be objectively specified and whose probability of occurrence is independent of the actions or characteristics of the person on whom they impinge. This is the definitional framework used in laboratory experiments on stress wherein noxious physical (e.g., noise, heat, crowding) or psychological (e.g., failure, competition) stimuli are imposed on randomly assigned subjects. It is also the basic definitional approach used in most studies of stressful life events, although it must be acknowledged that there is some tentativeness to the assumption that life events "assign themselves" randomly. If there is any validity to this assumption for at least some types of events, then this is the only definition of stress suitable for drawing causal inferences, because it is the only one for which independent and dependent variables are likely to be unconfounded.

In life-events research, there is controversy about whether events are most validly seen as falling into discontinuous categories or as falling along a continuous dimension of magnitude. In laboratory research, it is unlikely that heat and noise stressors would be conceptualized as falling along the same continuum. Similarly, in life-events research there is some evidence that particular types of stressors may have specific causal impact for certain disorders (e.g., exits from the social field and depression [Paykel, et al., 1969]). However, events are also commonly scaled along a continuum of magnitude.

Measurement of Stressful Life Events

Holmes and Rahe (1967) originally scaled life events in terms of the amount of readjustment they would require the average person to make. Paykel, Prusoff, and Uhlenhuth (1971) subsequently scaled events for the degree of upset they would normatively engender. The assumptions underlying such scaling procedures are borrowed from models of stress in the physical sciences. In Hooke's Law and Young's Modulus of Elasticity, a stressor (e.g., a weight) is quantified in terms of the load it places on an object (e.g., a string). The degree of distortion provoked in the object is assumed to be linearly related to the physical magnitude of the stressor. The assumed parallelism between stimulus and response dimensions provides the rationale for having subjects provide normative magnitude ratings of stimuli along a hypothetical response dimension. Even though life events are scaled along a putative response dimension, it is important to note that the weights were not literally derived, nor have they ever been successfully validated against direct measures of response disruption or symptoms. Indeed, the fact that correlations with most outcome variables are as high for simple counts of events as for summed magnitude scores (Rahe, 1974) suggests that the hypothetical magnitude dimension may lack validity. Although this is disappointing from the standpoint of the assumptions of the model, it also implies that stress scores are at least partially independent of symptoms and behavioral outcomes. Precisely such independence is required to test hypotheses about the causal relationship of stress to schizophrenia.

Defining stress in terms of objectively specifiable life events is a first step in operationalizing stress independently from schizophrenia. At least this strategy *attempts* to disentangle the independent variable from the welter of disturbances in arousal, disruptions in coping, cognitive eccentricities, and peculiarities of life-style that are known to be associated with the dependent variable. Of course, it remains open to question whether the scaling procedures currently in use do yield anything resembling an objective metric for stressors. The rationale, derived from principles of magnitude estimation in psychophysics (Stevens & Galanter, 1957), is solid, but no corresponding physical metric that could validate life-events scales exists.

But what about the second assumption: do the events included in current checklists assign themselves randomly across subjects? It is probably unsafe to assume that the majority of events included in the Holmes-Rahe Schedule of Recent Experiences (SRE) occur randomly, independent of the demographic characteristics and social circumstances of the respondents. Married respondents receive higher stress scores (Hendrie, Lachar, & Lennox, 1975), a finding that is not surprising since one can only experience a substantial number of stressors on the list if one is married. Spring (in preparation) found significant differences between patients and nonpatients on SRE scores for the prior three months. The rank ordering of the groups from highest to lowest number of life events was: controls, depressed patients, schizophrenics. When covariance techniques were used to equate the groups artificially on marital status, the between-group differences on life events vanished. The composition of the SRE appears biased toward events that can only occur to people in certain life circumstances: i.e., married, employed, or recently employed and involved in social relationships. Because many schizophrenics are single, unemployed, and socially isolated, they may be less likely than more socially integrated individuals to experience these stressors.

Attempts have been made to isolate a particular subset of events that occurs randomly across subjects. "Independent" or "fateful" life events are those that could not have been provoked by any behavior on the subject's part. Although it appears necessary for the sake of causal inference to focus particular attention upon fateful events, there are also some drawbacks to doing so. First, the domain of fateful events is quite limited, and event rates may be so low as to prevent meaningful comparison across groups. Second, even when examining events that are indisputably fateful, we cannot entirely free ourselves from the snare of confounding with preschizophrenic features and other causal factors related to schizophrenia. In inspecting the independent stressors preceding schizophrenic episodes in the Brown and Birley (1968) sample, Dohrenwend and Egri (1979) noted an excess of certain types of events. For example, in several instances the subject's parent was hospitalized for psychiatric disorder, committed suicide, or carried out actions probably symptomatic of mental illness. As Dohrenwend and Egri point out, these are not the types of events that occur randomly across individuals. Rather, they occur preferentially to people with a genetic predisposition to psychiatric disorder. Moreover, the impact of such fateful events may be augmented by peculiarities of the preschizophrenic's life-style, if, for example, the proband is an adult who lives with parents and has no other social ties.

A final difficulty with focusing attention only on fateful events is that agreement on which events belong in this category is far from perfect. Lists of "independent" events have been presented in at least five papers. Four of these sources have a priori specified categories of independent events. The fifth source (Brown & Birley, 1968) began with specific events reported by patients and sorted these according to whether they were "independent" or "possibly independent." Because of this difference in strategy, it is difficult to compare the Brown and Birley independent items with those on other tests. However, it bears noting that some of the types of events classed as independent by Brown and Birley would be explicitly excluded on other lists because they might be direct consequences of the proband's behavior. It is easier to make direct comparisons across studies that have specifically designated certain categories of independent events. Dohrenwend, Krasnoff, Askenasy, and Dohrenwend (1978); Dohrenwend (1974); Jacobs and Myers (1976); and Schwartz and Myers (1977) have all done so. Yet the *only* particular events commonly designated as independent on *all* of these lists have been those concerning deaths (of a spouse, of a child, of other family members or close friends, or of pets). What are the other types of "independent" events about which there is such disagreement?

One controversial category involves physical illness or injury to the respondent. All such items are excluded from the Dohrenwend et al. (1978) and Dohrenwend (1974) lists. Given the large body of evidence showing an association between psychopathology and physical illness (e.g., Eastwood, 1975; Dohrenwend, 1974), there is good reason to question whether physical illness may be a sign rather than a cause of emerging psychopathology.

However, even when events involving physical illness are removed, there is still relatively little commonality in the remaining events described as independent. It might be argued that the discrepancies arise from differences in the initial item pool of events. If the researchers all began with the same item pool, would they emerge with the same classification into independent and nonindependent? A comparison of the Jacobs and Myers (1976) and Schwartz and Myers (1977) lists refutes this premise. Both of these studies drew their control groups from a large community sample (Myers, Lindenthal, & Pepper, 1971) that had been surveyed for life events and mental health. Presumably, therefore, the life events examined in both studies were identical because the list had been established at the time of the community survey. By contrast, there are considerable differences between the events deemed independent in the two studies. It would surely be desirable for researchers to adopt a uniform set of independent events, so that findings would be more directly comparable across studies.

Although fateful events hold a special place in explanatory research on the etiology of schizophrenia, this certainly does not imply that they are the only stressors worthy of investigation. To the target population, other types of life events may appear to be of greater consequence. When Dohrenwend (1974) asked subjects to report freely on the last major event that changed their activities, he found that many psychiatric patients reported events related to psychiatric illness or its treatment. Consequently, a prudent strategy for research may be to sample a spectrum of categories of events, stratified according to their etiological implications. Dohrenwend et al. (1978) have advocated sampling three strata: (1) events involving physical illness or injury; (2) events related to the subject's psychological condition; and (3) events independent of physical or psychological health. Although the category of independent events may be most useful for testing a cause-effect relationship between stress and schizophrenia, efforts to describe fully and to understand the circumstances preceding psychosis must necessarily cast a broader net.

For descriptive purposes, it may be useful not only to sample a broad range of events, but also to make tandem use of subjective and objective stress ratings. Caplan (1975) has reported that for normal subjects the correlation between normative life-change scores and self-reports of readjustment is essentially zero. Grant, Gerst, and Yager (1976) report that psychiatric patients consistently assign events higher readjustment values than nonpatients, particularly for events concerned with marital-family relationships and physical health. If subjective distress were the only measure of stress, then any link with symptomatic distress might be explicable by response bias. However, if both subjective and objective scorings were used, then empirical support might be found for the clinical observation (Donovan, Dressler, & Geller, 1975; Beck & Worthen, 1972) that schizophrenia often follows subjectively traumatic but objectively trivial events.

Empirical Research on Remote Life Events

Given the constraints of space on the one hand and the abundance of the research literature on the other, this review must necessarily be highly selective. For a more thorough discussion of this material, the reader is referred to the chapter by Beuhring et al. (pp. 67–90) in this volume. Without wishing to belabor the point that there are many methodological pitfalls to be circumvented in measuring stress, it may bear repeating that all of these difficulties are exacerbated when the stressors to be measured are complex and when they are appraised over a long retrospective period. As Caplan (1975) points out, threatening or embarrassing events are particularly likely to be suppressed or forgotten. As an example, he reviews survey research showing that whereas hospitalizations for infectious and parasitic diseases are overreported, diseases of the breast and genitals are greatly underreported. He recommends that researchers be alert to problems in the reliable assessment of variables that may cause defensive distortion and selective forgetting. Following his advice, we begin by considering the data on fairly discrete events that can in principle be dated reliably, then move on to more subjective and defensively salient variables such as family atmosphere.

The stressors to be reviewed are the following: (1) psychological trauma occurring to the mother during pregnancy; (2) pregnancy and birth complications (PBCs); (3) early loss of a parent; and (4) adverse home conditions. We must note at the outset that these groupings are divisions of convenience rather than mutually exclusive categories. We describe the effects of a pregnant mother's loss of her spouse in the first category, although we expect that this may have some biological effects on the fetus, perhaps related to some of those observed in PBCs. We reserve early loss of a parent to pertain to deaths occurring after the proband is born, although the effects of this event on the remaining parent's interactions with the child might be similar, regardless of whether the death occurs pre- or postnatally. Finally, it is rare for any single study to evaluate separately the contribution of each stressor. (For an exception, see Beuhring et al., pp. 67–90, this volume.) Thus, in any given study, it is often the case that probands who have experienced one trauma, for example, PBCs, may also have suffered others, such as early parent loss or adverse home conditions.

Trauma Suffered by the Mother During Pregnancy In an elegant study, Huttunen and Niskanen (1978) focused on a single stressful life event: the death of a woman's spouse during her pregnancy and the effects of this maternal trauma on the child. Using death and birth registers for the city of Helsinki, Huttunen and Niskanen identified an experimental group of persons whose fathers had died before their births and a control group whose fathers died during the first year of their lives. They examined psychiatric and criminal registers to determine how many persons in each group had, by adulthood, been treated for psychiatric disorders or committed crimes leading to imprisonment. Rates of hospitalization and imprisonment were quite high for the combined groups, amounting to 10% of the sample, but they were significantly higher for the group with prenatal loss of a father. Moreover, cases of schizophrenia were significantly more common in the prenatal than postnatal trauma group, somewhat exceeding the general population expectancy of 1% incidence of schizophrenia. Increased incidence of schizophrenic offspring for mothers stressed during pregnancy was apparently not mediated by PBCs. In fact, PBCs were significantly more common psychiatric patients in the control group. The authors suggest that maternal stress has biological effects on the fetus and contributes to the formation of a vulnerable temperament in the offspring. This effect does not appear to be entirely specific for vulnerability to schizophrenia, since incidence of other disorders was also higher in the index group. Nonetheless, the data do suggest a formative effect of prenatal stress on vulnerability to psychopathology.

Pregnancy and Birth Complications McNeil and Kaij (1978) have reviewed the literature on schizophrenia and PBCs, the latter defined as general somatic deviations from the normal course of pregnancy, labor, delivery, and the early neonatal period. They conclude that PBCs are prevalent in the histories of schizophrenics. Moreover, among monozygotic (MZ) twins discordant for schizophrenia (one twin ill, the other well), there is an association between birth complications and schizophrenia. These data warrant cautious interpretation because they are largely derived from retrospective maternal report. However, they do suggest a possible formative effect of perinatal trauma on vulnerability to schizophrenia as well as other disorders (Pasamanick & Knoblock, 1961).

Is there any evidence that childhood manifestations of vulnerability follow the occurrence of PBCs? Perinatal complications have been linked with hyperactivity, variability of autonomic responses, low IQ, learning disabilities, and disorganization in childhood (Mednick, 1958; Pasamanick & Knoblock, 1961; Stabenau & Pollin, 1967; Pollin & Stabenau, 1968). In following up a sample of adolescents born to schizophrenic mothers, Mednick and Schulsinger (1968) found a subset who exhibited severe behavioral abnormalities by the fifth year of the study. Compared to matched "well" children of schizophrenics and children of normal parents, these "ill" high-risk children had a higher incidence of obstetric complications and showed galvanic skin response (GSR) anomalies. Mednick and Schulsinger (1974) later found GSR anomalies to be generally related to PBCs.

It appears that childhood behavioral abnormalities may follow perinatal complications, but it remains for a greater than chance association to be demonstrated prospectively. Because many years often elapse between birth and the observation of behavior disturbance, it will be important to examine intervening factors. In addition, where a connection between PBCs and childhood disturbance has been found prospectively, it remains to be determined whether the deviant children will progress toward schizophrenia in adulthood.

If there is a connection between PBCs and vulnerability to schizophrenia, how might it come about? The most widely held theory is that perinatal complications induce anoxia, which in turn engenders a minor form of brain injury that constitutes a component of the schizophrenia diathesis. But what causes PBCs? It is unlikely that PBCs are caused by maternal psychopathology because, as McNeil and Kaij (1978) conclude, reproduction by schizophrenics does not appear to entail a PBC incidence very different from that of the general population. It is possible that minor abnormalities in the developing fetus may create biological incompatibilities with the mother and disrupt the normal course of pregnancy. Another possible mechanism is that poor health and nutrition may mediate the relationship between PBCs and schizophrenia. Sameroff and Zax (1973a) and Pasamanick and Knoblock (1961) have suggested that poor maternal nutrition may produce PBCs and predict that the mother will have basic difficulties in caring for herself and the child. Another possibility is that both PBCs and less than optimum early mothering practices may be associated with certain maternal personality traits (Lapidus, 1970). For example, high maternal anxiety may lead to increases in muscle tension which complicate delivery, prompt the use of anesthesia, and increase the probability of complications (Sameroff & Zax, 1973b). In addition, the anxious mother may later be worried or ill at ease in child-rearing interactions, particularly if she associates the child with the difficulties she experienced in giving birth.

In sum, it appears that either PBCs themselves or other adverse conditions with which they are associated contribute formatively as nonspecific risk factors to psychopathologic vulnerability. It is to be hoped that further research will determine the magnitude of this association and the way it comes about.

Early Loss of a Parent Both Norman Garmezy (1974b) and Manfred Bleuler (1978) have reviewed the many studies demonstrating that a substantial number of persons who become schizophrenic either lose a parent or are separated from a parent for a prolonged period during childhood. Perhaps the most widely cited study is that of Wahl (1956), who found death of a parent or prolonged separation before the age of 15 in 41% of a large male schizophrenic sample. In Bleuler's study, the only significant excess in parental loss compared to the general population was for schizophrenic females, and that involved loss of a mother. Bleuler's findings are consistent with Wahl's in revealing a high incidence of deaths of same-sexed parents in the histories of schizophrenics. Bleuler concludes that consensus favors the existence of an excess of early parental loss in schizophrenia inasmuch as all studies comparing schizophrenics and normals show either no difference or more loss for schizophrenics, never less.

Findings suggest that early parental loss relates to vulnerability to various psychopathological disorders. Both Bleuler and Frank (1965) concluded that the incidence of early parental loss is even greater for neurotics, psychopaths, and addicts than for schizophrenics.

Do childhood manifestations of vulnerability follow close on the heels of bereavement? Rutter (1966) found that children referred to psychiatric clinics had experienced more parental deaths than controls. However, although most parent deaths occurred in early childhood, behavioral disturbances did not become serious until adolescence. It remains to be determined whether comparisons of behavior before and after bereavement would reveal subtler abnormalities provoked by trauma. It also remains to be investigated whether childhood disturbances that develop after stress are way stations on the pathway to adult schizophrenia.

There are some data on the association between parental loss and adolescent behavior disorder in children already genetically at risk for schizophrenia. The high-risk adolescents in Mednick and Schulsinger's (1968) "ill" group had suffered an excess of early maternal loss. Unfortunately, the lack of prebereavement baseline data prevents a clear interpretation that the abnormalities were contingent on the trauma. Moreover, mothers of the "ill" probands suffered from more severe psychiatric disorder than mothers of the "well" group, and fathers of the "ill" children were also more likely to be psychiatrically disturbed (B. Mednick, 1973). Consequently the effects of early childhood bereavement on adolescent behavior disorder are in this case confounded with those of the severe genetic loading for psychopathology and rearing by two disturbed parents. A similar confounding prevents examination of the effects of mother absence not due to death. Mother absence was associated with childhood disorder, but absent mothers were also more severely disturbed than other mothers.

The excess of early parent loss in the histories of psychiatric patients suggests the possibility of a formative effect of early bereavement on vulnerability. There is a need for carefully controlled prospective studies that obtain prebereavement comparison data and that examine the effects of early loss in populations at risk as well as in samples with no other known risk factors. If early loss can be disentangled from other sources of vulnerability, then it may become possible to evaluate its formative effect alone and its additive or interactive effect with other risk factors.

Childhood Home Life and Family Atmosphere Although the clinical literature relating schizophrenia to abnormalities of communication and parental role structure is very extensive, there is little empirical evidence that adverse family conditions preponderate in the early lives of preschizophrenic persons. Both Jacob (1975) and Leff (1978) were impressed by the lack of solid evidence that these conditions occur with any greater frequency in families of disturbed than normal offspring. Jacob (1975) and Hirsh and Leff (1975) concluded their reviews with the meager yield that parents of schizophrenics show greater conflict than parents of children with other conditions. A serious difficulty with many investigations is that it is exceedingly difficult to disentangle cause and effect. Disturbed communication might reflect a genetic predisposition to schizophrenia in both parent and child, or, even more likely, it might reflect the parents' response to the child's peculiarities (Liem, 1974).

Despite myriad weaknesses in the studies of family conditions, research in this area continues to proliferate. There is a consensus among researchers that the variables appraised are so subtle and complex that they elude adequate measurement. Manfred Bleuler (1978) has described this viewpoint eloquently, and, although his study of early home life conditions is not exempt from methodological pitfalls, it should be mentioned because its findings are suggestive. Bleuler retrospectively classified the childhood home conditions of 208 schizophrenic probands and their siblings as "horrible," "doubtful," or "normal." Child backgrounds were considered "horrible" if there was proof of long-term mistreatment, severe physical neglect, regular beatings or unreasonable punishment, or exploitation by forcing the child to work. The environment was also considered horrible if the child was regularly exposed to antisocial behavior of the parents (e.g., prostitution, drunken beatings), induced to beg or steal, involved in prolonged incest, or required to reinforce and become involved in the parents' psychopathological behaviors.

Bleuler judged that one third of the schizophrenic probands could be considered to have grown up under "horrible" conditions, and only one quarter could be considered to have been raised in a "normal" atmosphere. However, for an unmatched comparison group of alcoholics, conditions as children had been slightly worse. More than one third of the alcoholics seemed to have grown up under "horrible" conditions, and only one fifth under "normal" ones. Just as Bleuler found early parent loss to be more common in the histories of female schizophrenics, he found females more likely than males to have grown up under horrible childhood conditions and experienced a poor relationship with the mother.

Bleuler cites many case examples illustrating how common it is for adversities in childhood to be denied, only to have truly tragic conditions emerge on closer inquiry. However, on retrospective inquiry it is impossible to fathom whether the adult schizophrenic distorts the past through a lens of victimization, or indeed whether the preschizophrenic child provokes a misery-prone environment.

One of Bleuler's most interesting findings is the suggestion of a temporal relationship between the occurrence of horrible childhood conditions and the emergence of a schizoid personality. Only about half of the schizophrenic probands presented evidence of premorbid schizoid personalities, but schizoid features were associated with more adverse courses of illness. For the majority of schizoid persons, schizoid features were reported to have appeared in the early school years and seemed to become manifest in temporal proximity to horrible home conditions. These data might surely be questioned, since it is plausible that a retrospective effort after meaning might manufacture a temporal connection between the two occurrences when none in fact exists. However, they do suggest that if a traumatic childhood environment has a causal relationship to future schizophrenia, it may first produce a schizoid personality, and the psychosis will later develop against this background. To be certain, many disorders besides schizophrenia can arise from a schizoid personality, and many schizoids do not develop further disorders. Many siblings of the schizophrenics manifested schizoid features, and Bleuler suggests that here too an association existed with adverse home conditions. However, schizoid siblings frequently went on to develop a variety of personality disturbances besides schizophrenia. Bleuler proposes that the relationship between childhood adversity and later schizophrenia is found only for probands who are prepsychotically schizoid. Those schizophrenic probands who were not schizoid did not tend to show as much evidence of stressful conditions in childhood. A final caution is in order because it may be that both the childhood adversities and the development of schizoidia reflect a strong genetic loading for psychopathology. Horrible childhood conditions often arose because of schizophrenia, schizoid personality, alcoholism, or personality disturbance in proband parents.

Conclusions on Remote Stressors The first question we posed was: is there an excess of stress in the early lives of schizophrenics? The answer to this question appears to be yes. Preschizophrenics seem to suffer more than the normal incidence of pregnancy and birth complications as well as parent loss. Stressful family conditions have been more difficult to document, and it may also be that these are responses to the proband's eccentricities. However, although the histories of schizophrenics reveal more than the normal amount of stress, they do not seem to reveal more than those of other types of patient, and they certainly reveal more than those of other types of patient, and they certainly reveal nothing that normal children have not also experienced and accommodated to.

Do child stressors occur immediately before the emergence of signs of vulnerability? The evidence on this point is very weak, principally because of inadequacies in research design. It is established that early stress is frequently found in the histories of disturbed children. However, it is not clear that childhood stress statistically increases the probability of childhood disorder, nor is it clear that these child disorders are precursors of adult schizophrenia. Huttunen and Niskanen's (1978) findings suggest that early stress may increase the probability of adult disorder. But although the 10% incidence of psychiatric hospitalization and imprisonment in offspring with prenatal or neonatal loss of a father sounds very high, there are no control data to establish usual base rates of occurrence for these conditions. Both Mednick and Schulsinger's (1968) and Bleuler's (1978) findings suggest that among individuals at risk for schizophrenia adverse conditions may antedate the emergence of childhood behavioral abnormalities. However, given the confounding of adverse environmental conditions with parental genetic loading for psychopathology, and given the absence of prestress baseline data for the children, we cannot really determine whether childhood pathology precedes or follows on the heels of life stress. It is to be hoped that ongoing high-risk studies involving a closer monitoring of life stress and child vulnerability will provide the needed data.

Can early trauma permanently increase vulnerability to schizophrenia? It is too soon to tell. The major reason is that we have not yet determined whether trauma contributes any unique variance to risk for schizophrenia other than that variance that is associated with genetic risk. Most of the traumatic circumstances that have been investigated can be secondary effects of other causal factors in schizophrenia's etiology, particularly the factor of genetic liability. Thus, if the proband has a congenital predisposition to psychopathology by virtue of having a disturbed parent, he is also likely to encounter many stressors that are consequences of this fact. The disturbed parent may create a horrible home life, be absent for prolonged periods of time, and be likely to become physically ill or die. One way to determine whether these life traumas add any unique variance to the etiology of schizophrenia is to compare groups of probands who experience the genetic risk without the life trauma, those who experience the trauma without having the genotype, and others who have the genotype coupled with varying degrees of early trauma (e.g., early bereavement alone, early bereavement plus adverse home conditions). A related strategy has been proposed by Reider and Gershon (1978).

Empirical Research on Recent Life Events

Two of the best-designed studies of life events immediately preceding schizophrenia are those of Brown and Birley (1968) and Jacobs and Myers (1976). In a retrospective comparison of acute-onset schizophrenics and normal community controls,

Brown and Birley found that in the 3-week period before illness onset, schizophrenics experienced many more stressful life events than the controls did and many more than their own event rates in earlier time periods. During these 3 weeks, 46% of schizophrenics experienced at least one independent event, compared to 12% in earlier 3-week periods, and compared to 14% for controls in the 3 weeks before the interview. Brown, Sklair, Harris, and Birley (1973) later reported that the schizophrenic excess of life events in the final 3 weeks occurred in all categories of event severity, including events with little or no threatening implications.

Jacobs and Myers compared first-admission schizophrenics and community controls on life events reported to have occurred in the year before illness onset or interview. Patients reported 50% more events for the period, but the difference failed to reach significance when only independent events were considered. Fully 84% of schizophrenics compared to 50% of normals reported at least one undesirable event during the year. The difference between the two studies in findings for independent events may reflect the length of time used. At least for acute-onset patients, periods longer than 3 weeks to 6 months may dilute real differences between groups.

Although schizophrenics report more recent life events than normal controls, they appear to report fewer than depressed patients in the period before illness onset (Jacobs, et al., 1974; Clancy et al., 1973; Beck & Worthen, 1973). These findings do suggest that severe life events are less centrally involved in initiating episodes of schizophrenia than depression, but they do not rule out a role of stress in the onset of schizophrenia.

Are recent stressful life events a necessary precursor of schizophrenia? We can spell out the parameters of the uncertainty. In the Brown and Birley study, 60% of patients versus 19% of controls reported either independent or possibly independent events in the 3 weeks before onset/interview. In the Jacobs and Myers study, 40.3% of patients versus 29% of controls reported independent events for the preceding year. Other, nonindependent events were also more numerous for schizophrenics, and we cannot easily tease out which of these might be causes and which consequences of illness. Based on these findings, it appears that stress is frequently a precursor of schizophrenia, although it is not necessary in all cases.

We must note, however, that this interpretation should be treated cautiously for a variety of reasons. First, the schizophrenics in these samples may have been a select group particularly in the respect that their illness onsets could be clearly dated. The Jacobs and Myers sample may have included many schizophreniform and schizoaffective cases. Brown and Birley excluded 60% of the schizophrenic hospital population in trying to find cases of recent, datable onset.

A second caution stems from the observation that even relatively trivial events were frequent precursors of schizophrenia. Because such events are easily overlooked, it may be that incidence of stress preceding schizophrenia is somewhat greater than we now believe. Consequently, it will be important for future studies to assess comprehensively the sphere of "microevents," as Lewinsohn (1979) has suggested.

A third issue is a potentially more serious challenge to the premise that stress is a precursor of schizophrenia. Because most studies have been done retrospectively, it is likely that patients and family members trying to understand the origins of illness may be more strongly motivated than healthy controls to search the past for stressful precipitants. If this is true, then apparent differences in the incidence of stressful life events may be the spurious outcome of attitudinal or motivational factors. Because healthy community members are not equally pressed to explain their present condition, it seems very important for retrospective studies to use control groups that suffer some adversity equally in need of explanation. The possibility of using medical or surgical patients as controls is often dismissed because it is established that physical illness is associated with a high incidence of stressful life events (e.g., Schless et al., 1977). However, controls for the "effort after meaning" are essential. Moreover, studies comparing medical patients with mixed groups of psychiatric patients have demonstrated at least a minimum of specificity in life event precursors (Schless et al., 1977; Morrison, Hudgens, & Barchha, 1968; Brown et al., 1973).

A further observation is less a cautionary note than a recommendation for future research. The paradigm for investigating stress as a precursor of schizophrenia has thus far been a rather simple one: symptoms are observed at Time 2 and stressors are sought at Time 1. We have emphasized that the sequence of causal factors leading to schizophrenia occurs over a long time. Consequently, it seems important to undertake more sophisticated analyses of the temporal relationships among factors along the causal pathway.

First, it is necessary to learn more about the statistical independence of life events over time. Using a panel regression technique to reanalyze the Myers et al. (1975) community survey data, Eaton (1978) found some degree of association between events over time. However, he demonstrated that much of the nonindependence of life events over time is explained by their association with broad demographic variables such as age and sex. On the other hand, it remains possible that life events display greater associations across time for psychiatric patients. Brown and Birley (1968) found that for schizophrenics reporting an event in the final 3 weeks before illness onset, 75% also reported earlier events in the preceding 10 weeks. Of those patients with no event in the final 3 weeks, only 35% reported earlier events. No such pattern emerged for normal controls. Brown has introduced the term "difficulties" to describe chronic sources of strain, and he has differentiated difficulties from more discrete and time-limited life events. It is possible that one key feature of the life circumstances preceding schizophrenia is either the chronicity or the "snowballing" nature of the stressors. Serban (1975) has also suggested this hypothesis.

A second relationship that deserves further exploration is that between life events and behavior that precedes them. For the New Haven community sample, Eaton (1978) found almost a zero association between symptoms at Time 1 and life events at Time 2. In marked contrast, Gersten, Langner, Eisenberg, and Simcha-Fagan (1977) found, in a large community sample of children, that life events correlated equally well with behavior pathology before or after the events. The relevance of the Gersten et al. finding for research on stress and schizophrenia is its demonstration of the need to take into account the effects of the proband's prepsychotic and pre-event behavioral condition.

Finally, it is important to consider that there may be individual variations in the relationship between life events and symptom onset and that these may relate to differences in vulnerability to psychopathology. One of the few demonstrations of this possibility comes from the early work of Strecker (1922). Strecker examined 100 cases of "dementia praecox," almost all of whom were first episode cases. He categorized probands according to the severity of precipitating circumstances as well as according to presence or absence of hereditary background for psychosis. The proportion of probands genetically predisposed to psychosis was 45% for cases precipitated by severe adversity and 64% for cases with no discernible precipitant. Strecker concluded that the greater the genetic predisposition, the less the likelihood of finding severe stress as a precursor of schizophrenia.

Concluding Remarks

In examining whether stress is a precursor of schizophrenia, this chapter has cast its net over a broader segment of the life cycle than usual. Even the prenatal period has been scooped up into our net. We have taken this tack because we believe that schizophrenia is fundamentally a disorder that develops over a long time span. Even when inheritance at conception has set a high risk for schizophrenia, the 40–60% discordance for illness among MZ twins shows that the story at conception is incomplete. Apparently, it remains for life to flesh out the details by experiences creating further risks or buffers against illness. Just as the salient etiological factors accrue over time, so do the manifestations of illness often appear gradually.

Accordingly, we have emphasized that there may be multiple points of impact for stress in the etiology of schizophrenia. We suggest that it may be particularly worthwhile to pay careful attention to the effects of adversities early in life, where formative effects on vulnerability are likely to occur. Similarly, it may be fruitful to refine techniques that detect the early manifestations of vulnerability so that it becomes possible to examine prospectively whether these emerge on the heels of stressful circumstances. All in all, the evidence that early trauma can enhance vulnerability is quite suggestive, and further well-controlled studies are certainly warranted.

The findings on recent life events and schizophrenia do suggest that stress is often a precursor of schizophrenic episodes. However, we have noted certain methodological controls that would be useful to establish the generalizability and magnitude of these findings. Two points may bear repeating. One is that the population of adult schizophrenics is likely to be quite heterogeneous with respect to etiology and even premorbid level of vulnerability. It may prove essential to delineate more uniform groups along these parameters because it is likely that the contribution of stress to schizophrenia is different for each subset. The second point is that we will be unable to differentiate with certainty between formative and triggering effects of recent stress until we attempt to quantify and evaluate the relative contribution of vulnerability.

For any subpopulation of schizophrenics, at least three types of relationship might exist between stress and illness. It may be useful to end by examining these and considering what advantages could accrue from knowing of their existence. The first relationship, and the one that has been our primary concern, is that stress might be a cause of schizophrenia. It may contribute formatively to vulnerability, or it may trigger the expression of illness. It is not necessary that stress be the only factor in the causal formula for it to be of value in predicting and explaining the onset of schizophrenic episodes. For example, it may be that for most individuals stress leads to a syndrome of distress, coping breakdown, and demoralization when life circumstances outstrip the available coping resources (Dohrenwend & Egri, 1979; Zubin & Spring, 1977). In a person not otherwise predisposed to illness, the demoralization may resolve uneventfully, but, in a vulnerable person, it may blossom into an episode of psychopathology. If this is so, then demoralization following stress in a vulnerable person may be a sign that the proband has entered a period of high risk. Immediate preventive measures might then be taken, particularly because demoralization may be more responsive to supportive measures than schizophrenia itself.

It is also possible that in many cases stress is a sequel to psychopathology. This might arise if prodromal manifestations tended to involve the preschizophrenic in complex and difficult life situations or if the sporadic appearance of psychotic signs before the full-blown schizophrenic syndrome achieved the same effect. In this case, stress would be a consequence of the early symptoms of schizophrenia and would afford no understanding of how these symptoms originate. However, because it might ultimately prove easier to detect the snowballing of stressful life events than the prodromal symptoms, even this type of relationship might have certain practical advantages. In this case, stress might be an early marker of the onset of an episode, and it might "buy time" in which to attempt to abort psychotic decompensation. Such efforts would qualify as secondary rather than primary prevention, but they might still be effective.

Finally, it may be that for many patients there is truly no relationship between stressful life events and the occurrence of schizophrenia. How might we reconcile this with clinical impressions to the contrary? One might speculate that the very insistence by schizophrenic patients that stress caused them to fall ill has been the single greatest impetus to research in this domain. Mayer-Gross, Slater, and Roth (1969) noted that "the patient's mind is full of ideas concerned with the events which are presumed to have caused the attack" (p. 261). Manfred Bleuler (1978) claimed that:

In every instance the content of the later psychosis has something to do with the patient's childhood suffering. It is especially the case that the patient himself always senses a relationship between the development of his illness and his childhood suffering (p. 128).

If stress does not truly precede the onset of schizophrenia, how might such a subjective conviction of its effect come about? This might occur by what Clancy et al. (1973) described as the "collective system of rational thought," whereby human beings seek to attribute negative outcomes to pathogenic causes. Noxious life experiences are a natural target to explain illness. The subjectively felt but objectively untrue link between stress and illness would therefore provide no specific knowledge of schizophrenia but would be of more general use in understanding how ill people may explain and experience their illnesses.

On the other hand, if schizophrenics systematically linked their symptoms to life experiences by the type of "tour de force" that Mayer-Gross et al. considered so unlikely, then such a subjective connection would, regardless of its objective untruth, convey an advantage in understanding schizophrenia. When Freud's neurotic patients reported particular types of childhood sexual experiences, their reports did not correspond to reality. They were nonetheless useful in understanding and treating these patients because they revealed a particular kind of symbolic thinking that is at least symptomatic, if not productive, of neuroses.

We conclude, therefore, that the study of stress and schizophrenia continues to hold promise for identifying clues to the causes, predictors, and treatment of schizophrenia.

References

Andrews, G., & Tennant, C. Editorial: Life event stress and psychiatric illness. *Psychological Medicine,* 1978, *8,* 545–549.

Archibald, H. C., and Tuddenham, R. D. Persistent stress reaction after combat. *Archives of General Psychiatry,* 1965, *12,* 475–481.

Arieti, S. *Interpretation of Schizophrenia* (2nd ed.). New York: Basic Books, 1974.

Asarnow, R. F., Steffy, R. A., MacCrimmon, D. J., & Cleghorn, J. M. An attentional assessment of foster children at risk for schizophrenia. In L. Wynne, R. Cromwell, & S. Matthysse (Eds.) *Nature of schizophrenia.* New York: Wiley, 1978.

Asarnow, R. F., & MacCrimmon, D. J. Residual performance deficit in clinically remitted schizophrenics: A marker of schizophrenia? *Journal of Abnormal Psychology,* 1978, *87,* 597–608.

Beck, J. C., & Worthen, K. Precipitating stress, crisis theory, and hospitalization in schizophrenia and depression. *Archives of General Psychiatry,* 1972, *26,* 123–129.

Bleuler, E. *Dementia praecox or the group of schizophrenias.* New York: International Universities Press, 1950. (Originally published, 1911.)

Bleuler, M. *The schizophrenic disorders: Long-term patient and family studies.* New Haven: Yale University Press, 1978.

Bowers, M. B. *Retreat from sanity: The structure of emerging psychosis.* New York: Human Sciences Press, 1974.

Broen, W. E., & Storms, L. H. A theory of response interference in schizophrenia. In B. Maher (Ed.), *Progress in experimental personality research.* (Vol. 4). New York: Academic Press, 1967.

Brown, G., & Birley, J. L. Crises and life changes and the onset of schizophrenia. *Journal of Health and Social Behavior,* 1968, *9,* 203–214.

Brown, G., Harris, T., & Peto, J. Life events and psychiatric disorders: Part II. Nature of the causal link. *Psychological Medicine,* 1973, *3,* 159–176.

Brown, G., Sklair, F., Harris, T. O., & Birley, J. L. T. Life events and psychiatric disorders: Some methodological issues. *Psychological Medicine,* 1973, *3,* 74–87.

Brown, G. W. Meaning, measurement and stress of life events. In B. S. Dohrenwend & B. P. Dohrenwend (Eds.), *Stressful life events: Their nature and effects.* New York: Wiley, 1974.

Buchsbaum, M. S., Murphy, D. L., Coursey, R. D., Lake, C. R., & Zeigler, M. G. Platelet monoamine oxidase, plasma dopamine-beta-hydroxylase and attention in a 'biochemical high-risk' sample. In L. Wynne, R. Cromwell, & S. Matthysse (Eds.), *Nature of schizophrenia.* New York: Wiley, 1978.

Caplan, R. D. A less heretical view of life change and hospitalization. *Journal of Psychosomatic Research,* 1975, *19,* 247–250.

Chapman, L. J., Chapman, J. P., & Raulin, M. L. Scales for physical and social anhedonia. *Journal of Abnormal Psychology,* 1976, *85,* 374–382.

Clancy, J., Crowe, R., Winokur, G., & Morrison, J. The Iowa 500: Precipitating factors in schizophrenia and primary affective disorder. *Comprehensive Psychiatry,* 1973, *14,* 197–202.

Cole, J. O. Phenothiazine treatment in acute schizophrenia: Effectiveness. *Archives of General Psychiatry,* 1964, *10,* 246–261.

Davis, J. M. Overview: Maintenance therapy in psychiatry of schizophrenia. *American Journal of Psychiatry,* 1975, *132,* 1237–1245.

DeAmicis, L. A., & Cromwell, R. L. Reaction time crossover in process schizophrenic patients, their relatives and control subjects. *Journal of Nervous and Mental Disease,* 1979, *167,* 593–600.

Docherty, J. P., Van Kammen, D. P., Siris, S. G., & Marder, S. R. Stages of onset of schizophrenic psychosis. *American Journal of Psychiatry,* 1978, *135,* 420–426.

Dohrenwend, B. P. Problems in defining and sampling the relevant population of stressful life events. In B. S. Dohrenwend & B. P. Dohrenwend (Eds.), *Stressful life events: Their nature and effects.* New York: Wiley, 1974.

Dohrenwend, B. P., & Egri, G. Recent stressful life events and schizophrenia. Presented at the Conference on Stress, Social Support, and Schizophrenia, Burlington, Vermont, September 1979.

Dohrenwend, B. S., Krasnoff, L., Askenasy, A. R., & Dohrenwend, B. P. Exemplification of a method for scaling life events: The PERI Life Events Scale. *Journal of Health and Social Behavior,* 1978, *19,* 205–229.

Donovan, J. M., Dressler, D. M., & Geller, R. A. Psychiatric crisis: A comparison of schizophrenic and nonschizophrenic patients. *Journal of Nervous and Mental Disease,* 1975, *161,* 172–179.

Eastwood, M.R. *The relation between physical and mental illness: The physical status of psychiatric patients at a multiphasic screening survey.* Toronto: University of Toronto Press, 1975.

Eaton, W. W. Life events, social supports, and psychiatric symptoms: A re-analysis of the New Haven data. *Journal of Health and Social Behavior,* 1978, *19,* 230–234.

Eisler, R., & Polak, P. Social stress and psychiatric disorder. *Journal of Nervous and Mental Disease,* 1971, *153,* 227–233.

Eitinger, L., & Strøm, A. *Mortality and morbidity after excessive stress.* New York: Humanities Press, 1973.

Feighner, J. P., Robins, E., Guze, S. B., Woodruff, R. A., Winokur, G., & Munoz, R. Diagnostic criteria for use in psychiatric research. *Archives of General Psychiatry,* 1972, *26,* 57–58.

Feinstein, A. A critical overview of diagnosis in psychiatry. In V. M. Rakoff, H. C. Stancer, & H. B. Kedward (Eds.), *Psychiatric diagnosis.* New York: Brunner/Mazel, 1977, pp. 189–206.

Frank, G. H. The role of the family in the development of psychopathology. *Psychological Bulletin,* 1965, *64,* 191–205.

Friedman, M., & Rosenman, R. H. *Type A behavior and your heart.* New York: Knopf, 1974.

Garmezy, N. Children at risk: The search for the antecedents of schizophrenia. Part I. Conceptual models and research methods. *Schizophrenia Bulletin,* 1974a, *8,* 14–90.

Garmezy, N. Children at risk: The search for the antecedents of schizophrenia. Part II: Ongoing Research Programs, Issues and Intervention. *Schizophrenia Bulletin.* 1974b, *9*, 55–125.

Gersten, J. C., Langner, T. S., Eisenberg, J. G., and Simcha-Fagan, O. An evaluation of the etiologic role of stressful life-change events in psychological disorders. *Journal of Health and Social Behavior,* 1977, *18*, 228–244.

Goldberg, S. C., Schooler, N. R., Hogarty, G. E., & Roper, M. Prediction of relapse in schizophrenic patients treated by drug and sociotherapy. *Archives of General Psychiatry,* 1977, *34*, 171–184.

Grant, I., Gerst, M., & Yager, J. Scaling of life events by psychiatric patients and normals. *Journal of Psychosomatic Research,* 1976, *20*, 141–149.

Grunebaum, M., Weiss, J., Gallant, D., et al. Attention in young children of psychotic mothers. *American Journal of Psychiatry,* 1974, *131*, 887–891.

Guze, S. The future of psychiatry: Medicine or social science? *Journal of Nervous and Mental Disease,* 1977, *165*, 225–230.

Harlow, H. F., & Suomi, S. J. Induced depression in monkeys. *Behavioral Biology,* 1974, *12*, 273–296.

Hendrie, H. C., Lachar, D., & Lennox, K. Personality trait and symptom correlates of life change in a psychiatric population. *Journal of Psychosomatic Medicine,* 1975, *19*, 203–208.

Hirsch, S. R., & Leff, J. P. Abnormalities in the parents of schizophrenics. *Maudsley Monograph,* 1975, *22*.

Hogarty, G. E., & Ulrich, R. F. Temporal effects of drug and placebo in delaying relapse in schizophrenic outpatients. *Archives of General Psychiatry,* 1977, *34*, 297–301.

Holmes, T. H., & Rahe, R. H. The Social Readjustment Rating Scale. *Journal of Psychosomatic Research,* 1967, *11*, 213–218.

Holzman, P. S., Proctor, L. R., Levy, D. L., Yasillo, N. J., Meltzer, H. Y., & Hurt, S. W. Eye-tracking dysfunctions in schizophrenic patients and their relatives. *Archives of General Psychiatry,* 1974, *31*, 143–151.

Huttunen, M. O., & Niskanen, P. Prenatal loss of father and psychiatric disorders. *Archives of General Psychiatry,* 1978, *35*, 429–431.

Jacob, T. Family interaction in disturbed and normal families: A methodological and substantive view. *Psychological Bulletin,* 1975, *82*, 33–65.

Jacobs, S., & Myers, J. Recent life events and acute schizophrenic psychosis: A controlled study. *Journal of Nervous and Mental Disease,* 1976, *162*, 75–87.

Jacobs, S. C., Prusoff, B. A., & Paykel, E. S. Recent life events in schizophrenia and depression. *Psychological Medicine,* 1974, *4*, 444–453.

Jenkins, C. D., Hurst, M. W., & Rose, R. M. Life changes: Do people really remember? *Archives of General Psychiatry,* 1979, *36*, 379–384.

Jung, C. G. *Über die Psychologie der Dementia Praecox.* Marhold: Halle/Saale, 1907.

Kety, S. S., Rosenthal, D., Wender, P. H., & Schulsinger, F. The types and prevalence of mental illness in the biological and adoptive families of adopted schizophrenics. In D. Rosenthal & S. S. Kety (Eds.), *The Transmission of Schizophrenia.* New York: Pergamon Press, 1968.

Kornetsky, C., & Eliasson, M. Reticular stimulation and chlorpromazine: An animal model for schizophrenic overarousal. *Science,* 1969, *165*, 1273–1274.

Langfeldt, G. The prognosis in schizophrenia. *Acta Psychiatrica Scandinavica,* 1956, Suppl. 110, 1–66.

Lapidus, L. B. Cognitive control, parental practices and contemporary social problems. Proceedings of the 78th Annual Convention of the American Psychological Association. 1970, *5*, 427–428.

Lazarus, R. S. Cognitive and coping processes in emotion. In B. Weiner (Ed.), *Cognitive Views of Human Motivation.* New York: Academic Press, 1974.

Leff, J. P. Schizophrenia and sensitivity to the family environment. *Schizophrenia Bulletin,* 1976, *2*, 566–574.

Leff, J. Social and psychological causes of the acute attack. In J. K. Wing (Ed.), *Schizophrenia: Towards a new synthesis.* New York: Grune & Stratton, 1978.

Lewinsohn, P. M., & Talkington, J. Studies on the measurement of unpleasant events and relations with depression. *Applied Psychological Measurement,* 1979, *3,* 83–101.

Liem, J. H. Effects of verbal communications of parents and children: A comparison of normal and schizophrenic families. *Journal of Consulting and Clinical Psychology,* 1974, *42,* 438–450.

Marcus, L. M. Studies of attention in children vulnerable to psychopathology. Unpublished doctoral dissertation, University of Minnesota, 1972.

May, P. R. A. *Treatment of schizophrenia: A comparative study of five treatment methods.* New York: Science House, 1968.

Mayer-Gross, W., Slater, E., & Roth, M. (Eds.). *Clinical psychiatry* (3rd ed.). Baltimore: Williams & Wilkins, 1969.

McKinney, W. T., Kliese, K. A., Suomi, S. J., & Moran, E. C. Can psychopathology be reinduced in rhesus monkeys? *Archives of General Psychiatry,* 1973, *29,* 630–634.

McNeil, T. F., & Kaij, L. Obstetric factors in the development of schizophrenia: Complications in the births of preschizophrenics and in reproduction by schizophrenic parents. In L. Wynne, R. Cromwell, & S. Matthysse (Eds.), *Nature of Schizophrenia.* New York: Wiley, 1978.

Mechanic, D. Invited commentary on self, social environment and stress. In M. H. Appley & R. Trumbull (Eds.), *Psychological stress.* New York: Appleton-Century-Crofts, 1967.

Mednick, B. R. Breakdown in high-risk subjects: Familial and early environmental factors. *Journal of Abnormal Psychology,* 1973, *82,* 469–475.

Mednick, S. A. A learning theory approach to research in schizophrenia. *Psychological Bulletin,* 1958, *55,* 316–327.

Mednick, S. A. Breakdown in individuals at high risk for schizophrenia: Possible predispositional perinatal factors. *Mental Hygiene,* 1970, *54,* 50–63.

Mednick, S. A., & Schulsinger, F. Some premorbid characteristics related to breakdown in children with schizophrenic mothers. In D. Rosenthal & S. S. Kety (Eds.), *The transmission of schizophrenia.* New York: Pergamon Press, 1968.

Mednick, S. A., & Schulsinger, F. Studies of children at high risk for schizophrenia. In S. Mednick, F. Schulsinger, J. Higgins, et al. (Eds.), *Genetics, environment and psychopathology.* Amsterdam: North-Holland, 1974.

Meehl, P. E. Schizotaxia, schizotypy, schizophrenia. *American Psychologist,* 1962, *17,* 827–838.

Morrison, J. R. Hudgens, R. W., & Barchha, R. G. Life events and psychiatric illness. *British Journal of Psychiatry,* 1968, *114,* 423–432.

Myers, J. K., Lindenthal, J. J., and Pepper, M. P. Life events and psychiatric impairment. *Journal of Nervous and Mental Disease,* 1971, *152,* 149–157.

Nuckolls, C. B., Cassel, J., and Kaplan, G. H. Psycho-social assets, life crises and the prognosis of pregnancy. *American Journal of Epidemiology,* 1972, *95,* 431–444.

Pasamanick, B., & Knoblock, H. Epidemiologic studies on the complications of pregnancy and the birth process. In G. Caplan (Ed.), *Prevention of mental disorders in children.* New York: Basic Books, 1961, pp. 74–94.

Paul, S. Benzodiazepine receptors and psychopathological states. Presented at the Seventieth Annual Meeting of the American Psychopathological Association. Washington, D.C., March 1980.

Paykel, E. S., Myers, J. K., Dienelt, M. N., Klerman, G. L., Lindenthal, J. J., & Pepper, M. P. Life events and depression: A controlled study. *Archives of General Psychiatry,* 1969, *21,* 753–760.

Paykel, E. S., Prusoff, B. A., & Uhlenhuth, E. H. Scaling of life events. *Archives of General Psychiatry,* 1971, *25,* 340–347.

Phillips, L. *Human adaptation and its failures.* New York: Academic Press, 1968.

Pollin, W., & Stabenau, J. R. Biological, psychological and historical differences in a series of monozygotic twins discordant for schizophrenia. In D. Rosenthal & S. S. Kety (Eds.), *The transmission of schizophrenia.* New York: Pergamon Press, 1968.

Pope, H. G., & Lipinski, J. F. Diagnosis in schizophrenia and manic-depressive illness. *Archives of General Psychiatry,* 1978, *35,* 811–827.

Rabkin, J. G. Stressful life events and schizophrenia: A review of the research literature. *Psychological Bulletin,* 1980, *87,* 408–425.

Rabkin, J., & Struening, E. Life events, stress and illness. *Science.* 1976, *194,* 1013–1020.

Rahe, R. H. The pathway between subjects' recent life changes and their near-future illness reports: Representative results and methodological issues. In B. S. Dohrenwend & B. P. Dohrenwend (Eds.), *Stressful life events: Their nature and effects.* New York: Wiley, 1974.

Rahe, R. H. Life change measurement clarification. *Psychosomatic Medicine,* 1978, *40,* 95–98.

Rahe, R. H., & Arthur, R. J. Life change and illness studies: Past history and future directions. *Journal of Human Stress,* 1978, *4,* 3–15.

Rieder, R. O., & Gershon, E. S. Genetic strategies in biological psychiatry. *Archives of General Psychiatry,* 1978, *35,* 866–873.

Rierdon, J. Word associations of socially isolated adolescents. *Journal of Abnormal Psychology,* 1980, *89,* 98–100.

Rosenman, R. H., Brand, R. J., Jenkins, D., Friedman, M., Straus, R., & Wurm, M. Coronary heart disease in the Western Collaborative Group study: Final follow-up experience of 8-1/2 years. *Journal of the American Medical Association,* 1975, *233,* 872–877.

Rosenthal, D. *Genetic theory and abnormal behavior.* New York: McGraw-Hill, 1970.

Rutschmann, J., Cornblatt, B., & Erlenmeyer-Kimling, L. Sustained attention in children at risk for schizophrenia: Report on a continuous performance test. *Archives of General Psychiatry,* 1977, *34,* 571–575.

Rutter, M. Children of sick parents: An environmental and psychiatric study. *Maudsley Monograph,* 1966, *16.*

Salzinger, K. *Schizophrenia: Behavioral aspects.* New York: Wiley, 1973.

Sameroff, A. J., & Zax, M. Perinatal characteristics in the offspring of schizophrenic women. *Journal of Nervous and Mental Disease,* 1973a, *157,* 191–199.

Sameroff, A. J., & Zax, M. Schizotaxia revisited: Model issues on the etiology of schizophrenia. *American Journal of Orthopsychiatry,* 1973b, *43,* 744–754.

Schless, A. P., Teichman, A., Mendels, J., & DiGiacomo, J. N. The role of stress as a precipitating factor of psychiatric illness. *British Journal of Psychiatry,* 1977, *130,* 19–22.

Schneider, K. *Clinical psychopathology.* New York: Grune & Stratton, 1959.

Schwartz, C. C., & Myers, J. K. Life events and schizophrenia. I. Comparison of schizophrenics with a community sample. *Archives of General Psychiatry,* 1977, *34,* 1238–1241.

Seligman, M. E. P., & Groves, D. Non-transient learned helplessness. *Psychonomic Science,* 1970, *19,* 191–192.

Selyé, H. *The stress of life.* New York: McGraw-Hill, 1956.

Serban, G. Stress in schizophrenics and normals. *British Journal of Psychiatry,* 1975, *126,* 397–407.

Spring, B., & Zubin, J. Vulnerability to schizophrenic episodes and their prevention in adults. In G. W. Albee & J. M. Joffe (Eds.), *Primary prevention of psychopathology* (Vol. I). Hanover, N. H.: University Press of New England, 1977, pp. 254–285.

Stabenau, J. R., & Pollin, W. Early characteristics of monozygotic twins discordant for schizophrenia. *Archives of General Psychiatry,* 1967, *17,* 723–734.

Stevens, S. S., & Galanter, E. H. Ratio scales and category scales for a dozen perceptual continua. *Journal of Experimental Psychology,* 1957, *54,* 377–411.

Strauss, J. S., Harder, D. W., & Chaldler, M. Egocentrism in children of parents with a history of psychotic disorders. *Archives of General Psychiatry,* 1979, *36,* 191–200.

Strecker, E. A. A preliminary study of the precipitating situation in two hundred cases of mental disease. *American Journal of Psychiatry,* 1922, *1,* 503–536.

Suomi, S. J., Delizio, R., & Harlow, H. F. Social rehabilitation of separation-induced depressive disorders in monkeys. *American Journal of Psychiatry,* 1976, *133,* 1279–1285.

Suomi, S. J., & Harlow, H. F. Production and alleviation of depressive behaviors in monkeys. In J. Maser & M. Seligman (Eds.), *Psychopathology: Experimental models.* San Francisco: Freeman, 1977.

Uhlenhuth, E. H., Balter, M. B., Lipman, R. S., et al. Remembering life events. In J. S. Strauss, H. M. Babigian, & M. Roff (Eds.), *The origins and course of psychopathology: Method of longitudinal research.* New York: Plenum Press, 1977, pp. 117–132.

Ullman, L., & Krasner, L. *A psychological approach to abnormal behavior* (2nd ed.). Englewood Cliffs, N.J.: Prentice-Hall, 1975.

Venables, P. H. Input dysfunction in schizophrenia. In B. Maher (Ed.), *Progress in Experimental Personality Research* (Vol. 1). New York: Academic Press, 1964.

Wahl, C. W. Some antecedent factors in the family histories of 568 male schizophrenics of the United States Navy. *American Journal of Psychiatry,* 1956, *113,* 201–210.

Watt, N. F., Stolorow, R. D., Lubensky, A. W., & McClelland, D. C. School adjustment and behavior of children hospitalized for schizophrenia as adults. *American Journal of Orthopsychiatry,* 1970, *40,* 637–657.

Weiner, H. The illusion of simplicity: The medical model revisited. *American Journal of Psychiatry,* 1978, *135* (July supplement), 27–33.

Wing, J. K. *Reasoning about madness.* New York: Oxford University Press, 1978.

Wing, J. K., & Brown, G. W. Institutionalism and schizophrenia. London: Cambridge University Press, 1970.

Wohlberg, G. W., & Kornetsky, C. Sustained attention in remitted schizophrenics. *Archives of General Psychiatry,* 1973, *28,* 533–537.

Young, L. D., Suomi, S. J., Harlow, H. F., & McKinney, W. T. Early stress and later response to separation. *American Journal of Psychiatry,* 1973, *130,* 400–405.

Zubin, J., & Spring, B. Vulnerability—a new view of schizophrenia. *Journal of Abnormal Psychology,* 1977, *86,* 103–126.

Chapter 2

Cognition, Emotion, and Schizophrenia

GLENN SHEAN

College of William and Mary
Williamsburg, Virgina

Bleuler introduced the concept of schizophrenia in 1911, in part, to allow for the role of psychological factors in the formation of symptoms. He viewed schizophrenia not as a progressive deterioration toward dementia, as Kraepelin did, but as a condition characterized by a disorder of associations and a splitting of the basic functions of the personality.

Bleuler's concept of an associational disturbance in schizophrenia was rooted in the psychology of the late nineteenth century. With this concept, he attempted to specify a single underlying deficit, described in psychological terms but organic in origin, that would account for the diverse symptoms of this disorder.

For us the alteration of the thinking process, or elementarily expressed, of the association, is of special importance, and, as a matter of fact, nearly all the psychogenic symptoms can be derived from it. . . . In schizophrenia, it is the highest control which fails where it would be necessary to act, and this again must be referred to as a disturbance of the connections of all the individual functions. With this dismemberment of the connections, it is comprehensible that the logical function of thinking is disturbed by affective needs . . . (1924, pp. 205–206).

The concept of associational disturbance as the basis for schizophrenic thought disturbance has been variously interpreted by investigators over the past 70 years. However, there has been no general agreement as to the specific nature of this deficit.

Bleuler's emphasis on thought disturbance as the salient feature of schizophrenia has contributed to two traditional models for understanding psychological phenomena: the psychodynamic and the experimental.

The fact that the content of delusions and hallucinations almost always refers to some aspect of the patient's personal predicament has led psychodynamic theorists to view schizophrenic thought disturbance as a dynamically determined coping strategy designed to disguise, disown, and deny unacceptable emotions and thereby minimize or avoid personality disintegration. The basic formulation of the psychodynamic view has been stated by Arieti as follows:

Confronted with overpowering anxiety, when the patient cannot change or tolerate the unbearable aspects of his existence any longer, he has to change reality. But reality cannot change, and he has to change himself again in order to see reality in a different way. The psychotic transformation will enable him to experience himself and the environment in strange, unique ways . . . and yet the mechanisms he resorts to now are available to every human being; they are part of his human nature (1974, p. 215).

In this statement, Arieti implies an assumption common to many dynamically oriented clinical theorists, i.e., there are no qualitative differences between the thought processes of normals and schizophrenics.

From the psychodynamic perspective, thought disorder in schizophrenia is one aspect of a major cognitive transformation, a transformation in which one's attitude toward life has changed. In this process, certain ideas become predominant and repetitious, as if the existence of the patient hinged on them. Burnham (1966) has described the characteristics of this restructuring of the cognitive system as follows: (1) the boundaries between self and nonself are blurred; (2) the ability to distinguish between trivial and relevant events to the person is impaired; and (3) there is a severe impairment of normal discrimination between inner and outer mechanisms of control. In brief, the thought disturbance or cognitive restructuring observed in schizophrenia is understood as a defensive disposition to control one's emotional response to threatening experiences and situations (McReynolds, 1962).

A second general approach to the understanding of schizophrenia has grown out of Bleuler's emphasis on the associational disturbance. Many researchers have focused on the form rather than the content of schizophrenic thought disorder. Weiner (1966) has grouped theories of formal thought disorder according to three aspects of normal thought: (1) the capacity to scan information selectively, establishing and maintaining focus on that which is relevant and preventing the intrusion of irrelevant material; (2) the capacity to think abstractly; and (3) the capacity to reason logically about the relationships between objects and events. Theories of formal thought disorder have been thoroughly summarized and reviewed by Chapman and Chapman (1973) and therefore are only briefly sampled in this chapter.

1. McGhie and Chapman (1969) have postulated that the basic problem in schizophrenia is an inability to select, focus on, and regulate incoming information. The loss of the ability to direct attention focally leads to a growing inability to cope with diverse environmental stimuli which in turn generates increased anxiety and a sense of vulnerability. The authors speculate that a defect of the reticular system leads to a breakdown in the ability for selective attention, a flooding of consciousness with undifferentiated experience, and the anxiety-panic confusion associated with a schizophrenic episode.

Broen (1966) has also formulated a model of formal thought disorder. He speculates that disturbed schizophrenics show "response disorganization" in response to heightened drive levels. The result of this process is that the likelihood of various response alternatives becomes more equal for schizophrenics than for others. With increasing chronicity, patients respond to this disorganization of response hierarchies by narrowing their perception to only the most prominent stimuli. Broen has suggested that this process of response disorganization is most pronounced for nonparanoid patients.

Silverman (1964) has formulated a model that attempts to explain schizophrenic thought as the result of a defect in attentional processes. Rather than emphasizing the role of selective attention. Silverman's model focuses primarily on the degree to which stimuli are sampled from the environment. His research suggests that schizophrenics show either marked or minimal scanning. Paranoids appear to be excessive scanners while nonparanoid patients evidence the developmentally earlier pattern of minimal scanning. Silverman relates this evidence to clinical theory by speculating that nonparanoid (minimal scanner) patients avoid anxiety by directing their attention away from the environment and onto internal processes while paranoids utilize excessive scanning as a means of vigilance against a perceived hostile environment.

As is evident in the above brief review of "attentional deficit" models of schizophrenia, several theorists have attempted to differentiate between paranoid and nonparanoid patients in terms of their theoretical models. Most appear to attribute greater disturbance vulnerability to the nonparanoid group.

2. Many clinicians and researchers have been impressed by the concreteness of schizophrenic thought. Vigotsky (1934) has formulated a theory of schizophrenic thought which grew out of his model of the development of thought processes in normals. In Vigotsky's view, the development of thought is characterized by a series of states that ideally culminate in the ability to form abstract concepts. Abstract thought is equated with the ability to single out elements or qualities apart from the total concrete experience in which they are embedded. Schizophrenics fail to develop or regress to a preadolescent stage of complex thinking, i.e., they group objects using any kind of relationship that may be found rather than on the basis of an abstracted quality shared by all objects in the group.

Goldstein (1939) also developed a model of schizophrenic thought based on their having lost the ability to think abstractly. In his view, the abstract response has two primary differentiating features: it is reflective—reflective in that such responses involve a conscious decision to respond to objects as bearer of particular qualities or attributes rather than as a series of stimulus qualities that gain attention in a reflex-like manner—and it is voluntary. Goldstein's concepts have resulted in a great number of studies of the loss of the ability to abstract in schizophrenia; few, however, have attempted to test his concept of the role of conscious volition.

McGaughran (1954) has offered a reinterpretation of Goldstein's concept of concreteness. He has focused on an additional aspect of Goldstein's definition of concreteness, i.e., idiosyncratic groupings based on private symbolic meanings not shared by most people. McGaughran and Moran (1956, 1957) found no difference between paranoid schizophrenic and normal subjects on scores for level of abstraction, but they did find differences in the nature of their concepts. Schizophrenics tended to be more private, frequently with the quality of personal idiom and over-abstraction. It may be, as Chapman and Chapman (1973) have suggested, that schizophrenics tend to think and respond autistically rather than being unable to think abstractly.

Arieti (1974) has set forth an interesting reinterpretation of Bleuler's concept of associational disturbance, based in part on the earlier work of Von Domarus (1944). Arieti has pointed out that when an individual thinks logically, he organizes his thoughts according to a pattern or structure that leads toward an end or conclusion. If, however, he relaxes and allows his thoughts to arise spontaneously without exerting any selection or direction, ideas arise to consciousness seemingly for their own sake and not for any distant purpose. These associational processes are compatible with the basic laws of association (contiguity and similarity), i.e., ideas are still connected but lack structure, purpose, and conscious intention.

Arieti argues that in schizophrenia, contrary to Bleuler's view, disturbances in logic consist of *more* frequent occurrence of ideas connected by the laws of association. In other words, ideas are still connected by the principles of contiguity and similarity, but they lack logical continuity. In more advanced cases of schizophrenia, Arieti maintains that the ideas still tend to associate by similarity, but by a new type of similarity connected with the verbalization rather than the connotation, i.e., the associational link is a predicate of verbal quality (Von Domarus, 1944). The impairment of the capacity for logical continuity or intentionality in schizophrenic associations differentiates these individuals from normals and is a function of the extent of the fragmentation of the personality.

Arieti's explanation of the basis for schizophrenic thought disturbance is compatible with the dynamic view that threatening unconscious impulses and emotions, in the context of impaired interpersonal function, result in ego failure-fragmentation, which in turn results in the processes of thought disturbance described by Arieti.

A recent experiment by Schneider (1976) appears to support Arieti's interpretation of the schizophrenic thought disorder, as opposed to the attention deficit hypothesis. Schneider's results suggest that the mechanisms of selective attention are intact in delusional schizophrenics, but that some of the memory traces these persons judge as relevant are seldom judged relevant by normals. More specifically, Schneider found that material related to the delusional system affects the schizophrenic subject much the same way material which normals consider to be important affects normals.

If, indeed, schizophrenic patients do not suffer from a specific formal disturbance of thought, but rather utilize to the extreme psychological processes common to all of us as a means of preserving remnants of executive ego function, then several corollary hypotheses fall into place. First, their sense of vulnerability must result in a special sensitivity to the nonverbalized emotional tone of interpersonal communications (Lidz, 1973). Second, this sense of vulnerability may result in excessive reliance upon a select few cognitive mechanisms as self-protective strategies by which these persons are able to minimize the likelihood of threatening interactions and associated levels of emotional arousal. La Russo (1978) has substantiated this notion. Her research findings indicate that paranoid patients are more sensitive than normals to genuine nonverbal facial cues that communicate a particular stress or relief from that stress. The author speculates that if a person has learned in childhood that emotional expressiveness will result in rebuke, particularly if the rebuke is communicated covertly in double messages, the receiver has an enhanced likelihood of developing a particular sensitivity to particular cues.

The picture of schizophrenic thought that emerges from this review is one of growing reliance on idiosyncratic meanings and interpretation of events associated with increased severity of disturbance. The bizarre idiosyncratic nature of schizophrenic thought may be understood as the result of a process of disengagement and withdrawal from some or most aspects of interpersonal reality and a growing compensatory involvement in autistic fantasy. Inferred levels of vulnerability-sensitivity to threatening levels or patterns of interaction are likely to be linearly related to severity of disturbance. Different clinical subtypes can be understood as resulting from differing levels of vulnerability-disorganization and the ability of the individual to utilize cognitive (ego defensive) strategies to maintain personality integration and ward off anxiety arousing experiences.

The remainder of this chapter focuses on cognitive strategies by which schizophrenic patients manage their emotions and concurrently develop increasingly idiosyncratic ways of thinking.

In apparent contrast to the psychodynamic emphasis on the determining role of emotions, R. Lazarus (1977) has asserted that cognitive processes determine the quality and intensity of emotional reactions. More specifically, Lazarus maintains that cognitive processes underlie coping activities which, in turn, continually shape emotional reactions by altering the ongoing relationship between person and environment.

Lazarus (1973) maintains that the self-regulation of emotion goes beyond the proposition that people can inhibit the overt expression of emotion; self-regulation may also dampen, eliminate or alter the quality of emotional states (see also Lazarus, Coyne, & Folkman, pp. 218–239, this volume). According to this model, emotions are controlled by intrapsychic modes of coping, that is, the defense mechanisms. Coping strategies generally precede emotion, that is, they are anticipatory. Lazarus and his colleagues have conducted a number of experimental investigations to demonstrate that different cognitive sets (Speisman et al., 1964; Aas, 1958; Lazarus et al., 1963; Lazarus & Alfert, 1964) and personality variables (Lazarus et al., 1965; Speisman et al., 1964) may be important determinants of individual emotional reactions to stress (Averill et al., 1972). Neufeld (1975) has also reported evidence that the personality dimensions of repression-sensitization are related to subjects' response to experimental threat. In a more recent study, Le Fave and Neufeld (1980) report that both personality factors (physical-danger trait anxiety) and cognitive expectancy result in greater autonomic responding.

Beck (1971) has formulated a cognitive model of psychopathology based on the assumption that the input from external situations in both normals and psychiatric patients is molded in accordance with the cognitive schemas activated by the situation. The difference between normal and abnormal reactions, according to Beck, lies in the degree of correspondence between the conceptualization and the actual stimulus situation. In psychopathology, perseverative faulty conceptualizations (cognitive sets) such as those relevant to anger, abandonment, rejection, and loss are viewed as leading to sequences of perceptual distortion and prolonged inappropriate emotional arousal. According to Beck, typical cognitive patterns and feeling states are associated with particular categories of disturbance. Feeling states are considered to result from the particular cognitive strategies by which the person structures his or her reality.

It follows from this discussion that groups of schizophrenic patients may utilize different cognitive strategies to manage their emotions, and these strategies are associated with the different symptom pictures and levels of thought disturbance, i.e., continued perceptual distortion and prolonged inappropriate negative emotions are associated with excessive and rigid reliance on one or more cognitive strategies which at the same time preserve personality function and result in idiosyncratic thought.

Social Adjustment, Paranoid Signs, and Cognition

Clinical theorists have observed that paranoid thought evolves from a combination of denial of unacceptable feelings and impulses and projection of these feelings (Heilbrun & Norbert, 1971). Cameron (1963) has observed that paranoid persons use denial as a defense when something threatening has reached the preconscious or conscious level. The essence of the paranoid dynamism is viewed as rooted in a sense of inferiority and isolation that results in strategies designed to control, deny, and project feelings. The paranoid is depicted as a person haunted by fears of intimacy, dependency, and caring, as troubled by a remarkably insecure gender identity, as someone existing in a chronic state of anger originating in a profound sense of insecurity and ambivalence in the parent-child relationship. Conscious compensatory attitudes are evidenced in a strong sense of and preoccupation with personal and social injustices, and a compelling need to appear to self and others as controlled, strong, independent, and invulnerable (Zamansky, 1958).

In contrast, chronic nonparanoid patients have been described as vulnerable, sensitive individuals who are relatively ineffectual, frightened, puzzled, submissive people (Sullivan, 1956). This group is portrayed as withdrawn, vulnerable, and unusually sensitive to stress. Cameron (1963) has described chronic undifferentiated patients as individuals characterized by a global, cognitive disorganization which seriously impairs their ability to differentiate between different aspects of the environment. Their underlying mood is one of anxiety and dread which eventually results in the pathway to chronic schizophrenia, i.e., isolation-withdrawal, cognitive disorganization, autistic fantasy.

Investigation of the delusions of paranoid-reactive and process-nonparanoid patients indicates a greater degree of cognitive disorganization in the latter group (Shean, 1975; Baird & Shean, 1977). Process-nonparanoid patients express less coherent, more diffuse and extravagant beliefs than their paranoid counterparts. This evidence supports the clinical descriptions of process-nonparanoid patients as more disorganized-vulnerable-idiosyncratic in function than their paranoid counterparts.

Studies of schizophrenic patients have proven more productive when the heterogeneity within the schizophrenic sample is reduced by dividing patients according to pattern of disturbance, i.e., paranoid/nonparanoid, and prehospitalization adjustment, i.e., process-reactive (Goldstein, 1978; Schooler & Silverman, 1969). Psychophysiological studies indicate that process-nonparanoid patients are most likely to evidence both diminished differential autonomic responsiveness and reduced habituation of orienting responses, suggesting a defect in excitatory modulation in this group (Ax et al., 1970). Several researchers have suggested that the degree and pattern of disruption of excitatory modulation are related to premorbid adjustment and the presence or absence of paranoid signs (Venables, 1964). These studies suggest that process-nonparanoid patients evidence the greatest deficit in attention and excitatory modulation of arousal. Clinical studies also suggest that process-nonparanoid patients will be more likely to withdraw from novel stimulation, and to avoid attentional focusing which might result in threatening input because of failure to develop or a breakdown in the ability to modulate excitatory experiences. The ability of paranoid patients to focus attention and maintain cognitive functions after years under the deprived circumstances of institutionalization suggests that paranoid mechanisms of denial, intellectualization, and projection enable these individuals to reestablish and maintain a more adaptive level of excitatory modulation and attentional focusing.

Studies of Cognitive Strategies and Stress Control

Research with normal subjects indicates that autonomic arousal to threatening stimuli is modifiable where stimuli represent consistent signals for reinforcement (Martin et al., 1966). Normal subjects are differentially able to elicit and inhibit autonomic responses to avoidance stimuli, but only when they receive explicit instructions and several reinforcing trials. Post-training interviews suggest that subjects adopt a variety of cognitive strategies to control autonomic responses to discriminative stimuli.

A series of studies was designed to investigate the relationship between cognitive style of emotional control and schizophrenic subtype. In one study, groups of male paranoid-reactive and process-nonparanoid patients were reinforced (avoidance of an aversive stimulus) to modify autonomic responsiveness to differential excitatory and inhibitory avoidance stimuli (Shean & Faia, 1974). Schizophrenic subjects did not differ substantially from college students in their ability to perform the differential avoidance task. Subgroups of schizophrenic subjects also did not significantly differ in autonomic responsiveness to the discriminative stimuli. Subjects' responses to instructions during a post-experiment interview, however, did differ dramatically. Each paranoid-reactive subject reported difficulty in imagining situations or experiences that would stimulate the emotion of fear and thus enable him or her to respond to the excitatory stimulus. Autonomic responses indicated that these subjects were in fact responding to the excitatory stimulus at about the same level as nonparanoid subjects, but cognitive information was not consonant with this fact. Denial of emotions, such as anxiety or fear, was expressed in each case. Most subjects indicated that they believed they had learned to control their emotions so effectively and for so long that they doubted such feelings as fear could be reexperienced. Explanations given for the exertion of such control included experiences (real or fantasied) in dangerous occupations, hobbies, or athletic contests that necessitated the elimination or suppression of emotions such as fear.

Nonparanoid subjects, on the other hand, consistently reported little difficulty in imagining experiences that would make them fearful. In fact, everyday situations, such as crossing a heavily traveled street, thunderstorms, crowded shops, and people staring, were often mentioned as fearful stimuli for this group.

In summary, self-report data appear to support clinical descriptions of the paranoid patient as someone who controls certain threatening emotions through the cognitive strategies of denial and intellectualization, while process-nonparanoid patients appeared to be particularly vulnerable persons who withdraw to protect themselves from stressful situations that might seem quite routine and ordinary to most persons.

A second study was designed to test the hypothesis that paranoid-reactive patients deny or overcontrol certain unpleasant emotions such as anxiety and fear while process-nonparanoid patients are unable to control such feelings (Shean et al., 1974). Groups of schizophrenic subjects participated in a procedure designed to determine group differences in patterns of cognitive appraisal and response to stress. Results indicated that paranoid-reactive subjects underrate emotional reactions to stressful stimuli, i.e., these subjects evidenced greater heart-rate variability to stressful stimuli while rating the stimuli less disturbing than did process-nonparanoid subjects. Nonparanoid subjects, on the other hand, tended to rate stimuli as more stressful than their autonomic responses indicated (distributions of autonomic data and ratings were normalized for comparison). These findings support the clinical pictures of the groups already described here.

A follow-up study of groups of 20 paranoid-reactive underraters (ratings of stress stimuli below autonomic responsiveness) and 20 process-nonparanoid overraters (ratings of stress stimuli were higher than autonomic responses) was conducted to further delineate personality characteristics of the groups (Schmaltz & Shean, 1973). Several personality tests were administered (Byrne's Repression-Sensitization Scale, Eysenck Personality Inventory, Autonomic Perception Questionnaire, some items based on clinical literature and the 16PF) to each subject, and an item analysis of the entire test-item pool was conducted to ascertain which items, if any, discriminated between the groups. Individual items that did discriminate significantly between over- and underraters are listed in Tables 2-1 and 2-2.

The tendency of paranoid-reactive patients to deny experiencing fear or anxiety in the presence of stressful stimuli and for process-nonparanoid patients to evidence unusual sensitivity to stress was confirmed further in a study in which subjects were asked to view segments of a stressful film ("Subincision") and then rate the stress value of the film. Paranoids rated the film significantly less stressful than normals and nonparanoids, while nonparanoids rated the film as significantly more stressful than the other groups (Riley, 1973).

This series of investigations suggests that there may be quite different patterns of cognitive control of emotions that characterize reactive-paranoid and process-nonparanoid schizophrenic persons. In summary, it appears that the paranoid group may be referred to as "overcontrolled" persons who erect a cognitive structure and self concept which allows them effectively to deny that they are vulnerable to the day-to-day stressors that elicit feelings of anxiety, fear, and hurt in most of us. On the

Table 2-1 **Questions That Overraters Answered Significantly More Often Than Underraters**

1. I like mixing with people. (True)
2. I suffer from nerves. (True)
3. Most nights I go right to sleep without any trouble. (True)
4. I can look anyone in the eye and tell a lie with a straight face if I have reason to. (False)

Table 2-2 **Questions That Underraters Answered Significantly More Often Than Overraters**

1. I don't seem to care what happens to me. (False)
2. At times I feel like picking a fight with someone. (True)
3. There aren't many people you can trust. (True)
4. When you feel anxious do you experience accelerated heart beat? (No)

other hand, process-nonparanoid patients appear to be deficient in cognitive defensive strategies and associated control of feelings. This deficiency renders these persons unusually vulnerable and unable to cope with the stresses of day-to-day living and with few alternatives to autistic withdrawal.

Concluding Remarks

These findings can be considered little more than preliminary and suggestive. There are several obvious shortcomings in the methodology and approach, but the overall trend of the research reviewed in this chapter suggests that different patterns of cognitive function within the population we call schizophrenic play a role in the ability of each person to order his or her world, to make it predictable, safe, reasonable, and worth living in, and that these strategies play an important role in determining ongoing mood and permissible emotions. To withdraw completely into total apathy is to become a biological machine without emotions or feelings that relate to interpersonal reality. To become convinced that one is an exceptionally superior person, who is at the same time victim of the evil intentions of powerful others, salvages and overinflates a fragile form of self-esteem, floods one's consciousness with a self-justifying mood of self-righteous anger and resentment, and effectively denies one's own frailty, vulnerability, and need for interpersonal intimacy. Conceivably, intelligence, genetic inheritance, temperament, social class, and a myriad of other factors, in addition to life experience, contribute to the cognitive pathway taken by each person.

Further investigation is necessary to unravel the complex relationship between cognition-emotion and the clinical picture. These studies do suggest, however, that there are different cognitive strategies for controlling emotions that characterize paranoid-reactive and process-nonparanoid patients.

References

Aas, A. *Mutilation fantasies and autonomic responses.* Oslo: Oslo University Press, 1958.

Arieti, S. *Interpretation of schizophrenia.* New York: Basic Books, 1974.

Arnold, M. B. *Emotion and personality.* New York: Columbia University Press, 1960.

Averill, J. R., Olbrich, E., & Lazarus, R. S. Personality correlates of differential response to direct and vicarious threat: A failure to replicate previous findings. *Journal of Personality and Social Psychology,* 1972, *21,* 25–29.

Ax, A. F., Banford, J. L., Beckett, P. G., et al. Autonomic conditioning in chronic schizophrenia. *Journal of Abnormal Psychology,* 1970, *76,* 40–54.

Baird, P., & Shean, G. Delusions and Sartre's concept of "Bad Faith". Unpublished paper, 1977.

Beck, A. T. Cognition, affect and psychopathology. *Archives of General Psychiatry,* 1971, *24,* 495–500.

Bleuler, E. *Dementia praecox or the group of schizophrenias* (D. Sinkins, trans.). New York: International Universities Press, 1950. (German edition, 1911)

Bleuler, E. *Textbook of psychiatry* (A. A. Brill, trans.). New York: Macmillan, 1924.

Broen, W. E., & Storms, L. H. Lawful disorganization: The process underlying a schizophrenic syndrome. *Psychological Review,* 1966, *73,* 265–279.

Burnham, D. L. Varieties of reality restructuring in schizophrenia. In R. Cancro (Ed.), *The schizophrenic reactions.* New York: Brunner/Maxel, 1970.

Cameron, N. The development of paranoic thinking. *Psychological Review,* 1943, *50,* 219–228.

Chapman, L. J., & Chapman, J. P. *Disordered thought in schizophrenia.* New York: Appleton-Century-Crofts, 1973.

Goldstein, K. The significance of special mental tests for diagnosis & prognosis in schizophrenia. *American Journal of Psychiatry,* 1939, *96,* 575–587.

Goldstein, M. J. Further data concerning the relation between premorbid adjustment and paranoid symptomatology. *Schizophrenic Bulletin,* 1978, *4,* 236–241.

Heilbrun, A. B., & Norbert, N. Sensitivity to maternal censure in paranoid and nonparanoid schizophrenics. *Journal of Nervous and Mental Disease,* 1971, *152,* 45–49.

La Russo, L. Sensitivity of paranoid patients to nonverbal cues. *Journal of Abnormal Psychology,* 1978, *87,* 463–471.

Lazarus, R. S. Cognitive and coping processes in emotion. In A. Monat & R. Lazarus (Eds.), *Stress and coping.* New York: Columbia University Press, 1977.

Lazarus, R. S. The self-regulation of emotion. Paper delivered at symposium, Parameters of Emotion, Stockholm, 1973.

Lazarus, R. S. A cognitively oriented psychologist looks at biofeedback. *American Psychologist,* 1975, *30,* 553–561.

Lazarus, R. S., Speisman, J., and Mordkoff, A. The relationship between autonomic indicators of psychological stress: Heart rate and skin conductance. *Psychosomatic Medicine,* 1963, *25,* 19–30.

Lazarus, R. S., & Alfert, E. Short-circuiting of threat by experimentally altering cognitive appraisal. *Journal of Abnormal and Social Psychology,* 1964, *69,* 195–205.

Lazarus, R. S., Coyne, J. C., & Folkman, S. Cognition, emotion, and motivation: The doctoring of Humpty-Dumpty. In R. W. J. Neufeld (Ed.), *Psychological stress and psychopathology.* New York: McGraw-Hill, 1981.

Le Fave, M. K., and Neufeld, R. W. J. Anticipatory threat and physical danger trait anxiety: A signal-detection analysis of effects on autonomic responding. *Journal of Research in Personality,* 1980, *14,* 283–306.

Martin, R., Dean, S., & Shean, G. Selective attention and instrumental modification of the GSR. *Psychophysiology,* 1966, *4,* 460–467.

McGaughran, L. S. Predicting language behavior from object sorting. *Journal of Abnormal and Social Psychology,* 1954, *49,* 183–195.

McGaughran, L. S., & Moran, L. J. "Conceptual level" vs "conceptual area" analysis of object-sorting behavior of schizophrenic and nonpsychiatric groups. *Journal of Abnormal and Social Psychology,* 1956, *52,* 43–50.

McGhie, A., & Chapman, J. Disorders of attention and perception in early schizophrenia. *British Journal of Medical Psychology,* 1969, *34,* 103–116.

McReynolds, P. Perception and schizophrenia. In D. D. Jackson (Ed.), *Schizophrenia.* New York: Basic Books, 1962.

Neufeld, R. W. J. Effects of experimentally altered cognitive appraisal on "d" and response bias to experimental threat. *Journal of Personality and Social Psychology,* 1975, *31,* 735–743.

Riley, A. Effects of defensive orientation on stress reduction for paranoid and nonparanoid schizophrenics. Unpublished master's thesis, 1973.

Schmaltz, E., & Shean, G. Personality and cognitive appraisal of stress. Paper presented at annual meeting of the Southeastern Psychological Association, New Orleans, 1973.

Schafer, R. *Psychoanalytic interpretation in Rorschach testing.* New York: Grune & Stratton, 1954.

Schneider, S. J. Selective attention in schizophrenia. *Journal of Abnormal Psychology,* 1976, *85,* 167–173.

Schooler, C., & Silverman, J. Perceptual styles and their correlates among schizophrenic patients. *Journal of Abnormal Psychology,* 1969, *74,* 459–470.

Shapiro, D. *Neurotic styles*. New York: Basic Books, 1965.

Shean, G. A factor-analytic study of schizophrenic delusional thought. Paper presented at the Annual meeting of the Southeastern Psychological Association, 1975.

Shean, G., & Faia, C. Autonomic control, selective attention and schizophrenic subtype. *Journal of Nervous and Mental Disease*, 1975, *160*, 176–181.

Shean, G., Faia, C., & Schmaltz, E. Cognitive appraisal of stress and schizophrenic subtype. *Journal of Abnormal Psychology*, 1974, *83*, 523–528.

Silverman, J. The problem of attention in research and theory in schizophrenia. *Psychological Review*, 1964, *71*, 352–379.

Speisman, J. C., Lazarus, R. S., Mordkoff, A. M., & Davison, L. A. The experimental reduction of stress based on ego-defense theory. *Journal of Abnormal and Social Psychology*, 1964, *68*, 367–380.

Sullivan, H. S. *Schizophrenia as a human process*. New York: Norton, 1956.

Venables, P. H. Input dysfunction in schizophrenia. In B. A. Maher (Ed.), *Psychopathology*. New York: Academic Press, 1964.

Vigotsky, L. S. Thought in schizophrenia. *Archives of Neurology and Psychiatry*, 1934, *31*, 1063–1077.

Weiner, I. B. *Psychodiagnosis in schizophrenia*. New York: Wiley, 1966.

Zamansky, H. S. An investigation of the psychoanalytic theory of paranoid delusions. *Journal of Personality*, 1958, *26*, 410–425.

Chapter 3

Vulnerability to Environmental Stress: High-Risk Research on the Development of Schizophrenia*

TRISHA BEUHRING

University of Southern California
University Park, California

ROBERT CUDEK

University of Southern California
University Park, California

SARNOFF A. MEDNICK

University of Southern California
University Park, California
and
Psykologist Institut
Copenhagen, Denmark

ELAINE F. WALKER

Cornell University
Ithica, N. Y.

FINI SCHULSINGER

Psykologist Institut
Copenhagen, Denmark

The diathesis-stress model of schizophrenia (Rosenthal, 1970; also see Spring & Coons, pp. 13–54, this volume) suggests that the likelihood of a recent event precipitating a schizophrenic episode depends on the degree of preexisting vulnerability to this psychiatric disorder. A number of factors are thought to affect vulnerability. Studies of twin and familial concordance rates for schizophrenia suggest that there is a genetic component (Gottesman, 1979; Gottesman & Shields, 1972; Zerbin-Rudin, 1972). Retrospective studies of adult schizophrenics indicate that a history of somatic or familial stress may also play a formative role (see McNeil & Kaij, 1978). However, genetic concordance studies often suffer from sampling problems

*The study reported in this chapter was supported by UPHS NIMH Grant No. 31433, by an NIMH Postdoctoral Research Fellowship (No. F32MHO7916-01), and by a dissertation fellowship from the Scottish Rite Schizophrenia Research Program, NMJ, USA.

and tend to ignore the influence of deviant family interaction patterns on the development of psychopathology. Causal order is never satisfactorily established by retrospective studies of environmental variables because reports on early events frequently omit relevant information or are biased by knowledge of the clinical status of the subject.

More convincing support for the vulnerability aspect of the diathesis-stress hypothesis can be obtained from prospective, longitudinal studies of high-risk persons (Mednick & McNeil, 1968). The offspring of schizophrenics provide such a high-risk group. While only 1% of the general population is expected to develop schizophrenia, 10–16% of the children of schizophrenics will eventually manifest the disorder themselves (Gottesman & Shields, 1972; Yolles & Kramer, 1969). Studies of high-risk offspring who were raised in foster or adoptive homes indicate that a genetic predisposition contributes to the higher incidence of schizophrenia in this group (Heston, 1966; Rosenthal et al., 1971). This chapter reviews and presents converging evidence that a history of somatic or psychological stress may interact with genetic predisposition to increase further the vulnerability of high-risk offspring to schizophrenia. The role of three early environmental stressors will be considered: obstetric complications, parental absence during childhood, and institutional childcare.

Obstetric Complications

In recent years, there has been a proliferation of studies concerning the adverse effects of obstetric complications (OCs) on physical and behavioral development. Retrospective studies have found a significant relationship between OCs and a variety of subsequent disorders, including neurological and behavior problems (Pasamanick & Knoblock, 1966). Prospective studies also link OCs to an increase in neurological abnormalities (see Sameroff & Chandler, 1975) and, further, indicate that infants who suffer anoxia as a consequence of OCs may exhibit early personality differences (Graham et al., 1962) and impairments in social competence which may persist into the school years (Corah et al., 1965).

The results of retrospective studies of schizophrenics are compatible with these findings for the general population. The available studies, summarized by McNeil and Kaij (1978), indicate that a history of OCs is more characteristic of adult schizophrenics than of their normal siblings. Studies of monozygotic twins discordant for schizophrenia provide converging evidence because, with twins, the effects of OCs are independent of genetic variation. Such studies indicate that OCs, including anoxia, low birth weight, and soft neurological signs, occur more often among schizophrenic twins than among their co-twins (see McNeil & Kaij, 1978; Pollin & Stabenau, 1968). Within schizophrenic subsamples, OCs have been related to relatively early adult onset, poorer psychiatric outcome, and lower IQ. In keeping with the general literature, one study (Pollack & Greenberg, 1966, cited in McNeil & Kaij, 1978) found that OCs bore some relationship to abnormal EEG and psychological test evidence of central nervous system dysfunction, despite the fact that schizophrenics with neurological symptoms had ostensibly been excluded from their sample.

Taken together, these findings suggest that the physiological damage which frequently attends OCs may be a contributory factor in the etiology of schizophrenia.

OCs as a Predictor in High-Risk Samples To date, the only published studies which relate OCs in the births of high-risk offspring to their subsequent adult psychiatric status have emerged from the Danish high-risk project. Begun in 1962 by Mednick and Schulsinger, this longitudinal study has followed 207 high-risk offspring of chronically schizophrenic women and 104 low-risk offspring of control women. The offspring ranged from 9 to 20 years of age at the beginning of the project.

A 5-year follow-up (Mednick & Schulsinger, 1968) found that 20 of the high-risk offspring had experienced serious psychiatric or social breakdowns (not necessarily schizophrenia). Initial analyses suggested there were no significant differences in the frequency of individual OCs (such as anoxia) between the group of "sick" subjects and two comparison groups: 20 matched "well" high-risk offspring and 20 matched low-risk controls. However, a subsequent reanalysis (Mednick, 1970) found that *at least one* OC was more characteristic of the "sick" high-risk group, and less characteristic of the "well" high-risk group, than of the matched low-risk controls. This pattern of results led Mednick to suggest that OCs may exacerbate a genetic predisposition to psychopathology in high-risk offspring.

OCs have since been related specifically to schizophrenic symptoms. An intensive reassessment of the complete high- and low-risk samples was conducted in 1972 (Schulsinger, 1976): 15 schizophrenics and 29 borderline schizophrenics were identified in the high-risk group. Similar to the earlier findings for "sick" subjects, there was some indication that the schizophrenic high-risk subjects had experienced more OCs than the remaining high-risk subjects or the low-risk controls (Mednick et al., 1975). However, subsequent analyses (Mednick et al., 1978) showed that a weighted summary score of OCs predicted adult schizophrenia only for the high-risk males. This relationship was largely mediated by an association between OCs and abnormally high reactivity and fast recovery of the autonomic nervous system (ANS). Although OCs also predicted this ANS deviance in high-risk females, the deviancy was not in turn related to their manifestation of schizophrenic symptoms. This sex difference in effects has since been partly explained by the fact that female schizophrenics suffered less severe complications than male schizophrenics in relation to their same-sex controls (Feldman et al., Note 1).

In summary, the findings from the Danish project suggest that the somatic insults which accompany obstetric complications may to the same degree exacerbate a genetic predisposition to schizophrenia in high-risk offspring. Deviancies of the autonomic nervous system appear to be manifestation of this increased constitutional vulnerability, and they evidently mediate much of the relationship between obstetric complications and schizophrenia in the Danish high-risk males if not the females (Mednick et al., 1978). This is generally consistent with Mednick's (1958, 1962) theory that the combination of high ANS reactivity and very fast ANS recovery may result in a neurological predisposition to learned avoidant thinking, and hence schizophrenia. According to this formulation, the greater the reactivity of the ANS, the greater the anxiety in response to threatening or unpleasant stimuli, and the faster the recovery rate of the ANS, the faster and greater the anxiety-reducing reinforcement of avoidant responses such as irrelevant thoughts. In the present context, Mednick's theory suggests that the somatic stress of OCs may increase an inherited predisposition of high-risk offspring to respond in this way, thereby increasing the probability that they would learn to react to situational stress with the avoidant responses which are characteristic of schizophrenia.

Given this line of reasoning, it is tempting to speculate on the role that a history of psychological stress may play in fostering the expression or development of any such neurological predisposition. Mednick (1958) suggests that the constitutionally vulnerable person will have a tendency to learn progressively more avoidant responses if confronted with an unkind environment during childhood and adolescence. Although a variety of factors might combine to create this unkind environment, two are particularly likely to have an enduring effect: parental absence during childhood and institutional child-care. We consider the possible contribution of these early life stresses to increasing the vulnerability of high-risk offspring to schizophrenia in the following sections.

Institutional Child-Care

Several studies have assessed the development of institutionalized children in comparison to children raised in family settings (Yarrow, 1964; Wooten, 1962). Overall, the findings suggest that institutional child-care (ICC) has marked and pervasive negative effects. Institutionalized children are more depressed (Bowlby, 1956), have poorer language and cognitive abilities (Dennis, 1960), and are less assertive, responsive, and competent than family-reared children (Provence & Lipton, 1962; Taylor, 1968). Furthermore, some of these effects seem to be independent of the disruption caused by separation from the parents inasmuch as they are apparent in children institutionalized from birth (Brossard & Descarie, 1971; Dennis, 1960).

The predictive significance of institutional child-care has also been investigated by the Danish high-risk project. Stern, Mednick, and Schulsinger (1974) noted that there was a greater incidence of institutional child-care among the high-risk offspring who later suffered psychiatric and social breakdowns than among the matched high-risk and low-risk controls. Walker, Cudeck, Mednick, and Schulsinger (Note 2) have since found that amount of institutional child-care predicts later schizophrenic symptoms, but once again only for the high-risk males.

Parental Absence

Parental absence (PA) has also been linked to a variety of psychological and behavioral disorders in children. These disorders include delinquency (McCord,

McCord, & Thurber, 1962), sexual maladjustment (Biller, 1970), impaired cognitive functioning (Reis & Gold, 1977), and psychopathology (Weininger, 1972). In general, the earlier the separation and the longer its duration, the higher the incidence of maladjustment in the offspring (Marino & McCowen, 1976). The nature and extent of maladjustment sometimes varies with the sex of the absent parent, however, or with the sex of the child.

Paternal absence occurs more frequently than maternal absence and seems to have greater implications for the male offspring (Santrock, 1970). A consistently reported finding is that male children without fathers show more feminine patterns of sex-role development (Biller, 1968; Cox, 1976; Santrock, 1970; Sears, 1951). As a result, they may be subjected to greater stress, via cultural censure, than their father-reared peers (see Bardwick, 1971). Paternal absence has also been related to an increase in antisocial behavior in both males and females (Cox, 1976; Hetherington, 1972; Santrock, 1977).

Maternal absence during early childhood has been related to impaired emotional, cognitive, and physiological functioning in both male and female offspring (Marino & McCowen, 1976). In later years, children may show deficits in language ability and progressive retardation, depending on their age at the time of separation (Provence & Lipton, 1962; Yarrow, 1964).

In light of such findings, it is not surprising that a history of parental absence has also been associated with schizophrenia. Several retrospective studies have reported a higher incidence of parental absence among schizophrenics than in the general population (Brill & Liston, 1966; Dennehy, 1966; Gregory, 1958; Wray & McLaren, 1976). Hilgard and Newman (1963) found that separation due to the death of a parent, particularly the mother, was also more common in the histories of schizophrenics.

PA as a Predictor in High-Risk Samples Mednick and Schulsinger (1968) reported that a history of parental separation was especially characteristic of their high-risk subjects who suffered psychiatric and social breakdowns during the five years following the initiation of their study. After the 1972 reassessment, Mednick et al. (1975) observed that parental separation was far more common in the schizophrenic high-risk subjects than in those diagnosed as borderline schizophrenic or neurotic, or in those who did not exhibit any mental disorder. However, subsequent path analyses of the data (Mednick et al., 1978) indicated that the amount of parental absence predicted schizophrenic symptoms only for high-risk males. The longer the boys were separated from their parents, the more likely they were to develop schizophrenia as adults.

Although these outcomes were superficially consistent with the literature cited earlier, they were somewhat surprising when viewed from another perspective. All the mothers of the high-risk offspring were diagnosed schizophrenics. Thus, their offspring might have been expected to suffer from the *presence* rather than the *absence* of a deviant parent. For example, several studies indicate that exposure to a schizophrenic mother is detrimental to the children (Nameche, Waring, & Ricks, 1964;

Sobel, 1961). There is also evidence which suggests that disordered parental communication is a factor which precipitates psychopathology in the offspring (Goldstein et al., 1978). The apparent conflicts between these studies and the findings of the Danish high-risk project have since been resolved by a study which took both parental absence and the nature of substitute child-care into account, as we now see.

PA and ICC as Joint Predictors

Yarrow (1964) pointed out that maternal absence usually precipitates or coincides with placement of the offspring in a child-care institution, yet, few studies reporting behavioral correlates of separation have attempted to control for the confounding effects of institutionalization. Only by doing so, however, were Walker et al. (Note 2) able to clarify earlier findings (Mednick et al., 1975; Mednick et al., 1978) which paradoxically suggested that being removed from a schizophrenic mother was detrimental to the high-risk male. It now appears to have been detrimental only because it often resulted in their placement into a child-care institution. The more institutionalization following maternal absence, the more likely it was that high-risk males would later show symptoms of schizophrenia. Maternal absence was related to *decreases* in clinical symptoms among the males if they were placed in a foster home or with relatives instead. Conversely, a relationship between paternal absence and social impairment-antisocial behavior suggested that rearing by the schizophrenic mother alone may have had some additional adverse effect on the male offspring. In contrast to these results for high-risk males, however, few significant relationships emerged from the data for high-risk females. Amount of maternal absence only predicted to increases in later social impairment-antisocial tendencies among the females, while neither amount of institutionalization nor extent of paternal absence was predictive of their later clinical status.

As we said earlier, it is not too surprising that separation from a schizophrenic mother would be beneficial rather than detrimental to the offspring (Nameche, Waring, & Ricks, 1964; Sobel, 1961). What is less clear is why only the high-risk males were significantly affected. Nevertheless, other studies have reported comparable findings. Higgins (1974) observed that his male high-risk subjects showed more behavioral disturbances than the females as a function of being raised by a schizophrenic mother rather than a foster mother. Mother-reared males showed more asocial behavior and general withdrawal, and were described as more easily upset and irritated. Similar results were reported by Rutter (1970) in his study of 200 families, in which one of the parents was a psychiatric patient. He found that discord and disruption in the home were consistently and strongly associated with antisocial disorders, but only in the male offspring. Along the same lines, Rutter (1971) reported a decline in antisocial behavior in males separated from deviant parents and raised with normal foster parents. Thus it appears that parental absence and institutional child-care may have a greater, and sometimes different, effect on high-risk males than females.

Concluding Remarks

On the one hand, obstetric complications have been identified as somatic stressors which may exacerbate an inherited predisposition to schizophrenia in high-risk off-spring. On the other hand, parental absence and institutional child-care have been identified as factors in the rearing environment which may, in interaction with each other and genetic predisposition, contribute to the development of this disorder. Evidence of a relationship between these two classes of environmental stress (Drillien, 1964; Pollin & Stabenau, 1968) suggests the need for a study which examines their joint and independent contributions to increasing the vulnerability of high-risk offspring to schizophrenia. Such a study is presented below.

SCHIZOPHRENIA IN HIGH-RISK OFFSPRING: OCs, PA, AND ICC AS JOINT PREDICTORS

The following study was designed to examine simultaneously the role of obstetric complications, parental absence, and institutional child-care as antecedents to schizophrenia in high-risk offspring. The inclusion of obstetric complications as a predictor was not expected appreciably to alter the pattern of findings reported by Walker et al. (Note 2) for parental absence and institutional child-care because the current study was also based on data for the Danish high-risk sample. Rather, one aim was to determine whether the effects attributed to rearing environment were robust with respect to the somatic stressor. A second aim, in accord with the approach taken by Walker et al., was to define the dependent variable of schizophrenia in terms of symptom clusters (rather than a categorical diagnosis) in order to determine whether these environmental antecedents were differentially predictive of the various manifestations of the disorder. Last, the study sought to estimate the degree to which these three environmental factors jointly predicted each clinical symptom cluster, or syndrome.

High-Risk Subjects

The subjects in this study were the 207 Danish offspring of chronically schizophrenic mothers referred to previously (e.g., Walker et al., Note 2): 121 were males and 86 were females. The high-risk subjects were from 9 to 20 years old (average age, 15) at the initiation in 1962 of the longitudinal project from which they were selected. An extensive review of the selection rationale and background of the subjects is provided by Mednick et al. (1978). In the years since the study's beginning, 15 cases of schizophrenia, 58 cases of borderline schizophrenia, and a number of other manifestations of psychopathology were diagnosed among the high-risk offspring (see Mednick et al., 1975, and Schulsinger, 1976, for diagnostic procedures and criteria). The subjects ranged between 19 and 30 years of age at the time of the major reassessment in 1972 which provided the data on which these diagnoses were based.

Data

Because the sample was assessed in 1962 and 1972, two sets of data were available. During the initial contact in 1962, information was collected from midwife reports pertaining to the pregnancy and birth of each subject. An interview with the parents or parent substitutes also provided details about the child's rearing environment. Particularly relevant for current purposes were the data from that interview which related to the amount of parental absence and institutional child-care experienced by the high-risk offspring.

History of Obstetric Complications The births of Danish children are routinely attended by licensed midwives who assist in the delivery and who are acquainted with the course of pregnancy preceding it. The midwife reports, which are recorded in national registers, were examined for the data which pertained to obstetric complications. Altogether, 33 variables from the midwife reports were available, examples of which are mother's age and marital status, whether artificial help or anesthetics were required during delivery, and signs of prematurity or asphyxiation in the child.

In the previous work with these data (e.g., Mirdal et al., 1974), it was found that the occurrence of any individual OC in the sample was very low. In addition, these data were simply categorical records of various complications which were not readily amenable to statistical analysis. One solution to the problem was to assign a severity weight to each obstetric complication. Table 3-1 shows the weights assigned to the OCs used here. These weights were based on obstetrical research and clinical opinion (Mednick, 1970). Using this weighting scheme, three OC variables were constructed: (1) the sum of the weights for all OCs for each subject; (2) the total number of complications, without regard to severity weight; (3) the weight of the most severe OC.

History of Parental Absence and Institutional Child-Care Placement in an institution was not the inevitable result of separation from the parents. In some instances, children whose parents were unable to care for them were raised by another relative, close family friend, or foster parent. Consequently, amount of maternal absence, amount of paternal absence, and amount of institutional child-care were each subdivided into four age periods: amount occurring during the child's first year, second year, years 3–5, and years 6–10. Data on the amount of separation or institutionalization occurring during any age period was available only in a rough trichotomy. A score of 0 denoted no separation/institutionalization during the period; a score of 1 denoted some parental absence/institutionalization; and a score of 2 denoted sepa-

Table 3-1 **Severity Weights for Obstetric Complications**

0	1	2	3	4
No complications	Forceps used Caesarian section Placental defects Previous fetal loss Bleeding after delivery Adipositas Narrow pelvis Mother's illness during pregnancy Twins Labor time above 24 hours	Mother's serious illnesses Infarcts in the placenta Bad fetal position Dry birth Contractions of pelvis during delivery Primary uterine intertia (weak labor) Signs of prematurity with weight above 2500 grams Labor time above 36 hours	Secondary uterine inertia Bleeding during delivery Labor time above 48 hours	Asphyxia Umbilical cord complications Eclampsia Signs of prematurity with weight less than 2500 grams

ration (institutionalization) for most of the time period. Thus the most extreme set of scores would be 2-2-2-2, denoting separation or institutionalization for nearly all years from birth to age 10.

Clinical Symptoms as Adults In 1972, information pertaining to the current psychological functioning of the subjects was collected and used to make reliable clinical diagnoses (Schulsinger, 1976). These data included an extensive clinical interview and two standard psychiatric computer-scored interviews: (1) the Current and Past Psychopathology Scales (CAPPS: Endicott & Spitzer, 1972) and (2) the Present Status Examination, ninth edition (PSE: Wing, Cooper, & Sartorious, 1974).

The total number of clinical items available for each subject from the 1972 data was in excess of 700 items. To reduce the amount of information and increase reliability, the following data-reduction procedure was carried out (Mednick et al., 1978). Items were selected from the clinical interview, CAPPS, and PSE which pertained to eight syndromes: social impairment, antisocial tendencies, borderline schizophrenia, hallucinations and delusions, hebephrenic traits, thought disorder, paranoid traits, and autistic traits. After selection, each subset of 10 to 20 items was factor-analyzed, and the most salient items on the factor were retained to represent each syndrome. From these eight clusters of items, eight scores were calculated by summing the salient items for a particular syndrome. Table 3-2 shows the mean score for the eight syndromes according to diagnostic category and sex. It can be seen that these symptom scales are consistent with psychiatric conceptions of the various diagnoses.

These eight scales were moderately intercorrelated, so a second-order factor analysis was performed. This produced five higher-order factors. Three of these were

Table 3-2 **Mean Scores on Symptom Scales by Consensus Diagnosis**

	DIAGNOSES									
SYMPTOMS	SCHIZOPHRENIA		PSYCHOPATHY		OTHER PERSONALITY DISORDERS		NEUROSIS		NO ILLNESS	
	Males	*Females*	*Males*	*Females*	*Males*	*Females*	*Males*	*Females*	*Males*	*Females*
Social impairment	12.6	9.9	7.0	10.0	6.7	6.8	6.3	8.0	6.0	6.0
Antisocial tendencies	17.7	16.8	17.7	18.0	10.8	10.0	8.9	10.1	9.7	9.1
Borderline schizophrenic traits	10.8	9.2	5.0	7.0	5.4	6.2	5.9	5.7	5.0	5.2
Hallucinations and delusions	23.6	19.9	10.0	10.0	10.1	10.5	10.3	10.3	10.0	10.1
Hebephrenic traits	16.8	16.9	11.0	10.0	10.2	10.4	10.3	10.5	10.0	10.1
Thought disorder	10.1	7.9	4.0	4.5	3.6	3.8	3.5	4.3	3.9	3.0
Paranoid traits	7.9	7.2	5.3	6.0	5.1	5.8	5.1	4.8	4.9	4.5
Autistic traits	13.0	13.0	7.3	10.0	7.9	7.4	7.3	7.6	6.2	5.5

composed of pairs of scales—social impairment-antisocial tendencies, paranoia-autism, and borderline schizophrenia–hallucinations-delusions. Hebephrenic traits and thought disorder were retained as individual factors.

Path Analyses

Rationale These data were designed to explore the manner in which obstetric complications, parental absence, and institutional child-care are related to specific syndromes of schizophrenia. Operationally, the 1962 data on obstetric complications, parental absence, and institutional child-care were used to predict the clinical functioning of this high-risk sample as it was measured by the factor scores obtained from the 1972 assessment data.

Latent Variables and Their Indicators The unreliability and situational specificity of behavioral and clinical data such as these have been well documented (e.g., Bentler, 1980). Indeed, the cornerstone of measurement theory is that psychological phenomena are measured with error (Nunnally, 1967) and that construct validation and replication must be stressed if research findings are to be generalizable. In the present context, for example, maternal absence has been measured by four distinct variables corresponding to time periods in the child's life. Any one of the four variables might be criticized as too limited to be a useful, global measure of amount of maternal absence. However, using a composite of the four to represent this construct, or latent variable, is much less susceptible to the same criticism. The same holds true for the variables measuring amount of paternal absence, institutional child-care, and obstetric complications.

Using this reasoning, many researchers (e.g., Bentler, 1980) have argued that analyses should be based on latent variables rather than on the original measured variables which define them.

In addition to more accurate measurement of the constructs of interest, statistical analyses based on latent variables provide a more reliable picture of the relationships among constructs (Burket, 1964). Consequently, analyses in this study were based on latent variables. Table 3-3 presents a summary of the latent variables considered

Table 3-3 **Measured Variables Defining Each Latent Variable**

LATENT VARIABLE	MEASURED VARIABLES
Obstetric complications	1. Weighted sum of OCs 2. Total number of OCs 3. Weight of most severe OC
Amount of maternal absence	1. Maternal absence, year 1 2. Maternal absence, year 2 3. Maternal absence, years 3–5 4. Maternal absence, years 6–10
Amount of paternal absence	1. Paternal absence, year 1 2. Paternal absence, year 2 3. Paternal absence, years 3–5 4. Paternal absence, years 6–10
Amount of institutional child-care	1. Institutionalization, year 1 2. Institutionalization, year 2 3. Institutionalization, years 3–5 4. Institutionalization, years 6–10
Clinical construct 1	1. Social impairment 2. Antisocial tendencies
Clinical construct 2	1. Borderline schizophrenic features 2. Hallucination and delusion symptoms
Clinical construct 3	1. Hebephrenic symptoms
Clinical construct 4	1. Thought disorder
Clinical construct 5	1. Paranoia 2. Autism

and the measured, variables from the 1962 or 1972 data which served as their indicators. Because our interest lay in relationships which could not be explored with standard multiple-regression techniques, we used the computerized procedure described by Joreskog and Sorbom (1978) which permits "path analysis with latent variables," or structural equation modeling. This method, a generalization of regression theory, can be thought of as a regression analysis performed with factors rather than single variables as predictors.

As noted earlier, Walker et al. (Note 2) have already examined the prediction of clinical syndromes from parental absence and institutional child-care using this approach. The primary interest here was in the added effects of obstetric complications to the prediction of specific syndromes as a point of reference. Figure 3-1 presents a path diagram from Walker et al. (Note 2) which shows the effects of parental absence and institutionalization differentiated by sex of the offspring. The measured

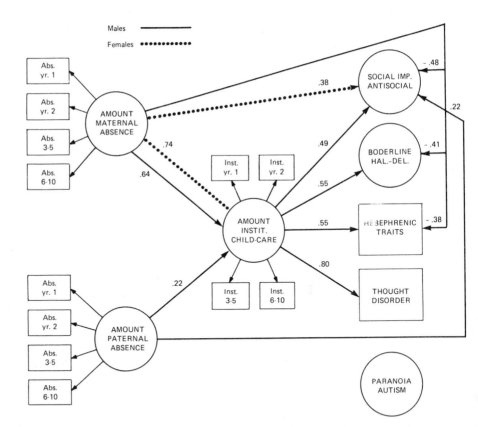

Fig. 3-1. Path diagram for the prediction of clinical symptoms from amount of maternal absence, paternal absence, and institutional child-care (Walker et al., Note 2). Circles represent constructs (latent variables); boxes represent measured variables defining the constructs; arrows between the constructs illustrate statistically significant path coefficients.

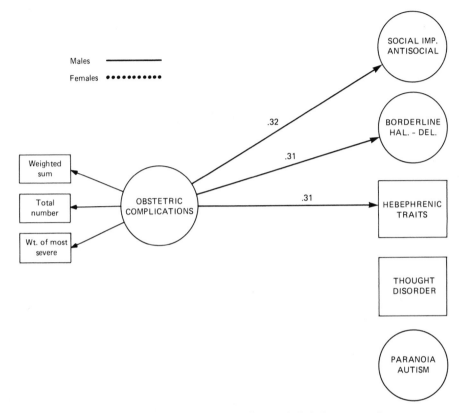

Fig. 3-2. Path diagram for the prediction of clinical symptoms from
obstetric complications.

variables are denoted by boxes, and the latent variables are shown as circles. The
solid lines illustrate the regression coefficients for male subjects, while broken lines
illustrate the coefficients for females. For clarity, only the statistically signficant
relationships have been depicted.

This study presents two additional analyses. In the first analysis, obstetric complications were used as the sole predictor of the clinical syndromes. The second analysis
simultaneously incorporated obstetric complications, parental absence, and institutional child-care as predictors of those syndromes. The differences between these
models was used to examine the interaction of biological and rearing-environment
factors in the prediction of schizophrenic symptoms.

Results

OCs as a Predictor Figure 3-2 summarizes the results for the prediction of clinical
syndromes from obstetric complications alone. It can be seen that OCs are useful
predictors of later psychopathology in high-risk males but not females. For the males,

OCs were significantly related to social impairment-antisocial traits, borderline schizophrenia–hallucinations-delusions, and to hebephrenic traits.

Just as the percentage of variance accounted for in multiple-regression analyses shows how successfully the independent variables predict the dependent variable, so the percentage of variance accounted for in the present analysis shows the strength of the relationships between OCs and clinical syndromes. The first panel of Table 3-4 lists the percentage of variance predicted in each clinical syndrome using a history of obstetric complications as the only antecedent construct. As the table shows, almost no variation in the data on psychopathological symptoms for females is accounted for by OCs. For males, 9–10% of the variance in social impairment-antisocial tendencies, borderline schizophrenia–hallucinations-delusions, and hebephrenic traits is significantly predicted by a history of obstetric complications.

OCs, PA, and ICC as Joint Predictors Figure 3-3 shows the independent and joint effects of obstetric complications, maternal absence, paternal absence, and institutional child-care.

Amount of separation from the parents accounted for 71% of the variance in the amount of institutionalization experienced by high-risk offspring, whether male or female. This relationship was most directly attributable to amount of maternal absence, as shown by the positive coefficients for the paths from maternal absence to institutional child-care. Note that paternal absence no longer directly predicted institutionalization of the males, as it did in the Walker et al. (Note 2) study. (A small correlation between the constructs of paternal absence and obstetric complications

Table 3-4   **Percentage of Variance in Clinical Symptoms Accounted for by Amount of Parental Absence, Institutional Child-Care, and/or Obstetric Complications**

	PREDICTORS					
	OBSTETRIC COMPLICATIONS ALONE		PARENTAL ABSENCE AND INSTIT. CHILD-CARE*		OBSTETRIC COMPLICATIONS, PARENTAL ABSENCE, AND INSTIT. CHILD-CARE JOINTLY	
CLINICAL SYMPTOMS						
	Males	*Females*	*Males*	*Females*	*Males*	*Females*
Social impairment– Antisocial tendencies	10%	1%	12%	5%	21%	4%
Borderline schizophrenia– Hallucinations-delusions	9%	1%	13%	8%	20%	8%
Hebephrenic traits	9%	0	9%	1%	16%	1%
Thought disorder	4%	1%	22%	3%	24%	4%
Paranoia-autism	1%	1%	3%	4%	3%	3%

*From Walker et al. (Note 2).

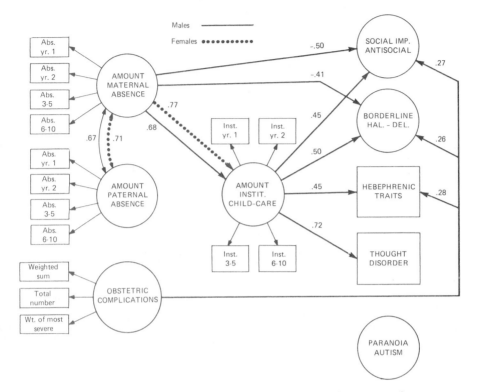

Fig. 3-3. Path diagram for the prediction of clinical symptoms from amount of maternal absence, paternal absence, institutional child-care, and obstetric complications.

may account for this altered finding.) Amount of paternal absence was only indirectly related to institutionalization of the male and female offspring via its correlation with amount of maternal absence (shown by curved lines). These results suggest that high-risk children were often institutionalized after separation from their mother because her absence left them without a caretaking parent in the home. This is consistent with the hypothesis that amount of maternal absence would strongly predict the amount of institutional child-care provided to her offspring. Obstetric complications did not add to this prediction. There was essentially no relationship between obstetric complications and amount of institutionalization (the correlation between these constructs was .07 for the males and .06 for the females). This suggests that OC-related deficits and resulting behavior problems were not an important factor in deciding whether to place or retain a high-risk child in an institution.

Amount of institutional child-care after parental separation predicted increases in symptoms of psychopathology, but only in the high-risk males. This is shown by the positive coefficients for the paths from institutionalization to the syndromes of borderline schizophrenia–hallucinations-delusions, social impairment-antisocial tendencies, hebephrenic traits, and thought disorder.

As observed by Walker et al., the relationship of maternal absence to increased symptoms in the male offspring was mediated by the effects of institutional child-care. When not accompanied by institutional child-care, maternal absence was associated with decreases in the manifestation of two clinical syndromes in the males. This is shown by the negative coefficients for the direct paths from maternal absence to borderline schizophrenia–hallucinations-delusions and social impairment-antisocial tendencies. The direct negative path to hebephrenic traits, which was also reported by Walker et al., missed statistical significance when OCs were included as an additional antecedent variable. Similarly, amount of maternal absence was no longer significantly related to increases in social impairment-antisocial tendencies in the female offspring. Paternal absence no longer directly predicted increases in these tendencies in high-risk males.

Overall, the pattern of findings reported by Walker et al. (Note 2) was not appreciably changed by including obstetric complications as an additional antecedent variable. None of the correlations between obstetric complications and maternal absence, paternal absence, or institutional child-care were statistically significant. Moreover, the magnitude of the coefficients for the direct paths from obstetric complications to three clinical syndromes in the males was approximately the same whether or not the child-rearing variables were included as predictors. This shows that the increased risk for schizophrenia associated with a history of OCs is independent of the amount of parental absence or institutionalization experienced by the high-risk offspring.

Discussion

Mednick et al. (1978) reported that parental absence increased the likelihood that high-risk males would manifest schizophrenic symptoms as adults. The results of Walker et al. (Note 2) made it clear that this relationship was mediated by the institutional child-care provided to many of those children after separation from their mothers. The results of the latter study were not appreciably altered in the present investigation by including obstetric complications as an additional antecedent variable. It is worth reiterating that obstetric complications were not related to type of rearing history. That is, few subjects in the high-risk sample experienced both obstetric complications and parental absence of institutional child-care. Thus, it appears that at least two distinct classes of environmental stress, somatic and child-rearing, may increase the probability of schizophrenia in high-risk male (if not female) offspring. This outcome lends some support to the idea that schizophrenia is not the inevitable result of a singular detrimental background, but rather that different forms of stress may interact with genetic predisposition to increase the likelihood of later psychopathology.

Prediction of Clinical Symptoms This discussion highlights the relationship of each predictor to later symptoms of schizophrenia. A complementary approach is to emphasize the extent to which manifestations of each specific syndrome are accounted for by a given set of predictors. The third panel of Table 3-4 shows the percentage of variance jointly accounted for in each clinical syndrome by obstetric complications, parental absence, and institutional child-care.

For males, obstetric complications (positive path), institutional child-care after separation (positive path), and maternal absence (direct negative path) jointly accounted for 20% of the variance in symptoms of borderline schizophrenia–hallucinations-delusions. The same predictors jointly accounted for 21% of the variance in the males' social impairment-antisocial tendencies and 16% of the variance in their hebephrenic traits (although the direct maternal-absence path missed statistical significance for the latter syndrome). Institutional child-care after separation was the only significant predictor of thought disorder in high-risk males, accounting for most of the 24% explained variance in that syndrome.

By contrast, no predictor was significantly related to these four syndromes in females (although there was a nonsignificant tendency for amount of maternal absence without institutionalization to predict increases in their social impairment-antisocial tendencies). Hence, it is not surprising that even as a group the environmental variables included in this study accounted for very little (1% to 8%) of the variance in the high-risk females symptoms of psychopathology.

A particularly interesting finding was that none of the environmental factors predicted increases in paranoia-autism, either for high-risk males or females. Even when considered jointly, they accounted for only 3% of the variance in this syndrome. However, it should be remembered that these outcomes are bound to underestimate the amount of variance in this and other syndromes which the variables actually explain. Approximately half of the eventual schizophrenics in the Danish high-risk sample were likely to have gone undetected at the time of the 1972 reassessment on which these analyses were based (Mednick et al., 1978).

Sex Differences in Exposure and Vulnerability to Environmental Stress The principal question raised by our findings is why obstetric complications, parental absence, and institutional child-care have a far greater effect on high-risk males than females. In fact, our results suggest that high-risk females are relatively impervious to the effects of early environmental stress, at least as it is represented by these somatic and child-rearing variables.

One explanation for these findings is that males may be exposed to comparatively greater stress in a given familial or institutional setting. While there is little research regarding the caretaking behavior of schizophrenic mothers, some evidence suggests that normal parents are less protective and indulgent with male children (Block, 1973; 1978) and that the annoyance threshold for male deviance is less than that for female deviance (see Eme, 1979). A suggestion that the institutional treatment of males may be qualitatively different from that experienced by females was obtained during interviews with the persons who were directors of the Danish institutions when these high-risk children attended. The evidence for consistently harsher treatment of males in either setting is not overwhelming, however (e.g., Maccoby & Jacklin, 1974), and the fact that only high-risk males were differentially affected by the type of substitute care provided after separation also argues against sex differences in *exposure* to stress as the sole explanation of our results.

An alternative explanation for the pattern of findings is that high-risk males may be constitutionally *more vulnerable* than the females to *any* form of environmental stress. Greater male susceptibility to a host of pre-, peri-, and postnatal biological insults is undisputed (Braine et al., 1966; Garai & Scheinfeld, 1968; Gottfried, 1973; Maccoby & Jacklin, 1974). In a review of the literature on childhood psychopathology, Eme (1979) concluded that males may be more vulnerable to psychological stressors as well. This hypothesis is consistent with our finding that only among males did the effects of maternal absence depend on the type of substitute care. Also consistent with that hypothesis are studies noting that male offspring of schizophrenic mothers (Higgins, 1974) and psychotic mothers or fathers (Rutter, 1970) are more likely to be adversely affected by rearing with a deviant parent. While Mednick (1958, 1962) hypothesized that abnormal reactivity of the autonomic nervous system (ANS) predisposes high-risk offspring to rapid avoidance learning in response to stress, he found that deviant ANS reactivity was predictive of later schizophrenia only among the high-risk males (Mednick et al., 1978). Taken together, these findings suggest that the same environmental stress may be experienced or reacted to differently by male and female high-risk offspring. That is, males may be constitutionally more vulnerable to the effects of psychological as well as somatic stressors. This explanation is not incompatible with the one offered earlier. Differential exposure and greater constitutional vulnerability may each contribute to the apparently greater effect of early environmental stress on high-risk males, at least as it is represented by obstetric complications, parental absence, and institutional child-care.

Three final points should be kept in mind, however, when evaluating the merits of a "differential vulnerability" explanation for the observed sex differences in the effects of stress. As noted already, only about half the eventual schizophrenics in the Danish high-risk sample were expected to exhibit symptoms of the disorder at the time of the 1972 reassessment (Mednick et al., 1978). Because the undiagnosed schizophrenics who experienced obstetric complications, parental absence, or institutional child-care were comparatively symptom-free that time, the true relationship of these variables to later psychopathology in females may have been obscured. That is, once the complete subsample of high-risk schizophrenics is identified, these environmental stressors may be shown to predict clinical symptoms in the females as well as in the males. It is still likely, however, that the prediction would be stronger for males, since approximately equal numbers of male and female schizophrenics and borderline schizophrenics were diagnosed at the time of this study. A second possibility is that the environmental stressors considered in this study have an equal impact on high-risk males and females, but the manifested symptoms of psychopathology take different forms: primarily schizophrenia for males; primarily other disorders, such as manic-depression, in females (see Mednick et al., 1978). While this hypothesis awaits investigation in the high-risk sample, it would still not account for the incidence of schizophrenia-related symptoms among the females. Finally, environmental stressors which differentially predispose high-risk females to schizophrenia may yet be identified. The latter outcome would mean that there are sex differences in response to specific types of stress, rather than to stress per se.

Regardless of interpretation, the findings of the Danish project suggest that the etiology of schizophrenia may in part be different for high-risk males and females. That is, generalizations concerning the interaction of environmental factors and genetic predisposition to schizophrenia may well be qualified by sex differences in the effects of stress. Confirmation of this observation awaits further follow-up and cross-validation on samples from other high-risk projects when their subjects reach maturity.

Independent Stressors or Genetic Correlates A major problem with concluding that any environmental factor exacerbates a genetic predisposition to schizophrenia is that the variable of interest may simply be a correlate of genetic variation among the schizophrenic mothers and hence among their high-risk offspring. For example, it has been suggested that obstetric complications are a manifestation of "schizophrenic genes" rather than a precipitating event. In a similar manner, earlier research (Mednick et al., 1978) has shown that the severity of maternal schizophrenia is related to the amount of separation from her children. Absent parents thus constitute a more deviant subgroup, and this deviance could be transmitted genetically or through modeling before the parents' departure. Both points deserve consideration.

Literature pertaining to the first point was reviewed by McNeil and Kaij (1978) who concluded that a greater maternal genetic loading for schizophrenia does not produce both obstetric complications and a greater genetic predisposition in her offspring. They noted that the majority of studies showed no differences in the incidence of OCs occurring in reproduction before versus after the onset of maternal schizophrenia. Nor was there a consistent relationship between OC rates and the severity of maternal schizophrenia. Similar findings have been reported for the Danish high-risk sample (Feldman et al., Note 1; Mednick et al., 1978). Thus, it appears reasonable to conclude that the obstetric complications which did occur served as independent environmental stressors which interacted with a genetic predisposition to schizophrenia, at least in the high-risk male offspring.

The outcomes reported by Walker et al. (Note 2), and reaffirmed in this study, provide evidence regarding the nature of maternal absence and institutional child-care effects on high-risk offspring. If amount of maternal absence is a correlate of the genetic loading for schizophrenia, then increasing separation from the schizophrenic mother should uniformly predict increased psychopathology in the offspring, regardless of the type of substitute care provided. Yet amount of maternal absence was related to more schizophrenic symptoms when the high-risk males were institutionalized and fewer schizophrenic symptoms when they were raised by a relative or foster parent. This pattern of findings is compatible with the view that separation from the schizophrenic mother was an independent (but not necessarily stressful) environmental factor which contributed to the prediction of schizophrenia, especially among high-risk males. Moreover, it suggests that institutional child-care after separation was a relatively independent source of stress which increased the probability of later psychopathology in high-risk males.

The latter conclusions must be regarded with caution, however, because it is possible that foster parents and relatives were more likely to accept the offspring of genetically "better" mothers than genetically "poorer" mothers, resulting in a correlation between type of placement and the children's inherited predisposition to schizophrenia. Similarly, preplacement characteristics of the offspring themselves could account for the apparently differential relationship of maternal absence to later psychopathology. Preexisting deviance in a high-risk child may influence the decision to place him or her in an institution rather than a foster home. Deviant children may already be more likely to develop schizophrenia, or may be more likely to suffer adverse effects from less than optimal institutional care. Earlier reports from this project have suggested that preplacement characteristics may be important in this regard (Herrmann, 1973; Mednick & Schulsinger, 1974). Thus, the differential relationship of maternal absence to clinical symptoms in high-risk males provides suggestive, but certainly not conclusive evidence that rearing-environment factors may help determine the probability of later schizophrenia in high-risk offspring.

Concluding Remarks

Obstetric complications, maternal absence, and institutional child-care are environmental factors which may independently, or in interaction, contribute to the prediction of schizophrenia in genetically high-risk males. Moreover, these variables appear to be differentially related to specific syndromes indicative of schizophrenia, despite the fact that the syndromes are moderately intercorrelated.

While each environmental variable was related to at least two of the five syndromes considered in our study, meaningful prediction of a given syndrome may depend on the joint consideration of several antecedents (see Hanson, Gottesman, & Heston, 1976). That is, multiple indicators may be more useful than single variables for the purpose of identifying individuals within the high-risk sample who are especially predisposed to a particular schizophrenic syndrome. The potential utility of multiple indicators is highlighted by the findings for three of the syndromes defined in our study: hebephrenic traits, borderline schizophrenia–hallucinations-delusions, and social impairment-antisocial tendencies. Both obstetric complications and institutional child-care after separation predicted increased manifestations of these syndromes in high-risk males. Conversely, joint consideration of the environmental predictors may suggest preventive courses of action. Separation from the schizophrenic mother, if accompanied by foster parenting or rearing with a relative, was associated with decreased manifestations of the same syndromes. Although these findings are still tentative, their overall pattern supports the conclusion reached by Gottesman and Shields (1972, as cited by Hanson et al., 1976, p. 149) that the "net result of a dynamic combination of genetic and environmental sources of liabilities and assets determines whether an individual with the necessary, but not sufficient, genetic predisposition crosses a threshold to clinical schizophrenia."

References

Bardwick, J. M. *Psychology of women: A study of biocultural conflicts.* New York: Harper & Row, 1971.

Bentler, P. M. Multivariate analysis with latent variables: Causal modeling. *Annual Review of Psychology*, 1980, *31*, 419–456.

Biller, H. B. A multi-aspect investigation of masculine development in kindergarten age boys. *Genetic Psychology Monographs*, 1968, *76*, 89–139.

Biller, H. B. Father absence and the personality development of the male child. *Developmental Psychology*, 1970, *2*, 181–201.

Block, J. H. Conceptions of sex roles: Some cross-cultural and longitudinal perspectives. *American Psychologist*, 1973, *28*, 512–529.

Block, J. Another look at differentiation in the socialization behaviors of mothers and fathers. In F. Denmark & J. Sherman (Eds.), *Psychology of women: Future directions of research.* New York: Psychological Dimensions, 1978.

Bowlby, J. The effects of mother-child separation. *British Journal of Medical Psychology*, 1956, *29*, 211–249.

Braine, M. D., Heimer, C., Wortis, H., & Freedman, A. M. Factors associated with impairment of the early development of prematures. *Monographs of the Society for Research in Child Development*, 1966, *31* (4, Serial 106).

Brill, N., & Liston, E. Parental loss in adults with emotional disorders. *Archives of General Psychiatry*, 1966, *14*, 307–314.

Brossard, M., & Descarie, T. The effects of three kinds of social stimulation on the development of institutionalized infants. In C. Lavatelli (Ed.), *Readings in child development and behavior.* New York: Harcourt, Brace, 1971.

Burket, G. R. A study of reduced rank models for multiple prediction. *Psychometric Monographs*, 1964, *12*.

Corah, N. L., Anthony, E. J., Painter, P., Stern, J. A., & Thurston, D. L. Effects of perinatal anoxia after seven years. *Psychological Monographs*, 1965, *79*, 3, whole No. 596.

Cox, M. J. The effects of father absence and working mothers on children. *Dissertation Abstracts International*, 1976, *36*, 3640.

Dennehy, C. M. Childhood bereavement and psychiatric illness. *British Journal of Psychiatry*, 1966, *112*, 1049–1069.

Dennis, W. Causes of retardation among institutional children: Iran. *Journal of Genetic Psychology*, 1960, *96*, 47–59.

Drillien, C. M. *The Growth and Development of the Prematurely Born Infant.* Baltimore: Williams & Wilkins, 1964.

Eme, R. F. Sex differences in childhood psychopathology: A review. *Psychological Bulletin*, 1979, *86*, 574–595.

Endicott, J., & Spitzer, R. Current and past psychopathology scales (CAPPS). *Archives of General Psychiatry*, 1972, *27*, 678–687.

Feldman, P. M., Mednick, S. A., Schulsinger, F., & Fuchs, F. Schizophrenia in children of schizophrenics: Pregnancy and birth complications. *British Journal of Psychiatry,* accepted for publication.

Garai, J., & Scheinfeld, A. Sex differences in mental and behavioral traits. *Genetic Psychology Monographs,* 1968, *77,* 169–199.

Goldstein, M., Rodnick, E., Jones, J., McPherson, S., & West, K. Familial precursors of schizophrenia spectrum disorders. In L. Wynne, R. Cromwell, & S. Mathyse (Eds.), *The Nature of Schizophrenia: New Approaches to Research and Treatment.* New York: Wiley, 1978.

Gottesman, I. I. Schizophrenia and genetics: Toward understanding uncertainty. *Psychiatric Annals,* 1979, *9,* 26–37.

Gottesman, I. I., & Shields, J. *Schizophrenia and genetics: A twin vantage point.* New York: Academic Press, 1972.

Gottfried, A. W. Intellectual consequences of perinatal anoxia. *Psychological Bulletin,* 1973, *80,* 231–242.

Graham, F. K., Ernhart, C. B., Thurston, D. L., & Croft, M. Development three years after perinatal anoxia and other potentially damaging newborn experiences. *Psychological Monographs,* 1962, *76,* 3, whole No. 522.

Gregory, I. Studies of parental deprivation in psychiatric patients. *American Journal of Psychiatry,* 1958, *115,* 432–442.

Hanson, D. F., Gottesman, I. I., & Heston, L. L. Some possible childhood indicators of adult schizophrenia inferred from children of schizophrenics. *British Journal of Psychiatry,* 1976, *129,* 142–154.

Herrmann, E. Long-range effects of early parental separation experiences in children with high- and low-risk for schizophrenia. Unpublished doctoral dissertation, New School for Social Research, 1973.

Heston, L. L. Psychiatric disorders in foster-home reared children of schizophrenic mothers. *British Journal of Psychiatry,* 1966, *112,* 819–825.

Hetherington, E. M. Effects of father absence on personality development in adolescent daughters. *Developmental Psychology,* 1972, *7,* 313–326.

Higgins, J. Effects of child rearing by schizophrenic mothers. In S. A. Mednick, F. Schulsinger, J. Higgins, & B. Bell (Eds.), *Genetics, environment and psychopathology.* Amsterdam: North-Holland Publishing Co., 1974.

Hilgard, J. R., & Newman, M. F. Parental loss by death in childhood as an etiological factor among schizophrenics and alcoholic patients compared with a non-patient community sample. *Journal of Nervous and Mental Disorders,* 1963, *137,* 14–28.

Joreskog, K. G., & Sorbom, D. *LISREL IV user's guide.* Chicago: National Educational Resources, 1978.

Maccoby, E. E., & Jacklin, C. N. *The psychology of sex differences.* Stanford: Stanford University Press, 1974.

Marino, C. D., & McCowen, R. J. The effects of parent absence on children. *Child Study Journal,* 1976, *6,* 165–182.

McCord, J., McCord, W., & Thurber, E. Some effects of paternal absence on male children. *Journal of Abnormal and Social Psychology,* 1962, *124,* 1424–1432.

McNeil, T. F., & Kaij, L. Obstetric factors in the development of schizophrenia: Complications in the births of preschizophrenics and in reproduction by schizophrenic parents. In L. C. Wynne, R. L. Cromwell, & S. Mathyse (Eds.), *The nature of schizophrenia: New approaches to research and treatment.* New York: Wiley, 1978.

Mednick, S. A. A learning theory approach to research in schizophrenia. *Psychological Bulletin,* 1958, *55,* 316–327.

Mednick, S. A. Schizophrenia: A learned thought disorder. In G. Nielsen (Ed.), *Clinical psychology.* Proceedings of XIV International Congress of Applied Psychology. Copenhagen: Munksgaard, 1962.

Mednick, S. A. Breakdown in individuals at high risk for schizophrenia: Possible predispositional perinatal factors. *Mental Hygiene,* 1970, *54,* 50–63.

Mednick, S. A., & McNeil, T. F. Current methodology in research on the etiology of schizophrenia: Serious difficulties which suggest the use of the high-risk group method. *Psychological Bulletin,* 1968, *70,* 681–693.

Mednick, S. A., & Schulsinger, F. Some premorbid characteristics related to breakdown in children with schizophrenic mothers. *Journal of Psychiatric Research,* 1968, *6(1),* 267–291.

Mednick, S. A., & Schulsinger, F. Studies of children at high risk for schizophrenia. In S. A. Mednick, F. Schulsinger, J. Higgins, & B. Bell (Eds.), *Genetics, environment and psychopathology.* Amsterdam: North-Holland Publishing Co., 1974.

Mednick, S. A., Schulsinger, H., & Schulsinger, F. Schizophrenia in children of schizophrenic mothers. In A. Davids (Ed.), *Childhood personality and psychopathology: Current topics, 2.* New York: Wiley, 1975.

Mednick, S. A., Schulsinger, F., Teasdale, T. W., Schulsinger, H., Venables, P. H., & Rock, D. R. Schizophrenia in high-risk children: Sex differences in predisposing factors. In G. Gerban (Ed.), *Cognitive defects in the development of mental illness.* New York: Bruner/Mazel, 1978.

Mirdal, G., Mednick, S. A., Schulsinger, F., & Fuchs, F. Perinatal complications in children of schizophrenic mothers. *Acta Psychiatrica Scandinavica,* 1974, *50,* 553–568.

Nameche, G., Waring, M., & Ricks, D. Early indicators of outcome in schizophrenia. *Journal of Nervous and Mental Disease,* 1964, *139,* 232–240.

Nunnally, J. C. *Psychometric theory.* New York: McGraw-Hill, 1967.

Pasamanick, E., & Knoblock, H. Retrospective studies on the epidemiology of reproductive casuality: Old and new. *Merrill-Palmer Quarterly,* 1966, *12,* 7–26.

Pollin, W., & Stabenau, J. R. Biological, psychological, and historical differences in a series of monozygotic twins discordant for schizophrenia. In D. Rosenthal & S. S. Kety (Eds.), *The transmission of schizophrenia.* New York: Pergamon Press, 1968.

Provence, S., & Lipton, R. C. *Infants in institutions.* New York: International Universities Press, 1962.

Reis, M., & Gold, D. Relation of paternal availability to problem solving and sex-role orientation in young boys. *Psychological Reports,* 1977, *40,* 823–829.

Rosenthal, D. *Genetic theory and abnormal behavior.* New York: McGraw-Hill, 1970.

Rosenthal, D., Wender, P. H., Kety, S. S., Welner, J., & Schulsinger, F. The adopted away offspring of schizophrenics. *Journal of Psychiatry,* 1971, *128,* 307–311.

Rutter, M. Sex differences in children's responses to family stress. In E. Anthony & C. Koupernki (Eds.), *The child in his family.* New York: Wiley, 1970.

Rutter, M. Parent-child separation: Psychological effects on the children. *Journal of Child Psychology and Psychiatry,* 1971, *12,* 233.

Sameroff, A. J., & Chandler, M. J. Reproductive risk and the continuum of caretaking casualty. In F. D. Horowitz (Ed.), *Review of child development research* (Vol. 4). Chicago: University of Chicago Press, 1975.

Santrock, J. W. Paternal absence, sex typing and identification. *Developmental Psychology,* 1970, *2,* 264–272.

Santrock, J. W. Effects of father absence on sex-typed behaviors in male children. *Journal of Genetic Psychology,* 1977, *130,* 3–10.

Schulsinger, H. A ten-year follow-up of children of schizophrenic mothers: Clinical assessment. *Acta Psychiatrica Scandinavica,* 1976, *53,* 371–386.

Sears, P. S. Doll play aggression in normal young children: Influence of sex, age, sibling status and fathers absence. *Psychological Monographs,* 1951, *65,* 6, whole No. 323.

Sobel, E. Children of schizophrenic parents. *American Journal of Psychiatry,* 1961, *118,* 512–517.

Stern, S., Mednick, S. A., & Schulsinger, F. Social class, institutionalization and schizophrenia. In S. A. Mednick, F. Schulsinger, J. Higgins, & B. Bell (Eds.), *Genetics, environment and psychopathology.* Amsterdam: North-Holland Publishing Co., 1974.

Taylor, A. Deprived infants: Potential for affective adjustment. *American Journal of Orthopsychiatry,* 1968, *38,* 835–845.

Walker, E. F., Cudeck, R., Mednick, S. A., & Schulsinger, F. Effects of parental absence and institutionalization on the development of clinical symptoms in high-risk children. Submitted for publication.

Weininger, O. Effects of parental deprivation: An overview of literature and report on some current research. *Psychological Reports,* 1972, *30,* 591–612.

Wing, J. K., Cooper, J. E., & Sartorious, N. *The measurement and classification of psychiatric symptoms.* New York: Cambridge University Press, 1974.

Wooten, B. A social scientist's approach to maternal deprivation. In *Deprivation of Maternal Care.* Geneva: World Health Organization, 1962, Public Health Paper 14.

Wray, S. R., & McLaren, E. Parent-child separation as a determinant of psychopathology in children: A Jamaican study. *West Indian Medical Journal,* 1976, *25,* 251–257.

Yarrow, L. J. Separation from parents during early childhood. *Review of Child Development Research,* 1964, *1,* 89–136.

Yolles, S., & Kramer, M. Vital statistics. In L. Bellak & L. Loeb (Eds.), *The schizophrenic syndrome.* New York: Grune & Stratton, 1969.

Zerbin-Rudin, E. Genetic research and the theory of schizophrenia. *International Journal of Mental Health,* 1972, *1,* 42–62.

Part II

AFFECTIVE DISORDERS

Chapter 4

Loss as a Source of Stress in Psychopathology

CHARLES G. COSTELLO

University of Calgary
Calgary, Alberta

The very word "loss" has a melancholy ring about it, and many of those interested in the physiological and psychological effects of loss want to know if it is one of the causes of depression. This chapter, therefore, concentrates on the possible contribution of loss in the etiology of depression.

An exhaustive review of the work in each of the relevant areas of research need not be attempted because many thorough reviews are already available. A review of work on the effects of loss of a mother in the early life of humans has been done by Michael Rutter (1972) in his book on the general topic of maternal deprivation; Mineka and Suomi (1978) have reviewed the investigations of the effects of social separation in monkeys; Dohrenwend and Dohrenwend's (1974) book, *Stressful Life Events: Their Nature and Effects,* provides a good coverage of the immediate effects on adult humans of stressful life events, including those which involve loss; Bloom, Asher, and White (1978) have reviewed the literature concerning marital disruption as a stressor. The more consistent findings from all of these areas of research, the common and sometimes questionable assumptions, and some of the methodological problems are brought together here.

For our purposes, *loss* refers to the actual loss of someone or something to whom or to which an attachment had probably grown. The loss may have occurred naturally or may have been experimentally produced. In neither case is it easy to point to the demonstrable effects of loss acting alone. Here, as in previous reviews of such investigations, it is abundantly clear that loss can be considered to be only one factor among many acting to increase a person's *vulnerability* to stress and psychopathology or acting directly to *provoke* stress and psychopathology. It is also painfully obvious that we are far from having determined the specific contribution loss itself makes, either acting alone or in interaction with other variables. As Brown and Harris (1978) have proposed, those words "vulnerability" and "provoke" simply provide a useful way to conceptualize the role of loss in producing stress and psychopathology.

Loss may act as a *provoking agent* in that it is one of the immediate causal antecedents of a particular episode of stress and/or psychopathology. Loss may also be a *vulnerability factor* in that it enhances a person's sensitivity to later pathogenic stimuli, which may include losses acting as provoking agents. Losses which increase a person's vulnerability do not, according to Brown and Harris, play any role in the later onset of particular episodes of stress or psychopathology in the absence of a provoking agent. From the analysis of their own data on early loss of a mother, life events, and depression they concluded that the early loss acted as a vulnerability factor. Brown and Harris's conclusion has been questioned as we see later, and, at the present time, it would be preferable to leave open the possibility that, in some circumstances, an early loss may increase the likelihood of the later onset of stress and psychopathology, even in the absence of any environmental provoking event. A loss could, of course, act as both a vulnerability factor *and* as a provoking agent in that its immediate effects are to provoke stress and/or psychopathology and its delayed effects are to act as a vulnerability factor.

Let us, first of all, review the more consistent findings, the assumptions, and some of the methodological problems in each of the following areas of research: (1) the immediate effects of separation from mothers and peers in preadult human and nonhuman primates; (2) the long-term effects of separation from mothers and peers in preadult nonhuman primates; (3) the long-term effects of parental loss in preadult humans; and (4) the effects of loss occurring in the adult years of humans. In reviewing each area of research, some comment is made on the interpretation of the data proposed, and in the final section, the role of loss in producing stress and psychopathology is reconsidered.

The Immediate Effects of Separation from Mothers and Peers in Preadult Human and Nonhuman Primates

In the early 1950s, John Bowlby and his associates at London's Tavistock Clinic began to publish their series of papers reporting that human infants separated from their mothers went through a phase of "protest" followed by a phase of "despair."

Upon reunion with the mothers, the infants were observed to show a "detached" attitude. These three phases in the responses of children to separation from their mothers, particularly the first two phases of "protest" and "despair," have been generally accepted as established facts. For instance, Mineka and Suomi (1978) wrote that:

The early work of Spitz (1946), Robertson and Bowlby (1952) and Bowlby (1960[b]) indicated that young human children often display a biphasic response to prolonged physical separation from their mothers. Immediately after the act of separation the children tended to be highly agitated and distressed, a phase that Bowlby termed *protest*. This phase was typically followed, after several days, by a phase of dejection and social withdrawal termed *despair* (p. 1377).

Suomi and Harlow (1977) wrote: "One form of depression exists for which cause, course, and one form of effective cure are relatively well-known and documented. It is *anaclitic depression,* also known as dependency depression" (p. 136). Suomi and Harlow went on to describe the phases of "protest," "despair," and "detachment." They noted that anaclitic depression "is *not* an inevitable consequence of separation from mother. Even in Spitz's original definitive report only approximately 20% of his institutionalized subject population experienced anaclitic depression." They concluded, however, that "because anaclitic depression has a documented etiology, a well-defined sequence of symptoms and at least one form of therapy that appears to be generally successful, it is perhaps the most easily modeled form of depression" (p. 137). They also conlcuded, like so many workers with nonhuman primates, that "anaclitic depression remains an attractive starting point for pursuit of a viable monkey model" (p. 137).

Researchers with nonhuman primates are not the only ones who have accepted the observations of Bowlby and his associates. The child psychiatrist, Michael Rutter, wrote:

Short-term effects [of maternal deprivation] have been most studied with respect to children admitted to hospital or to a residential nursery (Vernon, Foley, Sipowicz, & Schulman, 1965; Yarrow, 1964). There is good evidence that many (but not all) young children show an immediate reaction of acute distress and crying (what has been called the period of "protest") followed by misery and apathy (the phase of "despair") and finally there may be a stage where the child becomes apparently contented and seems to lose interest in his parents ("detachment" in Robertson's and Bowlby's terms) (Bowlby, 1958, 1962, 1968; Robertson & Bowlby, 1952). That these reactions occur is well established. What remains controversial is their clinical significance and the psychological mechanisms involved (1972, pp. 29–30).

Let us take a brief look at the nature of the data concerning these phases in the responses of human children to prolonged separation from their mothers. The observations of John Bowlby and James Robertson are clinical ones, with no attempt at objectivity and no measures of interobserver reliabilities. The number of cases in each report is always small, or sometimes, as in Robertson and Bowlby (1952), it is unstated. Bowlby (1960a) apologetically noted that "we have no large series of well-observed cases to quote" (p. 91). In his second paper, the one referred to by Mineka and Suomi (1978), Bowlby (1960b) relied quite heavily on the data reported by Heinicke (1956). (Heinicke's report is considered in more detail later on.) Those data were obtained from only six children, and Bowlby (1960b) himself commented, "In view of the small number of children and the possible errors due to time sampling, too great weight must not be set on these [data]" (p. 26). The variable of separation is confounded in many cases with that of illness and the administration of anesthetics for surgery. For instance, the 2-year-old girl, Laura, in Robertson's (1952) film, *A Two-Year-Old Goes to Hospital,* is in the hospital for an umbilical hernia and on the second day receives a general anesthetic for surgery. For a day or two afterward, the child is, as the voice-over says, "subdued." But there is no clear indication of despair, and her subdued appearance might very well be a residual effect of the anesthetic.

Many of Bowlby's papers do not, in actuality, present any new data in relation to his hypothesized stages of "protest," "despair," and "detachment." The papers present either discussion of his attachment theory or references to the same small set of observations that he and his Tavistock colleagues made. In some instances, a paper does not emphasize responses to separation at all. Bowlby (1958), referenced by Rutter (1972) in the passage quoted above, reviews the clinical observations and theoretical ideas related to the concept of attachment but presents no data related to separation. Rutter (1972) also references Bowlby (1968). In that paper, Bowlby reports no data of his own or of others on the behaviors of children during separation. He does refer to the data of Heinicke and Westheimer (1965) on the behavior of children during reunion with the parents. (This study of Heinicke and Westheimer [1965] receives consideration later.) The third Bowlby paper (1962) to which Rutter (1972) refers presents data concerning the incidence of childhood loss in psychiatric patients and delinquents but no data on the immediate effects of separation in human infants. Bowlby (1962) does make brief references to the data in Robertson and Bowlby (1952), Robertson (1953), Bowlby (1953), and Heinicke (1956). As already noted, Robertson and Bowlby (1952) present a number of clinical observations of an unknown number of children. Robertson's (1953) paper in *Nursing Times* is very similar to the Robertson and Bowlby (1952) paper and adds nothing more. In his 1953 paper, Bowlby presented examples of "protest" and "detachment" in 49 cases observed by his team at the Tavistock Clinic, but he does not refer to the "despair" phase.

The reports by Heinicke (1956) and Heinicke and Westheimer (1965) are far more systematic than those of Bowlby and Robertson, but they do not provide much in the way of evidence for the hypothesized sequence of phases in response to separation. Heinicke (1956) compared six children placed in a residential nursery with six placed in a day nursery. The children were around 2 years old, and the two groups did not differ in relation to the occupation of the father, the income level of the family, or nationality. The reason for the placement of the day children was that the mother had to work to supplement the family income. The mother of four of the residential children was pregnant and "going into confinement"; in one case, the mother was sick; and, in one case, the parents took a holiday. The differences in reasons for placement of the day-nursery and residential-nursery children might very well be important to any differences observed between the two groups in response to separation. But in any case, the differences themselves, though suggesting more "protest" in the residential children, provide little evidence in relation to the presence of "despair." When the occurrence of specific categories of behavior is expressed as a percentage of the total activity of the child, the residential children show more crying for their parents. When the total period of separation is broken down, the difference in percentages of time crying is significant only at 10–12 days after initial separation (residential children, 10.2%; day children, 2.0%). The residential children also show more resistance to nurses' demands. For the total period of separation, the residential children resisted 47.1% of the time, the day children, 18.7% of the time—a significant difference. The residential children also show more severe hostility (3.6% of total activity over the total period of separation) than the day children (0.4%).

These data, then, provide some support for the hypothesized "protest" phase. The two groups do not differ significantly in inactivity when this is expressed as a percent of total activity (residential group, 0.7%; day group, 0.2%), nor do they differ in eating. These are the only two measures that seem relevant to the concept of "despair." Heinicke himself does not refer in his paper to "despair," "sadness," or "depression," interpreting his findings, which mainly have to do with "protest," in terms of anxiety.

Heinicke and Westheimer (1965) reported the data on 10 children who had been placed in a residential nursery and 10 control children who were not separated from their mothers. It is not possible to analyze this study in detail here, but we can note the observations on the separated children. Heinicke and Westheimer say that at the moment of separation seven children began to cry, commenting that "the word 'scream' is really more appropriate." Heinicke and Westheimer also note that "longing for the return of the parents in a form of crying for 'Mummy' and 'Daddy' dominated the child's behavior during the first three days" (1965, p. 162). But their figures do not substantiate this statement. They show that crying constituted a mean of between 4 and 5% of total activity during the first three days. Hostile behavior of a mild sort accounted for around 4.5% of total activity, and more severe hostility for about .45% of behavior during the first three days. By the fourteenth day of separation, these figures had increased to 6.25% and 2.20%, respectively. They present no data for despair or sadness alone but do include some for the spontaneous appearance of "sadness-resignation, excessive cheerfulness, and injury to the self." Heinicke and Westheimer focused their analysis of this unusual constellation of behaviors on the two days after the visit of the father, which occurred around the twelfth day of separation, noticing that "in only four cases did the two raters disagree." But disagreement in four out of ten cases would be considered too much by most research- ers. After reexamination of the data, the raters agreed that the above constellation of behaviors occurred in eight out of the ten children. These data cannot be consid- ered supportive of the hypothesized "despair" phase, if indeed they can be considered particularly relevant to the hypothesis.

There is little doubt about the existence of processes of attachment of children to mothers and the stressful effects of brief separations from the mother. A large body of data supports the presence of these phenomena (see Ainsworth et al., 1978, for a recent review). But no good evidence supports the hypothesis that the processes of "protest" and "despair" occur in the child's response to prolonged separation from the mother. The problem is important, and one which needs more careful investi- gation. In such investigations, it will be important to carry out a functional analysis of postseparation behaviors, particularly the ways in which a child's behaviors relate to the behaviors of others in the situation. (This problem is considered in more detail later.)

The data obtained by some investigators of nonhuman primates suggest that sep- aration of infants from the mother does result in behaviors of a "protest" and "despair" sort (Seay, Hansen, & Harlow, 1962; Hinde, Spencer-Booth, & Bruce, 1966; Kaufman & Rosenblum, 1967; Schlottman & Seay, 1972; Singh, 1975). But some investigators have not observed "protest" and "despair" following separation from the mother. Rosenblum and Kaufman (1968) did not observe those behaviors in bonnet macaque infants separated from their mothers. Preston, Baker, and Seay (1970) separated patas monkey infants from their mothers and found "protest" but not "despair." Similar results were found by Jensen and Tolan (1962) for separated pigtail macaques and by Kaplan (1970) and Jones and Clark (1973) who observed agitation in squirrel monkey infants separated from their mothers but found no evi- dence of "despair." Lewis, McKinney, Young, and Kraemer (1976) found evidence of "protest" and "despair" in only one out of five studies of the effects of separating infant rhesus monkeys from their mothers. Mineka and Suomi (1978) commented that "similar variation in response to separation was found long ago in human pri- mates. In Spitz's (1946) original study, only about one-fourth of his population of separated infants exhibited the syndrome [of "protest-despair"]" (p. 1379). In actuality, Spitz (1946) presents no observations on "protest" in any of his population, restricting himself to the discussion of signs of depression. In any case, Pinneau's (1955) cogent criticisms of Spitz's work cast doubt on using Spitz's data.

No certain explanations exist for the differences in findings on the effects of sep- aration in nonhuman primates. In general, the age of the subjects at the time of separation has not been found to account for the conflicting data, although Suomi, Collins, and Harlow (1973) found that rhesus monkeys separated from their mothers at 90 days of age showed more severe reactions than monkeys separated at 60 or 120 days of age. Nor has evidence been reported for sex differences in the effects of mother-infant separations in monkeys.

A finding that has attracted particular attention has been the differences in response to separation between bonnet *(M. radiata)* and pigtail *(M. nemestrina)* macaques. Kaufman and Rosenblum (1969a) found that bonnet infants who were adopted by "aunts" after separation from the mother did not show the depressive reaction of pigtail infants that they had observed in their previous studies (Kaufman & Rosenblum, 1967a, 1967b). They noted that the pigtail infants were not adopted by "aunts." Although this difference between bonnets and pigtails in "social structure" has been emphasized by most commentators on the Kaufman and Rosenblum findings, Kaufman and Rosenblum (1969b) and Kaufman (1973) have noted temperamental differences between the two species which may or may not be related to the differences in group structure. Bonnet adult females appear to have a relaxed maternal disposition. They are less likely to retrieve or otherwise protect their infants and at the same time are more tolerant of the continued closeness of their growing infants, permitting them access to the nipple more often and punishing them less often. As a consequence, bonnet infants appear to be more secure, leave their mothers and go farther away, and spend more time than pigtails in social play. The data in support of these statements can be found in Kaufman and Rosenblum (1969b) and Kaufman (1977).

That the differences in social structure should not be overemphasized is indicated by Kaufman's (1973) report of observations of bonnets who showed no distress when separated from mother and when *no* substitutes were available during the separation. These data, referred to in Kaufman (1973), have not yet been published in detail, and in a personal communication, Kaufman (Note 1) has commented that their findings that bonnets showed no postseparation distress, even when no substitutes were available, probably had to do with the situation in which separation took place rather than being related to a species characteristic. Nevertheless, the role of the nature of preseparation attachment in determining the effects of separation in monkeys may be particularly worth investigating.

In humans, Heinicke and Westheimer (1965) found that the smaller the amount of the mother's affection before separation, the more the child, during separation, avoided observers (two correlations examining this were .59 and .19) and expressed hostility in doll play (correlation .28). On the other hand, they cried less for their parents (correlation .52).

No systematic data appears to relate preseparation attachment behavior in monkeys to their behavior during separation. But Hinde and Spencer-Booth (1971) found that those infants whose attempts to gain ventro-ventral contact had been rejected least by their mothers and who had to play the least role in maintaining proximity with her when off her tended to be the least distressed after reunion.

All of these comparisons are, of course, of the most tenuous sort. Kaufman and Rosenblum took the mothers away, leaving the infant monkeys in their social group, and Heinicke and Westheimer observed children taken away from their mothers and put into nurseries—a considerable procedural difference which certainly is an important determinant of the monkey's response to separation (Hinde & Davis, 1972; Hinde & McGinnis, 1977). Monkeys taken from their mothers and placed in unfamiliar environments show a long protest phase, whereas when the mother is taken away, leaving the infant in a familiar environment, the infant more quickly goes into the despair phase.

Kaufman and Stynes (1978) have recently reported an observation of depression induced in a bonnet macaque infant. They formed a group with both pregnant pigtail and bonnet females that lived together for over a year and in which four pigtails and one bonnet were born. The bonnet infant at 5 months of age underwent a separation in which his mother and all the other bonnets were removed. The infant, ignored by the pigtail adults, became agitated for three days as it tried to make contact. This was followed on the fourth day by postural collapse and social withdrawal. The authors noted that the depressive response of this single bonnet infant might have been idiosyncratic, but they do not think it likely as the infant was typical developmentally and behaviorally. They suggest that even for bonnets "when confronted by a forbidding and frustrating social environment there apparently remains no plan that works, and helplessness ensues, i.e., depression occurs" (p. 74).

Even if one were to conclude from the data that sufficient evidence of similarities exists in the response to separation from the mother in nonhuman primates and humans, one could not assume that this is a specific kind of response to separation from a *mother*. It also seems that similar kinds of responses of "protest" and "despair" can be observed in monkeys separated from *peers* during the first year of life when they have been reared with the peers and without mothers from early infancy (Suomi et al., 1976; Suomi et al., 1975; Suomi, Harlow, & Domek, 1970). Erwin, Brandt, and Mitchel (1973) found that, as with maternal separations, the strength of attachment before peer separation was related to the severity of the subsequent separation. Also, for both maternal and peer separation, the more socially inadequate the reunion environment, the greater the probability of long-term depressive symptoms (Suomi & Harlow, 1975).

Some recent reports have included data on the physiological effects of separation. Reite, Kaufman, Pauley, and Stynes (1974) removed the mothers of four pigtail monkeys from the cage when the monkeys were between 22 and 33 weeks of age. The infants were left in intact social group pens. Immediately after separation, the infants were "behaviorally agitated, exhibited increased motor activity of a restless 'searching' nature, and frequent 'cooing,' the plaintive distress call of the young macaque. The onset of agitation was accompanied by pronounced elevation of both heart rate and body temperature lasting up to several hours" (p. 364). During the first night, REM sleep and heart rate decreased markedly in all infants, and, in three of the four infants, body temperature dropped below the lowest baseline value. Body temperature and heart rate dropped in all four infants the next day when they all showed depressive behavioral characteristics. The authors commented that the initial response of agitation with elevations in body temperature and heart rate is compatible with a state of organismic hyperarousal and increased energy expenditure and might be seen to function adaptively in the attempt to regain the mother. The behavioral depression with hypothermia and bradycardia might, they suggested, either be interpreted in terms of Engel's (1962) conservation-withdrawal theory or it might be considered as intrinsically maladaptive, "a manifestation of disturbed CNS physiology resultant from the stress of separation" (p. 366).

Hunt, Smotherman, Lowe, McGinnis, and Levine (1977) and Levine, Mendoza, Coe, Smotherman, and Kaplan (1977) reported increases in cortisol levels in infant squirrel monkeys separated from their mothers, but the cortisol levels were not significantly correlated with the behavioral reactions of the monkeys.

Kramer and McKinney (1979) reported data on the effects of combining separation experiences and the administration of biogenic amine-depleting agents. Among the pharmacological agents investigated was alpha-methyl-para-tyrosine (AMPT), which depletes the catecholamine neurotransmitters, norepinephrine, and dopamine. They found that AMPT increased huddling and decreased locomotion in rhesus monkeys separated from the peer groups in which they had been reared from the first month of life. Some of the monkeys were separated from their mothers at birth, individually reared in a laboratory nursery for the first month of life, and then housed alone in wire mesh cages. Kramer and McKinney found that in order to produce despair-like behavior in these chronically isolated animals the dosage of AMPT which had significantly amplified the "despair-like" separation behaviors of peer-reared monkeys had to be increased 10 to 20 times. These findings suggest that AMPT is particularly potent in amplifying the stressor effects of separation from conspecifics to which an early attachment had been formed.

The data from the studies with nonhuman primates would probably be much more useful to us if we had more data on the immediate effects on children of prolonged parental separation. The immediate effects of the child's separation from a parent due to divorce would probably repay investigation despite the difficulty of controlling for the confounding variables. Some very general observations of the stressful effects on children of their parents' divorce have been presented by Kelly and Wallerstein (1976), Stuart and Abt (1972), Toomin (1974), and Wallerstein and Kelly (1975), but we need much more systematic data than they have presented. There are data indicating that recent separation from parents, either due to their divorce or due to the death of a parent, is related to the probability of psychiatric disorder in children. Kalter (1977) reported that 32.6% of 387 children referred to a department of psychiatry had experienced a parental divorce, twice the rate of occurrence for children of divorce in the general population of the United States. Rutter (1966) examined the case histories of 739 children with neurotic or behavior disorders attending the Maudsley Hospital Children's Department. The observed rate of parental death for the disturbed children was compared with the expected rate calculated from the Registrar General's figures. The calculation was made separately for each year during the child's lifetime according to the parents' age, sex, and marital status in that year so that variables that have been found to be related to death rates could be controlled. The expected rate of total parental death was 34.6, while the observed rate was 88. The expected rate of paternal death was 20.3, the observed rate, 52. The expected rate of maternal death was 14.3, the observed rate, 36. All of these differences are statistically significant. But one cannot, of course, simply conclude that parental death caused the disturbance in the children. Data on the time between the parental death and the onset of the child's disturbance were not available for all the cases. But in 36% of the 69 children for whom data were available, five or more years had elapsed between bereavement and onset of illness. In thirteen of the cases, parental death occurred after the onset of the child's illness.

To summarize, we can note: (1) that there is a lack of good data on the immediate effects of prolonged separation on a child; (2) that separation of infant monkeys from mothers or peers with whom they have been reared *may* result in "protest" and "despair" behaviors; (3) that although intriguing data suggest that more relaxed monkeys and more flexible social structures reduce the stressful effects of separation, no firm conclusions can be drawn at this point; and (4) that some data suggest that the "despair" which is experimentally induced in monkeys by social separation is mediated by the same biochemical processes that underlie clinical depressions.

The Long-Term Effects of Separation from Mothers and Peers in Preadult Nonhuman Primates

The long-term effects of preadult separation from mothers and peers in nonhuman primates has not been extensively researched, and the few available data can be reviewed briefly. Hinde and Spencer-Booth (1971) found that the tendency for infant monkeys separated from their mothers to be more prone to try to maintain contact with their mothers upon reunion and less prone to interact with peers than infants that had not been separated lasted in some cases as long as two years following reunion. Mitchell, Harlow, Griffin, and Møller (1967) found that monkeys separated from their mothers for *2-hour* periods during the first year of life were more withdrawn than controls when exposed to novel stimuli during adult years. Some data also suggest that separation from peers may have similar long-term effects. Suomi, Harlow, and Domek (1970) found that four rhesus monkeys repeatedly separated from peers with whom they had been reared from birth (without mothers) showed as severe "agitation" followed by "despair" after twenty 4-day separations as they did on the first such separation. It was also found that "their social behavior at age 9 mo., following the separations, was virtually identical to their behavior at age 3 mo., prior to the separations, in sharp contrast to the rapid and broad behavioral maturation traditionally reported for similar monkeys not subjected to separation" (p. 164). Unfortunately, because the monkeys were in isolation during the 4-day separation periods, one cannot be sure how much isolation itself or separation contributed to the behavior observed.

A study of separation effects in adolescent monkeys by Suomi, Eisele, Grady, and Harlow (1975) indicates the possible importance of isolation alone in producing "depressive behaviors." Their monkeys were reared in nuclear families of four mother-father pairs. Five-year-old monkeys were separated from their family units and housed in one of three conditions for 120 days. Some of the monkeys were placed with familiar peers, others were placed with strangers, and others were housed individually. All of the group-housed adolescents showed mild reactions to separation from their families, whereas the individually housed monkeys showed the "protest" and "despair" similar to those shown by separated infants. Mineka and Suomi (1978), referring to recent work from their laboratory, found that repeated separations of peer-reared adolescent monkeys resulted in increasingly severe depressive effects. The protest phase dropped out, and the monkeys, when separated, went immediately into the despair phase.

Data relevant to a vulnerability hypothesis of the effects of early loss were presented by Young, Suomi, Harlow, and McKinney (1973). They separated infant monkeys from their peers for 30 days in infancy. Later, during adolescence, the monkeys were subjected to repetitive daily separations of 23 hours per day. Unlike control monkeys that had not been separated in infancy, the monkeys separated in infancy exhibited depression-like behaviors in response to adolescent separations. In their review, Mineka and Suomi (1978) noted that more recent studies suggest (1) that early experience with separation may predispose monkeys to react more severely than nonseparated monkeys only to the first in a series of adolescent separations and (2) that monkeys responded severely to separation in their second year only if they had responded severely to the separation in the first year.

The Long-Term Effects of Parental Loss in Preadult Humans

The relation between preadult parental loss and adult psychiatric disorders has long been a controversial issue and the controversy has not yet ended. Some investigators have found significant differences between patients and controls in the incidence of early parental death (Archibald, 1962; Barry & Lindemann, 1960; Hilgard & Newman, 1963; Norton, 1952). Others have failed to find any such significant difference (Brill & Liston, 1966; Granville-Grossman, 1966; Gregory, 1966; Munro, 1966; Pitts, Meyer, Brooks & Winokur, 1965). But, as Birtchnell (1970a) has pointed out, a serious defect in these early studies was the failure to consider the incidence of early parent death in adequate detail—with respect to the year of loss, for instance. High incidences during early years can be canceled out by lower incidences during later years, so that the total incidences before a certain age may be similar for patients and controls. In some studies, the sex and the age of the patient have also been ignored. The importance of these points is illustrated in Birtchnell's (1970a) data. In a study of 500 patients and 500 controls, Birtchnell found that the incidence of early parental death (i.e., before age 20) for patients was 29.4% (144/489) and for controls 24.3% (115/473)—a nonsignificant difference. But incidence of early parental death (i.e., before age 20) in patients under age 40 was 25.5% (52/204) and in controls under 40 was 16.9% (34/201)—a significant difference. When the period from age 0 to 9 is considered, 17.7% of the patients (85/489) had lost a parent and 11.3% of the controls (53/473)—also a significant difference. The loss of a father showed a greater degree of disproportionate representation in the patients than did the loss of a mother (see Table 4-1), and only the difference for fathers is significant. But when the period from 0 to 4 is considered, the difference between patients and controls in the incidences of both loss of mother and loss of father was significant (see Table 4-2).

These disproportionate numbers of parental losses in the patients are due primarily to losses suffered by daughters. When the data are separately analyzed for the sex of the patients, the above pattern of significant findings is found for daughters but not for sons.

The sex of the patient has also been found to be important in the comparison of moderately and severely depressed patients. First let us look at the findings in general. In his further analysis of the data from the 500 patients and 500 controls presented in his 1970a paper, Birtchnell (1970b) found that the incidence of parent death from age 0 to 19 for the depressed patients was 28.3% (65/231) and for the nondepressed 29.6% (60/214)—a nonsignificant difference. When the depressed patients were classified into two groups of moderately and severely depressed patients, the incidence of parent death from age 0 to 19 was significantly higher in the severely depressed group, 37.2% (35/94), than in the moderately depressed group, 25.2% (37/148). No statistical difference existed between the two groups of depressives in relation to early loss of the father, but one did appear in relation to loss of the mother: severely depressed, 22.34% (21/94); moderately depressed, 6.42% (95/148). Once again, this effect was most marked for daughters (severely depressed, 23.4% [18/77]), suffered early loss of mother; moderately depressed, 3.7% [35/94]) than for sons (severely depressed, 17.6% [3/17]); moderately depressed, 11.1% [6/54]).

Two considerations make one a little cautious about these data. First, depression was rated retrospectively from case histories. Birtchnell devised his own scale of depression for the task, and we have no psychometric information on the scale in general and no data on the reliability of the ratings of depression in this particular study. Second, the period from 0 to 19 years is a long one if one is concerned about the effects of *early* parental loss. The pattern of results for earlier years is the same as those for the period 0 to 19 years, but Birtchnell reports the results of statistical tests only for the latter complete period. This is probably due to the small numbers of cases involved when shorter age ranges were considered.

Table 4-1 **The Incidence of Father and Mother Deaths Before Age 9 for 489 Patients and 473 Controls**

	PATIENTS	CONTROLS
Father death	45.5(18.7%)	27.5(11.8%)
Mother death	39.5(15.9%)	25.5(10.9%)

From data presented in Birtchnell, 1970a.

Table 4-2 **The Incidence of Father and Mother Deaths in the Age Period 0–4 Years for 489 Patients and 473 Controls**

	PATIENTS	CONTROLS
Father death	22(8.9%)	7.8(4.4%)
Mother death	25(10.1%)	11.5(4.9%)

From data presented in Birtchnell, 1970a.

Table 4-3 **The Incidence of Parent Death Occurring Before Age 10 in 2699 Depressed Patients Compared with Expected Values Calculated from a General Population Sample of 3425 Subjects**

	LOSS OF FATHER		LOSS OF MOTHER		LOSS OF EITHER PARENT	
	SONS	DAUGHTERS	SONS	DAUGHTERS	SONS	DAUGHTERS
Observed	51	120*	36*	80*	87	200*
Expected	47.1	92.4	25.6	58.9	82.7	151.3

From data presented in Birtchnell, 1972.
*Significantly greater than expected.

The sex of the patient was also an important factor in Birtchnell's (1972) study in which he compared with expected numbers the incidence of parent death occurring before the age of 10 in five diagnostic groups including depressed patients (total N = 2699). The expected numbers were based on the age distribution within the diagnostic groups and were calculated from a general population sample of 3425 subjects contacted by letter (replies were received from 3425/4000 subjects—85.6%). The results for the depressed patients are presented in Table 4-3. It can be seen that, although there is a significantly greater loss only of mothers in male depressives, the female depressives had a significantly greater loss of fathers and mothers.

The higher incidence of paternal loss in female depressives found in the Birtchnell (1972) study was not found in the Brown, Harris, and Copeland (1977) study of 458 women selected at random in Camberwell, an inner-city district of London. They found that loss of a mother, but not of a father, before the age of 11 was significantly associated with depression. Twenty-two percent of the women who had suffered from depression during the year before interview and 6% of the normal women (i.e., the rest of the community sample) had lost a mother before age 11. They also found that women who had suffered a severe life event or difficulty were much more likely to have developed depression in the year before interview if they also had an early loss of mother. Their data are presented in Table 4-4.

As already noted, it is extremely difficult to separate the causal effects of a loss itself from the possibly stressful circumstances preceding and following the loss. Brown and Harris (1978) presented some data suggesting that the effect of loss of a mother before age 11 was not due to the discontinuity and social upheaval that may result. They divided the group of women in the community who had lost a mother before 11 into two groups: 23 women who had lost contact with their fathers at some time soon after the loss of their mothers and 16 who had maintained continuous contact with their fathers (or, in rare cases, another person such as a grandmother who had already been living with them). They found that 30% of those with discontinuous contact had been depressed in the 12 months before interview, compared with 56% of those in continuous contact. Brown and Harris noted that exam-

Table 4-4 **Percentage of Women in a General Population Study Who Suffered an Onset of Psychiatric Disorder in the Year of Study by Whether They Had a Severe Event or Major Difficulty and Whether They Suffered Loss of a Mother or Father Before Age 11**

	LOSS OF MOTHER BEFORE 11		LOSS OF FATHER BEFORE 11 (EXCLUDING 30 WOMEN WITH A LOSS OF MOTHER BEFORE 11)	
	YES	NO	YES	NO
Severe event or major difficulty	47 (7/15)	17* (26/150)	20 (3/15)	17 (23/135)
None	0 (0/15)	2 (4/239)	0 (0/17)	2 (4/222)

From data presented in Brown, Harris, & Copeland, 1977.
*P < .01; other differences are not significant at the .05 level.

ination of the data from their investigations of patients confirmed this result, but they do not present the data. Brown, Harris, and Copeland (1977) concluded from the findings related to loss of a mother before age 11 that the loss increases the vulnerability of a woman to severe life events and difficulties, a position that is developed in more detail in Brown and Harris (1978).

This conclusion has been criticized by Tennant and Bebbington (1978). The criticism has been elaborated in detail in Bebbington (in press), who argues that the procedure of partitioning 2 × 2 × 2 contingency tables is a questionable approach to the analysis of causal models. The reason is that propositions in epidemiology may be intransitive, with the result that it is possible simultaneously to refute and to confirm predictions supporting a single model on a single set of data using the method of Brown and his colleagues of partitioning contingency tables. Bebbington (in press) reanalyzed the Brown, Harris, and Copeland (1977) data in Table 4-4, using the procedure of log-linear analysis (Everitt, 1977). He concludes from the results that the loss of a mother before 11 is more parsimoniously described as a separate provoking agent than as a vulnerability factor. As Bebbington (in press) notes, the results of the log-linear analysis are disconcerting because the model of vulnerability has a strong intuitive appeal and because it is unclear how early loss of a mother could act as a provoking agent for an illness in the adult years.

Perhaps even more disconcerting is the fact that Brown, Harris, and Copeland (1977) did not find a significantly high incidence of loss of mother or father before age 11 in 114 female patients with a diagnosis of primary depression. They argued that this apparent inconsistency between the results for patients and the cases found in the community sample could be explained by the fact that loss of mother before age 11 not only increases the chances of developing psychiatric disorder, it also correlates with other factors that tend to lower chances of contacting a psychiatrist. For supporting documentation, they referred to pages 239–240 of another paper—Brown, Bhrolchain, and Harris (1975)—but the relevant data do not appear to be there. The data can be found, however, in footnote 15 on page 362 of Brown and Harris (1978). The data indicate that loss of mother before age 11 is significantly associated with low intimacy with the husband (gamma = .56) and with having three or more children under 14 at home (gamma = .40). There are also data suggesting that the second factor—having three or more children under 14 at home—is associated with a reduced likelihood of contacting a psychiatrist. Brown and Harris (1978), referring to the psychiatric cases discovered in the community sample, noted:

Of those with fewer than three children under fourteen at home, 83 percent (10/12) of those not employed and 50 percent (8/16) of those employed had seen their general practitioners. Of those with three or more children under fourteen at home, only 11 percent (1/9) had done so, irrespective of whether they were employed (p < .01) (p. 188).

In view of Bebbington's (in press) caveats concerning this piecemeal approach to complex contingency data, one would wish to see confirmation of these results with larger samples and perhaps other forms of analyses before accepting the explanation for the difference between community cases and patients.

Brown, Harris, and Copeland (1977) did find a significant difference in the incidence of *other* forms of past loss when patients (49% suffered such losses) were compared with normal women in the general population (28% suffered such losses). *Other* losses were loss of mother between ages 11 and 17, loss of father or sibling before age 17, loss of a child at any age through death (including stillbirth) or adoption, and loss of a husband by death. Brown and his colleagues argued that such *other* past losses can only raise the chances of women developing depression by acting as a *vulnerability* factor since, they wrote, it seems unlikely that such loss could play an etiological role on its own, producing depression after many years of incubation. They went on to argue that because it is only through a provoking agent that a vulnerability factor can have some effect, one would expect a correlation of provoking agents and vulnerability factors in any population suffering from the provoked condition. So, past other loss, if it acts as a vulnerability factor, should be correlated with the presence of events or difficulties in the 9 months before onset. Brown and his colleagues presented the data appearing here in Table 4-5 and commented that, whereas there is no significant correlation between *other kinds of past loss* and the presence of events or difficulties, loss of mother before age 11 among the patients conforms exactly to these predictions (Brown, Harris, & Copeland, 1977, p. 7).

In actuality, however, the contingency between loss of mother before age 11 and the presence of events or difficulties is not significant. The argument also seems unsound in that they set out to demonstrate that "other past losses" are acting as vulnerability factors and refer to the nearly significant data for "loss of mother" in

Table 4-5 Patients with: (a) Loss of Mother Before 11; (b) Other Forms of Past Loss (Excluding Those wtih Loss of Mother Before 11) by Whether There Was an *Absence* of a Severe Event or Major Difficulty Before Onset

	A		B	
			OTHER PAST LOSS (EXCLUDING 12 PATIENTS WITH LOSS OF	
	LOSS OF MOTHER BEFORE 11		MOTHER BEFORE 11)	
	Loss	*No loss*	*Loss*	*No loss*
	%	%	%	%
	8	26	30	26
N =	(12)	(100)	(48)	(52)
	NS		NS	

From brown, Harris $ Copeland, 1977, p. 7, italics in title added

support of the argument. Again Bebbington's (in press) paper makes one worry about such arbitrary partitioning of such complex contingency tables.

In summarizing the last two sections, we can note that (1) although infant monkeys continue to manifest "protest" and "despair" after a series of separations, in adolescent monkeys "protest" diminishes with repeated separations; (2) social separation early in the life of nonhuman primates may increase their vulnerability to later separations, but apparently only if they had responded severely to the early separation; (3) whether we are considering psychiatric problems in general or depression in particular, females tend to show a greater than normal incidence of both loss of a mother and loss of a father. There is some slight indication that the incidence of loss of a mother is higher in male depressives.

The Effects of Loss Occurring in the Adult Years of Humans

During the last decade, much research has been devoted to the connections between life events and illness. Losses of various kinds have been included in such studies, but the specific effects of losses, as contrasted with other life crises, have rarely been isolated. We shall proceed to review the data from those rare studies after examining the data from studies of the effects of losing a spouse through death.

The problem with most of the studies on widows and widowers is that quite unsystematic observations have been made and qualitative rather than quantitative analyses have been done. For instance, Marris (1958), Lopata (1973), Parkes (1972), and Glick, Weiss, and Parkes (1974) have made interesting observations of those who have lost a spouse, the observations sometimes covering long periods after the death of the spouse. But one cannot assess the reliability or validity of their data, and subject attrition has been a big problem. For instance, Glick, Weiss, and Parkes (1974) planned to interview their widows and widowers 3 weeks, 8 weeks, and 13 months after the death of the spouse. Of the 191 widows and 83 widowers contacted, only 108 widows (56%) and 50 widowers (60%) agreed to partipate. For a variety of reasons (e.g., the subject had been separated from the spouse at the time of the spouse's death), 27 widows and 13 widowers were ineligible or unsuitable. Twenty-eight widows and 14 widowers refused any further interviews, and 3 widows had moved away. At the end of the investigation, only 49 widows (26% of those contacted) and 19 widowers (19% of those contacted) had completed all the interviews, and this casts serious doubt on the generalizability of any findings of the study.

It would be unwise to dismiss completely the observations of these writers because they suggest hypotheses to be tested in more systematic studies. These observations indicate that after the death of a spouse: (1) symptoms generally associated with clinical depression, such as guilt feelings, insomnia, loss of weight, and loss of interest, may occur; (2) somatic distress may accompany acute grief; (3) the behaviors and experiences of acute grief are similar across cultures; (4) there is often an obsessional review of the death and circumstances surrounding the death; and (5) a widow's adjustment to the loss may take 2 to 4 years.

Phenomena that have not been generally noted or about which there is some controversy are: (1) hallucinations of the dead husband may occur up to 10 years after his death (Rees, 1971), and (2) when the loss is unanticipated, the likelihood of recovering from it is reduced (Glick, Weiss, & Parkes, 1974).

There are no firm data on the incidence of clinical depression after the death of a spouse. Bornstein and Clayton (1972) interviewed 92 widows and widowers 12 months after the death of a spouse using the Feighner criteria (Feighner et al., 1972) for a diagnosis of depression:

The subject had to describe a low mood characterized by feeling depressed, sad, despondent, discouraged, blue, low mood not further differentiated, or any other term such as lost or numb, plus 5 of the following 8 symptoms for a diagnosis of *definite* depression and 4 of the 8 symptoms for a diagnosis of *probable* depression: (1) loss of appetite or weight loss, (2) sleep difficulties including hypersomnia, (3) fatigue, feeling restless, (4) loss of interest, (5) difficulty concentrating, (6) feelings of guilt, (7) wishing to be dead or thoughts of suicide. (Bornstein & Clayton, 1972, p. 470; italics in original.)

Nine of the subjects were found to be definitely depressed and seven were probably depressed. The diagnosis relied on retrospective data, inasmuch as the cluster of symptoms "had to be present since the death of a spouse." In these circumstances, it would be important to have some evidence of interdiagnostician reliability. It would also be necessary to obtain incidence data from a control group of some sort before anything could be decided about the significance of the incidence data from the bereaved group. In Carey's (1977) investigation, 119 (54%) of 221 widows and widowers agreed to be interviewed 13 to 16 months after their loss. Carey used an eight-item adjustment scale developed from an initial list of 40 questions. Carey reported that "a factor analysis clearly indicated that a one-factor solution was appropriate. A factor loading of .50 was used as a cutoff point. He also reported a Kuder-Richardson Formula 20 reliability coefficient of .86. The eight items were: (1) Is loneliness a serious problem for you? (2) Do you feel you are about to go to pieces once a month or more? (3) Are you sometimes so unhappy that you would not care if you died tomorrow? (4) Are you at peace and content most of the time? (5) Do you often feel depressed (sad, blue, low, despondent)? (6) Is depression a serious problem for you? (7) Do you cry frequently? (8) Do you sometimes feel your life is futile and empty? Carey noted that "a shortened version of the questionnaire was also given to 100 married people approached randomly in and around the hospital, the same area from which the widowed respondents came" (1977, p. 127). The responses were scored on a 3-point scale and arbitrary cutoff points were used to classify the respondents into those who were "depressed," "of average adjustment," "well-adjusted." Carey found that only 3.5% of the married were in the depressed category compared to 25% of the widowed, and 82.5% of the married were in the well-adjusted category compared with 50% of the widowed.

This cannot be taken as firm evidence for the greater incidence of depression in the widowed for two reasons. First of all, one would need to know more about the psychometric properties of the adjusted scale, particularly its relation to other self-report scales of depression. Indeed, one wonders why a new scale had to be developed when so many are readily available. Second, the control group, though "approached randomly," was not a true random sample. Some data presented by Carey also cast doubt on the comparability of the two groups: "The married sample was 50 percent male, as compared to 34 percent male for the widowed sample. Of the married persons 20 had college degrees, as compared to 13 percent of the widowed." Differences on these variables are disconcerting in view of the vast literature indicating important sex and social-class differences in the incidence of depression (Bebbington, 1978).

Paula Clayton and her colleagues have written a series of papers on bereavement and depression. The first (Clayton, Desmarais, & Winokur, 1968) reported data from interviews with the relatives of 30 people who had died in a hospital. The plan was to contact the relatives of 50 people who had died, but for one reason or another, the relatives of 20 of the deceased could not be contacted. The relative was asked about symptoms and feelings for three different time periods: "ever before (including terminal illness)," "during the terminal illness," "since the death." A symptoms inventory, designed by Cassidy, Flanagan, Spellman, and Cohen (1957) was used. During bereavement, symptoms such as depressed mood, sleep disturbance, crying, difficulty in concentrating, loss of interest in TV, newspapers, and friends, and anxiety attacks occurred frequently. The greatest frequency was for depressed mood, which occurred in 41% of the 39 relatives interviewed, and the lowest frequency was anxiety attacks, which occurred in 21% of the 39 relatives interviewed. The authors concluded that "it seems implicit then from these findings that there is such an entity as 'reactive depression' but that it is seldom seen by the psychiatrist" (p. 177). The fact that the authors put "reactive depression" in quotation marks suggests that they do not believe that this is the same as reactive depression as generally used in the psychiatric literature, but the paper does not make their position on this clear. In any case, the data cannot be considered as providing strong support for a significant incidence of clinical depression after bereavement for the following reasons: (1) because of the number of refusals, we cannot have much confidence in the generalizability of the findings; (2) there are no data on the reliability of the assessment of symptoms; and (3) data on constellations of symptoms rather than on each symptom, taken separately, would have been more relevant to the question of the incidence of clinical depression during bereavement.

The next five papers from Clayton and her colleagues are based on some portion of the same sample of bereaved spouses and married controls. The general sampling procedures and methods of assessment need outlining before our review of the findings reported in the individual papers. Using a table of random numbers, the listing in obituaries, and information on death certificates, 188 widows and widowers were contacted and 109 (58%) agreed to be interviewed. There were 76 widows and 33 widowers in an age range of 20 to 89, with a mean of 61.5. Each of the 109 bereaved persons was matched in age with 3 same-sexed people from the same voting district and, after 207 potential controls were contacted, the final control group of 109 married people was selected.

Clayton, Halikas, and Maurice (1971) reported data from interviews with the widows and widowers 6 to 35 days after the death of their spouses. The authors noted that their results are similar to those found in Clayton, Desmarais, and Winokur (1968). Crying, depressed mood, sleep disturbance, difficulty in concentrating or poor memory, anorexia or weight loss, and the use of sleep and nerve medicines were common in widows and widowers in the bereavement period. Clayton, Halikas, and Maurice (1972) looked at the constellations of symptoms for the data reported in the Clayton, Halikas, and Maurice (1971) paper. The Feighner criteria (Feighner et al., 1972) described earlier were used. Twenty-two subjects were diagnosed as definite depression and 16 as probable depression. The 38 subjects were then compared with the remainder of the 109 subjects who did not receive a diagnosis of depression. They were compared on 53 demographic, social, and physical variables. One social variable that showed a significant difference was that fewer of those with reactive depression had children in a geographical area they considered close. More of the depressed felt hopeless, felt they were a burden, and felt lonely.

Bornstein, Clayton, Halikas, Maurice and Robins (1973) interviewed 92 of the original 109 subjects within 17 months of the death of the spouse. The mean time after death was 13 months and the range was 12 to 20 months. Using, once again, the Feighner criteria for classification of depression, they found that of the 38 subjects who had been diagnosed as depressed, 1 month after the death, 16 could still be diagnosed as depressed at this follow-up. Of the 71 subjects who were not diagnosed depressed 1 month after the death, 4 were now diagnosed as depressed. It should be noted that of the original 38 depressed, no follow-up was done on two of them because one had died and one refused a second follow-up interview; and of the original 71 who were not depressed, 15 were not followed up because 3 had died and 12 refused a second interview. When the depressed and the nondepressed group at this follow-up were compared, no significant differences were found in previous psychiatric history or family history of psychiatric problems. It was found that only two of the 16 depressed subjects lived with their families at the time of the last interview compared with 35 of the 76 nondepressed subjects. It was also found that 50% of the depressed group had never attended church before the death, compared with 17% of the nondepressed. Interestingly, whereas 75% of the depressed group had experienced death among relatives before, 96% of the nondepressed group had previously experienced death among relatives. The general conclusion of the authors was:

This follow-up study, in conjunction with data taken from the one month interview, leads us to conclude that grief is grief and is not a model for psychotic depression. Although some of our patients had depressive symptoms, none could be called psychotic at 13 months. Thus, while the normal depression of widowhood served as an excellent model for the depression resulting from a *clear-cut* loss, it is also different from clinical affective *illness* and should be considered separately in studies of affective disorders in psychiatric patients (Bornstein et al., 1973, p. 566; italics in original).

The problems connected with deciding when the loss through death can be considered to be causally related to the subsequent depression is indicated by the findings of Clayton and her associates reported in their fourth paper (Clayton et al., 1973). Of the 92 subjects who were interviewed around 13 months after the death, spouses of 81 of the bereaved had had illnesses of more than 5 days, and these were chosen for further investigation. They were divided into two groups; those whose spouses had short terminal illnesses (6 months or less) ($N = 46$) and those subjects ($N = 35$) whose spouses had longer terminal illnesses (more than 6 months). The subjects were given the interview to assess symptoms for the following time periods: during the illness of the spouse, since the death, and 1 year after the death. Nineteen of the 81 subjects had symptoms justifying a diagnosis of depression or probable depression during the illness. At 1 month after the death, 13 of the 19 were still depressed. Of the 62 who were not depressed during the terminal illness, 15 had developed a depressive illness 1 month after the death. The authors commented, "This difference is significant at the .01 level by chi-square, indicating that if 'anticipatory grief' is present the subject is much more likely to have a post-mortem depression than if it is not observed" (p. 49). Glick, Weiss, and Parkes (1974) reported that 34% of the widows interviewed said they were upset by the pain suffered by their spouse before his death, and 40% were upset by the deterioration in his physical appearance.

Clayton (1975) reported data concerning the effect of living alone on bereavement symptoms. One man was excluded from the original sample of 109 widows and widowers because he was in a nursing home with a chronic brain syndrome. Sixty-one of the 108 people were living alone 1 month after the death, 40 were living with children, 4 with siblings, and 3 with parents. The average age of those living alone was 65 and for those living with others, 58—a significant difference. There was no significant difference on other demographic variables, including sex. Using Feighner's criteria for depression, 34% of those living alone and 36% of those living with others were given a diagnosis of depression. At a 1-year follow-up of 89 people, 52 were living alone and 37 were living with others. Again, the only significant demographic difference between the groups was in age, the means being 63 and 57, respectively. Twenty-seven percent of those living alone received a diagnosis of depression against 5% of those living with others—a significant difference. Clayton concluded that at 1 month after the loss of a spouse it is the bereavement itself, rather than the effects of loneliness or social isolation, that "influences the occurrence of depressive symptoms." She played down the findings at 1 year. "It may be that those living alone experience more depressive syndromes than those living with someone a year after bereavement" (p. 136).

Only Birtchnell (1970a) and Brown, Harris, and Copeland (1977) seem to have considered the relation between deaths other than spouse deaths occurring later in life and psychiatric illness. When comparing the patients and controls, Birtchnell (1970a) found that in the patient group there were almost twice as many parent deaths in the most recent 5-year period than in the previous 5 years (97 versus 50) with little difference between the two periods for controls (72 versus 70). When sons and daughters were considered separately, this pattern of findings was the same for both sexes, but significant only for the daughters. The figures are presented in Table 4-6. Birtchnell noted that women are perhaps more sensitive than men to the death of a parent and suggests that this may be because they are more often involved in the terminal nursing of the deceased patient. Birtchnell (1970a) also found that the incidence of parental deaths over the 20 years before admission for depressed

Table 4-6 **The Incidence of Parent Death for Patients and Controls in Relation to Sex of the Bereaved and Recency of Loss**

	No. of Years Before Admission	Patients	Controls
Sons	1–5	44	38
	6–10	21	34
Daughters	1–5	53	34
	6–10	29	36

From data presented in Birtchnell, 1970a.

patients was 51.6% and for nondepressed patients, 51.0%. When the severely depressed were compared with the moderately depressed, the incidence of recent death was significantly higher in the severely depressed: 55/90 (66.3%) versus 59/142 (46.8%). The difference between the two groups of depressed patients was significant only in relation to mother deaths. Without arguing for the proposition in detail, Birtchnell noted that it was likely that a higher proportion of psychotic patients were included in the severely depressed group.

Brown, Harris, and Copeland (1977) presented interesting data relating past loss to the distinction between psychotic and neurotic depression. Apart from this overall classification of the 114 depressed patients, they divided each diagnostic subgroup in half to produce the most and least psychotic groups and the most and least neurotic groups. The patients were also rated independently of the psychotic-neurotic distinction in terms of the *severity* of their condition at the time of their admission into treatment. The authors commented that "although psychotic patients tended to be rated as more severe, these two ratings are, to a considerable extent, independent of each other" (p. 8). In actuality, the relationship between the two ratings (their Table VI, p. 9) is a significant one. In relation to the psychotic-neurotic distinction and past losses, they found that more of the most psychotic patients had past losses than did the least psychotic patients (77% versus 55%), and both these incidences exceeded that for the neurotic group (39%).

These differences were significant. No data were presented for the two halves of the neurotic group. When loss through death was distinguished from other kinds of losses, it was found that:

"77 per cent of the most psychotic, 42 per cent of the least psychotic and 16 per cent of the neurotic group had had a past loss through death ($p < .01$). By contrast, none of the most psychotic, 13 per cent of the least psychotic and 22 per cent of the neurotic group have had a past loss other than death ($p < .01$)" (Brown, Harris, & Copeland, 1977, p. 9).

Data were also presented to show that within the psychotic group, severity of symptoms is highly related to loss by death, and within the neurotic group, severity is related to other forms of loss. But because the severity ratings are significantly related to the psychotic and neurotic ratings, these data on severity cannot be taken to be additional independent data. Data analyses were also presented for an independent series of 70 consecutive female in-patient admissions suffering from depression, with results similar to those above. These results could not be accounted for by the fact that the psychotic patients were older than the neurotic patients. The authors noted the similarity between their results indicating a relationship between severity of depression and early loss through death and those of Birtchnell (1970) (presented earlier here). It should be noted that Birtchnell's data refer only to parental death before age 20, whereas Brown's data included deaths of people other than patient parents and included losses up to 2 years before the date of interview.

A fair amount of work has been done relating life events in general to the onset of depression. Rather than reviewing all of this work, we should concern ourselves with those investigations that have focused on life events involving a loss.

Paykel, Myers, Dienelt, Klerman, Lidenthal, and Pepper (1969) reported the results of an investigation of life events experienced by 185 depressed patients in the 6 months immediately preceding the onset of the depressive symptoms. The diagnosis of depression was based on data obtained with an expanded version of the Hamilton Rating Scale for Depression (Hamilton, 1960). Information on life events experienced in the 6 months before interview was also obtained from 185 controls from the general population matched with the patients for age, sex, marital status, social class, and race. Thirty-three life events were examined, and for 8 of them the differences between the depressed and the controls were significant, the events occurring to a significantly greater extent among the depressed patients. Three events involved loss—marital separation, death of an immediate family member, and departure of a family member from home. In the other five events, the loss is not so obvious—increase in arguments with spouse, start of new type of work, serious illness of a family member, serious personal illness, and change in work conditions. The authors also selected two groups of events from the list of 33. One group, called *entrances,* consisted of events that involved the introduction of a new person into the social field: engagement to be married, marriage, birth of a child, a new person in the home. The other group, called *exits,* included events that involved departure from the social field: death of a close family member, separation, divorce, a family member leaving home, marriage of a child, a son drafted for military service. Entrances were reported by 21 depressed patients and 18 controls—an insignificant difference—whereas exits were reported by 46 depressives and only 9 controls, a significant difference. The authors drew attention to the fact that, despite the stronger relationship between exits and depression than between entrances and depression, the events reported by the depressives which distinguished them from the controls were quite diverse. And, in fact, most of the 33 events recorded were more frequent in the depressives.

In some instances, the lack of significant findings for particular events may have been due to the small numbers involved. This point has been discussed in more detail by Paykel (1973), who also brings up another important point in relation to the findings of the 1969 study. He referred the findings—46 out of 188 depressives having a life event of an exit nature compared with 9 out of 185 controls—to the general population. Using an estimate of 2% for the incidence of new cases in the 6 months in which the data were collected, he noted that out of 10,000 subjects in the general population, there would be 9,800 nondepressives and 200 new depressives. Using the findings from the 1969 study, one would expect that in 5% of the normals, that is, 490 subjects, an exit would have occurred and in 25% of the depressives, that is, 50 subjects, an exit would have occurred. The total number of subjects who would have experienced exits would, therefore, be 490 + 50 subjects. Fifty of these, that is, 9%, would have become depressed. In other words, less than 10% of the subjects who experienced exits would have become clinically depressed, suggesting that the greater part of the variance in determining depression must be attributed to something else.

Paykel and Tanner (1976) investigated the occurrence of life events in 30 previously recovered, depressed women undergoing clinical relapse in a controlled trial of maintenance treatment with amitriptyline and psychotherapy and in 30 matched patients who did not relapse. Overall, patients who relapsed experienced significantly more life events in the 3 months before relapse and especially in the month immediately preceding it. But they did not find any specific relationship between exit events and relapse. This might have been due, as the authors point out, to the fact that there were too few exits for reliable analysis.

The distinction between entrance events and exit events would seem to be a useful one. But, as we have noted, exit events themselves seem to make only small contributions to depressive illness. Also, the finding that exit events occur with greater frequency for psychiatric problems in general (Myers, Lindenthal, & Pepper, 1971; Lindenthal, Pepper, & Ostrander, 1972) suggests that the relationship between such exit events and depression is not a specific one.

Brown and Harris (1978) have presented evidence strongly in support of the etiological role of severe life events in depression. They also commented that "reading through the descriptions of events leaves us in no doubt that loss and disappointment are the central features of most events bringing about clinical depression" (p. 103). But they use the concept of loss in a broad manner, and it also includes threats of loss. For instance, one category of loss they have listed is "separation or threat of it, such as death of a parent, or a husband saying he is going to leave home." Including threats of loss, as well as actual loss, makes it impossible to relate their data to the other data reviewed in this chapter. Another category refers to a person's sense of loss rather than to an objective loss: "an unpleasant revelation about someone close that forces a major reassessment of the person and the relationship, such as the loss of one's conception of a relationship after finding out about a husband's unfaithfulness."

Somewhat surprisingly, little in the way of hard data exists on the stress and psychopathological responses to separation and divorce. Hetherington, Cox, and Cox (Note 2) reported that both men and women experienced anxiety and depression after separation from their spouses, but they do not present supporting data for their statement. Briscoe, Smith, Robins, Marten, and Gaskin (1973) presented data indicating that "psychiatric illness is associated with marital turmoil and divorce," but their data do not permit one to draw any clear conclusions about the temporal relations between divorce and psychiatric illness. Goode (1949) noted that "there is no consistently traumatic pattern consequent on the divorce itself" but did not present the relevant data. Smith (1971) reported that 11% of the 880 seriously disturbed patients attending a regional mental health center and 2% of a random population sample of 2414 had been separated or divorced in the previous year. More detailed probing of a smaller sample of the patients (N is not clear from the report) indicated that for nonalcoholics the divorce or separation occurred for 46% of the patients before the onset of the illness and for 54% after onset. In general, as Bloom, Asher, and White (1978) have noted, "persons who are divorced or separated have been repeatedly found to be overrepresented among psychiatric patients, and persons who are married and living with their spouses have been found to be underrepresented" (p. 869), but what causes what has not yet been determined.

In summarizing this section, we can note that: (1) there are some intriguing observations on the stressful effects of the death of a spouse, but the methodological weaknesses of the studies make it impossible to draw any firm conclusions; (2) there is some evidence suggesting that deaths of close people other than spouses may be among the causal antecedents of depression, particularly more severe and/or psychotic depressions; (3) recent losses other than those resulting from deaths may play a causal role in depression, but loss seems to be but one of a complex set of causal factors; and (4) there are a considerable amount of data indicating that separated or divorced people are at higher risk for psychopathology than married people. But there are no data clearly indicating that the breakup of a marriage causes psychopathology.

A Reconsideration of the Role of Loss as a Source of Stress in Psychopathology

Two basic but questionable assumptions seem to be made by many who are interested in the relations between loss, stress, and psychopathology. (1) Losses early in life increase the probability of psychopathology later in life because early losses have immediate stressful effects. These stressful effects impair some attribute necessary for the normal functioning of the organism later in life. For instance, in humans, an early loss may reduce a person's self-esteem. And (2) The immediate stressful effects of losses later in life are basically the same as those resulting from losses early in life.

Some researchers who investigate social separation in nonhuman primates would probably wish to accept only the second assumption noted above. In other words, they would argue, as Mineka and Suomi (1978) and Suomi and Harlow (1977) seem to do, that social separation in young nonhuman primates produces effects similar to the anaclitic depression produced by social separation in human children. They might then, like Suomi and Harlow (1977), acknowledge that "there exists some question about whether anaclitic depression is representative of adult depressions" (p. 137), but assume pro tem that it is, again like Suomi and Harlow, who wrote, "Our choice of depression as a psychopathological disorder to model in monkeys was not made indiscriminately. Depression is one of the most widespread psychiatric problems known to man" (1977, p. 134). But the argument is a most tenuous one. As we have seen, the data on anaclitic depression are poor, and the issue of whether anything like adult forms of depression occur in children is a controversial and inadequately studied one (Costello, in press, a & b; Lefkowitz & Burton, 1978).

Workers with nonhuman primates seem to be quite cautious about accepting the first assumption noted two paragraphs above. For instance, to take the Wisconsin group again as representative, Mineka and Suomi noted, "In the human literature it has often been reported that individuals who have experienced traumatic social loss as children may be predisposed to respond to social loss as adults with a strong depressive reaction. . . . Actually the evidence supporting this position is not unequivocal" (1978, p. 1388). It is indeed those working with humans who seem to accept the first assumption. For instance, Brown and Harris (1978) noted that their data:

suggest early loss of a mother leads . . . to changes in the personality of the woman herself. It is certainly not unlikely that loss of a mother before eleven may have an enduring influence on a woman's sense of self-esteem, giving her an on-going sense of insecurity and feelings of incompetence in controlling the good things of the world (pp. 239–240).

The particularly questionable component of this assumption is that it is the *traumatic* effects of the early loss that increases a person's vulnerability. As we have seen, no firm data establishes that such losses in childhood do have immediate traumatic effects. And an alternative explanation of the effects of early loss of a mother or, indeed, a father, certainly exists in that an important source of modeling and encouragement for the development of social skills is absent. In other words, it is not the trauma of parental loss that is important but rather the impoverishment in the child's social environment produced by the absence of the parent. A considerable amount of data now indicates the detrimental effects of either mother or father absence on the social development of children (Lamb, 1976; Rutter, 1972). Other data, as Lewinsohn's (1974) theory of depression predicts, indicates that social skills are deficient in those adults prone to become depressed (Weissman & Paykel, 1974). More generally, there is evidence that poor social skills in children are not only a good indicator of current problems but are also a good predictor of later difficulties (Hartup, 1976; Roff, 1970; Rutter, 1978).

Some theoreticians deemphasize the trauma of early loss, postulate that it is parental absence that is important, but also postulate that the parental absence results in a central unitary impairment. So, for instance, Seligman (1975) has said that depression occurs when the organism perceives that its responses and reinforcements are independent events. He has also suggested that:

maternal deprivation results in a particularly crucial lack of control. Mother is the primary partner in the dance of development, the fountain of synchronies with the infant's responses, and the main object of his contingency analyses. His sense of mastery or of helplessness develops from the information provided by mother's responses to his actions. If mother is absent, a profound sense of helplessness should arise—particularly if no surrogate, or an unresponsive one, is provided. Presumably even a mechanical mother, but one that danced with the infant and provided synchronies, would stave off helplessness (p. 146).

Seligman is probably right in attributing the detrimental effects of early maternal loss to impairment in development, but the impairment is not necessarily a learned helplessness one. As Mineka and Suomi (1978) have noted, "There is as yet no evidence bearing on the question of whether a separated organism is retarded at learning that its responses can bring gratification or relief."

Insofar as Bowlby (1969, 1973) emphasizes that one of the chief functions served by an attachment object is that of providing a base of security from which the infant can explore and learn about the environment, he too seems to be giving importance to the detrimental effects of the consequent absence of the lost object. But his main emphasis still seems to be on the traumatic emotional impact of the loss. In the first part of a recent two-part paper (Bowlby, 1977a), he noted that any of a number of experiences, including "discontinuities of parenting," "persistent threats by parents not to love a child," "threats by parents to abandon the family," "can lead a child, an adolescent, or an adult to live in constant anxiety lest he lose his attachment figure and, as a result, to have a low threshold for manifesting attachment behaviour," or the person, as a result of such experiences, will:

have reacted to them differently by inhibiting attachment feeling and behaviour and disclaiming, perhaps even mocking, any desire for close relations with anyone who might provide love and care. . . . As in the case of anxious attachment, there is likely to be much underlying resentment which, when elicited, is directed against weaker persons, and also unexpressed yearning for love and support (Bowlby, 1977a, all above quotes from p. 207).

In the second part of the paper (Bowlby, 1977b), one of the psychotherapist's tasks is described as evoking memories of disrupted attachments "not simply as unhappy occurrences but in terms of the pervasive influence they are exerting in the present on the patient's feelings, thoughts and actions" (Bowlby, 1977b, p. 423). Those who base their observations and ideas on those of Bowlby usually assume that the trauma of either early losses or severely impaired parental relationships results in a basic deficiency in the potential for forming attachment. So, for instance, Rynearson (1978) has recently written of how a human may displace an overdetermined need for attachment to pets.

Concluding Remarks

In conclusion, we can only end as we began by noting that, though, on an intuitive basis, one would expect loss to produce both stress and psychopathology, and, though the expectation has been put to the test of research on many occasions, we are still far from knowing under what circumstances and by what means loss may produce stress and psychopathology. Researchers, whatever their preferred theories, must attempt to answer some very important questions soon: (1) What are the responses of children to prolonged separation, and how are these responses affected by individual differences between the children in constitution, personality, and previous experiences of separation, for example? To what extent are the responses of such children affected by the responses of others with whom the children are interacting? (2) Is there an increased probability of a syndrome of depression (i.e., a constellation of depressive behaviors) in children who have recently experienced the loss of a parent? What are the similarities and differences between such a syndrome and the syndromes of depression occurring in adults? And (3) does loss in adults specifically increase the probability of the onset of the syndromes of depression or are the probabilities of the onset of other psychopathological conditions also increased?

References

Ainsworth, M. D. S., Blehar, M. C., Waters, E., & Wall, S. *Patterns of attachment: A psychological study of the strange situation.* Hillsdale, N.J.: Erlbaum, 1978.

Archibald, H., Bell, D., Miller, C., & Tuddenham, R. D. Bereavement in childhood and adult psychiatric disturbance. *Psychosomatic Medicine,* 1962, *24,* 343–351.

Barry, H., Jr., & Lindemann, E. Critical ages for maternal bereavement in psychoneurosis. *Psychosomatic Medicine,* 1960, *22,* 166–179.

Bebbington, P. E. The epidemiology of depressive disorder. *Culture, Medicine and Psychiatry,* 1978, *2,* 279–341.

Bebbington, P. E. Causal models and logical inference in epidemiological psychiatry. *British Journal of Psychiatry,* in press.

Birtchnell, J. Recent parent death and mental illness. *British Journal of Psychiatry,* 1970, *116,* 289–297. (a)

Birtchnell, J. Early parent deaths and mental illness. *British Journal of Psychiatry,* 1970, *116,* 281–288. (b)

Birtchnell, J. Early parent death and psychiatric diagnosis. *Social Psychiatry,* 1972, *7,* 202–210.

Bloom, B. L., Asher, S. J., & White, S. W. Marital disruption as a stressor: A review and analysis. *Psychological Bulletin,* 1978, *85,* 867–894.

Bornstein, P. E., & Clayton, P. J. The anniversary reaction. *Dseases of the Nervous System,* 1972, *33,* 470–471.

Bornstein, P. E., Clayton, P. J., Halikas, J. A. Maurice, W. L., & Robins, E. The depression of widowhood after thirteen months. *British Journal of Psychiatry,* 1973, *122,* 561–566.

Bowlby, J. Some pathological processes set in train by early mother-child separation. *Journal of Mental Science,* 1953, *99,* 265–272.

Bowlby, J. The nature of the child's tie to his mother. *International Journal of Psychoanalysis,* 1958, *39,* 350–373.

Bowlby, J. Separation anxiety. *International Journal of Psychoanalysis,* 1960, *41,* 89–113. (a)

Bowlby, J. Grief and mourning in infancy and early childhood. *Psychoanalytic Study of the Child,* 1960, *15,* 9–52. (b)

Bowlby, J. Childhood bereavement and psychiatric illness. In D. Richter, J. M. Tanner, Lord Taylor & O. L. Zangwill (Eds.), *Aspects of psychiatric research.* London: Oxford University Press, 1962.

Bowlby, J. Effects on behaviour of disruptions of an affectual bond. In J. D. Thoday & A. S. Parkes (Eds.), *Genetic and environmental influences on behaviour.* London: Oliver & Boyd, 1968.

Bowlby, J. *Attachment and loss: I. Attachment.* New York: Basic Books, 1969.

Bowlby, J. *Separation: Anxiety and anger.* New York: Basic Books, 1973.

Bowlby, J. The making and breaking of affectional bonds: I. Aetiology and psychopathology in the light of attachment theory. *British Journal of Psychiatry,* 1977, *130,* 201–210. (a)

Bowlby, J. The making and breaking of affectional bonds: II. Some principles of psychotherapy. *British Journal of Psychiatry,* 1977, *130,* 421–431. (b)

Brill, N., & Liston, E. Parental loss in adults with emotional disorders. *Archives of General Psychiatry,* 1966, *14,* 307–313.

Briscoe, C. W., Smith, J. B., Robins, E., Marten, S., & Gaskin, F. Divorce and psychiatric disease. *Archives of General Psychiatry,* 1973, *29,* 119–125.

Brown, G. W., & Harris, T. *Social origins of depression: A study of psychiatric disorder in women.* London: Tavistock, 1978.

Brown, G. W., Harris, T., & Copeland, J. R. Depression and loss. *British Journal of Psychiatry,* 1977, *130,* 1–18.

Brown, G. W., Ní Bhrolcháin, M., & Harris, T. Social class and psychiatric disturbance among women in an urban population. *Sociology,* 1975, *9,* 225–254.

Carey, R. G. The widowed: A year later. *Journal of Counseling Psychology,* 1977, *24,* 125–131.

Cassidy, W. L., Flanagan, N. B., Spellman, M., & Cohen, M. E. Clinical observations in manic-depressive disease. *Journal of American Medical Association,* 1957, *164,* 1535–1546.

Clayton, P. J. The effect of living alone on bereavement symptoms. *American Journal of Psychiatry,* 1975, *132,* 133–137.

Clayton, P., Desmarais, L., & Winokur, G. A study of normal bereavement. *American Journal of Psychiatry,* 1968, *125,* 168–178.

Clayton, P. J., Halikas, J. A., & Maurice, W. L. The bereavement of the widowed. *Diseases of the Nervous System,* 1971, *32,* 597–604.

Clayton, P. J., Halikas, J. A., & Maurice, W. L. The depression of widowhood. *British Journal of Psychiatry,* 1972, *120,* 71–78.

Clayton, P. J., Halikas, J. A., Maurice, W. L., & Robins, E. Anticipatory grief and widowhood. *British Journal of Psychiatry,* 1973, *122,* 47–51.

Costello, C. G. Childhood depression: Three basic but questionable assumptions in the Lefkowitz and Burton critique. *Psychological Bulletin,* 1981. (a)

Costello, C. G. Childhood depression. In E. J. Mash & L. G. Terdal (Eds.), *Behavioral assessment of childhood disorders.* New York: Guilford Press, 1981. (b)

Dohrenwend, B. P., & Dohrenwend, B. S. *Stressful life events: Their nature and effects.* New York: Wiley, 1974.

Engel, G. L. Anxiety and depression-withdrawal: The primary affects of unpleasure. *International Journal of Psychoanalysis,* 1962, *43,* 49–108.

Erwin, R., Brandt, E. M., & Mitchell, G. Attachment formation and separation in heterosexually naive preadolescent rhesus monkeys *(Macaca mulatta). Developmental Psychobiology,* 1973, *6,* 531–538.

Everitt, B. S. *The analysis of contingency tables.* London: Chapman & Hall, 1977.

Feighner, J. P., Robins, E., Guze, S. B., Woodruff, R. J., Winokur, G., & Munoz, R. Diagnostic criteria for use in psychiatric research. *Archives of General Psychiatry,* 1972, *26,* 57–63.

Glick, I. O, Weiss, R. S., & Parkes, C. M. *The first year of bereavement.* New York: Wiley, 1974.

Goode, W. J. Problems in post-divorce adjustment. *American Sociological Review,* 1949, *14,* 394–401.

Granville-Grossman, K. L. Early bereavement and schizophrenia. *British Journal of Psychiatry,* 1966, *112,* 1027–1034.

Gregory, I. Retrospective data concerning childhood loss of a parent. *Archives of General Psychiatry,* 1966, *15,* 354–361.

Hamilton, M. A rating scale for depression. *Journal of Neurology, Neurosurgery and Psychiatry,* 1960, *23,* 56–61.

Hartup, W. W. Peer interaction and the behavioral development of the individual child. In E. Schopler & R. S. Reichler (Eds.), *Psychopathology and child development.* New York: Plenum, 1976.

Heinicke, C. Some effects of separating two-year-old children from their parents: A comparative study. *Human Relations,* 1956, *9,* 105–176.

Heinicke, C., & Westheimer, I. *Brief separations.* New York: International Universities Press, 1965.

Hetherington, E. M., Cox, M., & Cox, R. Divorced fathers. *Family Coordinator,* 1976, *25,* 417–428.

Hetherington, E. M., Cox, M., & Cox, R. Stress and coping in divorce: A focus on women. Unpublished manuscript, 1977. (Available from E. M. Hetherington, Department of Psychology, University of Virginia, Charlottesville, Virginia, 22901).

Hilgard, J., & Newman, M. Parental loss by death in childhood as an aetiological factor among schizophrenic and alcoholic patients compared with a non-patient community sample. *Journal of Nervous and Mental Diseases*, 1963, *137*, 14–28.

Hinde, R. A., & Davies, L. Removing infant rhesus from mother for 13 days compared with removing mother from infant. *Journal of Child Psychology and Psychiatry*, 1972, *13*, 227–237.

Hinde, R. A., & McGinnis, L. Some factors influencing the effects of temporary mother-infant separation: Some experiments with rhesus monkeys. *Psychological Medicine*, 1977, *7*, 197–212.

Hinde, R. A., & Spencer-Booth, Y. Effects of brief separations from mothers on rhesus monkeys. *Science*, 1971, *173*, 111–118.

Hinde, R. A., Spencer-Booth, Y., & Bruce, M. Effects of 6-day maternal deprivation on rhesus monkey infants. *Nature*, 1966, *210*, 1021–1033.

Hunt, L. E., Smotherman, W. P., Lowe, E. L., McGinnis, L., & Levine, S. Separation and adrenocortical responsiveness in mother and infant rhesus macaques. *Abstracts for the American Society of Primatologists*, 1977, *1*, 19.

Jensen, G. D., & Toleman, C. W. Mother-infant relationship in the monkey *Macaca nemestrina:* The effect of brief separation and mother-infant specificity. *Journal of Comparative and Physiological Psychology*, 1962, *55*, 131–136.

Jones, B. C., & Clark, D. L. Mother-infant separation in squirrel monkeys living in a group. *Developmental Psychobiology*, 1973, *6*, 259–269.

Kalter, N. Children of divorce in an outpatient psychiatric population. *American Journal of Orthopsychiatry*, 1977, *47*, 40–51.

Kaplan, J. The effects of separation and reunion on the behavior of mother and infant squirrel monkeys. *Developmental Psychobiology*, 1970, *3*, 43–52.

Kaufman, I. C. Mother-infant separation in monkeys: An experimental model. In J. P. Scott & E. C. Senay (Eds.), *Separation and depression*. Washington, D. C.: American Association for the Advancement of Science, 1973.

Kaufman, I. C. Developmental considerations of anxiety and depression: Psychobiological studies in monkeys. In T. Shapiro (Ed.), *Psychoanalysis and contemporary science*. New York: International Universities Press, 1977.

Kaufman, I. C. Personal communication, March 27, 1979.

Kaufman, I. C., & Rosenblum, L. A. Depression in infant monkeys separated from their mothers. *Science*, 1967, *155*, 1030–1031. (a)

Kaufman, I. C., & Rosenblum, L. A. The reaction to separation in infant monkeys: Anaclitic depression and conservation-withdrawal. *Psychosomatic Medicine*, 1967, *29*, 648–675. (b)

Kaufman, I. C., & Rosenblum, L. A. The waning of the mother-infant bond in two species of macaque. In B. M. Foss (Ed.), *Determinants of infant behavior* (Vol. 4). London: Methuen, 1969. (a)

Kaufman, I. C., & Rosenblum, L. A. Effects of separation from mother on the emotional behavior of infant monkeys. *Annals of the New York Academy of Science*, 1969, *159*, 681–695. (b)

Kaufman, I. C., & Stynes, A. J. Depression can be induced in a bonnet macaque infant. *Psychosomatic Medicine*, 1978, *40*, 71–75.

Kelly, J. B., & Wallerstein, J. S. The effects of parental divorce: Experiences of the child in early latency. *American Journal of Orthopsychiatry*, 1976, *46*, 20–32.

Kraemer, G. W., & McKinney, W. T. Interactions of pharmacological agents which alter biogenic amine metabolism and depression: An analysis of contributing factors within a primate model of depression. *Journal of Affective Disorders*, 1979, *1*, 33–54.

Lamb, M. E. (Ed.). *The role of the father in child development*. New York: Wiley, 1976.

Lefkowitz, M. M., & Burton, N. Childhood depression: A critique of the concept. *Psychological Bulletin*, 1978, *85*, 716–726.

Levine, S., Mendoza, S. P., Coe, C. L., Smotherman, W. P., & Kaplan, J. The pituitary-adrenal response as an indication of attachment in mother and infant squirrel monkeys. *Abstracts for the American Society of Primatologists*, 1977, *1*, 22.

Lewinsohn, P. M. A behavioral approach to depression. In R. J. Friedman & M. M. Katz (Eds.), *The psychology of depression: Contemporary theory and research*. Washington, D.C.: V. H. Winston, 1974.

Lewis, J. K., McKinney, W. T., Young, L. T., & Kraemer, G. W. Mother-infant separation in rhesus monkeys as a model of human depression: A reconsideration. *Archives of General Psychiatry*, 1976, *33*, 699–705.

Lopata, H. Z. *Widowhood in an American city*. Cambridge, Mass.: Schenkman, 1973.

Marris, P. *Widows and their families*. London: Routledge & Kegan Paul, 1958.

Mineka, S., & Suomi, S. J. Social separation in monkeys. *Psychological Bulletin*, 1978, *85*, 1376–1400.

Mitchell, G. D., Harlow, H. F., Griffin, G. A., & Møller, G. W. Repeated maternal separation in the monkey. *Psychonomic Science*, 1967, *8*, 197–198.

Munro, A. Parental deprivation in depressive patients. *British Journal of Psychiatry*, 1966, *112*, 443–457.

Myers, J. K., Lindenthal, J. J., & Pepper, M. P. Life events and psychiatric impairment. *Journal of Nervous and Mental Disease*, 1971, *152*, 149–157.

Myers, J. K., Lindenthal, J. J., Pepper, M. P., & Ostrander, D. R. Life events and mental status: A longitundal study. *Journal of Health and Social Behavior*, 1972, *13*, 398–406.

Norton, A. Incidence of neurosis related to maternal age and birth order. *British Journal of Social Medicine*, 1952, *6*, 253–258.

Parkes, C. M. *Bereavement: Studies of grief in adult life*. New York: Basic Books, 1972.

Paykel, E. S. Life events and acute depression. In J. P. Scott & E. C. Senay (Eds.), *Separation and depression*. Washington, D.C.: American Association for the Advancement of Science, 1973.

Paykel, E. S., Myers, J. K., Dienelt, M. N., Klerman, G. L., Lindenthal, J. J., & Pepper, M. P. Life events and depression: A controlled study. *Archives of General Psychiatry*, 1969, *21*, 753–760.

Paykel, E. S., & Tanner, J. Life events, depressive relapse and maintenance treatment. *Psychological Medicine*, 1976, *6*, 481–485.

Pinneau, S. R. Infantile disorders of hospitalism and anaclitic depression. *Psychological Bulletin*, 1955, *52*, 429–452.

Pitts, F., Meyer, J., Brooks, M., & Winokur, G. Adult psychiatric illness assessed for childhood parental loss and psychiatric illness in family members—a study of 748 parents and 250 controls. *American Journal of Psychiatry*, 1965, *121*, supplement, i–x.

Preston, D. G., Baker, R. P., & Seay, B. M. Mother-infant separation in patas monkeys. *Developmental Psychology*, 1970, *3*, 298–306.

Rees, W. D. The hallucinations of widowhood. *British Medical Journal*, 1971, *4*, 37–41.

Riete, M., Kaufman, I. C., Pauley, J. D., & Stynes, A. J. Depression in infant monkeys: Physiological correlates. *Psychosomatic Medicine*, 1974, *36*, 363–367.

Robertson, J. *A two-year-old goes to hospital*. New York: New York University Film Library, 1952. (Film)

Robertson, J. Some responses of young children to loss of maternal care. *Nursing Times*, 1953, *49*, 382–386.

Robertson, J., & Bowlby, J. Responses of young children to separation from their mothers. *Le Courier: Centre International de L'Enfance*, 1952, *2*, 131–142.

Roff, M. Some life history factors in relation to various types of adult adjustment. In M. Roff & D. F. Ricks (Eds.), *Life history research in psychopathology* (Vol. I). Minneapolis: University of Minnesota Press, 1970.

Rosenblum, L. A., & Kaufman, I. C. Variations in infant development and response to maternal loss in monkeys. *American Journal of Orthopsychiatry*, 1968, *38*, 418–426.

Rutter, M. *Children of sick parents: An environmental and psychiatric study.* London: Oxford University Press, 1966.

Rutter, M. *Maternal deprivation reassessed.* Baltimore Harmondsworth: Penguin Books, 1972.

Rutter, M. Early sources of security and competence. In J. S. Bruner & A. Garton (Eds.), *Human growth and development.* Oxford: Clarendon Press, 1978.

Rynearson, E. K. Humans, pets and attachment. *British Journal of Psychiatry,* 1978, *133,* 550–555.

Schlottmann, R. C., & Seay, B. M. Mother-infant separation in the Java monkey *(Macaca irus). Journal of Comparative and Physiological Psychology,* 1972, *29,* 334–340.

Seay, B. M., Hansen, E. W., & Harlow, H. F. Mother-infant separation in monkeys. *Journal of Child Psychology and Psychiatry,* 1962, *3,* 123–132.

Seligman, M. E. P. *Helplessness: On depression, development and death.* San Francisco: Freeman, 1975.

Singh, M. E. Mother-infant separation in rhesus monkeys living in natural environments. *Primates,* 1975, *16,* 471–476.

Smith, W. G. Clinical life-events and prevention strategies in mental health. *Archives of General Psychiatry,* 1971, *25,* 103–109.

Spitz, R. A. Anaclitic depression: An inquiry into the genesis of psychiatric conditions in early childhood II. *Psychoanalytic Study of the Child,* 1946, *2,* 313–342.

Stuart, I. R., & Abt, L. E. (Eds.). *Children of separation and divorce.* New York: Grossman, 1972.

Suomi, S. J., Collins, M. L., & Harlow, H. F. Effects of permanent separation from mother on infant monkeys. *Developmental Psychology,* 1973, *9,* 376–384.

Suomi, S. J., Collins, M. L., Harlow, H. F., & Ruppenthal, G. C. Effects of maternal and peer separations on young monkeys. *Journal of Child Psychology and Psychiatry,* 1976, *17,* 101–112.

Suomi, S. J., Eisele, C. J., Grady, S. A., & Harlow, H. F. Depression in adult monkeys following separation from nuclear family environment. *Journal of Abnormal Psychology,* 1975, *84,* 576–578.

Suomi, S. J., & Harlow, H. F. Effects of differential removal from group on social development of rhesus monkeys. *Journal of Child Psychology and Psychiatry,* 1975, *16,* 149–164.

Suomi, S. J., & Harlow, H. F. Production and alleviation of depressive behaviors in monkeys. In J. Maser & M. E. P. Seligman (Eds.), *Psychopathology: Experimental models.* San Francisco: Freeman, 1977.

Suomi, S. J., Harlow, H. F., & Domek, C. J. Effect of repetitive infant-infant separation of young monkeys. *Journal of Abnormal Psychology,* 1970, *76,* 161–172.

Tennant, C., & Bebbington, P. E. The social causation of depression: A critique of the work of Brown and his colleagues. *Psychological Medicine,* 1978, *8,* 565–575.

Toomin, M. K. The child of divorce. In R. E. Hardy & J. G. Cull (Eds.), *Therapeutic needs of the family: Problems, descriptions and therapeutic approaches.* Springfield, Ill.: Charles C Thomas, 1974.

Vernon, D. T. A., Foley, J. M., Sipowicz, R. R., & Schulman, J. L. *The psychological responses of children to hospitalization and illness.* Springfield, Ill.: Charles C Thomas, 1965.

Wallerstein, J. S., & Kelly, J. B. The effects of parental divorce: Experiences of the preschool child. *Journal of the American Academy of Child Psychiatry,* 1975, *14,* 600–616.

Weissman, M. M., & Paykel, E. S. *The depressed woman: A study of social relationships.* Chicago: University of Chicago Press, 1974.

Yarrow, L. J. Separation from parents during early childhood. In M. L. Hoffman & L. W. Hoffman (Eds.), *Review of child development research,* 1964, *1,* Russell Sage Foundation, New York.

Young, L. D., Suomi, S. J., Harlow, H. F., & McKinney, W. T. Early stress and later response to separation. *American Journal of Psychiatry,* 1973, *130,* 400–405.

Chapter 5

Stress and Depression: A Cognitive Perspective*

BRIAN F. SHAW

The University of Western Ontario
London, Canada
and University Hospital
London, Canada

Theoretical and empirical work on both stress and depression in the past decade has been extensive. As a result, the terms "stress" and "depression" are widely recognized by professional and lay people. Without denying the value of the constructs, one shared characteristic is the overapplication of the terms. Both concepts have engendered considerable conceptual confusion because they have been employed to define a wide range of human behavior ranging from discrete responses to complete syndromes.

Complicating the present situation, there is a growing literature that relates depression and stress. For example, McLean (1976, p. 298) noted that "microstressors acting cumulatively, and in the absence of compensatory positive experiences,

*This work was supported in part by grants from the Medical Research Council of Canada (MA-6370), the Ontario Mental Health Foundation (#777-79/80), and the National Institute of Mental Health (U.S.) (#MH-35016-01).

Drs. Keith S. Dobson and R. W. J. Neufeld kindly provided valuable comments on an earlier draft of the chapter.

can be potent sources of depression." In this view, depression results if the person is unable to cope with the accumulating environmental stress. From a psychobiological perspective, Goodwin and Bunney (1973) have concluded that "depression is frequently associated with physiologically significant stress." In an attempt to clarify various conceptual models of depression, Akiskal and McKinney (1975, p. 299) posited that "stress or frustration beyond the coping ability of the individual disrupts the functional integrity of the reinforcement system (in the diencephalon) that consequently results in depression."

Clearly the concepts of stress and depression are related, but what is the nature of the relationship? Is there evidence for a functional or causative relationship? Not all persons who experience stress beyond their coping ability become depressed. The fact that some people become depressed while others develop different stress-related symptoms (Paykel et al., 1969; Anisman, 1978) calls a simple stressor-syndrome relationship into question. Are there common factors that reduce a person's ability to cope with stress *and* that precipitate the unique set of affective, cognitive, behavioral, and physiological changes of depression? What is the nature of the stressors that are associated with depression?

Before attempting to answer these complex questions, relevant assumptions about stress and depression must be clarified. Lazarus and Launier (1978) viewed stress as a relative phenomenon defined as "any event in which environmental or internal demands (or both) tax or exceed the adaptive resources of an individual." In relating external demands of the environment and the internal demands of the individual to the resources of the individual, they employed the notion of an active cognitive commerce between the individual and the environment. A person is under stress when demands begin to tax or exceed his/her resources and thus, the process is multidimensional, requiring internal and external data for precise understanding.

Depression, unlike stress, is defined in terms of a response system. Characteristic responses include changes in mood (e.g., sadness, irritability, crying), physiology (e.g., decreased appetite, sleep, and sexual interest; somatic agitation), behavior (e.g., social withdrawal, procrastination), and cognition (e.g., self-criticism, negative expectations, hopelessness). To develop comparability in studies of depression, Feighner, Robins, Guze, Woodruff, Winokur, and Munoz (1972) and Spitzer, Endicott, and Robins (1978) proposed research criteria for primary depression that have received general acceptance. Depression may be defined as a syndrome characterized by dysphoric mood, loss of energy, agitated or retarded activity levels, loss of interest, feelings of guilt, self-criticism, decreased concentration, suicidal ideation, decreased appetite, decreased sexual drive, and sleep difficulty. If these symptomatic changes last for at least one month in the absence of other psychiatric conditions, such as schizophrenia, alcoholism, or organic brain syndromes, a diagnosis of depression can be made. For research studies a multiple-criteria approach including subjective and objective severity data on the subject's response as well as diagnosis is most desirable (see Shaw, 1979, for detailed discussion).

Suicidal behavior is not necessarily a concomitant of depression (Lester, 1972) but a related consequence. Depression can be distinguished from normal sadness and a grief reaction, but these terms are often confused in the literature. Akiskal and McKinney (1975) commented on the importance of differentiating "normal depression" from so-called "clinical depression." According to Zung (1973), the researcher's task is to define why most people undergo transient and minor fluctuation in response to stress, while 5% of men and 10% of women become depressed (Goodwin & Bunney, 1973). To assist this differentiation, "sadness" is the term recommended to represent normal mood fluctuation. Normal sadness may be accompanied by psychophysiological changes, but changes in self-concept, adaptive behavior, and vegetative patterns are not found for more than a few days. Studies that employ only a subjective measurement of depression (e.g., many of the studies on college students) are, for greater certainty, best viewed as studies on "sadness" until more cross-sample replications are completed. This conservative stance may prove to be misguided if findings on "depressed" college students are consistent with the clinical population, but at present the position prevents unwarranted generalizations.

Another condition that has often been associated with depression is grief. Since Freud's (1917) paper on mourning and melancholia, there has been considerable opinion that grief is a type of depression or vice versa. This chapter adopts the position that depression differs from normal grief in one main area, namely, the cognitive symptoms are not typical of the normal grief reaction. Lindemann's (1944) observations on persons in acute grief are remarkably similar to the previous description of depression. The features of grief included: a marked tendency to sighing respiration, loss of energy and fatiguability, gastrointestinal symptoms (loss of appetite and nausea), guilt, hostile or irritable reactions, and decreased interest in activities. Averill (1968) discussed the relationship between grief and depression in detail. He considered depression to be a more general phenomenon and proposed that "pathological grief reactions," including a lowering of self-esteem, be considered similar to clinical depression.

Freud's (1917) view that mourning and melancholia have the same symptoms except that the disturbance of "self-regard" is absent in mourning has essentially been confirmed by the studies of Clayton, Halikas, and Maurice (1971, 1972). Notably in Clayton et al.'s 1972 study, only 35% of bereaved persons experienced clinical depression as defined by the diagnostic criteria for depression (Feighner et al., 1972). This finding supports the possibility that stress-moderating-intensifying factors in addition to bereavement per se determine the abnormal reactions. In this chapter, the psychological factors that will differentiate between normal grief and abnormal grief are considered. Abnormal grief is characterized primarily by an extended period of grief and "distorted reactions" (Lindemann, 1944) that result in significant personality and physical changes. In abnormal grief, cognitive distortion of one's self, one's experiences, and the future emerge. Later in the chapter, the characteristics of the cognitively predisposed person are explained, and then an attempt to integrate depression as a function of grief and other stressors is made.

The main task at hand, then, is to review the literature relating stress and depression with a major emphasis on the question: Are there predisposing factors that, in an interaction system with stress, result in depression? A cognitive theoretical framework is employed to examine predisposing factors. It is assumed that stress can act as a catalyst for depression in certain cognitively predisposed people. The present work views stress in a way similar to that of Lewis (1934), Leff, Roatch, and Bunney (1970), Paykel, Myers, Dienelt, Klerman, Lindenthal, and Pepper (1969), and Thomson and Hendrie (1972). As a function of the continuous interaction between stress and specific cognitive processes, a person may develop a set of beliefs that he/she is unable to cope. By adopting a cognitive framework, human beings are seen as information processors motivated to reduce the demands of the external environment. Stress, by definition, must be viewed idiosyncratically because individuals appraise stressors differently and "depressogenic stressors" for person A may not be so for person B.

The subtypes of depression are not discussed in relation to stress here. Many investigators employ subtypes to clarify their clinical diagnoses and treatment plans. Two particular dichotomies, endogenous-reactive and primary-secondary, have been widely used. The "endogenous" group of patients represents individuals with more physiological symptoms (e.g., psychomotor retardation or agitation; weight loss; middle insomnia and early morning awakening) and who have not experienced significant life stressors before the onset of depression. "Reactive" depressed patients have experienced precipitating stressful events (see Kiloh & Garside, 1963; Goodwin & Bunney, 1973). The "primary" depressed group represents persons who manifest signs and symptoms of depression (Robins & Guze, 1969) as a primary disorder of mood. The "secondary depression" group includes individuals who have a preexisting *nonaffective* disorder (e.g., schizophrenia) or medical illness (e.g., rheumatoid arthritis, hypothyroidism) and who experience depressive symptoms in addition to these conditions.

Research on the subtypes of depression has been inconsistent. Leff, Roatch, and Bunney (1970) concluded that both the incidence and types of stressful life events that occurred in the endogenous group were similar to the reactive group. Similarly, Andreasen and Winokur (1979) indicated that neither substantiate differential symptom patterns nor treatment response between primary and secondary depressed groups have been found. A reasonable conclusion at present is that stable dimensions of depression with acceptable predictive validity and etiological significance have yet to be determined.

The subtypes of bipolar-unipolar depressions are not addressed here. The evidence on this subgrouping is such that only the studies on unipolar depressed groups are reviewed. Studies on genetic factors in the bipolar (or manic-depressive) group (see Leonard, 1968; Perris, 1966; Winokur, Clayton, & Reich, 1969) led to the conclusion that this group should be discussed independently.

Stress in the Development of a Predisposition to Depression

In this section, the characteristics of individuals predisposed to depression are described, followed by the conditions that may precipitate such a predisposition.

Extreme caution must be exercised in interpreting or generalizing speculations about predisposing factors to depression. While there have been many experimental studies on the different cognitive, behavioral, and physiological characteristics of depressed persons and "normals," few studies have examined the changes in depressed persons over time. Fewer yet have investigated predisposing characteristics in predictive longitudinal studies (if any, in fact, have been done to date).

Models of depression must give an account of the predisposing features. For example, physiological models tend to stress genetic factors as illustrated by Akiskal and McKinney's (1975) hypothesized functional impairment of the diencephalic centers of reinforcement and "predisposing 'leaky' presynaptic membranes or decrease in post-synaptic receptivity" (p. 300). McLean (1975) in his review noted that the specific evidence for a genetic predisposition for depression is inconclusive. Similarly, personality characteristics using traditional "traits" have not been predictive (see Becker, 1974, and Chodoff, 1972, for reviews).

From a cognitive viewpoint what are the defining characteristics of a predisposed person? The best-developed cognitive model is Beck's (1967) "cognitive triad" model of depression. He posited that a negative view of the self, one's experiences, and the future was critical to the development of depression.

This assumes that the predisposed person processes information about stressors under the influence of a factor (labeled the "self"). The self contains memories that are subsumed under highly salient, negative attributes. The predisposed person believes he/she lacks an attribute essential for happiness and effective coping, such as intelligence, motivation, conscience, or attractiveness. These negative self-percep-tions may not generalize to a negative self-concept or self-theory[1] (i.e., the person may have a perception of the self and acknowledge "good or worthwhile" attributes as well as the negative attributes). A generalized negative self-theory may be reflected in the statement, "I'm a worthless person." In depression, from a cognitive perspective the shift from negative self-percepts to a negative self-theory is critical. The model predicts that once the individual generalizes his/her percepts into a negative view of the self, the probability of a depressive reaction is high, although at this point one cannot predict when this reaction may occur.

The cognitive model assumes: (1) the negative attributes are psychologically more powerful than the positive attributes (i.e., the negative attributes have a greater effect on the processing of stimuli); and (2) the negative attributes are a function of a person's personal standards and are not necessarily consensually validated notions. Thus, the predisposed person may believe he/she is inferior in some attribute, despite the fact that he/she is above the norm. This view of self-perception directly follows James's (1890) definition of self-esteem as the ratio between aspirations and achievements. Vulnerability to depression, then, is in part a function of the generality of the

---

[1]The term "self-theory" (Epstein, 1973) is used instead of "self-concept" to reflect the idea of one's view of the self as a conceptual tool that serves in part "to organize the data of experience in a manner that can be coped with effectively" (p. 407).

negative self-perceptions. The person who believes he/she is a "loser" (Beck, 1967) in areas of life that are considered vitally important is the person who is prone to depression.

Once a negative view of the self is established, Beck's (1967) descriptions of negative views of experiences and of the future are natural consequences within the information-processing model. If a person perceives himself/herself in a negative way, then new stimuli in the form of environmental experiences or future predictions will be affected. Information from the environment is selected or "filtered" in such a way as to create maximum possible consonance within the system. Thus, positive stimuli will be distorted, related to the negative aspect of self. People change over time because the system is a transactional one in which environmental stimuli alter the self, and vice versa, creating new outcomes as information about the self is processed (Shaw, 1979). In other words, the self has a major role in information processing (Epstein, 1973), but the very process involved changes the "self" over time. The experimental studies supporting the differential effects of depression on information processing are reviewed later in the chapter.

There is a small but significant literature on the early life experiences that correlate with a predisposition to depression (McClure, Stern, & Costello, 1970). The role of bereavement in childhood may be considered as one type of trauma or loss that, according to Abraham (1924), predisposes the person to depression. Brown (1961) reported a study of 216 depressed patients compared to two control groups (medical in-patients and the British orphanhood census). The depressed patient group suffered childhood bereavement—death of a parent before age 15—in 41% cases compared with 16% and 12% respectively for the two control groups. Brown's (1961) study has been criticized on a number of methodological grounds, one being his use of normal control groups instead of other psychiatric groups (see Beck, 1974).

Other studies relating childhood bereavement and depression have not produced reliable findings (Akiskal & McKinney, 1975) primarily because of inconsistent methodologies. In one well-designed study, however, Beck, Sethi, and Tuthill (1963) also found a significantly greater incidence of a loss of a parent in high-depressed than in nondepressed psychiatric patients. Nevertheless, in this study, 27% of the high-depressed group reported the loss of a parent before age 16; and thus, if we accept these findings as fact, we still have to account for the early predisposing events of the other 73% of the population.

Certain child-rearing practices of parents are correlated with subsequent high self-esteem (Coopersmith, 1967). High self-esteem, as defined by self-confidence, school achievement, and peer relationships, was found in children who were reared under conditions of acceptance (allowing for the possibility of dissent within limits), clear definition of the rules of the family, and respect for actions within the rules. The necessity of standards for behavior is important because the "absence or limited presence of such defined standards apparently leave the child uncertain of his success and failure and lessens the likelihood that he will judge his performance as 'successful'" (Coopersmith, 1967, p. 246).

Few studies have investigated treatments for low self-esteem children. Dweck (1975) assessed whether "helpless children" (who can be viewed as low self-esteem children) could learn to deal more effectively with failure. Dweck and Repucci (1973) had previously demonstrated that children who interpret failure to mean the situation is beyond their control (i.e., they have "learned that they are helpless") do not persevere with a problem-solving task despite the fact that they were performing as well as others. Children who were trained to reattribute their failures to a lack of effort instead of a lack of ability maintained or improved their performance (Dweck, 1975). In general, low self-esteem children do not get this type of training, and thus the early experiences that leave children with a sense of helplessness could be considered predisposing conditions for depression. The self-theories related to these experiences may be characterized by the cognitions "I'm a failure. Nobody cares for me."

McLean (1975) and Lewinsohn (1974) point to deficits in social skill (the ability to obtain positive reinforcement from the social environment) as antecedents of depression. While not restricting their formulation to childhood per se, the early years are an important period when skills such as assertiveness, verbalization, and social judgment are typically learned. According to the social skills model, poor social skills lead to marginal social interactions, less social recognition, lower self-esteem, and ultimately vulnerability to depression. This paper assumes that social skill deficits interact with the negative self-theory (e.g., "I'm ugly so people wouldn't want to talk to me"). The cause of such developments is not easily understood, but it is assumed that social insults in the form of peer rejection enhance the negative self-theory and thus can be viewed as a factor predisposing the person to depression.

A reformulation of Seligman's learned helplessness model of depression (see Abramson, Seligman, & Teasdale, 1978, and Miller & Seligman, pp. 149–178, this volume) introduced another paradigm in which a negative self-theory may develop. From the learned helplessness perspective, past experience in an environment where responding and reinforcement are noncontingent results in specific attributions of the experience. If the attributions are internal and stable (e.g., "I'm a failure because I'm too stupid"), then the person will probably behave in a pattern similar to depressed persons (i.e., he/she will manifest learned helplessness). These attributions may be learned in childhood. Dweck (1975) found the criticisms of teachers to be consonant with internal, stable attributions (e.g., inability) made by fourth-grade girls. It may be that negative or "depressogenic" attributions about the self are reinforced in some ways by the natural environment. In the absence of disconfirmation by parents or significant others, the seeds of future depression may begin to develop at this stage.

What type of cognitions does the predisposed person manifest? Beck (1967), using the dreams of depressed patients in psychotherapy, characterized the patient's thought content as characterized by a "loser" theme. The thinking of the depressed persons reflected a systematic bias that was negatively self-referential but not easily recognized by the person. Hauri (1976) in his study of the dreams of recovered depressed and control subjects found a significantly greater proportion of negative, unpleasant dreams in the depressed group. He concluded that the negative ideation was not simply a concomitant of the depressed state but had a more permanent quality in the thinking of "depression-prone" persons. Unfortunately, a prospective study of two groups of subjects, one with depressed dreams and one with nondepressed dream ideation, would be required to determine the validity of the hypothesized predisposition.

Beck (1963) outlined a number of thinking errors observed in depression (for example, overgeneralization, the process of drawing a general conclusion on the basis of a single incident). Although there have not been controlled studies on this observation, it is unlikely that the errors are unique to depression. Harrow and Quinlan (1977) studied schizophrenic, depressed, and personality-disordered patients and concluded that disordered thinking is influenced by acute psychopathology, including depression.

Investigators interested in possible deficits in "information processing" have determined a number of cognitive deficits related to depression. Hemsley and Zawada (1976) reported that depressed and schizophrenic subjects were comparable in their performance on a short-term memory task. In the terms of Broadbent's (1970) theory of information processing, both groups manifested evidence of a "filtering" inefficiency. Russell and Beekhuis (1976) also found similar free-recall performance in schizophrenic and psychotic depressed subjects whose performance was inferior to that of normal subjects. They concluded that the recall impairment was primarily a function of an inability to use perceived structuring of the list during recall.

Byrne (1976) studied choice reaction times in depressed and normal control subjects. He found that both decision time and movement time were lowered in depression. The results were interpreted to indicate an impairment in the central information-processing mechanism. Research assessing the information-processing capabilities in depression continues, including Neufeld's (pp. 240–270, this volume) provocative paradigm.

Studies on the recall of depressed patients for different types of material sheds light on their characteristic cognitive processes. Lishman (1972) and Lloyd and Lishman (1975) found that depressed subjects tended to recall material with a higher negative tone. The speed of recall for pleasant memories was higher than for unpleasant memories. The results indicated that the selective recall of negative experiences tends to be specific to the depressive episode. Depressed patients also tend to underestimate the amount of experimental reinforcement received when asked to recall the results of a past performance. Similar results have been reported with college student subjects (Nelson & Craighead, 1977; Wener & Rehm, 1975; Dobson & Shaw, in press).

Giles (1980) investigated the basic tenet of Beck's (1967) cognitive model of depression, namely, that depressed persons, compared to nondepressed psychiatric and normal controls, manifest systematic and negative distortions of the self, the world, and the future. Within the three experimental groups, female subjects were assigned to either a success or failure condition and either an interpersonal problem-solving task or a card-sorting task.

The results confirmed the major hypotheses. Depressed persons, compared with others: (1) reported a lower probability of achieving a given goal in a task-oriented situation; (2) set lower standards for their performances; (3) evaluated their performance to be worse than others; (4) expected failure during the task when the outcome in fact was uncertain; and (5) predicted a lower likelihood of success in tasks of a similar nature in the future regardless of feedback (success or failure). These perceptions were independent of the subjects' actual performance. In general, normal subjects judged their performance to be superior to others, independent of the actual performance; nondepressed psychiatric patients considered their performance to be average; and the depressed patients rated their performance as below average, independent of success or failure feedback. This normal positive bias has also been reported by Lewinsohn (Mischel, Chaplin, & Barton, 1980).

Interestingly, Rizley (1978), in a study of depressed college students following an impersonal number-guessing task, found that depressed subjects rated internal casual factors (effort and ability) to be more important determinants of failure but less important determinants of success than did nondepressed subjects. These results, if replicated with depressed patients, and taken together with the Giles (1980) findings, suggest a relatively stable process of thinking during depression. Expectations of failure may be related to a constellation of stable attributions about the self, with the result that future subjective probability estimates are negatively biased.

In summary, the person predisposed to depression probably manifests the following characteristics:

1. A decidedly negative self-theory. This characteristic is best observed in situations involving skilled behaviors. It is important to observe this characteristic across trials with various types of tasks (e.g., impersonal and interpersonal problem-solving tasks). By eliciting the person's subjective probabilities of success, the observer will note lower than average estimates and the initial prediction of failure. Following the task, the depression-prone person will tend to attribute success to external factors, and failure to internal factors. The depression-prone person will not manifest the "positive bias" of judgment as seen in normals (see Mischel, Ebbeson, & Zeiss, 1976).

2. A tendency toward errors of logic in the appraisal of situations. External stress situations, especially those involving personal evaluation, tend to be appraised as very important. Coping inabilities are viewed as fixed characteristics (e.g., "I'll never be able to change").

3. A family history characteristic of low self-esteem children. These people are "reared under conditions of rejection, uncertainty, and disrespect, have come to believe they are powerless and without resource or recourse. They feel isolated, unlovable, incapable of expressing and defending themselves" (Coppersmith, 1967, p. 250).

4. A personal history of depression. Obviously, the best predictor of future behav-

ior is past behavior, and depending on the age of the person, past episodes of depression are predisposing to future episodes (Beck, 1967).

5. A "failure" schema.[2] This last characteristic is the most theoretical at present. Following Beck's (1967) description, the depression-prone person is vulnerable to idiosyncratic stressors that in turn result in self-judgments of inadequacy and expectations of failure.

Stress: Catalyst for Depression

From a cognitive perspective, specific stressors impinge on the predisposed person, precipitating the negative schemas and, subsequently, a depressive reaction (Beck, 1967). The actual mechanism is, of course, theoretical, but it offers an acceptable account of the development of depression. The prototype of the specific stressors that activate negative schemas are those that are "reminiscent of the original traumatic experience" (Beck, 1967, p. 278).

What are the types of situations that engender enough stress to precipitate depression? There have been three approaches to this problem. Beck (1967; 1976) described three types of event: (1) situations that lower a person's self-esteem (e.g., failing an examination, being fired, being jilted by a lover); (2) situations that involve a thwarting of important goals or posing an insoluble dilemma (e.g., conflict about marriage because of parents' influence); and (3) physical disease or abnormality that activates ideas of physical deterioration or death. Often the illness can be traced to past experiences the person has had with family members (e.g., mother was overprotective during illness). Beck (1967) also noted that depression seems to arise from a series of stressful situations rather than from one situation. McLean (1976) makes a similar point when he discusses "microstressors acting cumulatively."

Other investigators have studied external life stressors and depression (see review by Dohrenwend and Dohrenwend, 1974; for an assessment of the role of "loss" as a case in point, see Costello, pp. 93–124, this volume). Lazarus and Launier (1978) criticized this type of research which is based on the Holmes and Rahe (1967) model because the person is seen as a "passive victim of adventitious events." This criticism is well founded, and the strict environmentalist position is also rejected here.

Paykel et al. (1969) reported that hospitalized depressed patients had experienced more stressful life events in the 6 months before hospitalization than had matched control subjects from the community. Losses in particular characterized the depressed patients. Brown, Harris, and Peto (1973) also found a relationship (in their view a causal relationship) between life events and the onset of depression. Nevertheless, as cogently discussed by McLean (1976), only a small proportion (15–30%) of depressed patients actually experience the major, infrequently occurring life-stress events, as measured by the Social Adjustment Rating Scale (Holmes & Rahe, 1967).

---

[2]A schema is defined as a nonspecific but organized representation of prior experiences (Neisser, 1967).

Schless, Schwartz, Goetz, and Mendels (1974) examined the significance that depressed patients attach to life events. Depressed in-patients viewed a wide variety of events as more stressful than did nondepressed subjects, and these judgments were interpreted as independent of the severity of depression and the level of recovery. They questioned whether the patient's perceptions were a function of depression or some personality predisposition to depression. The ratings of the depressed subjects did not reveal specific items that were stressful in general, lending support to the notion that stressful events are idiosyncratic. No direct relationship was found between specific events (i.e., exits versus entrances) and depression. They concluded that depression is characterized by an "alarm reaction" whereby all events are seen as threatening. The third approach to the study of life events and depression is the positive events (pleasant events) approach of Lewinsohn and his colleagues (McPhillanny & Lewinsohn, 1971; Graf, 1973; MacPhillanny & Lewinsohn, 1974). They propose that a common antecedent of depression is a decrease in the pleasant events experienced by a person. Depression is hypothesized to be a function of a low rate of response-contingent positive reinforcement.

The work with positive events has also been extended to "punishing" events (Lewinsohn, 1975), as both types may reduce the rate of reinforcement. The two approaches, positive and negative events, are sampled by two inventories designed to provide estimates of the response-contingent positive reinforcement (or punishment) experienced by a person in the past month.

Lewinsohn and Amenson (1978) identified 49 pleasant and 35 unpleasant "mood-related events" that discriminated between the depressed and nondepressed groups. It appears from this research that some specificity can be given to the environmental events that are related to depression. Depressed subjects rated all of the aversive events, particularly the mood-related items, as more aversive than the nondepressed subjects, a finding that supports the findings of Schless et al. (1974).

To this point, we have considered the changes in the environment that may result in stress and ultimately depression. Another equally potent source of stress is the internal demands that people make of themselves. These internal demands can be seen as personal expectations or aspirations; in other words, the goals that a person sets for himself/herself. The stress related to the attempted attainment of internal standards has been long recognized in psychology. Psychoanalytic writers (Freud, Abraham) discussed the superego, a constellation of expectations learned primarily from the parents. Rogers (1951), in his study of self-esteem, introduced the "ideal-self" to capture these self-expectations.

What might lead a person to make unrealistically high demands on himself/herself? Perhaps it is an attempt to equalize past negative memories (e.g., parental disappointments). Certainly, people's tendency to attempt to "make up" for one's mistakes or losses in a short time is well known in gambling situations. An analogy could be made to depressed people who may maintain high internal standards while trying to lower the expectations of others by predicting failure (see Epstein, 1973).

McLean (1976) discussed unreasonable goal setting as a depression-related microstressor. He listed two stages of goal setting, a problematic area for depressed people: first, one must discriminate what is and is not attainable in the environment; and second, one must establish a feedback loop whereby goals are altered as a function of attainment or changing environmental conditions. One might add that in order to appraise the situation, one must also correctly appraise personal abilities (e.g., intelligence, strength, endurance, coping skills).

In my experimental work, two types of internal demands, the need to succeed interpersonally (affiliation need) and the need to succeed intrapersonally (achievement need), are considered. Other investigators (e.g., Groesbeck, 1958; Gotlib & Asarnow, 1979) have studied these dimensions with reference to mood variation and depression. Achievement abilities refer to one's work skills and intelligence as measured experimentally by problem-solving tasks such as card-sorting (Loeb, Beck, & Diggory, 1966) and anagrams (Miller & Seligman, 1975). Affiliation abilities may be observed in interpersonal problem situations such as those measured by the means-end problem-solving task (Platt & Spivack, 1972). These internal demands could be matched with the Endler and Okada (1974) stressor types labeled "interpersonal threat" and "ego-threat." It is unlikely that these dimensions will be sufficient measures of a person's internal demands. The main point is that it may be important to define and study empirically the interaction between environmental demands, internal demands, and the person's perceived ability to cope.

Depression: The Interaction of Stress and the Predisposed Person

The main thesis here is that certain cognitively predisposed persons who are under significant levels of stress will experience symptoms of depression. This formulation allows for the fact that not everyone who experiences high levels of stress (i.e., external and internal demands exceed coping resources) becomes depressed. Under high stress conditions, some people may develop a range of disorders (e.g., gastrointestinal disorders [Beck, 1976], schizophrenia [Zubin & Spring, 1977], compulsive behaviors, [Neufeld, pp. 240–270, this volume]).

This view does not presume that the depression-prone person will inevitably become clinically depressed under stress. The severity, chronicity, and pervasiveness of the stress process is assumed to affect the nature of the depressive response. The critical assumption, however, is that the stressors impinge on specific negative self-schema. In depression-prone people, sad moods are apt to result under lower levels of stress or when the stressors do not impinge on specific schema. The notion of a cognitive threshold under which a person experiences sadness and over which he/she becomes depressed (McLean, 1976) may be useful.

Once a person experiences depression, there is a higher probability that he/she will become depressed again within 10–20 years (Beck, 1967; Morrison et al., 1973).

Clinically, the severity and chronicity of the depression have been observed to increase with subsequent depressive episodes. It may be that the threshold for depression is lowered as a result of the increasing availability of the negative self-schema. The predisposition to depression can be seen as a process changing over time as a function of experience. The fact that the availability and potency of the cognitive schema change is, of course, necessary if the probability of future depressions is to be lowered.

Following the stress model of Lazarus and Launier (1978), in addition to the environmental and internal demands, the third aspect of the stress response concerns the person's coping resources. People who do not have a range of coping styles may be prone to psychological disorders including depression. Wide individual differences in the response to the same environmental event have been observed (Lazarus & Launier, 1978; Grinker & Spiegel, 1945). Anisman (1978; see also Anisman & Lapierre, pp. 179–217, this volume) proposed that the differences may reflect the fact that events are perceived differently (for example, see Glass & Singer, 1972). He also suggested that people may differ in coping style and that the neurochemical changes engendered by stress may be subject to individual differences. Therefore, given the same event (e.g., an insult to one's self-esteem), "some individuals may exhibit one form of pathology (e.g., primarily behavioural depression), whereas other individuals may exhibit an entirely different array of changes (e.g., the so-called psychosomatic syndrome)" (Anisman, 1978, p. 156–157).

To place a discussion of coping strategies and depression into context, consider the example of a depressive cognitive appraisal from Lazarus and Launier (1978). A person anticipating an upcoming job interview appraises the situation as threatening (i.e., there is a high likelihood of being rejected for the job). The anticipation of a threat is considered a primary appraisal in Lazarus' model. The secondary appraisal (which concerns coping resources and options and has implications for reappraisal and coping) was:

"As things stand now I will probably be rejected. This is a very damaging outcome because I have no other job opportunities. If I had the ability to deal effectively with the interview, I could be hired, but I don't have the ability. Moreover, there is no one to help me. The situation is hopeless" (p. 30).

This type of negative self-referential appraisal is frequently found in the thought records of depressed patients (see Beck et al., 1979).

Once a person appraises an event in such a negative manner, it is assumed that he/she will engage in the process of coping. In this case, it is probable that the aforementioned appraisal will require an effort to regulate the feelings of sadness rather than to solve the problem of the person's inability to handle interviews. The regulation of emotions and problem solving to alter the stressful person-environment interactions are the two major coping functions.

The modes of coping in the Lazarus and Launier (1978) model have been labelled information seeking, direct action, inhibition of action, and intrapsychic coping. Depressed people attempt to cope with their affective distress in a variety of ways. If we consider our example of the person with a negative appraisal of his/her ability to deal effectively with the interview, any of the four coping modes may be employed in an attempt to alter his/her sadness and hopelessness. Information seeking might involve seeking reassurance from family members. Inhibition of action may involve withdrawing from others, or retiring to bed in the hope of easing the painful affect. Intrapsychic modes include reviewing one's positive characteristics in an attempt to balance the perceived inabilities (these positive attributes are typically minimized in depression, Beck, 1970). Direct action modes are potentially the most harmful to the depressed person. Examples may be seeking employment below the person's actual ability because of his/her perceived inability in interviews or in extreme cases, suicide attempts to escape the painful affect (Beck, 1976).

These examples concern the depressed person's characteristic coping styles and are, of course, hypothetical. Once a person makes a negative self-referential appraisal, it is difficult to refocus attention on the precipitant or cause of the sad affect (e.g., the inability to handle interviews and the lack of external assistance). If the attempts to cope with the sadness are ineffective (and some, like withdrawing from others, are likely to be), then the resultant stress may lead to a clinical depression.

Once a person becomes depressed, significant changes in the transactions with the environment can be expected. According to the usual clinical observations, a depressed person is more vulnerable to stress than when he/she is nondepressed (Schless et al., 1974). Thus, stress acts to exacerbate and maintain the depression.

One stressor of interest here is bereavement. The grief reaction, as described previously, is similar to the depressive reaction, except that there is little or no change in self-theory. What conditions result in an abnormal grief reaction, where grief is prolonged, and, over time, the self-theory may be altered?

Gauthier and Marshall (1977) give an excellent clinical account of patients who experience "overwhelming and prolonged grief reactions." If the family, friends, and perhaps even the bereaved person decide that the best course is to avoid grief reaction altogether, an abnormal grief reaction can be predicted. Gauthier and Marshall (1977) found that a common finding is the "conspiracy of silence, whereby friends and relatives withhold information about the death, avoid discussing the dead person, remove all signs (clothes, photographs, etc.) of him or her, and forestall the involvement of the grieving person in the funeral and burial procedures" (p. 40). They suggest that during the time of the abnormal grief reaction (which may last for 20 years or longer) the person learns to deal with emotional information in a similar fashion, blocking all thoughts of the upsetting stimulus. This coping strategy (often labelled "denial"), if prolonged, may be an important condition leading to the alteration of the person's self-theory. How does the person perceive the reaction of others who encourage the avoidance of grief? One reported that perception is an unrealistic belief in personal causation (e.g., "Something I did resulted in death"). Another is the self-perception of inadequacy ("I'm too weak to handle pressure"). One might wonder whether the abnormal grief reaction and alterations in the self-theory are similar to the responses of bereaved children, who may not be cognitively able to understand the reasons for their parents' death.

Stress as an Exacerbator of Depression

According to Beck (1967), a feedback loop is established leading to the "downward spiral" of depression. The person's negative cognitions, sad affect, apathy, and physiological symptoms interact. For example, some depressed patients first notice a change in their energy level, a sense of fatigue and lack of motivation. The perception of these changes ("I'm too tired") influences future expectations ("I can't do anything") leading to withdrawal ("There's no use in trying") and sadness ("I can't even do the simplest things"). Once a person is depressed, the environment may become "overwhelming and hostile."

Coyne's (1976) description of the depressed person's environment emphasizes the importance of the "changing environment." Coyne, in fact, believes that significant others create an interpersonal environment characterized by their irritability and guilt, concurrent with statements of acceptance and support. He proposed that depressed people may require different social skills to deal with their environment when they are depressed than they do when interacting with "a more stable, normal environment." During depression the actual effect of stressors change to the point that the negative aspects of even typically innocuous situations (e.g., selecting clothes to wear, deciding what food to eat) become highly salient. As one patient said, "When you look around and all you can see is a future of failures, what's the use in trying?" This sense of hopelessness acts not only to accelerate the "downward spiral of depression" (Beck, 1967) but also to precipitate suicidal behavior (Kovacs, Beck, & Weissman, 1975).

Some experimental studies have examined alterations in physiology in response to stressors during depression. Biological changes in endocrine systems (e.g., growth hormone, 17-OHCS, MHPG) have been investigated in order to validate the amine hypothesis in depression. The basic "amine" theory (see Anisman, 1978; Goodwin & Bunney, 1973) is: depression results when there is a biologically significant decrease in the amines (e.g., catecholamines, indoleamine) at the level of the synaptic gap in the central nervous system. Metabolites of the amines are studied in depressives and controls, and initially the evidence for the theory looked promising indeed (Schildkraut, 1970). Some studies, however, have found that stress is a key mediating variable in these changes (Stern, McClure, & Costello, 1970). One possible approach to these data is that a consequence of depression is an increased vulnerability to stress, and thus the measured changes are related to the stress response.

Lewinsohn, Lobitz, and Wilson (1973) presented data indicating that female depressed subjects showed less habituation to an aversive stimulus (electric shock) than did psychiatric controls and normals. These data may be interpreted to indicate that females when depressed are increasingly vulnerable to stressors over time. It is clear, however, that more work is needed on the responsiveness of depressives to a variety of external stressors, including physical threat (e.g., electric shock), before conclusions are drawn.

There have been reports that depression is related to poor parenting and marital communication, further stressors that would probably exacerbate depression. McLean (1976) concluded that "parental depression inextricably involves other members of the family." He noted that poor parenting practices were concurrent with parental depression and cited data from interviews with depressed parents, the social learning literature on modeling, and Coopersmith's (1967) research on self-esteem to support his contention.

In a study on 2299 adults aged 18 to 65, Ilfeld (1977) found evidence that the social stressors of marriage and parenting were closely related to depression. Ilfeld's (1977) theoretical position was that these social stressors preceded depression, but inasmuch as his data are correlational, causality cannot be determined. For the present purpose, it is sufficient to report that there is a significant relationship between the two variables, and hence one could view the continued stress of a marital relationship and of parenting as a factor in maintenance of depression.

Libet, Lewinsohn, and Javorek (1973) found that depressed people tend to be negative and aversive in their interactions, and it is not surprising that, over time, family and friends avoid them. Similarly, as depressed people usually do not engage in constructive behavior, they receive little recognition and become further disengaged from incentives (Klinger, 1975). The most important point to remember is that we are observing a transactive system between person and environment. Thus, when the depressed person interacts with the environment, the probability of experiencing stress and failure (interpersonal and intrapersonal) is higher than normal, and the vicious cycle continues. How then can the depression system be altered?

Management of Stress and Depression

This section briefly concerns some important conditions for the successful management of depression. The discussion must be considered in the context of data indicating that depression is self-limiting. On average, studies have shown that without treatment most depressions last between 6 and 18 months. What "treatments" are likely to reduce this prognosis? And what types of therapy or earlier training may prevent the predisposition to depressive reactions?

Psychologically, certain conditions must be established in the treatment of the depressed person. First, the person must battle to remain active, both physically and mentally. Depression by definition involves a decreased rate of behavior and interventions that increase the person's activity in the face of negative predictions are important. Senay (1973) described an initial energy expenditure in the depressive process, an expenditure that is followed by a dramatic decrease in behavior to return the energy level to homeostasis. Gradually, an increase of activity is required. Other types of therapy, such as Morita therapy (Kora, 1965), exercise (Griest et al., 1979) and sleep deprivation (Pflug, 1978), have utilized methods to increase action. Cognitive and behavior therapies have also addressed this intervention directly (see Beck et al., 1979). The solution of other problems is initially given secondary attention to the simple increase in activity.

A second therapeutic goal is to help the patient perceive stressors, either external or internal, accurately. There is a tendency for depressed persons to overvalue the importance of any one event (Beck, 1970; Giles, 1980). Stressful life events are likely to be distorted in such a negative manner that it may be impossible to develop coping strategies. Cognitive therapy trains the patient to reappraise the situation, looking for possible thinking errors such as overgeneralization or arbitrary inference (e.g., drawing a broad conclusion like "I'm stupid" on the basis of a single event). When a depressed person appraises a situation, he may be "drawn" to the negative aspects because of the nature of his/her thinking. By examining the situation with reference to possible information processing biases, there is a higher probability that distortions will be corrected.

A third goal of therapy is to help the person understand the range of symptoms of depression. Without this knowledge, symptoms such as decreased reaction time, decreased concentration, and the perception of fatigue may be difficult to comprehend. For example, fatigue is often a function of a heightened state of muscle tension known as hyperponesis (Stern, McClure, & Costello, 1970). Many patients, their relatives, and friends use attributes such as "laziness," "stupidity," or "senility" to explain the changes in depression. When depressed, given these symptoms, people need to change their expectations about their behavior. Depressed persons may view their condition as evidence of their "failure, worthlessness, incompetence . . ." rather than as a series of problems requiring treatment.

Concluding Remarks

As always, many more detailed investigations are needed to verify or refute past research and, particularly, theories. Testable hypotheses can be generated from the cognitive model of depression.

The negative self-concept, or self-theory, is one of the cornerstones of the cognitive model. It has been proposed that persons who have a negative self-theory are prone to depression, but the concept is such a broad one that it probably will not discriminate between disorders such as schizophrenia and anxiety (Epstein, 1976). The present analysis pointed to the specific, empirically based observations subsumed under the negative self-theory and related to depression. Further research that investigates the uniqueness of the reported findings to depression and within reliable subtypes of depression is needed.

The relationship between stress and depression is for the most part without empirical referents. Are there specific external or internal demands (stressors) that characterize the depressed person? Are there specific coping inabilities that lead to depression? In the stress literature, trait inventories to measure stress proneness have been developed (Endler & Okada, 1975). To date, no such psychometric device has been constructed to assess depression proneness, but efforts in this direction within an interactionist framework may be fruitful.

The "failure" or "loser" schema should be investigated particularly in a longitudinal study. If a constellation of thought content or process can be identified that predicts a depressive reaction and/or explains the experimental data, we will make significant advances in our understanding of the psychology of depression. Paradigms from cognitive psychology and the social cognition literature may reveal significant methods for the investigation of a prepotent "failure" schema in depression. These studies employ verbal learning techniques using recall memory and reaction time in an attempt to define the schema. An example of this approach is the work of Rogers, Kuiper, and Kirker (1977) who studied normals using the Craik and Lockart (1972) paradigm of depth of processing.

The goal of understanding the relationship between stress and depression is an important one. Depression, in and of itself, and because of its relationship to suicidal behavior, deserves critical study. The work toward a cognitive theory of depression continues.

References

Abraham, K. A short study of the development of the libido. In *Selected papers on psychoanalysis.* New York: Basic Books, 1960.

Abramson, L. Y., Seligman, M. E. P., & Teasdale, J. D. Learned helplessness in humans: critique and reformulation. *Journal of Abnormal Psychology,* 1978, *87,* 49–74.

Akiskal, H. S., & McKinney, W. T. Overview of recent research in depression. *Archives of General Psychiatry,* 1975, *32,* 285–305.

Andreasen, N. C., & Winokur, G. Secondary depression: Familial, clinical and research perspectives. *American Journal of Psychiatry,* 1979, *136,* 62–66.

Anisman, J. Neurochemical changes elicited by stress. In H. Anisman & G. Bignami (Eds.), *Psychopharmacology of aversively motivated behavior,* New York: Plenum, 1978.

Averill, J. R. Grief: its nature and significance. *Psychological Bulletin,* 1968, *70,* 721–748.

Beck, A. T. Thinking and depression. 1. Idiosyncratic content and cognitive distortions. *Archives of General Psychiatry,* 1963, *9,* 324–333.

Beck, A. T. *Depression: Clinical, experimental and therapeutic aspects.* New York: Harper & Row, 1967.

Beck, A. T. Cognitive therapy: Nature and relation to behavior therapy. *Behavior Therapy,* 1970, *1,* 184–200.

Beck, A. T. The development of depression: A cognitive model. In B. J. Friedman & M. M. Katz (Eds.), *The psychology of depression: Contemporary theory and research.* New York: Wiley, 1974.

Beck, A. T. *Cognitive therapy and the emotional disorders.* New York: International Universities Press, 1976.

Beck, A. T., Sethi, B. B., & Tuthill, R. Childhood bereavement and adult depression. *Archives of General Psychiatry,* 1963 *9,* 295–302.

Beck, A. T., Rush, A. J., Shaw, B. F., & Emery, G. *Cognitive therapy of depression: A treatment manual.* New York: Guilford Press, 1979.

Becker, J. *Depression: theory and research.* Washington, D. C.: V. H. Winston, 1974.

Bock, O. A. Alcohol, aspirin, depression, smoking, stress and the patient with gastric ulcer. *South African Medical Journal,* 1976, *50,* 293–297.

Brown, F. Depression and childhood bereavement. *Journal of Mental Science,* 1961, *107,* 754–777.

Brown, G. W., Harris, T. O., & Peto, J. Life events and psychiatric disorders: In Nature of causal link. *Psychological Medicine* 1973, *3,* 159–176.

Byrne, D. G. Choice reaction times and depression. *British Journal of Clinical and Social Psychology,* 1976, *15,* 149–156.

Chodoff, P. The depressive personality. *Archives of General Psychiatry,* 1972, *27,* 666–673.

Clayton, P. J., Halikas, J. A., & Maurice, W. L. The bereavement of the widowed. *Journal of Nervous and Mental Disease,* 1971, *32,* 597–604.

Clayton, P. J., Halikas, J. A., & Maurice, W. L. The depression of widowhood. *British Journal of Psychiatry,* 1972, *120,* 71–78.

Coopersmith, S. *The antecedents of self-esteem.* San Francisco: Freeman, 1967.

Coppen, A., Ghose, K., Rao, R., Bailey, J., & Peet, M. Mianserin and lithium in the prophylaxis of depression. *British Journal of Psychiatry,* 1978, *133,* 206–210.

Coyne, J. C. Toward an interactional description of depression. *Psychiatry,* 1976, *39,* 28–40.

Craik, F. I. M., & Lockhart, R. S. Levels of processing: A framework for memory research. *Journal of Verbal Learning and Verbal Behavior,* 1972, *11,* 671–684.

Dobson, K. S., and Shane, B. F. The effects of self-correction on cognitive distortions in depression. *Cognitive therapy and research,* in press.

Dohrenwend, B. S., & Dohenrenwend, B. P. *Stressful life events: Their nature and effects.* New York: Wiley, 1974.

Dweck, C. S. The role of expectations and attributions in the alleviation of learned helplessness. *Journal of Personality and Social Psychology,* 1975, *31,* 674–685.

Dweck, C. S., & Repucci, N. D. Learned helplessness and reinforcement responsibility in children. *Journal of Personality and Social Psychology,* 1973, *25,* 109–116.

Endler, N. S., & Okada, M. An S-R inventory of general trait anxiousness. Toronto: York University, Department of Psychology Report, 1974, *1.*

Endler, N. S., & Okada, M. A multidimensional measure of trait anxiety: The S-R inventory of general trait anxiousness. *Journal of Consulting and Clinical Psychology,* 1975, *43*(3), 319–329.

Epstein, S. The self-concept revisited. *American Psychologist,* 1973, *28,* 404–416.

Epstein, S. Natural healing processes of the mind: Acute schizophrenic disorganization. Unpublished manuscript, 1976.

Eysenck, H. J. The effects of psychotherapy: An evaluation. *Journal of Consulting Psychology,* 1952, *16,* 319–324.

Feighner, J. P., Robins, E., Guze, S. B., Woodruff, R. A., Winokur, G., & Munoz, R. Diagnostic criteria for use in psychiatric research. *Archives of General Psychiatry,* 1972, *26,* 57–63.

Freud, S. Mourning and melancholia. In *Collected Papers* (Vol. 4). London: Hogarth Press, 1950. (Originally published, 1917.)

Gauthier, J., & Marshall, W. L. Grief: A cognitive and behavioural analysis. *Cognitive Therapy and Research,* 1977, *1,* 39–44.

Giles, D. D. The cognitive triad: A test of the major assumptions in Beck's cognitive theory of depression. Unpublished doctoral dissertation, University of Western Ontario, 1980.

Glass, D. C., & Singer, J. E. *Urban stress,* New York: Academic Press, 1972.

Goodwin, F. K., & Bunney, W. E. Psychobiological aspects of stress and affective illness. In J. P. Scott & E. C. Senay (Eds.), *Separations and depression.* Baltimore: King, 1973.

Gotlib, I. H., & Asarnow, R. F. Interpersonal and impersonal problem-solving skills in mildly and clinically depressed college students. *Journal of Consulting and Clinical Psychology,* 1979, *47,* 86–95.

Griest, J. H., Klein, M. H., Eischens, R. R., & Faris, J. Antidepressant running. *Psychiatric Annals,* 1979, *9,* 23–33.

Grinker, R. R., & Spiegel, J. P. *Men under stress.* New York: McGraw-Hill, 1945.

Groesbeck, B. L. Toward description of personality in terms of configurations of motives. In J. W. Atkinson (Ed.), *Motives in fantasy, action and society.* Princeton: Van Nostrand, 1958.

Hauri, P. Dreams in patients remitted from reactive depression. *Journal of Abnormal Psychology,* 1976, *85,* 577–586.

Harrow, M., & Quinlan, D. Is disordered thinking unique to schizophrenia? *Archives of General Psychiatry,* 1977, *34,* 15–21.

Hemsley, D. R., & Zawada, S. L. "Filtering" and the cognitive deficit in schizophrenia. *British Journal of Psychiatry,* 1976, *28,* 456, 461.

Holmes, T. H., & Rahe, R. H. The social readjustment rating scale. *Journal of Psychosomatic Research,* 1967, *11,* 213–218.

Ilfeld, F. W. Current social stressors and symptoms of depression. *American Journal of Psychiatry,* 1977, *134,* 161–166.

James, W. *Principles of psychology.* New York: Holt, 1890.

Kiloh, L. G., & Garside, R. F. The independence of neurotic depression and endogenous depression. *British Journal of Psychiatry,* 1972, *121,* 183–196.

Klinger, E. Consequences of commitment to and disengagement from incentives. *Psychological Review,* 1975, *82,* 1–25.

Kora, T. Morita therapy. *International Journal of Psychiatry,* 1965, *1,* 611–645.

Kovacs, M., Beck, A. T., & Weissman, A. Hopelessness: An indicator of suicidal risk. *Suicide,* 1975, *5,* 98–103.

Lazarus, R. S., & Launier, R. Stress-related transactions between person and environment. In L. A. Pervin & M. Lewis (Eds.), *Internal and external determinants of behavior.* New York: Plenum, 1978.

Leff, M. J., Roatch, J. F., & Bunney, W. E. Environmental factors preceding the onset of severe depression. *Psychiatry,* 1970, *33,* 293–311.

Leonard, K. Über momopolare und bipolare endogene. *Psychosen der Nervenarzt,* 1968, *39,* 104–106.

Lester, D. *Why people kill themselves.* Springfield, Ill.: Charles C Thomas, 1972.

Lewinsohn, P. M. A behavior approach to depression. In R. J. Friedman & M. M. Katz (Eds.), *The psychology of depression: Contemporary theory and research.* New York: Wiley, 1974.

Lewinsohn, P. M. Engagement in pleasant activities and depression level. *Journal of Abnormal Psychology,* 1975, *84,* 729–731.

Lewinsohn, P. M., & Amenson, C. S. Some relations between pleasant and unpleasant mood-related event depression. *Journal of Abnormal Psychology,* 1978, *87,* 644–654.

Lewinsohn, P. M., & Graf, M. Pleasant activities and depression. *Journal of Consulting and Clinical Psychology,* 1973, *41,* 261–268.

Lewinsohn, P. M., Lobitz, W. C., & Wilron, S. "Sensitivity" of depressed individuals to aversive stimuli. *Journal of Abnormal Psychology,* 1973, *81* (3), 259–263.

Lewinsohn, P. M., Lobitz, W. C., & Wilron, S. "Sensitivity" of depressed individuals to aversive stimuli. *Journal of Abnormal Psychology,* 1973, *81* (3), 259–263.

Libet, J., Lewinsohn, P. M., & Javorek, F. The construct of social skill: An empirical study of several measures on temporal stability, internal structure, validity, and situational generalizability. Unpublished manuscript, University of Oregon, 1973.

Lishman, W. A. Selective factors in memory. 2: Affective disorders. *Psychological Medicine,* 1972, *2,* 248–253.

Lloyd, G. G., & Lishman, W. A. Effects of depression on the speed of recall of pleasant and unpleasant experiences. *Psychological Medicine,* 1975, *5,* 173–180.

Lewis, A. J. Melancholia: A historical review. *Journal of Mental Science,* 1934, *80,* 1–42.

Lindemann, E. Symptomatology and management of acute grief. *American Journal of Psychiatry,* 1944, *101,* 141–148.

Loeb, A., Beck, A. T., & Diggory, J. Differential effects of success and failure on depressive and non-depressed patients. *Journal of Nervous and Mental Disease,* 1971, *152*(2), 106–114.

MacPhillamy, D. J., & Lewinsohn, P. M. Pleasant events schedule. Unpublished report, University of Oregon, 1971.

MacPhillamy, D. J., & Lewinsohn, P. M. Depression as a function of desired and obtained pleasure. *Journal of Abnormal Psychology,* 1974, *83,* 651–657.

McLean, P. D. Depression as a specific response to stress. In I. G. Sarason & C. D. Spielberger (Eds.), *Stress and anxiety* (Vol. 3). Washington D.C.: Hemisphere, 1976. (a)

McLean, P. D. Parental depression: Incompatible with effective parenting. E. J. Mash, L. C. Handy, & L. A. Hammerlynck (Eds.), *Behavior modification approaches to parenting.* New York: Bruner/Mazel, 1976. (b)

Mischel, W., Ebbesen, E. B., & Zeiss, A. M. Determinants of selective memory about the self. *Journal of Consulting and Clinical Psychology,* 1976, *44,* 92–103.

Miller, W. R., & Seligman, M. E. P. Depression and learned helplessness in man. *Journal of Abnormal Psychology,* 1975, *84,* 228–238.

Morris, J. B., & Beck, A. T. The efficacy of antidepressant drugs: A review of research (1958 to 1972). *Archives of General Psychiatry,* 1974, *30,* 667–674.

Morrison, J., Winokur, G., Crowe, R., & Clancy, J. The Iowa 500: the first follow-up. *Archives of General Psychiatry,* 1973, *29,* 678–682.

Neisser, U. *Cognitive psychology.* New York: Appleton-Century-Crofts, 1967.

Nelson, R. E., & Craighead, W. E. Selective recall of positive and negative feedback, self-control behavior and depression. *Journal of Abnormal Psychology,* 1977, *86,* 379–388.

Neufeld, R. W. J. On decisional process instigated by threat: Some possible implications for stress-related deviance. In R. W. J. Neufeld (Ed.), *Psychological stress and psychopathology.* New York: McGraw-Hill, 1981.

Paykel, E. S., Myers, J. K., Dienelt, M. N., Klerman, G. L., Lindenthal, J. J., & Pepper, M. P. Life events and depression. *Archives of General Psychiatry,* 1969, *21,* 753–760.

Perris, C. A study of bipolar (manic-depressive) and unipolar recurrent depressive psychoses. *Acta Psychiatrica Scandanavica* 1966, *42* (suppl. 194), 7–189.

Pflug, B. The influence of sleep deprivation on the duration of endogenous depressive episodes. *Arch Psychiatrie Nervenko,* 1978, *225,* 173–177.

Platt, J. J., & Spivack, G. Problem-solving thinking of psychiatric patients. *Journal of Consulting and Clinical Psychology,* 1972, *39,* 148–151.

Rizley, R. Depression and distortion in the attribution of causality. *Journal of Abnormal Psychology,* 1978, *87,* 32–49.

Robins, E. and Guze, S. D. Classification of affective disorders: The primary-secondary, the endogenous-reactive, and the neurotic-psychotic concepts. In T. A. Williams et al. (Eds.), *Recent advances in the psychobiology of the depressive illnesses.* Washington: U.S. Government Printing Office, 1969.

Rogers, C. R. *Client-centered therapy.* Boston: Houghton Mifflin, 1951.

Rogers, T. B., Kuiper, N. A., & Kirker, W. S. Self-reference and the encoding of personal information. *Journal of Personality and Social Psychology,* 1977, *35*(9), 677–688.

Russell, P., & Beekhuis, M. Organization in memory: A comparison of psychotics and normals. *Journal of Abnormal Psychology,* 1976, *85,* 527–534.

Schildkraut, J. *Neuropsychopharmacology and the affective disorders*. Boston: Little, Brown, 1970.

Schless, A. P., Schwartz, L., Goetz, G., & Mendels, J. How depressives view the significance of their life events. *British Journal of Psychiatry*, 1974, *125*, 406–410.

Senay, E. C. General systems theory and depression. In J. P. Scott & E. C. Senay (Eds.), *Separation and depression*. Baltimore: King, 1973.

Shaw, B. F. Theoretical and empirical foundations of a cognitive model for depression. In P. Pliner, K. Blankstein, & I. Spigel (Eds.), *Perception of emotion in self and others*. New York: Plenum, 1979.

Stern, J. A., McClure, T. N., & Costello, C. G. Depression: Assessment and aetiology. In C. G. Costello (Ed.), *Symptoms of psychopathology*. New York: Wiley, 1970.

Thompson, K. C., & Hendrie, H. C. Environmental stress in primary depressive illness. *Archives of General Psychiatry*, 1972, *26*, 130–132.

Wener, A. E., & Rehm, L. P. Depressive affect; a test of behavioral hypotheses. *Journal of Abnormal Psychology*, 1975, *84*, 221–227.

Winokur, G., Clayton, P. V., & Reish, T. *Manic-depressive illness*. St. Louis: Mosby, 1969.

Zubin, J., & Spring, B. Vulnerability—a new view of schizophrenia. *Journal of Abnormal Psychology*, 1977, *86*, 103–126.

Zung, W. From art to science: the diagnosis and treatment of depression. *Archives of General Psychiatry*, 1973, *29*, 328–337.

Part III

THEORY AND RESEARCH ON STRESS BEARING ON PSYCHOPATHOLOGY

Chapter 6

The Reformulated Model of Helplessness and Depression: Evidence and Theory*

SUZANNE M. MILLER   *MARTIN E. P. SELIGMAN*

Temple University   *University of Pennsylvania*
Philadelphia, Pennsylvania   *Philadelphia, Pennsylvania*

When human beings (and animals) are exposed to uncontrollable events, they exhibit four sets of deficits: (1) motivational, which consists of retarded initiation of voluntary responses (i.e., people give up trying); (2) cognitive, which involves difficulty in learning new response-outcome contingencies (i.e., people have trouble learning that new outcomes are controllable); (3) emotional, particularly depressed affect; and (4) lowered self-esteem.

The learned-helplessness model has been proposed to account for this symptomatology. As originally stated, the model's major premise for helplessness was that exposure to (and perception of) present uncontrollability (usually) produced the expectation of future uncontrollability. This expectation, in turn, produced the helplessness deficits. In other words, people who perceive themselves to be in a helpless (uncontrollable) situation come to expect to be helpless in the future. As a result of

*Supported by MH 19604 to Martin E. P. Seligman, RR 09069 to W. R. Miller and NSF Grant BNS76-22943 A02 to the Center for Advanced Study in the Behavioral Sciences.

149

this expectation, they show motivational, cognitive, emotional, and self-esteem deficits.

This model has also been extended to account for the large subset of depressions which are characterized by parallel symptomatology. In the case of such "helplessness" depressions, individuals were thought to have a generalized expectation of uncontrollability which, in turn, was responsible for the occurrence of generalized depressive deficits.

A revised version of the model has recently been proposed, in order more adequately to accommodate the burgeoning findings of recent research with helpless and depressed individuals (Abramson, Seligman, & Teasdale, 1978). The reformulated model is more consistent with the available evidence than the original theory, and it stresses the role of attributional states and attributional styles in helplessness and depression, respectively, as modulators of the expectation of future uncontrollability. That is, the way in which a person construes the cause of his/her present helplessness determines when and where he/she will expect to be helpless in the future.

In this paper, we begin with a brief review the reformulated model and detail its predictions for helplessness and depression. We then go on to present the recent evidence and evaluate its fit to the model.

Statement of the Reformulated Helplessness Model

The major new premise of the reformulated model for explaining helplessness is that it posits an attributional state which intervenes between the perception of uncontrollability and its extrapolation to the future as an expectation of future uncontrollability. The major new premise of the model for explaining depression is that it postulates an insidious attributional style that filters failure in such a way as to produce the four deficits broadly, long lastingly, and directed toward self.

Here is a brief statement of the attributional premise of the reformulated view of *helplessness.* When individuals perceive that they are in a helpless (failure) situation, they ask themselves why they can't do anything. The nature of the cause they assign determines in what new situations and across what span of time the expectation of future helplessness (and hence the four deficits) will be likely to recur. A person considers three relevant attributional dimensions: (1) *stability:* he or she may decide that the cause of failure is due to stable factors, such as low IQ, which will persist into the future, or that the cause of failure is due to unstable and transient factors, such as being sleep-deprived, which will not recur. An attribution to stable factors produces chronic deficits, whereas an attribution to unstable factors produces transient deficits; (2) *globality:* he or she may attribute failure to global factors ("I'm incompetent at everything"), which will produce failure in a wide variety of circumstances, or failure may be attributed to specific factors ("I'm incompetent at flower-arranging") which will produce failure only in similar circumstances. An attribution to global factors produces deficits across different situations, whereas an attribution to specific factors produces deficits in the original situation alone. And finally, (3) *internality:* an attribution to internal factors ("It's due to something about me") produces self-esteem loss, whereas an attribution to external factors ("It's due to something about the world") does not. Conversely, in controllable (success) situations, making a specific, unstable, and external attribution for success facilitates generalized, chronic, and self-esteem deficits.

Three main predictions of the attributional premise of the reformulated model can now be stated: (1) a stable attribution for failure (and an unstable attribution for success) predicts helplessness deficits even after a lapse of time in the original situation; (2) a global attribution for failure (and a specific attribution for success) predicts that helplessness deficits will recur even when the situation changes; and (3) an internal attribution for failure (and an external attribution for success) predicts the occurrence of self-esteem deficits.

In brief, the reformulated view of *depression* goes like this: The person expects that highly aversive outcomes are probable (or that highly desired outcomes are improbable). As in helplessness, he/she expects that no response in his/her repertoire will change the likelihood of these events (expectation of uncontrollability). In addition, the person has an insidious attributional style which tends to make stable attributions for failure (but unstable attributions for success); to make global attributions for failure (but specific attributions for success); and to make internal attributions for failure (but external attributions for success). So people who typically expect to be helpless about outcomes, and who construe the cause of their helplessness in global, stable, internal terms, are more prone to suffer depression and to show depressive symptomatology.

One final major premise of the reformulated model has to do with the severity of the deficits in both helplessness and depression. The intensity of motivational and cognitive deficits is determined by the strength and the certainty of the expectation of uncontrollability. That is, the more a person expects to be helpless, the more passive and cognitively retarded he/she will be. The intensity of self-esteem and affective deficits is determined jointly by the certainly of uncontrollability *and* the importance of the event. That is, people who have strong expectations of helplessness, particularly with respect to events that are important to them, will feel sadder and worse about themselves. None of the evidence we review, however, directly addresses the severity premise.

In summary, the reformulated learned-helplessness model (like the original model) proposes that when people expect to have no control over important outcomes, they show the symptoms associated with learned helplessness and some subsets of naturally occurring depression. In addition, the reformulated model proposes that the expectation of future helplessness is, in turn, governed by the types of attributions that a person makes for his/her state of helplessness. It should also be clear that, according to this view, the attributions made for one's helplessness (and the subsequent expectation of helplessness) have a special status. These cognitive states are not simply another symptom of helplessness or depression. They play a causal role in precipitating such symptomatology, and they are viewed as more primary mechanisms which precede the helplessness and depressive deficits and predict when and where such deficits will appear. Specifically, people who attribute the causes of their helplessness to stable factors expect to be helpless whenever the original situation recurs and therefore continue to exhibit passivity, retarded learning, and sadness in that situation. People who attribute the causes of their helplessness to global factors expect to be helpless even when the situation changes and so exhibit the motivational, cognitive, and affective deficits across a wide range of situations. People who make internal attributions for their helplessness ("I can't do it but others can") exhibit low self-esteem and feelings of worthlessness. Finally, people who consistently construe the causes of their helplessness in global, stable, internal terms are more at risk for depression.

Evidence

We discuss four classes of evidence: (1) studies which measure attributional states and styles and correlate them with helplessness and depressive deficits; (2) studies which manipulate attributional states and try to produce the predicted deficits; (3) studies which are consistent (or inconsistent) with the model but which neither measure nor manipulate attributions; and (4) traditional but inadequate ways of testing the model.

Within each class, existence of the motivational and cognitive deficits is mainly provided by performance deficits in failure to escape noise instrumentally, failure to solve anagrams and discrimination problems, and failure to see patterns in anagrams. The self-esteem and emotional deficits are tapped via self-report.

Measuring Attributional States and Styles Attributional states and styles have been measured in four populations: (1) with depressed and nondepressed college students; (2) with depressed and nondepressed psychiatric in-patients; (3) with depressed and nondepressed school children; and (4) with helpless and nonhelpless school children.

DEPRESSED AND NONDEPRESSED COLLEGE STUDENTS The results of three previously reported studies show that depressed and nondepressed college students differ in the internality of their attributional state following failure. Klein, Fencil-Morse, and Seligman (1976) found that depressed subjects attributed failure on a discrimination task to internal factors (e.g., "I'm incompetent"), whereas nondepressed subjects attributed failure to external factors (e.g., "The task was unfair"). Similarly, in an experiment by Rizley (1978) depressed subjects rated internal factors (especially effort) as a more important cause of failure than did nondepressed subjects. Conversely, depressed subjects rated the internal factor of ability as a less important cause of success than did nondepressed subjects. Finally, Garber and Hollon (1980) found that when depressed subjects predicted their own performance on a skill task, they did not change their expectancy for future success following success or failure feedback. That is, when they succeeded or failed on a given trial, it had no effect on their expectation that they would succeed or fail on the next trial. However they showed the appropriate expectancy changes when extrapolating success for the performance of others. This suggests that while depressed subjects do not believe that *they* have the requisite skill to produce the outcome, they believe that these skills are available to others. Therefore, they perceive themselves to be in an internal (or "personally") helpless situation, rather than in an external (or "universally") helpless situation.

In a study of depressed and nondepressed students, Hammen and Krantz (1976) found no initial differences in expectation for success on an interpersonal judgment task which they were about to perform or in self-evaluation ratings. However, following failure on the task, depressed subjects rated their personal qualities more negatively and lowered their expectations for future success on a similar task more than nondepressed subjects. These results show that depressives, compared to nondepressives, generate more internal (as reflected by self-ratings) as well as more stable (as reflected by lowered expectancy) attributions for failure. Moreover, in response to stories depicting problematic situations (e.g., "Being alone on a Friday night"), depressed women selected more depressed-distorted cognitions (e.g., "Upsets me and makes me start to imagine endless days and nights by myself") than nondepressed women; they also selected fewer nondepressed-nondistorted response options (e.g., "Doesn't bother me because one Friday night alone isn't that important").

In attributional terms, "distorted" cognitions are reducible (see Miller et al., 1980) to the tendency to ascribe internal-stable-global causes for failure and external-unstable-specific attributions for success. In follow-up work (Kratz & Hammen, 1980), a similar pattern of depressive-distorted cognitions have been observed in depressed psychiatric in-patients and when normal subjects role play being depressed. Among students, test-retest data revealed that both high depression and high distortion predicted high levels of depression eight weeks later. Among depressed psychiatric in-patients, those classified as "distorters" remained more depressed following treatment than those who did not distort. These results suggest that certain characteristic cognitive styles operate to sustain depressed mood. However, given that distorters tended to be more depressed than nondistorters to begin with, it is not possible to draw unequivocal conclusions about the depression-perpetuating role of distortion without further (multiple regression) analyses of these data.

Hollon and Kendall (1980) developed and administered a 30-item "Automatic Thoughts" questionnaire, which was found to discriminate the characteristic cognitive styles of depressed and nondepressed students. Two main differentiating factors emerged. The first factor indicated more perceptions of personal maladjustment (e.g., "I'm so disappointed"; "something has to change") among depressed subjects; the second factor indicated a more negative view of the self and a more negative view of the future among the depressed sample. For example, depressed students endorsed items such as "I'm a failure"; "I'm a loser" (negative self-concept) and "my future is bleak"; I'll never make it" (negative expectations). Although attributions were not directly assessed, negative self-concept is consistent with and may be reducible to the tendency to make internal attributions for one's failures and external attributions for success, and negative expectations are consistent with and may be reducible to the tendency to make stable and global attributions for one's state (Seligman, 1980).

Haley and Strickland (1977) directly measured one causal style, the tendency to make internal versus external atrributions for academic outcomes among college students, using the adult version of the Crandall Intellectual Achievement Response Scale. In two separate studies, they found that externality for positive outcomes was positively correlated with depression on the Zung scale. There was also a trend toward a positive relation between internality for negative outcomes and depression.

Here is the most direct evidence that college students with depressed symptoms have the predicted attributional style. Seligman, Semmel, Abramson, and Von Baeyer (1979) developed an attributional style scale for adults to test whether or not depressives have the attributional style that the model predicts. The scale consists of 12 questions of the form shown in Table 6-1.

Half of the situations are about good events, and half are about bad events. As can be seen, the subject is asked to imagine vividly each of the situations and to state what the major cause would have been if it happened to him. He then rates the internality of the cause, its stability, its globality, and the importance of the event.

We found a clear depressive attributional style. Using a sample of 143 undergraduates in Psychology 1 of the University of Pennsylvania, we correlated the Beck

Table 6-1 **Sample Question from the Adult Attributional Style Scale**

YOU HAVE BEEN LOOKING FOR A JOB UNSUCCESSFULLY FOR SOME TIME.

1. Write down *one* major cause _____

2. Is the cause of your unsuccessful job search due to something about you or something about other people or circumstances? *(Circle one number)*

| Totally due to other people or circumstances | 1 | 2 | 3 | 4 | 5 | 6 | 7 | Totally due to me |

3. In the future when looking for a job, will this cause again be present? *(Circle one number)*

| Will never again be present | 1 | 2 | 3 | 4 | 5 | 6 | 7 | Will always be present |

4. Is the cause something that just influences looking for a job or does it also influence other areas of your life? *(Circle one number)*

| Influences just this particular situation | 1 | 2 | 3 | 4 | 5 | 6 | 7 | Influences all situations in my life |

5. How important would this situation be if it happened to you? *(Circle one number)*

| Not at all important | 1 | 2 | 3 | 4 | 5 | 6 | 7 | Extremely important |

Seligman, Abramson, Semmel, & Von Baeyer, 1979.

Depression Inventory (Beck, 1967) with our attributional style scale. For bad outcomes, depression (as measured by the Beck Depression Inventory correlated with internality ($p < .0001$), stability ($p < .0001$), and globality ($p < .0001$). As for good outcomes, depression correlated with externality ($p < .01$), instability ($p < .002$) but not significantly with specificity (Seligman et al., 1979).

We then went on to ask whether this insidious way of construing causality *actually causes* depression or merely *correlates with* it. In a prospective pilot study, college students of various attributional styles faced the Psychology 1 midterm examination and rated what grade they would consider a failure before they took it. We then looked at those students who actually got a grade low enough for them to consider it a failure. Who became depressed on the Beck Depression Inventory (BDI) and who did not? We found that the students who, 8 weeks before, had made stable and global attributions for failure on the attributional style questionnannaire, tended to become depressed ($r = .63$, $p < .05$). Lyn Abramson and M. Seligman have replicated this experiment on a larger sample and found that a preexisting internal attributional style for failure predicts depression after perceived failure on the midterm, as well. So, our general prediction is that it is the combination of a preexisting internal, stable, and global way of construing causality for negative events, followed by an actual encounter with failure, that puts one at risk for depression.

In summary, the evidence is quite strong that college students with depressive symptoms make internal, stable, and global attributions for failure and the reverse for success, as predicted by the reformulation of the learned helplessness model of depression. But this is merely a correlation, and depression could easily flip this insidious attributional style in. Evidence that the attributional style antedates and causes depression is at best tentative, and proposed future research will test the causal hypothesis more conclusively.

DEPRESSED AND NONDEPRESSED PSYCHIATRIC IN-PATIENTS Eidelson (1977) assessed the relation between depression and, indirectly, attributional style among male psychiatric in-patients. Three main results emerged among nonschizophrenics. The more depressed an individual: (1) the more helpless he felt to attain important life goals; (2) the less likely he thought that he would achieve these goals; and (3) the more he tended to perceive others as having more control over important life goals than he himself had. So depressed patients report themselves as being in a helpless and hopeless situation (indicating a stable and global attribution for their plight), and we infer that they further attribute this state to internal factors (personal helplessness).

Raps and Seligman (1980) used our attributional style scale to measure whether or not adult depressed in-patients diagnosed by RDC criteria had the predicted depressive attributional style. We found this to be the case. Depressed in-patients at the Northport Veterans Administration Hospital ($N = 30$) were significantly more internal ($p < .023$), stable ($p < .0001$), and global ($p < .0001$) for failure for negative events than were control medical in-patients ($N = 64$). Attributions for positive events were in the predicted direction as shown by Table 6-2).

Table 6-2 **Depressed (*N* = 30) versus Nondepressed (*N* = 61) Patients on Attributional Style Component**

ATTRIBUTIONAL STYLE MEASURE	GROUP	MEAN	SD	SE	t VALUE (df = 89)	p 2 TAILED
(ISG+) − (ISG−) Composite Score	ND	4.32	3.11	.40	5.31	.0001
	D	0.30	3.90	.71		
ISG+	ND	16.32	2.21	.28	2.21	.03
	D	14.93	3.81	.70		
ISG−	ND	12.01	2.73	.35	4.22	.0001
	D	14.64	2.91	.53		
(I+) − (I−)	ND	1.18	1.36	.18	3.55	.001
	D	0.03	1.63	.30		
(S+) − (S−)	ND	1.47	1.20	.15	4.83	.0001
	D	0.01	1.64	.30		
(G+) − (G−)	ND	1.67	1.32	.17	4.74	.0001
	D	0.26	1.37	.25		
I+	ND	5.49	.83	.11	2.43	.017
	D	4.93	1.33	.24		
S+	ND	5.53	.82	.11	2.72	.008
	D	4.90	1.39	.25		
G+	ND	5.31	1.16	.15	0.76	NS
	D	5.10	1.41	.26		
I−	ND	4.30	1.18	.15	2.31	.023
	D	4.90	1.12	.20		
S−	ND	4.05	.90	.12	3.75	.0001
	D	4.89	1.16	.21		
G−	ND	3.65	1.37	.17	4.00	.0001
	D	4.8+	1.29	.24		

*I = Internal; S = Stable; G = Global; + = positive events, − = negative events. The higher the value, the more internal, stable, or global; e.g., *(ISG+) − (ISG−)* = Sum of I, S, G scroes for positive events minus the sum of I, S, G scores for negative events.

In summary, depressed patients, like subclinically depressed students, have the predicted attributional style. Because there has been no appropriate longitudinal study of this group, we cannot determine whether the insidious style is causal, but ongoing research will test this more conclusively.

DEPRESSED AND NONDEPRESSED SCHOOL CHILDREN Leon, Kendall, and Garber (1960) administered the recently developed "Cognitive Processes Inventory for Children" to a large sample of youngsters in grades 3 to 6. The questionnaire consists of 8 situations, such as competing in an athletic activity or moving into a new neighborhood. For each situation, the child responds to 4 forced-choice situations which include: (1) what the child would like to have happen; (2) his/her expectation that the outcome will be positive or negative; (3) his/her attribution for the cause, either internal or external; and (4) whether positive or negative affect is associated with the event. These results showed that children who reported high depression (as assessed by the Childhood Depression Inventory) attributed negative events to internal causes more than nondepressed children did. In addition, children rated as depressed by their parents (on the Personality Inventory for Children) attributed positive outcomes to external causes more than children rated as nondepressed. Other findings showed that internal attributions for positive events led to more positive affect, while both internal and external attributions for negative events were negatively correlated with positive affect.

Kaslow, Tannenbaum, Alloy, Abramson, and Seligman (1980) developed an attributional style scale for children and adolescents (the Kastan Scale) which parallels the adult attributional style scale exemplified in Table 6-1. Unlike the adult version, it is not open-ended, but consists of 48 questions of the form shown in Table 6-3. What the Kastan Scale accomplishes is to take each of the six attributional dimensions (internal, stable, global × good versus bad events) and pose the child with 48 situations in which all of the dimensions—save one—are held constant, and the child makes a choice of the most likely cause. So, for example, to find out whether or not children tend to make external versus internal attributions for negative events, 8 questions of the form in question 10 occur in the questionnaire. In question 10, the two alternative answers to the question "a good friend tells you that he hates you" are both specific and unstable, but one ("my friend was in a bad mood that day") is external and the other ("I wasn't nice to my friend that day") is internal. The child's score for internality for bad events is simply the number (out of 8) of internal attributions about bad events he chooses for all possible combinations of stability and globality. The gross measure of the child's attributional style for negative events is simply the sum of his internality, stability, and globality scores for negative events.

To test both for the psychometric properties of the scale, its correlations, and its causal relationship to later depression, we gave this scale, along with the Childhood Depression Inventory (Kovacs & Beck, 1978) to a group of 92 third to sixth graders of the Germantown Friends School in Philadelphia twice, separated by 3 months.

Across 3 months, *attributional style seems stable* in our youngsters (all $p <$ .0001). Attributional style for positive events correlates with itself 3 months later ($r = 70$); attributional style for negative events correlates with itself 3 months later ($r = .58$); and the composite score for attributional style for both positive and negative events correlates with itself 3 months later ($r = .72$).

Attributional style correlates highly with depression measured at the same time. The correlation of the composite attributional style (ISG+ − ISG−) with depression is .62 ($p <$ .0001). The correlation of depression with an attributional style for

Table 6-3

---

10. A good friend tells you that he hates you.

    SP-US   E   a. My friend was in a bad mood that day.
          I   b. I wasn't nice to my friend that day.

11. You tell a joke and no one laughs.

    SP-ST   I   a. I do not tell jokes well.
          E   b. The joke is so well known that it is no longer funny.

12. Your teacher gives a lesson and you do not understand it.

    I-US   GL   a. I didn't pay attention to anything that day.
         SP   b. I didn't pay attention when my teacher was talking.

13. You fail a test.

    E-SP   ST   a. My teacher makes hard tests.
         US   b. The past few weeks my teacher has made hard tests.

14. You gain a lot of weight and start to look fat.

    SP-ST   E   a. The food that I have to eat is fattening.
          I   b. I like fattening food.

15. A person steals money from you.

    E-ST   SP   a. That person is dishonest.
         GL   b. People are dishonest.

16. Your parents praise something that you make.

    SP-ST   I   a. I am good at making some things.
          E   b. My parents like some things I make.

17. You play a game and you win money.

    E-ST   GL   a. I am a lucky person.
         SP   b. I am lucky when I play games.

18. You almost drown when swimming in a river.

    I-GL   ST   a. I am not a very careful person.
         US   b. Some days I am not a careful person.

---

positive events being external, unstable, and specific is .52 ($p < .0001$), and the correlation of attributional style for negative events being internal, stable, and global taken together is .51 ($p <. 0001$). Each of the six separate attributions all correlate significantly with depression. The differences between the most depressed quartile of the students and the least depressed quartile are highly significant on attributional style. (All relevant $p < .001$.) So this is a strong hint that there is an insidious attributional style which correlates with and may be a risk factor for depression among youngsters.

Does the insidious attributional style cause depression? In order to ask this question, we subjected our data at the two different times to both the standard multiple regression analyses and to crosslag panel techniques (Kenny, 1973). The results of our analyses are consistent with causal effects of attributional style at Time 1 of depression at Time 2. The regression equations show a significant unstandardized regression coefficient of attributional style at Time 1 on depression at Time 2, particularly for negative events, and a very substantial coefficient for the effect of depression at Time 1 on depression at Time 2.

In the crosslag panel analysis, the six relevant correlations are: attribution at Time 1 and depression at Time 2, .51; attribution at Time 2 and depression at Time 1, only .29; attribution at Time 1 and attribution at Time 2, .58; depression at Time 1 and depression at Time 2, .80; attribution at Time 1 and depression at Time 1, .51; attribution at Time 2 and depression at Time 2, .34. We are encouraged, therefore, in our hypothesis that an insidious and stable attributional style that youngsters have does predispose them to depressive symptomatology.

The most clinically relevant subgroup of our pilot sample is the quartile of our third to sixth graders with the most severe depression symptomatology. These youngsters score 12 or greater on the CDI and thus fall into the "moderate-to-severe" range of depression (Kovacs & Beck, 1977). Both crosslag panel correlation and multiple regression techniques indicate that both attributional style at Time 1 and depression at Time 1 predict depression at Time 2, indicating significant causal effects in this quartile. For the crosslag panel analysis, the correlation of attribution at Time 1 with depression at Time 2 is .55, whereas the correlation for depression at Time 1 and attribution at Time 2 is only .25; the stability of attribution is .64, the stability of depression is .68; the correlation of attribution at Time 1 with depression at Time 1 is .41, with the correlation between attribution at Time 2 and depression at Time 2 being .58. So we have tentative evidence that when a child tends to construe the causes of his/her failures as being internal, stable, and global, that child is at risk for future depressive symptomology. Current research will test this more definitively.

HELPLESS AND NONHELPLESS SCHOOL CHILDREN Dweck and her associates have undertaken a series of studies which show pronounced differences in attributional styles and states between helpless (failure-oriented) and nonhelpless (master-oriented) grade-school children. In her initial investigation, Dweck and Repucci (1973) found that children who persisted in the face of failure typically attributed helplessness to lack of effort, whereas those who showed deteriorated performance typically attributed failure to lack of ability. Both styles are equally internal, but lack of effort is alleged to involve attributions to an unstable, specific, as well as controllable factor (e.g., "if I try harder, I can do better"). Lack of ability, on the other hand, is alleged to involve attributions to a stable, global, as well as uncontrollable factor (e.g., "I'm stupid and there is nothing I can do about it"). When characteristically helpless children were taught to reattribute failure to lack of effort, they were able to maintain or improve performance following a helplessness induction (Dweck, 1975).

Interestingly, girls, compared to boys, were more likely to display this insidious attributional style, to become helpless in the face of failure, to sustain this helplessness over time, and to transfer helplessness effects to a novel situation (Dweck & Bush, 1976; Dweck, Goetz, & Strauss, 1978). These six differences were consistent with naturally occurring teacher feedback in the classroom, which stressed lack of motivation in the case of boys and lack of ability in the case of girls (Dweck et al., 1978).

In a recent study by Diener and Dweck (1978), moment-to-moment changes in problem-solving strategies and spontaneous verbalizations were assessed as helpless and mastery-oriented children worked on a discrimination task. Although no differences emerged between the two groups prior to failure, striking differences were evident following failure. Helpless children began to use ineffectual strategies and showed a progressive decline in the sophistication of the strategies they employed. Mastery-oriented children continued to perform at the same level and some began to employ even more sophisticated strategies. These performance differences were consistent with the disparity in on-going cognitions between the two groups. The helpless group began to make causal attributions for their failure, attributing it to lack or loss of ability. They also uttered a good deal of task-irrelevant talk and expressed negative affect about the task. In contrast, mastery-oriented children did not make causal attributions for their failure. Instead, they engaged in self-instruction and self-monitoring, expressed positive affect, and remained optimistic about the chances of success. As predicted by the model, then, the performance of helpless children deteriorates after failure, and this deterioration is associated with what appears to be a global, stable, and internal attributional state (inability). The performance of mastery-oriented children does not deteriorate, and rather than generating insidious attributions for failure, they focus on ways of remedying the situation.

Diener and Dweck (1979) have recently replicated these results, and, further, found that helpless children, as compared to mastery-oriented children, were less likely to attribute success to ability, they expected poor future performance, and they believed other children would do better than they had done. That is, helpless children tended to make unstable, specific, and external attributions for success. Mastery-oriented children showed the reverse pattern.

Diener and Dweck's work also suggests differential *perception* of success and failure, in addition to differential attributions, between helpless and mastery-oriented children. Helpless children do not seem to perceive accurately that they have succeeded while mastery-oriented children do not seem to perceive accurately that they have failed. Other research has shown similar differential perception of noncontingency (Alloy & Abramson, 1979), of social skills (Lewinsohn et al., 1979) and of performance (DeMonbreun & Craighead, 1977) between depressed and nondepressed individuals. This chapter is about the attributional and expectancy status of helpless and depressive cognitions, and we do not attempt to address the perceptual issue here. Nonetheless, we view the issue as an important one, and future work should attempt to distinguish those deficits which follow from perceptual biases and those which follow from attributional and expectancy biases.

We would also like to speculate on an attributional analysis of the perceptual differences observed in the Diener and Dweck study. To the extent that a child makes an unstable, specific attribution for failure on a given trial, he/she will expect to succeed—not fail—on future trials. As such, he/she will not label his/her performance on the task *as a whole* as a failure, but as an *anticipated success*. Therefore, he/she will not be generating ongoing attributions for having failed, will not show deficits, and will report expectation of future success. This will make the child look like he/she has not accurately processed his/her poor performance on any given trial. The converse logic can be applied to a child who makes an unstable, specific attribution for success. We are not sure that this analysis captures the entire success-failure labelling difference, but we tentatively suggest that it may explain some part of the phenomenon.

To summarize the sweep of results, helpless and depressed students, depressed inpatients, and helpless and depressed children show the predicted insidious attributional style, which is characterized by internal, stable, and global attributions for failure and external, unstable, and specific attributions for success. Proposed research will concentrate on a more fine-grained analysis of this style, and the following three classes of experiment will be conducted: (1) an examination of the recurrence of depressive and helplessness deficits, over time, among people who differ on the stability dimension but who are matched for internality and globality; (2) an examination of the generality of depressive and helplessness deficits over diverse situations, among people who differ on the globality dimension but who are matched for stability and internality; (3) an examination of self-esteem deficits among people who differ in internality but who are equated for stability and globality; and (4) an examination of the causal role of this attributional style in putting people at risk for depression.

Manipulating Attributional States The results of four studies provide some degree of support for the revised helplessness model (Roth & Kubal, 1975; Tennen & Eller, 1977; Klein et al., 1976; Abramson, 1977). These studies were conducted before the statement of the reformulated theory, and therefore did not keep the three attributional dimensions distinct nor manipulate them as cleanly as more recent studies. Nonetheless, their results led to the development of the new theory (see Abramson, et al., 1978, for a more thorough review).

Roth and Kubal (1975) found that subjects who failed on an "important" concept-formation task, which supposedly predicted success at college, subsequently manifested performance deficits on a concept-formation task in a new experiment. On the other hand, subjects who failed on an "unimportant" concept-formation task, described as a simple learning task, did not. "Important" subjects presumably made a more global, stable, and internal attribution for their failure than "unimportant" subjects, evoking the expectation of noncontingency on a similar task in a new situation.

Tennen and Eller (1977) conducted a follow-up study in which subjects were induced to attribute failure on discrimination problems to their own inability (global, stable, internal) or to the difficulty of the task (specific, external, unstable) by telling them that the problems were getting easier or harder respectively. Only subjects who made a global-stable-internal (inability) attribution showed performance deficits on a different task (anagrams) in a separate experiment, whereas specific-unstable-external (task difficulty) attribution subjects showed improved performance.

Only one experiment bears on the self-esteem predictions of the helplessness model (Abramson, 1977), but unfortunately it was conducted before the reformulation was stated. Subjects pretreated with inescapable noise were led to attribute their failure to internal or external factors. The internal "personally helpless" group was told that the majority of subjects solved the problem. The external "universally helpless" group was told that solving the problem was a matter of luck. As predicted by the reformulation, both universally and personally helpless subjects showed cognitive, performance, and mood deficits on a second instrumental task: they expected to fail on the second task, became more depressed, and did worse (see also Klein et al., 1976). However, only the personally helpless group showed decrements in self-esteem. The problem with this study is that the attributions made by personally helpless subjects were probably also more global and stable than attributions made by universally helpless subjects. Therefore, it has not been unequivocally demonstrated that self-esteem deficits are due exclusively to an internal attributional state, and the research proposed below will rectify this.

Among more recent work, Friedlander and Chartier (1980) have conducted a parallel experiment to Abramson's in which they assessed the helplessness-alleviating potential of personal versus universal success. They found that when helpless subjects were exposed to a self-attributed mastery experience ("the amount of unpleasantness you experience is dependent on your skill and ability to find the solution") or to an other-attributed mastery experience ("I'll *tell* you what response to make so you won't have to figure anything out"), performance deficits were equally alleviated in each case. This evidence supports the reformulated model which specifies that either internal or external attributions for success should reverse helplessness deficits as long as the attribution for prior failure shifts to a more specific, unstable one. Only self-attributed success should augment self-esteem, but the present study did not assess self-esteem changes.

Pasahow (1980) pretreated subjects with unsolvable discrimination problems and led one group to attribute their failure to global factors (e.g., "this task is highly predictive of how people perform on all other psychology tasks"). A second group was led to attribute their failure to specific factors (e.g., "this task has no relation to other psychology tasks"). A third group received no attributional instructions, and a fourth control group performed a neutral task. All groups then tried to solve anagrams. Subjects in the global attribution and no attribution groups showed anagram performance deficits relative to subjects in the specific attribution and control groups. The latter two groups did not differ. So specific attributions for prior failure do not produce subsequent helplessness, presumably because the expectation of noncontingency is not generalized to a new situation. In line with this, subjects in the specific attribution group made more specific attributions for initial failure (although they did not differ along the internality or stability dimensions), believed the task was a poorer predictor of performance, and expected to do much better on the anagrams than the other failure groups.

The final main result was that subjects' global-specific attribution ratings (when treatment condition was controlled for) did not predict anagram performance. From our point of view, this does not pose a crushing problem for two reasons. First, Pasahow's measure of attribution was a top-of-the-head, unvalidated one. Second, our notion of attribution is not rooted in any privileged way in phenomology or self-report. Individuals do not have to be able to report accurately on their attributional state for such attributions to exist, although it would be nice if they did and this could be validly measured. We view attributions as hypothetical constructs, where *subjective reports* of attributional state are just one—nonprivileged—instance of the existence of such a state.

Dyck, Vallentyne, and Breen (1979) manipulated both attributions for failure and duration of the failure experience. Subjects were exposed to either short- (12 trials) or long-duration (30 trials) failure on a concept-formation task. An "incompetence" group was shown norms indicating that most people performed well on the problem and was allowed to observe a confederate succeed on 83% of the trials (global as well as internal and stable attribution). A second "task-difficulty" group was shown norms indicating that most people performed poorly and also observed a confederate fail on 83% of the trials (specific as well as external and unstable attribution). Two failure groups received no attributional information, and two additional groups experienced either long- or short-duration success. All subjects subsequently attempted a second concept-formation task and then went on to a second experiment where they worked on soluble tracing puzzles. Under long-duration failure, subjects in the incompetence and no-attribution groups showed performance deficits on both a similar and a different task. In contrast, subjects who attributed their failure to task difficulty performed as well as successful controls. Thus, when the attribution for failure is specific, the expectation of helplessness does not generalize, and no deficits are produced.

Under short-duration failure, the pattern of results was reversed, with "task-difficult" (but not "incompetence") subjects showing subsequent performance deficits. These results replicate those of Wortman, Panciera, and Shusterman (1976), who also found that "incompetence" attributions reversed helplessness deficits, whereas "task-difficulty" attributions did not. Taken together, these experiments show that "incompetence" subjects are only motivated to reassert control after a brief, but not after a prolonged, experience with failure. This suggests that the so-called reactance effect is a product of a transient attributional state (see also Hanusa & Schultz, 1977). When more asymptotic attributions are produced, the predicted helplessness effect emerges. Manipulation checks in the Dyck et al. (1979) study showed that while the "task-difficulty" group made more attributions to task difficulty for their failure, the "incompetence" group made more attributions to insufficient effort. Although insufficient effort may initially be construed as an unstable characteristic which motivates subjects to try harder, it is likely to be construed as a more stable characteristic after prolonged failure, undermining a subject's motivation. It is, of course, the expectancies produced by a subject's asymptotic—and not his transient—attributions that are of prime importance for helplessness theorizing.

The results of Abramson (1977) and Klein et al. (1976) appear to contradict those of Dyck et al. (1979), with only the first two studies finding generalized performance deficits in both the "incompetence" (personally helpless) *and* "task-difficulty" (universally helpless) groups. This suggests that "task-difficulty" subjects in the Abramson and Klein et al. studies made a more global and stable attribution for failure than in the Dyck et al. study. There are a number of procedural variations that make this a likely explanation for the discrepancy. For example, "task-difficulty" subjects in the Abramson study received information that the training task was basically unsolvable, i.e., a guessing game dependent on luck and chance. If the test task was viewed in the same way, subjects would have expected to be helpless (which they did) and would have shown the corresponding deficits. In contrast, "task-difficulty" subjects in the Dyck et al. study were told that the training task was solvable, but the majority of the subjects failed to solve it. Faced with a new task, they would have expected it to be solvable as well (which it was). This time, they were not shown norms indicating that the majority of subjects failed to solve it and so they did not expect to be helpless. This would have reversed performance deficits.

Another relevant procedural difference was that subjects in the Dyck et al. study construed the test task as part of a separate experiment, whereas subjects in the other two studies construed the test task to be part of the same experiment. This would have exaggerated the extent to which "task-difficulty" (universally helpless) subjects in the Abramson and Klein et al. studies generalized their expectancy of noncontingency.

In one final recent experiment, attribution for failure was also directly manipulated (Carver, Blaney, & Scheier, 1980). Subjects were first given difficult-to-unsolvable anagrams by one experimenter and were then presented with an unsolvable line-tracing task by a second experimenter. When subjects were told that poor performance on the anagrams was predictive of poor performance on the line-tracing task (a global attribution for failure), they persisted less on the second task then subjects who were told that poor performance on the anagrams was predictive of good performance on the line-tracing task (specific attribution for failure). However, the performance deficit only emerged when subjects had a mirror present during the line-tracing task. In a second experiment, subjects given a specific attribution for failure actually showed enhanced performance when a mirror was present.

The authors view these results as contrary to the learned-helplessness model, because performance deficits should occur following a global-attribution for failure, whether or not subjects perform in front of a mirror. Instead, they interpret the findings as evidence for the role of "self-focus" in failure. When a person fails, a discrepancy is created between oneself and one's standard of comparison. Self-focus enhances this effect and leads to attempts to reassert control (increased persistence) if individuals expect to succeed, or to withdrawal (decreased persistence) if individuals expect to fail.

There are several objections to this analysis. In the first place, no independent evidence establishes that subjects in the mirror-present conditions engaged in more self-focusing than subjects in the mirror-absent condition. Second, other evidence shows that when subjects perform a task they are told is "hard," helplessness deficits are reversed (see below). This may have undermined the potency of the failure manipulation in the majority of subjects, and some additional factor (such as a mirror) may have been necessary to obtain the helplessness effect. For example, there is evidence (Gur & Sackeim, 1979) that self-confrontation per se can be arousing, especially following failure, and this heightened arousal may account for the emergence of deficits in the global attribution, mirror-present failure condition. Other problems with the study include the absence of an untreated control group and the absence of an attributional manipulation check.

The results may thus be due to either the so-called self-focus effect or to increased arousal following failure plus self-confrontation in the global mirror-present group. In addition, subjects who have a mirror present make more internal attributions for outcomes than in the absence of a mirror (Duval & Wicklund, 1973; Buss & Scheier, 1976). To the extent that internal attributions tend to be more global than external attributions, it could enhance the deficits in the global-attribution mirror-present group. The present experiment is inadequate to discriminate among these various hypotheses, and further research is needed to resolve this issue.

In summary of the attribution manipulation studies, the results show that when subjects make an internal attribution for their helplessness, they probably show more self-esteem deficits than when the attribution is to external factors. When subjects attribute their helplessness to global and stable factors, they probably show more broad-ranging and long-lasting performance deficits than when the attribution is to specific and unstable factors. However, most of the studies cited suffer from methodological confounds which limit the crispness and generality of the conclusions. First and foremost, only two experiments (Pasahow, 1980; Carver, Blaney, & Scheier, 1980) successfully manipulated one single atrributional dimension (globality) while holding the others constant. Second, it is hard to gauge the effectiveness of the global and stable manipulations because subjects did not necessarily view the training and test phases as nonassociated separate experiments (see, for example, Abramson, 1977; Dyck et al., 1979; Friedlander & Chartier, 1980; Klein et al., 1976; Pasahow, 1980).

Having presented the major methodological criticisms of this research, let us briefly list the class of manipulation experiments that we propose to test the model adequately. (1) manipulate globality, holding internality and stability constant, and assess the generality of performance deficits across different situations; (2) manipulate stability, holding internality and globality constant, and assess recurrence of performance deficits over time; and (3) manipulate internality, holding globality and stability constant, and assess self-esteem deficits.

Indirect, but Relevant Evidence We now review a number of studies which, while not intended as direct tests of the reformulated model, have obtained results which are *interpretable* as either confirming or disconfirming the attributional analysis. However, we offer only cautious speculation about the attributional relevance of these experiments because the relevant attributions were neither directly measured nor manipulated.

Three of the studies (Douglas & Anisman, 1975; Klein & Seligman, 1976; Teasdale, 1978) were performed prior to the reformulation and helped to lead to it; so they cannot be counted as independent evidence.

Douglas and Anisman (1975) showed that subjects became helpless following failure on simple, but not complex, training tasks. Subjects who failed on a simple task ("that anybody should have been able to do") presumably made a more global, internal attribution than subjects who failed on a complex task. According to the authors, subjects in the simple condition expected to succeed, but instead failed, and it is this violation of expectancies that accounts for the observed deficits. We believe, however, that it is the attributions which the subject makes in this condition that determine his expectancy of future success (and hence his performance). Attributional theorists have further suggested that individuals are more likely to engage in a causal analysis when faced with an unexpected outcome. We disagree. We believe that individuals typically make attributions (not necessarily phenomonological) following failure and that unexpected failure (when one has anticipated success) merely leads to a *more* global and stable attribution than expected failure.

Klein and Seligman (1976) administered solvable therapy problems to depressed and helpless subjects and found that the experience with success worked to reverse the performance deficits. Similarly, in an experiment by Teasdale (1978), real experience with solvable problems worked to reverse performance deficits although simply recalling an earlier success experience did not. For both studies, it seems reasonable that subjects who are exposed to a solvable therapy experience shifted their attribution for failure from global and internal factors to more specific and external ones.

Among more recent studies, Schwartz (1980) has conducted a fascinating experiment which is amenable to an attributional analysis of helplessness. He was interested in evaluating how the effectiveness of a helplessness manipulation would be influenced by what individuals already knew about helplessness (the demand characteristics, if you will). Three groups of undergraduate subjects were pretreated with escapable noise, inescapable noise, or with no exposure to noise. Subjects in a fourth inescapable group differed from the standard inescapable group in one crucial respect: they were all students in an introductory course, in which the instructor had described the learned helplessness phenomenon in animals and briefly mentioned that the effect had been demonstrated in humans. Although the standard inescapable group showed performance deficits in an anagram test task, such deficits were not observed in the informed inescapable group. So knowledge of what learned helplessness is supposed to do to you may reverse helplessness deficits. We suggest that such knowledge shifts the attribution for failure from an internal and global one ("I'm stupid") to a more external and specific one ("this experiment is designed to make me do poorly").

Brown and Inouye (1978) have similarly shown that other factors besides direct exposure to uncontrollability can influence helplessness effects (see also Chartier, 1980; DeVellis, DeVellis, & McCauly, 1978). Three groups of subjects watched a model perform unsuccessfully at an anagram task under conditions where they perceived themselves to be either equal in competence to the model, superior in competence, or had no information. Subjects in the equal competence and no information conditions later performed more poorly on anagrams than superior competence subjects. It is suggested that perceived similarity in competence modulates the effects of modeled helplessness, with subjects in the equal competence condition making a more internal, stable attribution as a result of the model's failure than subjects in the superior competence condition. Indeed, equal competence subjects expected to solve fewer anagrams themselves, and these expectancy judgments accurately predicted anagram performance.

Several investigators have shown that helplessness affects generalize to a similar as well as a dissimilar test task, if the test task is given in the same room by the same experimenter (e.g., Douglas & Anisman, 1975). In contrast, Tiggemann and Winefield (1978) found that subjects pretreated with inescapable noise did not become helpless on a dissimilar test task given by a different experimenter in a different room. The most likely explanation is that subjects' attributions were too specific to produce an expectation of uncontrollability in the new test task, but, because attributions were not measured, we cannot be sure (see also Cole & Coyne, 1977).

A series of studies by Nation and his colleagues have investigated factors which work to sustain responding in the face of failure (Nation and Massad, 1978; Nation, Cooney, & Cartell, 1979; Nation, Cooney, & Taylor, 1979). In the typical procedure, subjects are pretreated with solvable, unsolvable, or no discrimination problems and then receive continuous "success therapy" on an instrumental task. In addition, a separate group of unsolvable subjects receives *partial* "success therapy" (combined success and failure). Finally, all subjects are tested for resistance to extinction, or "persistence," on an unsolvable instrumental task. The main findings are that continuous and partial success therapy reverse performance deficits and sad affect for unsolvable subjects during the therapy phase. However, only partial reinforcement therapy produces greater persistence during the unsolvable extinction phase, and the persistence is enhanced when (1) the therapy phase is extended; (2) the therapy and extinction tasks are similar; and (3) the therapy task is difficult. Indeed, helpless subjects receiving partial reinforcement therapy persist for a longer time than all other subjects (helpless and nonhelpless), whereas helpless subjects receiving continuous reinforcement therapy persist for a shorter time than all other subjects.

The authors interpret these results as supporting a frustration-theory account of persistence, which states that failure-produced frustration becomes counterconditioned to approach responses in subjects who experience partial reinforcement. When such subjects are exposed to extinction, they make an association between frustration-produced stimuli and the instrumental-approach response, which operates to sustain responding (Amsel, 1967, 1971); that is, partial reinforcement subjects have learned to associate frustration with upcoming reinforcement and so continue to respond even when they are experiencing failure.

The reformulated helplessness model offers an alternative account of superior resistance to extinction among partial reinforcement subjects. A subject who has had partial reinforcement therapy has been exposed to a combination of successes and failures. When faced with failure on a given trial, he comes to expect success on a later trial. Therefore, in explaining why he fails, he attributes it to a more unstable and possibly specific cause. When he encounters failure during extinction, he again makes the attribution to an unstable, specific cause, and so he continues to respond. In contrast, a subject who has had continuous success therapy has only had experience with success but not failure. Therefore, he had not had an opportunity to make attributions for his failure during therapy, and these attributions have not been bent in the specific, unstable direction.

This analysis also applies to the results of a recent experiment by Chapin and Dyck (1976). Children experiencing reading difficulties were trained with success only (easy sentences) or with partial reinforcement (a combination of hard and easy sentences). Two partial reinforcement schedules were used: either one failure preceeding each success or between one and three failures preceeding each success. Partial reinforcement increased persistence on failure-inducing hard-test sentences, but only in the three-failure training condition. The other procedures were only effective when subjects also received attributional retraining which emphasized that failure was due to lack of effort (see also Dweck, 1975). Attributional retraining increases persistence by changing the attribution for failure from stable to unstable. Children who experience multiple failure followed by success probably already make an unstable attribution for failure, and so attributional retraining is redundant.

An attributional analysis can also explain why immunization prevents helplessness deficits from emerging in solvable test situations. For example, in an experiment by Jones, Nation, and Massad (1977), subjects received either 0%, 50%, or 100% success on discrimination problems prior to pretesting with unsolvable discrimination problems. Subjects in the 50%-success group failed to show performance deficits on both instrumental and anagram test tasks. Similarly, Dyck and Breen (1976) found that subjects exposed to combined success and failure on a concept-formation task showed fewer performance deficits in a "new" experiment with anagrams than subjects exposed to simple failure. Presumably, initial experience with combined success and failure produces a more specific, unstable attribution for failure than initial experience with either success alone or failure alone. Therefore, subjects do not generalize the expectation of helplessness to a new, controllable situation (see also Prindaville & Stein, 1980; Thornton & Powell, 1974). Again, since attributions were not measured, this is speculation only.

The results of two final experiments appear to bear on the reformulation. In an experiment by Frankel and Snyder (1978), subjects pretreated with solvable or unsolvable discrimination problems were tested on anagrams described as moderately or extremely difficult. Prior experience with unsolvable problems only led to deficits when the anagrams were described as moderately difficult. When helpless subjects believed the test task was extremely difficult, they performed as well as non-helpless subjects. In a follow-up experiment, playing allegedly "distracting" music to helpless subjects similarly reversed anagram deficits (Snyder et al., 1980).

The authors contend that these results are contrary to helplessness theory because the expectation of uncontrollability (and hence the performance deficits) should increase, not decrease, with the perceived difficulty of the test task. Instead, they favor a "self-esteem" explanation which says that subjects try to protect their self-esteem following failure on one task by withholding effort on a subsequent task. Because failure on a task which is extremely difficult or which is performed under distracting conditions is not a further threat to self-esteem, subjects are not motivated to withhold effort.

We propose an alternative account which is in line with the reformulation. Consider the attribution a subject makes when he has failed on one task and achieves his first success on a new task. If he is performing under moderately difficult conditions, he is likely to make a relatively external, unstable, specific attribution for success ("it might be me, but . . ."). If, on the other hand, he is performing under extremely difficult conditions, he will make a more internal, stable, global attribution for success ("I'm brilliant"). The latter, but not the former, set of attributions will lead relatively more to the expectation of future success and will reverse performance deficits. Further work is needed to discriminate between the two hypotheses, and we are in the process of doing it.

One further study is worth reporting. Brown, Harris, and Copeland (1977) assessed the factors disposing toward severe depression in a large-scale sample of working-class women in London, England. They found that loss of a mother by death before age 11 significantly increased the risk of depression among women who had experienced a major recent loss. The presence of any one of three "invulnerability factors" mitigated against the development of depression: (1) having an intimate relationship with a husband; (2) having full or part-time employment; and (3) *not* having 3 or more children under the age of 14 at home.

We speculate on the following attributional account of these findings. When a young girl loses a mother by death, the most important source of reinforcement in her life disappears and never comes back. Moreover, she is helpless to control the situation in any way, and she makes a global and stable attribution for her state ("Death has taken her away from me forever"). Such a foundational experience will make it more likely for her to explain later loss in global and stable terms, resulting in severe depression. The invulnerability factors have one important element in common: they provide evidence of her ability to gain important reinforcers and thereby transform the attributions she makes for her present failures into more unstable and specific ones.

Overall, then, we have reviewed studies showing that a broad range of factors, such as prior knowledge, imitation, partial reinforcement, self-handicapping, strategies, and early loss, interact with and moderate helplessness effects. We have speculated that all these factors may operate through attributional channels and might therefore be accommodated within an attributional framework. Confirmation of this analysis awaits further research.

Traditional but Inadequate Ways of Testing the Model Both the locus of control construct (Rotter, 1966) and the ability-effort–task difficulty-luck distinctions (Weiner et al., 1971) are traditional but inadequate measures for testing the reformulation unambiguously.

Several investigators have explored the relationship between learned helplessness and Rotter's (1966) locus of control construct. This refers to the extent to which individuals believe that reinforcers are under their own control or are under the control of external factors. "Internals" believe that their own responses determine the nature and extent of the reinforcers they receive, whereas "externals" believe that reinforcers are determined by external factors, such as luck, chance, or fate. Although this line of research has generated some interesting findings which bear on helplessness, they are uninterpretable within the attributional framework. From the point of view of the reformulated model, the internality construct collapses several independent dimensions together.

First and foremost, locus of control confounds internality with control and externality with lack of control. However, internality is not equivalent to having control and externality is not equivalent to being helpless. This is illustrated in Table 6-4, where beliefs about oneself are plotted against beliefs about others. The self-other dichotomy defines the internal-external dimension: an outcome is internally attributed whenever an individual believes that the outcome is more or less likely to be contingent on one of his/her actions than on the actions of relevant others (Cells 2 and 3), whereas an outcome is externally attributed whenever the individual believes

Table 6-4 **Personal Helplessness and Universal Helplessness**

Other	SELF	
	THE PERSON EXPECTS THE OUTCOME IS CONTINGENT ON A RESPONSE IN HIS REPERTOIRE.	THE PERSON EXPECTS THE OUTCOME IS NOT CONTINGENT ON ANY RESPONSE IN HIS REPERTOIRE.
The person expects the outcome is contingent on a response in the repertoire of a relevant other.	1	Personal helplessness 3 (internal attribution)
The person expects the outcome is not contingent on a response in the repertoire of any relevant other.	2	Universal helplessness 4 (external attribution)

that the outcome is equally likely to be controllable or uncontrollable by relevant others as by himself/herself (Cells 1 and 4).

Note that Cells 3 and 4 both represent situations in which helplessness occurs, because by definition the person expects that the outcome is not contingent on any response in his/her repertoire. Yet an internal attribution is made in only one case (Cell 3) and an external attribution in the other case (Cell 4). Whenever a person believes that all responses in his/her own repertoire are independent of the desired outcome but other people can make responses that produce the outcome, then he/she makes an internal attribution for his/her helplessness (Cell 3). For example, if a person tries hard at math but fails, he/she is personally helpless because of a belief that when other relevant people try hard at math, they succeed. Therefore, he/she concludes that failure is due to some personal characteristic, such as inability, insufficient concentration, etc. Conversely, when the person believes that the outcome is independent of all responses in his/her own *and* other people's repertoire, then he/she makes an external attribution for helplessness (Cell 4), e.g. "the test was unfair." This is therefore a case of universal helplessness, and the person makes an external attribution for his plight. Similar (but inverse) logic applies to Cells 1 and 2, where the individual has control.

In Bandura's (1977) terms, personally helpless people have low self-efficacy expectations—they believe that they lack the requisite skills—combined with high outcome expectations—they believe that other people exist who have the requisite skills. Universally helpless people have low self-efficacy expectations combined with low outcome expectations—they believe that no one has the skills to produce the outcome. So internality is also orthogonal to self-efficacy, just as it is to control.

The second problem with the locus-of-control instrument is that the stable-unstable attributional dimension is not assessed independently of the internal-external dimension, even though the two dimensions are logically orthogonal (see Abramson et al., 1978; Weiner et al., 1971). This is a problem because the internal-external locus of the causal explanation merely deduces the presence or absence of self-esteem deficits. However, it is the stability (and globality), and not the internality, of the attribution that determines the recurrence of performance deficits over time (and situations). It is only to the extent that internal attributions for failure tend in nature to be more stable than external attributions that one would expect "internals" to show more recurrent helplessness deficits than "externals" (see also Weiner et al., 1971, on the relation between internality, stability, and changes in expectancy for success).

Third, and perhaps more important, there is no independent measurement of the global-specific dimension, even though it is logically orthogonal to both the internality and stability dimensions. The globality of the attribution determines the generality of the deficits across situations, and internal factors are often more global than external factors. To the extent that this is so, and only to the extent that this is so, one would predict more generalized helplessness deficits among "internals" than among "externals."

Fourth and finally, the locus-of-control construct collapses beliefs about control across negative and positive outcomes. Internals believe that both positive and negative reinforcers are response-contingent, whereas externals do not believe that either type of reinforcer is response-contingent. According to the reformulation, however, internal-global-stable attributions for failure do not necessarily cohere with internal-global-and stable attributions for success. Instead, the insidious attributional state of helpless individuals—and the insidious attributional style of depressed individuals—is thought to involve internal-global-stable attributions for failure coupled with the converse, external-specific-unstable attributions for success.

With the above (almost grave) limitations in mind, let us briefly review some of the recent locus-of-control findings as they have been alleged to bear on helplessness. In two experiments by Albert and Geller (1978), externals who had been pretreated with an unsolvable prediction task manifested subsequent performance deficits on a serial learning task, whereas internals performed as well or better than successful controls. Cohen, Rothbart, & Phillips (1976) showed that both internals and externals made helpless showed deteriorated performance on a similar test task, but only helpless externals showed deteriorated performance on a dissimilar test task.

Pittman and Pittman (1979) investigated susceptibility to helplessness as a function of amount of experience with uncontrollability. When subjects were exposed to a mild dose of uncontrollability on a discrimination task, only externals performed worse on a subsequent anagrams task. Internals, instead, tended to show a reactance effect, performing better on the subsequent task. These results parallel those of the two studies already reported. In contrast, after a high level of helplessness training, both internals and externals manifested performance deficits, and helpless internals actually performed worse than helpless externals.

Similarly, Benson and Kennelly (1980) found performance deficits for internals pretreated with high helplessness while externals were not impaired by high helplessness. Instead, the performance of externals pretreated with a high level of *controllability* was actually enhanced.

Taken together, these studies reveal that externals are more susceptible to uncontrollability than internals when the level of helplessness training is low. But when the level of uncontrollability is high, internals may be even more vulnerable to helplessness manipulations than externals. We speculate that internals, who expect to have control, initially make a more specific, unstable attribution for their failure than externals. Having this transient attributional state, they do not succumb to helplessness induction. Indeed, they tend to try harder after low degrees of helplessness training. After prolonged exposure to uncontrollability, a more asymptotic attributional state is evoked in which the attribution for failure may shift to more global and stable factors. This interferes with subsequent adaptive responding. In contrast, externals are less debilitated—if at all—by prolonged exposure to helplessness. This suggests that their asymptotic attributions for failure may be more specific and unstable than those made by internals. In the absence of any direct data, this analysis must remain speculative at best.

The second traditional, but inadequate, means of testing the model arises from the work of Weiner and his colleagues in achievement-related situations (e.g., Weiner et al., 1971). They operate from the premise that there are four major causes which individuals consider in accounting for success and failure. These are ability, effort, task difficulty, and luck. The internality and stability dimensions are thought to map onto these causes, with ability being an internal-stable attribution, effort being an internal-unstable attribution, task difficulty, an external-stable attribution, and luck, an external-unstable attribution. However, as Weiner (1979, p. 3) and Abramson et al. (1978) have emphasized, the placement of any particular cause within a given dimension can vary, both over time and between people. We concur, and we would like to underscore the fact that the ability-effort–task difficulty-luck distinctions do not map onto these dimensions. For example, Ostrove (1978) has shown that effort can be construed either as a stable or unstable cause. When individuals have been led to believe that effort is an unstable characteristic, they change their expectancies for future success if they are performing under motivating conditions. However, they do not change their expectancies for future success when they believe effort is a stable (invariant) characteristic. Table 6-5 illustrates how the four causal attributions systematically violate Weiner's original mapping. Within internal causes, ability can be construed as an unstable attribute and effort, as a stable attribute. Similarly, within external causes, task difficulty can be construed as an unstable attribute and luck, as a stable attribute.

A second, related problem has to do with whether these four causal attributions are those actually generated by individuals in naturally occurring situations. Recent research by Falbo and Beck (1979) indicates that only 23% of 2495 spontaneously generated attributions could be classified as one of the four causal elements. Moreover, different types of causes were assigned to explain success and failure. Weiner

Table 6-5 **Formal Characteristics of Attribution and Some Examples Which Violate Weiner's Mapping**

| | INTERNAL | | EXTERNAL | |
DIMENSION	STABLE	UNSTABLE	STABLE	UNSTABLE
Global *Failing student*	Laziness	Having a cold, which makes me stupid.	People are usually unlucky on the GRE.	ETS gave experimental tests this time which were too hard for everyone.
Specific *Failing student*	Math always bores me.	Having a cold, which ruins my arithmetic.	People are usually unlucky on math tests.	Everyone's copy of the math test was blurred.

Note: ETS = Educational Testing Service, maker of graduate record examinations (GRE).

(1979, p. 4) has similarly concluded that there are other salient causes of success and failure besides the four traditional ones, and that restricting options to these four might lead to false conclusions. It is for these two reasons that we have devised attributional scales (Seligman et al., 1979; Kaslow et al., 1980) that have subjects rate the degree of internality, stability, and globality of the causal attributions they generate for success and failure.

Bearing in mind, then, that there may be some difficulties in interpretation of the following findings, let us review some of the relevant research. Within the achievement context, a series of studies by Covington and Omelich (1979a and b; 1980a and b) examined the effect of success and failure on causal attributions. For example, in response to hypothetical academic situations, they found that positive self-evaluation followed success, but only if subjects perceived themselves as high in ability or as having expended effort (Covington & Omelich, 1980a). Conversely, under failure conditions, negative self-evaluation (shame) was greatest when individuals believed that they lacked ability or had expended high effort (Covington & Omelich, 1979a). Least shame was experienced under low effort. These data confirm the model, insofar as ability and effort both reflect internally attributed outcomes. As predicted, internal attributions for failure produced self-esteem deficits, whereas internal attributions for success produced self-esteem increments. They further found that repeated failure led to increased doubts about one's skills, and attributions tended to shift to low ability. This shift elicited a greater degree of shame. This attributional shift (and accompanying shame) was particularly salient in low self-confidence individuals (Covington & Omelich, 1980b). Moreover, both ability and effort ascriptions for failure depressed expectancies of future success, and expectancies predicted future performance (Covington & Omelich, 1979b). It seems probable that ability and effort are viewed by these individuals as stable, global (and uncontrollable) attributes which reduce the likelihood of improving performance.

One final study is worth reporting. Tennen (1980) had depressed and nondepressed students succeed or fail on anagram tasks. Depressed subjects attributed failure more to effort and success more to luck than did nondepressed subjects. In addition, following a success, depressed subjects were more depressed and had a lower expectancy of future success. Performance deficits were most salient among the depressed group when they were led to believe that effort expenditure was important. Attributing failure to effort, which can be viewed as a stable (and uncontrollable) characteristic, would lead to lowered expectancy of future success (and deteriorated performance). Attributing success to luck, which can be viewed as an unstable (and uncontrollable) characteristic, would similarly decrease expectancies of future success.

To summarize, repeated failure and depression lead subjects to attribute their helplessness to internal, stable, global (and uncontrollable) factors: ability and effort. Conversely, success is attributed to an external, unstable, specific (and uncontrollable) factor: luck. The internality of failure attributions and the externality of success attributions are both associated with decrements in self-esteem.

Concluding Remarks

In conclusion, we have outlined the attributional premise of the reformulated helplessness model. It says that when individuals fail, those who make internal, stable, and global attributions for their failures will lose self-esteem and show long-lasting and broad helplessness deficits. Conversely, with success, those who make internal, stable, and global attributions for their success will be less vulnerable to loss of self-esteem and show shorter and more specific helplessness deficits. A depressive attributional style is one in which an individual habitually makes internal, stable, and global attributions for failure and external, unstable, and specific attributions for success. We have reviewed the evidence as of this data that bears on the reformulation. We find strong evidence for the existence of the postulated depressive attributional style. Studies which measure the attributions which depressives make almost universally have found the predicted results and a new attributional style scale exists which provides strong evidence for such a correlation. The evidence gathered from experiments from which attributions are manipulated is considerably less strong but in the predicted direction. We find that two classes of studies on helplessness—those using the Rotter locus-of-control scale and those using the effort-ability–task difficulty-luck distinction—are difficult to interpret on conceptual grounds, although they also tend to support the reformulation. We see two promising and needed directions of research on the reformulation: first, to find out whether or not the attributional style causes depressive deficits; and second, to manipulate and measure a single attributional dimension while holding the other two attributional dimensions constant.

References

Abramson, L. Y. *Universal versus personal helplessness: An experimental test of the reformulated theory of learned helplessness and depression.* Unpublished doctoral dissertation, University of Pennsylvania, 1977.

Abramson, L. Y., Seligman, M. E. P., & Teasdale, J. Learned helplessness in humans: Critique and reformulation. *Journal of Abnormal Psychology,* 1978, *87,* 49–79.

Albert, M., & Geller, E. S. Perceived control as a mediation of learned helplessness. *American Journal of Psychology,* 1978, *91,* 389–400.

Alloy, L. B., & Abramson, L. Y. The judgment of contingency in depressed and nondepressed students: Sadder but wiser? *Journal of Experimental Psychology: General,* 1979 *108*(4), 441–485.

Amsel, A. Partial reinforcement effects on vigor and persistence. In K. W. Spence & J. T. Spence (Eds.), *The psychology of learning and motivation: Advances in research and theory* (Vol 1). New York: Academic Press, 1967.

Amsel, A. Frustration, persistence, and regression. In H. D. Kimmel (Ed.), *Experimental psychology: Recent research and theory.* New York: Academic Press, 1971.

Bandura, A. Self-efficacy: Toward a unifying theory of behavioral change. *Psychological Review,* 1977, *84,* 191–215.

Benson, T. S., & Kennelly, K. *A reexamination of the relationship between locus of control and learned helplessness.* Unpublished manuscript, University of Texas at Arlington, 1980.

Brown, I., & Inouye, D. K. Learned helplessness through modeling: The role of perceived similarity in competence. *Journal of Personality and Social Psychology,* 1978, *36,* 900–908.

Brown, G. W., Harris, T., & Copeland, J. R. Depression and loss. *British Journal of Psychiatry,* 1977, *130,* 1–18.

Buss, D. M., & Scheier, M. F. Self-consciousness, self-awareness, and self-attribution. *Journal of Research in Personality,* 1976, *10,* 463–468.

Carver, C. S., Blaney, P. H., & Scheier, M. F. Reassertation and giving up: The interactive role of self-directed attention. Unpublished manuscript, University of Miami, 1980.

Chapin, M., & Dyck, D. G. Persistence in children's reading behavior as a function of N-length and attribution retraining. *Journal of Abnormal Psychology,* 1976, *85,* 511–515.

Chartier, G. M. Learned helplessness, learned competence, and direct vs. observational learning. Unpublished manuscript, Arizona State University, 1980.

Cohen, S., Rothbart, M., & Phillips, S. Locus of control and the generality of learned helplessness in humans. *Journal of Personality and Social Psychology,* 1976, *34,* 1049–1056.

Cole, C. S., & Coyne, J. C. Situational specificity of laboratory-induced helplessness. *Journal of Abnormal Psychology,* 1977, *86,* 615–623.

Covington, M. V., & Omelich, C. L. Effort: The double-edged sword in school achievement. *Journal of Educational Psychology,* 1979, *71,* 169–182. (a)

Covington, M. V., Omelich, C. L. Are causal attributions causal? A path analysis of the cognitive model of achievement motivation. *Journal of Personality and Social Psychology,* 1979, *37*(9), 1487–1504. (b)

Covington, M. V., & Omelich, C. L. It's best to be able and virtuous too: Student and teacher evaluative responses to successful effort. Unpublished manuscript, University of California, Berkeley, 1980. (a)

Covington, M. V., & Omelich, C. L. Mastery learning and learned helplessness. Unpublished manuscript, University of California, Berkeley, 1980. (b)

DeMonbreun, B. G., & Craighead, W. E. Distortion of perception and recall of positive and neutral feedback in depression. *Cognitive Therapy and Research,* 1977, *1,* 311–329.

Devillis, R. F., Devellis, B. M., & McCauly, C. The vicarious acquisition of learned helplessness. *Journal of Personality and Social Psychology,* 1978, *36,* 894–899.

Diener, C. I., & Dweck, C. S. An analysis of learned helplessness: Continuous changes in performance, strategy, and achievement cognitions following failure. *Journal of Personality and Social Psychology,* 1978, *36,* 451–462.

Diener, C. I., & Dweck, C. S. An analysis of learned helplessness: II. The processing of success. Unpublished manuscript, University of Illinois, 1979.

Douglas, D., & Anisman, H. Helplessness or expectation in congruency: Effects of aversive stimulation on subsequent performance. *Journal of Experimental Psychology: Human Perception and Performance,* 1975, *1,* 411–417.

Duval, S., & Wicklund, R. A. Effects of objective self-awareness on attribution of causality. *Journal of Experimental Social Psychology,* 1973, *9,* 17–31.

Dweck, C. S. The role of expectations and attributions in the alleviation of learned helplessness. *Journal of Personality and Social Psychology,* 1975, *31,* 674–685.

Dweck, C. S., & Bush, E. S. Sex differences in learned helplessness: Differential debilitation with peer and adult evaluators. *Developmental Psychology,* 1976, *12,* 147–156.

Dweck, C. S., Davidson, W., Nelson, S., & Enna, B. Sex differences in learned helplessness: II. The contingencies of evaluative feedback in the classroom. III. An experimental analysis. *Developmental Psychology,* 1978 *14*(3), 268–276.

Dweck, C. S., Goetz, T. E., & Strauss, N. Sex differences in learned helplessness: IV. An experimental and naturalistic study of failure generalization and its mediators. Unpublished manuscript, University of Illinois, 1978.

Dweck, C. S., & Repucci, N. D. Learned helplessness and reinformcement responsibility in children. *Journal of Personality and Social Psychology*, 1973, *25*, 109–116.

Dyck, D. G., & Breen, L. J. Learned helplessness, immunization and task importance in humans. Unpublished manuscript, University of Manitoba, 1976.

Dyck, D. G. Vallentyne, S., Breen, L. J. *Journal of Experimental Social Psychology*, 1979, *15*, 122–132.

Eidelson, J. I. *Perceived control and psychopathology.* Unpublished doctoral dissertation, Duke University, 1977.

Falbo, T., & Beck, R. C. Naive psychology and the attributional model of achievement. *Journal of Personality*, 1979, *47*, 185–195.

Frankel, A., & Snyder, M. L. Poor performance following unsolvable problems: Learned helplessness or egotism? *Journal of Personality and Social Psychology*, 1978, *36*, 1415–1423.

Friedlander, S., & Chartier, G. M. Self-attributed mastery and other-attributed mastery in the alleviation of learned helplessness. Unpublished manuscript, Arizona State University, 1980.

Garber, J., & Hollon, S. Universal versus personal helplessness in depression: Belief in uncontrollability or incompetence. *Journal of Abnormal Psychology*, 1980, *89*, 56–66.

Gur, R. C., & Sackeim, H. A. Self-deception: A concept in search of a phenomenon. *Journal of Personality and Social Psychology*, 1979, *37*, 147–169.

Haley, W. E., & Strickland, B. R. Locus of control and depression. Paper presented at Eastern Psychological Association, 1977.

Hammen, C. L., & Krantz, S. Effect of success and failure on depressive cognitions. *Journal of Abnormal Psychology*, 1976, *85*, 577–586.

Hanusa, B. H., & Schultz, R. Attributional mediators of learned helplessness. *Journal of Personality and Social Psychology*, 1977, *35*, 602–611.

Hollon, S. D., & Kendall, P. C. Cognitive self-statements in depression: Development of an automatic thoughts questionnaire. Unpublished manuscript, University of Minnesota, 1980.

Jones, S. C., Nation, J. R., & Massad, P. Immunization against learned helplessness in man. *Journal of Abnormal Psychology*, 1977, *86*, 75–83.

Kaslow, N., Tannerbaum, R., Alloy, L. B., Abramson, L. Y., & Seligman, M. E. P. Depression and childhood attributional style. Unpublished manuscript, University of Pennsylvania, 1979.

Kenny, D. A. Crossing and synchronous common factors in panel data. In A. S. Goldberger & O. D. Duncan (Eds.), *Structural equation models in the social sciences*. New York: Seminar Press, 1973.

Klein, D. C., Fencil-Morse, E., & Seligman, M. E. P. Learned helplessness, depression, and the attribution of failure. *Journal of Personality and Social Psychology*, 1976, *33*, 508–516.

Klein, D. C., & Seligman, M. E. P. Reversal of performance deficits and perceptual deficits in learned helplessness and depression. *Journal of Abnormal Psychology*, 1976, *85*, 11–26.

Kovacs, M., & Beck, A. T. An empirical-clinical approach toward a definition of childhood depression. In J. G. Schulterbrandt & A Raskin (Eds.), *Depression in childhood*. New York: Raven, 1977.

Krantz, S., & Hammen, C. Assessment of cognitive bias in depression. *Journal of Abnormal Psychology*, 1979, *88*, 611–619.

Leon, G. R., Kendall, P. C., & Garber, J. Depression in children: Parent, teacher, and child perspectives. Unpublished manuscript, University of Minnesota, 1980.

Lewinsohn, P. M., Mischel, W., Chaplin, W., & Barton, R. Social competence and depression: The role of illusory self-perceptions. *Journal of Abnormal Psychology*, 1980, *89*(2), 203–312.

Miller, S. M., Bandura, A., Beck, A. T., & Seligman, M. E. P. Toward a unified cognitive theory of depression. Unpublished manuscript.

Nation, J. R., & Massad, P. Persistence training: A partial reinforcement procedure for reversing learned helplessness and depression. *Journal of Experimental Psychology: General*, 1978, *107*, 436–451.

Nation, J. R., Cooney, J. B., & Cartell, K. E. Durability and generalizability of persistence training. *Journal of Abnormal Psychology*, 1979, *88*, 121–136.

Nation, J. R., Cooney, J. B., & Taylor, D. A. The therapeutic efficiency of persistence training as a function of task difficulty in therapy. Unpublished manuscript, Texas A & M University, 1979.

Ostrove, N. Expectations for success on effort-determined tasks as a function of incentive and performance feedback. *Journal of Personality and Social Psychology,* 1978, *36,* 900–916.

Pasahow, R. J. The relation between an attributional dimension and learned helplessness. Unpublished manuscript, University of Pennsylvania, 1980.

Pittman, N. L., & Pittman, T. S. Effects of amount of helplessness training and internal-external locus of control on mood and performance. *Journal of Personality and Social Psychology,* 1979, *37,* 39–47.

Prindaville, P., & Stein, N. Predictability, controllability, and inoculation against learned helplessness. *Behavior Research and Therapy,* 1978, *16,* 263–271.

Raps, C., & Seligman, M. E. P. Reversal of cognitive and affective deficits associated with depression and learned helplessness by mood elevation among patients. Unpublished manuscript, Northport, Virginia, 1980.

Rizley, R. Depression and distortion in the attribution of causality. *Journal of Abnormal Psychology,* 1978, *87,* 32–48.

Roth, S., & Kubal, L. Effects of noncontingent reinforcement on tasks of differing importance: Facilitation and learned helplessness. *Journal of Personality and Social Psychology,* 1975, *32,* 680–691.

Rotter, J. B. Generalized expectancies for internal vs. external control of reinforcement. *Psychological Monographs,* 1966, 80 (1, Whole No. 609).

Schwartz, B. Knowledge of helplessness effects prevents helplessness effects. Unpublished manuscript, Swarthmore College, 1980.

Seligman, M. E. P. Behavioral and cognitive therapy for depression from a learned helplessness point of view. In L. Rehm (Ed.), *Behavioral Approaches in Depression,* 1980.

Seligman, M. E. P., Abramson, L. Y., Semmel, A., & Von Baeyer, C. Depressive attributional style. *Journal of Abnormal Psychology,* 1979, *88*(3), 242–247.

Snyder, M. C., Smollen, B., Strenta, A., & Frankel, A. A comparison of egotism, negativity and learned helplessness as explanations for poor performance after unsolvable problems. Unpublished manuscript, Dartmouth College, 1980.

Teasdale, J. D. Effects of real and recalled success on learned helplessness and depression. *Journal of Abnormal Psychology,* 1978, *87,* 155–164.

Tennen, H. Depression, learned helplessness and the perception of the causes of success and failure. Unpublished manuscript, State University of New York at Albany, 1980.

Tennen, H., & Eller, S. S. Attributional components of learned helplessness and facilitation. *Journal of Personality and Social Psychology,* 1977, *35,* 265–271.

Thornton, J. W., & Powell, G. D. Immunization to and alleviation of learned helplessness in man. *American Journal of Psychology,* 1974, *87,* 351–367.

Tiggemann, M., & Winefield, A. H. Situation similarity and the generalization of learned helplessness. *Quarterly Journal of Experimental Psychology,* 1978, *30,* 725–735.

Weiner, B. A theory of motivation for some classroom experiences. *Journal of Educational Psychology,* 1979, *71,* 3–25.

Weiner, B., Frieze, C. H., Kukla, A., Reed, L., Rest, S., & Rosenbaum, R. M. *Perceiving the causes of success and failure.* Morristown, N.J.: General Learning Press, 1971.

Weiner, B., & Litman-Adizes, T. An attributional, expectancy-value analysis of learned helplessness and depression. In. J. Garber & M. E. P. Seligman (Eds.), *Human helplessness: Theory and research,* New York: Academic Press, 1980.

Wortman, C. B., Panciera, L., Shusterman, L., Hibscher, J. Attributions of causality and reactions to uncontrollable outcomes. *Journal of Experimental Social Psychology,* 1976, *12,* 301–316.

Chapter 7

Neurochemical Aspects of Stress and Depression: Formulations and Caveats*

HYMIE ANISMAN   *YVON D. LAPIERRE*

Carleton University   Royal Ottawa Hospital
Ottawa, Ontario   Ottawa, Ontario

Introduction

Whether or not stress is a precipitating factor in clinical depression has been a subject of considerable debate. Some researchers have concentrated on the cognitive changes induced by stress and their relationship to depression, whereas others have been concerned primarily with the physiological consequences of stress as the immediate antecedent of depression. This is not to say that all investigators accept a primary role of stress in promoting affective disorders. Akiskal and McKinney (1975) have summarized the three basic positions in this respect.

1. Stress is not a precipitating factor in clinical depression; rather, its role is that of precipitating hospitalization among individuals who are already depressed (Hudgens, Morrison, & Barchha, 1967).

2. Depressed individuals will exhibit increased reactivity to stress. In essence, the stress reaction may be symptomatic of depression but will not itself induce such episodes (Slater & Roth, 1969).

*Contributions of H. A. were supported in part by Grants A9845 and MA 6486 from the Natural Science and Engineering Research Council and from the Medical Research Council.

3. Given a genetic predisposition to the illness, stress will provoke affective disorders (Akiskal & McKinney, 1973; Leff, Roatch, & Bunney, 1970; Paykel, 1973, 1974; Paykel, Myers, & Denielt, 1970).

To these formulations it can be added that:

4. Stress may induce depression in some people, provided that the mechanisms (experiential or organismic) to cope with stress are not available.

5. Stress does not influence all forms of depression in the same way, just as it may not necessarily influence all people in the same manner. Indeed, persons exhibiting a common set of symptoms cannot be assumed to have common underlying physiological deficits or experiential histories.

Given the difficulties of assessing the relationship between stress and depression, it is not particularly surprising to find these discordant views. As indicated by several researchers, analysis of the stress-depression topography may be exceedingly difficult. Among other things, with few exceptions the research approach has been one of a retrospective nature. Accordingly, it is often difficult to discern when the patient's self-report is to be accepted as valid. After all, the depressed person's perception of his/her stress history is colored by his/her current affective state. To be sure, we would not be surprised to learn that an incident ordinarily considered a minor inconvenience would, among depressed patients, be considered a major problem. On the other hand, it has been reported that stressful events may not readily be disclosed by the depressed individual (Goodwin & Bunney, 1973), thus challenging the traditional view that reactive and endogenous forms of depression can be differentiated on the basis of whether a stressful antecedent to depression can be identified. Furthermore, environmental insults that are interpreted as stressful to one person may not be viewed as such by a second person. Therefore, subjective evaluations made by therapists concerning the stress history of the depressed person may have little bearing on the reality of the situation as the patient perceives it. Indeed, in considering stressors that promote depression, it is not sufficient to evaluate only the contribution of major traumas (e.g., family breakdown, death in the family), but rather a series of everyday life events, any one of which may appear rather innocuous, may represent a potent stressor.

The purpose of this chapter is to offer an analysis of the relationship between stress and depression. In so doing, we evaluate current theoretical models of depression based primarily or exclusively on cognitive processes as well as models that emphasize neurochemical factors. Then we describe the neurochemical changes produced by stress, pointing out that several common features exist between stress-induced behavioral-neurochemical changes and the behavioral-biochemical factors associated with depression.

Clinical Depression:
Symptomatology and Characterization

A broad range of symptoms is associated with depression, although it should be understood that considerable interindividual differences occur in this respect. A person's affect may range from a mild downheartedness or indifference to a state of despondency or despair. Sadness per se does not reflect a clinical depression. However, as the sadness becomes more acute, a clinical syndrome may develop, characterized by affective, cognitive, and physiological symptoms (see review in Katz & Hirschfeld, 1978).

Typically, the mood of the depressed person will fluctuate over the course of a day. Although diurnal variations of mood vary between individuals, it is most common for the patient to be most depressed upon awakening, followed by increased spirits as the day progresses. Associated with the depressed mood is a deterioration of cognitive abilities, less effective intellectual functioning, and altered perception of the self and others. The patient often withdraws and develops an ideation characterized by guilt and by thoughts of death and suicide. These become more intense and eventually may progress to a delusional psychotic state.

In some people, motor activity and speech may slow considerably, and the voluntary and vegetative functions may become retarded. Anxiety is a common accompaniment, and this may result in agitated depression. This agitation is related to a motoric phenomenon rather than to an acceleration of psychic processes.

Physical accompaniments of the depressed mood and diminished intellectual functioning are bodily complaints leading to hypochondriasis, a loss of appetite, and subsequent loss in weight. Sleep functions are disturbed and gastrointestinal functions may become retarded. Finally, genitourinary functions become inhibited, resulting in decreased libido and loss of sexual abilities.

Characterization of the depressive syndrome must include genetic, personality, age, and psychodynamic factors. Heredity appears to have a role in the predisposition to depression, although specification of the inherited factors is still a matter of speculation. Some evidence, however, shows that bipolar patients have a higher incidence of genetic predispositions than the unipolar depressives (Murphy, Goodwin, & Bunney, 1972; see review in Winokur, 1978). Moreover, experiments reported by Winokur (1969, 1978) provisionally suggest that the genetic predisposition may take place through the Xga blood system which shares a common locus with color blindness on the short arm of the X chromosome. Gershon (1978) has also suggested that catechol-O-methyl transferase, the enzyme that degrades catecholamines extraneuronally, may prove to be a genetic marker for affective illness.

Although depression is not restricted to any age group, it has been reported that the incidence of depression increases with age (Landoni & Ciompi, 1971). In fact, depression in the older age group has particular characteristics (e.g., anxiety and psychotic features) leading to the diagnostic label of involutional depression. Thus, it is not unlikely that the mechanisms underlying depression in older populations may differ in some respects from the depressions seen in other age groups.

In addition to genetic and organismic factors, we later show that experiential (environmental) factors contribute largely to the incidence of depression. Moreover, it appears likely that these factors interact with personality variables in determining clinical outcome. Because a multiplicity of factors may be associated with affective illnesses, conceptualization of the depressive syndrome should not be restricted to a single model but rather viewed as the result of an interplay of several different factors. Moreover, depression does not necessarily reflect a single physiological process but may best be considered as a consequence of the interplay between several different physiological processes.

Biochemical Correlates of Depression

Biochemically based studies attempting to correlate body chemistry with depression have followed two major lines of research. The initial attempts to relate depression to physiological processes were concerned with hormonal factors. Subsequently, a greater attention centered on the neurochemical correlates of depression.

Hormonal Correlates STEROIDS The involvement of the pituitary-adrenocortical axis in depression has received considerable attention. Interest in this relationship stemmed from the observation that the antidepressant activity of imipramine could be potentiated by the administration of the synthetic steroid, dexamethasone. Subsequent work conducted by Carroll, Curtis, and Mendels (1976a, b) on the role of the neuroendocrine regulation system in depression made extensive use of the dexamethasone suppression test. In particular, it was found that following administration of dexamethasone, escape from the suppressant effects on ACTH and cortisol release occurred earlier in depressed than in nondepressed populations. It appears that hypothalamic-pituitary-adrenal activity is higher among depressed patients, particularly of the endogenous type, because the release from the dexamethasone suppression is most prominent in the endogenous type of depression and is not evident in neurotic depressives.

Plasma corticosterone production among depressed patients has been found to correlate with changes in rating scores on items related to emotional arousal and psychotic disorganization, and with severity of depression (Carroll & Davies, 1970; Davies, Carroll, & Mowbray, 1972; Gibbons, 1964; Sachar et al., 1970). The question of mechanisms subserving adrenal cortical activity in depression were clarified by Carpenter and Bunney (1971) who demonstrated that the central control mechanism continues to function normally in depression, but peripheral production and clearance rates of steroids are increased, thus maintaining a normal 24-hour plasma concentration. These findings may suggest that depression is associated with a hypothalamic dysfunction as well as a peripheral one.

Although the aforementioned studies were conducted with depressed patients once the illness was well established, an interesting prospective investigation was carried out with parents of terminally ill children. In this instance, parents were monitored throughout the terminal phase of their child's illness and during the bereavement period (Hoffer et al., 1972 a, b). Overall, it was found that levels of cortical excretion did not alter substantially with the death of the child. However, in the subpopulation exhibiting the highest adrenal cortical excretion, the degree of active mourning and grief was most pronounced. Moreover, among subjects with low adrenal cortical excretion rates prior to the loss, there was a significant increase with death of the child, whereas among subjects with high baseline levels of steroids, a drop in steroid excretion was evident during bereavement. Taken together, it would appear that change of adrenal cortical activity in reactive depression is highly individualized, and attempts to relate adrenal activity with depression must consider basal activity rates.

HUMAN GROWTH HORMONE Nocturnal release of the growth hormone becomes irregular during depression. This irregularity of growth hormone secretion applies to the depressive syndromes in general, but it is an aid in the distinction between unipolar and bipolar illness. Lower growth hormone secretion was found to occur in unipolar than in bipolar depressives or in normals. Moreover, the growth hormone release was proportional to the severity of the depression (Schildkraut et al., 1975).

SEX HORMONES The introduction of oral contraceptives resulted in early reports of depression associated with their use (Kaye, 1963). The incidence of depression in oral contraceptive users was estimated at 5–7% (Malek-Ahmadi & Behrmann, 1976). However, subsequent to the initial reports concerning the precipitation of depression by oral contraceptives, the increased incidence of depression in users of oral contraceptives became doubtful on the basis of matched and control comparative studies (Fleming & Seager, 1978).

THYROID Thyroid hypofunction may present a clinical syndrome suggestive of depression, and, as such, it must be considered in the differential diagnosis of the latter. The findings of Prange et al. (1969) on the potentiation of the antidepressant activity of imipramine in certain subgroups of depressed females led to further studies of the pituitary-thyroid axis. It was found that central and peripheral mechanisms remained normally responsive during depression, despite a therapeutic benefit derived from hormonal treatments (Whybrow et al., 1972).

Neurochemical Correlates of Depression Several recent reviews have dealt extensively with the potential role of the biogenic amines, norepinephrine and serotonin, in the mediation of affective disorders. Accordingly, we present only a limited review of this literature here and encourage the reader to consult the various reviews and original investigations for more comprehensive analyses of the various hypotheses (see Coppen, 1967; Goodwin & Bunney, 1973; Murphy, Campbell, & Costa, 1978; Post & Goodwin, 1978; Schildkraut, 1970, 1978; Whybrow & Laverty, 1973; van Praag, 1978).

The discovery of effective antidepressants in the late 1950's opened a new field of investigation into the affective disorders. Two main hypotheses based on deficencies of norepinephrine (Schildkraut, 1970, 1975, 1978; Bunney & Davis, 1965) and serotonin (Murphy, Campbell, & Costa, 1978; van Praag, 1974, 1978) were advanced. Subsequent to the formulation of these hypotheses, it was suggested that mania may be associated with increased utilization of central catecholamines (see reviews in Baldessarini, 1975; Bunney, 1975; Bunney & Davis, 1965; Sachar & Coppen, 1975) or that mania was a reflection of receptor supersensitivity resulting from a deficency of catecholamines (Bunney, 1975; Bunney & Murphy, 1975). Still other investigators suggested that acetylcholine might be related to depression (e.g., Janowski et al., 1972).

Although the various hypotheses initially adhered to monistic etiological concepts, it has become increasingly more evident that a "balance" between neurotransmitter systems might be the most appropriate working formulation with which to assess the etiological factors associated with depression. For the purpose of simplicity, we review the evidence supporting each of the hypotheses individually, but the reader should consider that the two positions are not mutually exclusive.

To reiterate, a detailed examination of the adequacies or inadequacies of the various hypotheses is not the major purpose of this chapter, and we provide only a limited review of this literature. In doing so, however, we do introduce the various research strategies that have been used to assess the relationship between brain monoamines and depression.

Serotonin (Indolamine) Hypothesis POSTMORTEM STUDIES Examinations of the brains of suicide victims, although not an extremely reliable source of information on the premorbid functioning of a person, may provide leads for more systematic investigations. Consistent with the hypothesis that serotonin (5-HT) might be related to depression, Shaw, Kemps, and Ecclestone (1967) reported that 5-HT appeared in lower concentrations in the hindbrain of suicide victims relative to a control group of accident or acute illness victims. Subsequently, Pare, Yeung, Price, and Stacey (1969) measured 5-HT, as well as its metabolite, 5-hydroxyindole acetic acid (5-HIAA), among suicide victims. Again, decreased concentration of 5-HT was noted among the suicide victims, but concentrations of 5-HIAA did not differ from controls. Further studies conducted by Bourne, Bunney, Colburn, Davis, Davis, Shaw, and Coppen (1968) and by Beskow, Gottfries, Roos, and Winblad (1976) indicated that the decreased levels of 5-HT were, in fact, accompanied by decreased concentrations of the metabolite, 5-HIAA. Finally, analyses of relatively discrete brain regions revealed that the reduction of 5-HT among depressed suicide victims was localized mainly to the raphe nuclei (Lloyd et al., 1974).

Without question, analysis of postmortem brain tissue must be considered cautiously. Among other things, drugs consumed by the depressed or control subjects may influence monoamine levels. Moreover, there is no certainty that all depressed subjects should have been considered in a unitary fashion, or for that matter, it is not certain that supposedly nondepressed accident victims were, in fact, not depressed. Finally, owing to the rapid degradation of monoamines even after death, the interval between death and tissue extraction must be critically controlled. Despite these caveats, it is significant that a fair degree of consistency has been observed between studies, pointing to a relationship between central 5-HT and depression.

BLOOD STUDIES The platelet has been used as a cellular model for the study of peripheral metabolism of 5-HT (Murphy, 1972). Although decreased accumulation of 5-HT was reported among depressed individuals in some studies, other investigators have observed no such differences (see Murphy et al., 1978, for a review). Furthermore, it does not appear that blood platelet serotonin is correlated with changes of mood or severity of depression (Murphy, 1972).

With respect to monoamine oxidase (MAO), the enzyme that degrades monoamines intraneuronally, it was observed that blood platelet MAO was lower in bipolar patients than in control subjects; differences, however, were not evident between unipolars and controls (Murphy & Costa, 1975; Murphy, Belmaker, & Wyatt, 1974). These data provisionally suggest a differentiation of etiological factors between unipolar and bipolar patients.

URINE STUDIES In general, peripheral indoleamine activity does not appear to be correlated with mood. Specifically, basal excretion of the urinary metabolites of 5-HT and tryptophan were not found to differ between depressed and nondepressed subjects. Moreover, loading with tryptophan and pyridoxine did not significantly alter urinary metabolite excretion relative to control subjects (Fraser, Pandy, & Mendels, 1973).

CEREBROSPINAL FLUID STUDIES Cerebrospinal fluid (CSF) is typically obtained from the lumbar spinal region. An estimate of 5-HT is derived by measuring its principal metabolite, 5-HIAA. However, because serotonergic nerve endings occur in the brain and the spinal cord, 5-HIAA is of mixed spinal and cerebral origin. To some extent, the mixed sources for 5-HT and 5-HIAA are probably responsible for the equivocal results obtained in the initial attempts to assess indoleamine activity in CSF. That is, some authors reported a slight or nonsignificant decrease in 5-HIAA production (Bowers, Heninger, & Gerbode, 1969; Papeschi & McLure, 1971), whereas others found no decrease at all (Goodwin & Post, 1974). A second factor which may have contributed to the variable results obtained concerns the heterogeneity of the depressive groups examined. Indeed, when the depressions were restricted to the so-called vital type, a lower CSF concentration of 5-HIAA was observed (van Praag & Korf, 1971b).

In order to decrease the variation contributed by the mixed spinal and cerebral 5-HT, the probenicid technique was introduced. The administration of probenicid inhibits the active transport of 5-HIAA from the central nervous system (CNS). Thus, the adulteration of the metabolite is largely prevented, and the metabolite production over a unit of time (as opposed to metabolite present at any given point in time) can be estimated. That is to say, because 5-HIAA concentrations increase linearly for several hours after probenicid treatment, the accumulation of 5-HIAA can be viewed as an indicant of the synthesis and utilization rates of the parent amine. Thus, lowered accumulation of 5-HIAA indicates a functional or absolute deficiency of 5-HT neuronal activity (see van Praag, 1978, for a more detailed description of the procedures and rationale).

Using the probenicid technique, several investigators indicated decreased accumulation of 5-HIAA in vital depressions (Bowers, 1969; van Praag, Korf, & Puite, 1973). The decreased accumulation was more pronounced in a bipolar than a unipolar group (van Praag, 1969; Roos & Sjostrom, 1969; see Murphy et al., 1978, and van Praag, 1978, for reviews). Further, van Praag and Korf (1971) also reported a bimodal distribution with respect to 5-HIAA accumulation, with only 40% of depressives exhibiting values below the expected range of variation of control subjects. Thus, two distinct groups, homogeneous in psychopathological terms but heterogeneous biochemically, may exist.

As in the case of postmortem analyses, determination of CSF monoamine metabolites is not without problems, even when the probenicid technique is employed. For instance, the probenicid treatment may have a stressful component to it by virtue of the fact that it may induce nausea and also requires that subjects remain immobile for several hours prior to the spinal tap (to avoid influences of motor activity on amine metabolites). This, of course, may alter neurochemical activity. Second, substantial within- and between-day variation of 5-HT activity can be expected among both depressed and control subjects, making longtitudinal analyses of 5-HIAA more informative, perhaps, than a single determination. Third, the possibility should be considered that the so-called control population may have neurological deficits that could potentially influence monoamine activity. Finally, as indicated by van Praag and Korf (1971b), several distinct populations of depressives showing similar behavioral profiles but differing biochemically may exist. Accordingly, observation of large within-group variance should not be surprising. It is comforting that, despite these caveats, the CSF data have yielded results relatively consistent with those derived from postmortem determinations. However, we should underscore that these findings do not suggest a causal relationship between monoamine levels but simply serve to indicate that a correlation exists between monoamines and depression.

THERAPEUTICS The most powerful evidence in favor of a causal role of monoamines in depression is gleaned from the finding that pharmacological treatments that influence 5-HT activity may also influence the symptoms of depression.[1] The first tricyclic antidepressant, imipramine, was demonstrated to have effects on central monoamines (including serotonin, norepinephrine, and dopamine). The more specific 5-HT reuptake inhibitor, chlorimipramine, was also found to have antidepressant activity, although it should be mentioned that this compound also has effects on catecholamines (Bertilsson, Asberg, & Thorun, 1974; and see Sulser, 1978). Chlorimipramine has a somewhat different profile than imipramine. Indeed, the therapeutic efficacy of antidepressants varies between individuals, suggesting that each drug has a preferential therapeutic action for different types of depression (see Kupfer & Detre, 1978).

PRECURSOR STUDIES The rationale for precursor studies is that if depression is associated with a relative or absolute deficiency of monoamines at the postsynaptic receptor sites, then increasing the concentration of the amine by precursor loading should promote recovery from the depression. This is not an absolute prerequisite for justification of the hypothesis because the deficiency may reflect receptor deficits rather than levels of the amine per se, but, if observed, it would lend veracity to a neurochemically based hypothesis.

Tryptophan and 5-hydroxytryptophan (5-HTP) are precursors of serotonin and are administered to depressed patients alone or in combination with MAO inhibitors.

---

[1]In considering pharmacological therapies of depression, as well as other psychological disturbances, it should be emphasized that alleviation of symptoms does not imply effects on etiological mechanisms. Thus, a drug treatment could eliminate or reduce a subset of symptoms (e.g., dealing with motoric or vegetative functions) but leave unchanged the depressed mood or intellectual functioning.

The findings with tryptophan alone are equivocal. While Coppen, Shaw, Hersberg, and Maggs (1967) found tryptophan to be a potent antidepressive, other investigators were not able to substantiate these results (Dunner & Goodwin, 1972; Bunney, Murphy, & Goodwin, 1970). With respect to 5-HTP, this substance might be expected to be more effective than tryptophan as an antidepressive because it is nearly totally converted to serotonin. The reports on the effects of 5-HTP were variable, but they did indicate that in a subgroup of unipolar depressives this drug is beneficial as an antidepressive (Takahashi, Condo, & Keto, 1975; van Praag et al., 1972). Furthermore, the effectiveness of 5-HTP as an antidepressive has been shown when administered in combination with chlorimipramine (van Praag, 1978b; van Praag et al., 1972; Walinder et al., 1975).

Catecholamine Hypothesis: Norepinephrine As indicated earlier, the catecholamine hypothesis as proposed by Schildkraut deals primarily with the involvement of norepinephrine as a biological substrate of depression. To reiterate briefly, it was assumed that depression is related to a functional or absolute decline of brain norepinephrine. However, as recently indicated by Schildkraut (1978), this does not exclude the possibility of other neurotransmitters being involved in depression.

POSTMORTEM STUDIES Relatively few studies are available where brain concentrations of norepinephrine (NE) were determined among suicidal victims of depression. However, it has been reported that concentrations of norepinephrine in hindbrain and hypothalamus did not differ between depressed suicides and controls (Bourne et al., 1968; Pare et al., 1969). On the other hand, Birkmayer and Riederer (1975) found that among depressives who died from causes other than suicide, levels of NE and 5-HT were lower than in a control population. Thus, it seems that a role of NE in depression, based on postmortem analyses, must be considered, at best, as highly provisional.

METABOLITES IN BLOOD AND URINE Consistent with the catecholamine hypothesis of depression, studies where patients served as their own controls during and after depressive illness indicated that renal excretion of norepinephrine and its metabolite, normetanephrine, were decreased during the depressive period (Greenspan et al., 1969; Bunney & Davis, 1965). Normetanephrine reflects not only CNS activity but also peripheral NE activity. Thus, these data offer only very provisional support for a catecholamine hypothesis. The principal norepinephrine metabolite of the CNS is 3-methoxy-4-hydroxy phenylglycol (MHPG). Inasmuch as 50% of urinary MHPG originates from the brain, it may be regarded as an indicant of central norepinephrine activity, albeit it too is contaminated by peripheral catecholamine activity (Maas et al., 1973). Low excretion rates of MHPG are taken to indicate relatively slow release of central NE, whereas a high excretion rate suggests relatively high rates of NE utilization.

Although decreased MHPG is not evident in all depressives, several reports are available suggesting that decreased MHPG occurs in some forms of depression. While Fawcett, Maas, and Dekermenjian (1972) reported lower MHPG levels among depressed than nondepressed people, other investigators found that MHPG excretion was lower among manic-depressives than in characterological depressions

(Schildkraut, 1974; Schildkraut et al., 1973; see also Beckman, St. Laurent, & Goodwin, 1975). Similarly, Maas, Dekermenjian, and Jones (1973) reported that bipolar patients were more apt to have low MHPG excretion rates than other types of depressives.

As predicted by the catecholamine hypothesis, it has been reported that MHPG excretion rates are higher among manic than among depressed individuals, although contradictory data are available in this respect (see Bond, Jenner, & Sampson, 1972; Bunney, Goodwin, & Murphy, 1972; Greenspan et al., 1970; Jones, Maas, & Dekermenjian, 1973). Finally, it is of heuristic and practical import to note that the efficacy of drug treatments vary among patients exhibiting high versus low MHPG excretion rates. Whereas patients with high MHPG excretion rates respond favorably to amitryptaline, those patients exhibiting low MHPG excretion rates are more positively influenced by imipramine and desmethylimipramine (Beckman & Goodwin, 1975; Maas, Fawcett, & Dekermenjian, 1972; Schildkraut, 1972).

CEREBROSPINAL FLUID STUDIES Determination of MHPG concentrations in CSF have yielded inconsistent results. Although some investigators reported decreased concentrations of the NE metabolite among depressed patients (Gordon & Oliver, 1971; Post et al., 1973), other investigators found no such effect (Shopsin et al., 1972). Interestingly, however, Shopsin et al. did report that MHPG concentrations were higher in manic than in control subjects and that these concentrations approached control values with alleviation of the mania following lithium treatment.

TYROSINE The data concerning the norepinephrine precursor, tyrosine, has not provided compelling evidence in favor of the catecholamine hypothesis. However, it has been demonstrated that in a subgroup of depressives an elevation of tyrosine that exceeds control values occurs in plasma following oral administration of the compound. These data suggest slower production of norepinephrine from the precursor substance in this subgroup of depressives (Takahashi et al., 1968).

CATECHOL-O-METHYL-TRANSFERASE (COMT) COMT plays an important role in the extraneuronal degradation of norepinephrine and other catecholamines, and this might indicate the relationship between catecholamine activity and depression. It has been found that COMT is reduced by about 50% in women with unipolar depression, and to a lesser degree among women with bipolar depression (Cohn, Dunner, & Axelrod, 1970; Dunner et al., 1971). More recently, enzyme activity was found to be increased in agitated depressives and decreased in retarded depressives (Shulman, Griffith, & Diewold, 1978). The fact that the COMT changes in depression occur exclusively among women suggest either that activity of this enzyme is only a correlate of depression or that the mechanisms underlying depression in women differ from those subserving depression in men.

MONOAMINE OXIDASE (MAO) Monoamine oxidase is a complex of enzymes which are involved in the intraneuronal degradation of catecholamines as well as serotonin. MAO activity has been assessed in brains of suicide victims and in plasma of depressed patients. In both instances, however, the data derived are not conclusive. It has been reported that MAO activity was reduced by 20–40% among suicide victims relative to a comparable group that died of causes other than suicide (Gottfries, Oreland, & Wibeig, 1975). Unfortunately, it was not clear whether the suicides occurred in an exclusively depressed population, thus limiting the conclusions that can be drawn.

With respect to plasma MAO activity, values exceeding normal were reported among some women with severe endogenous depression (Klaiber et al., 1972). The elevation of MAO activity was normalized by administration of conjugated estrogens in high doses. In contrast to these results, in other studies (e.g., Murphy & Weiss, 1972) a 50% decrease of MAO activity was evident in bipolar depression. These results were corrected to account for the normally expected increase of central and peripheral MAO activity that occurs with increasing age (Robinson et al., 1972).

CYCLIC AMP Norepinephrine crosses the synaptic cleft and activates adenylate cyclase, an enzyme present in the postsynaptic cell membrane. This enzyme activates cyclic AMP, the so-called second messenger, which produces the physiological response in the second neuron. In depression, because of a deficiency of monoamines, we would expect to find lower concentrations of cyclic AMP. Consistent with this prediction, urinary collection of cyclic AMP indicated decreased values in depressives and increased values among manic patients (Sinanam et al., 1975). Subsequent studies, however, indicate that the role of urinary cyclic AMP in depression is of dubious significance because of the ambiguity as to whether it is primarily derived as a result of motor activity or as a result of the depressed affect (Sebens & Korf, 1975).

Dopamine Dopamine (DA), like norepinephrine, is a central neurotransmitter in addition to being a precursor to norepinephrine. The study of this amine in depression has been considerably less extensive than that of norepinephrine. This may have arisen in part because of the fact that dopamine has been most closely aligned with motor activity rather than affective states (see Kelly, 1978; Iversen, 1978, for reviews). However, with the recent contentions that dopamine may be involved in processes subserving reward (reinforcement), it would not be surprising to find renewed interest in this transmitter in the analysis of depression (see Wise, 1978).

POSTMORTEM STUDIES As in the case of norepinephrine, the data concerning dopamine levels in postmortem analyses have been inconsistent. In studies involving depressed patients that had committed suicide, dopamine levels were not found to differ from a control population (Moses & Robins, 1975; Pare et al., 1969). However, among depressed patients who died from causes other than suicide, reduced dopamine levels were reported (Birkmayer & Riederer, 1975).

CEREBROSPINAL FLUID STUDIES The majority of studies have revealed decreased concentrations of the DA metabolite homovanillic acid (HVA), in lumbar CSF of depressed individuals, suggesting a decrease of dopamine utilization (Bowers, Heninger, & Gerbodi, 1969; Brodie, Sack, & Siviver, 1975; McLure, 1973; Mendels et al., 1972; Nordin, Ottosson, & Roos, 1971; Paeschi & McLure, 1972). These lowered lumbar HVA concentrations were more pronounced in retarded depressives than in nonretarded forms of depression, which, in turn, were lower than in a control group. The latter two groups did not consistently differ from one another significantly (Mendels et al., 1972). It has also been reported that HVA concentrations were lower in unipolar than bipolar depressives (Ashcroft et al., 1973; van Praag & Korf, 1975), although contradictory reports are available in this respect (Paeschi & McLure, 1971). Furthermore, the degree of HVA reduction was not found to correlate with severity of depression. Indeed, some evidence suggests that motor activity promotes the higher HVA concentrations in lumbar CSF by quasimechanical means (Goodwin & Post, 1975; Post et al., 1973; Sachar & Coppen, 1975).

The probenicid technique permits an evaluation of dopamine turnover by assessing the accumulation of HVA in the CSF. In vital depression, principally of the unipolar variety, decreased HVA has been observed, indicating decreased cerebral turnover of dopamine (van Praag & Korf, 1971). The occurrence of decreased HVA concentration was accompanied by a state of motor retardation. Administration of L-DOPA which normalized HVA concentrations was not accompanied by reductions of depression, but it did largely eliminate the retarded motor activity associated with the affective illness (van Praag, 1974).

PRECURSOR AND THERAPEUTIC STUDIES Attempts at treatment of depression with high and low doses of L-DOPA have not been found to alleviate depression. As we just indicated, such treatments produced only a normalization of motor activity (Weiss et al., 1974). These results again suggest that the role of dopamine is restricted to the retarded depressions where motor disturbances are evident. Data suggesting otherwise, however, have been forthcoming from studies using nomifensin, a nontricyclic antidepressant that acts as a central dopamine agonist. Nomifensin was found to have superior therapeutic effects to chlorimipramine in patients with a subnormal response to probenicid before treatment (van Scheijn, van Praag, & Korf, 1977). Thus, dopamine may influence depression of a nonretarded variety in a restricted subpopulation of depressives. Whether or not a therapeutic effect is obtained through drug treatments is dependent on the particular compound employed.

Acetylcholine The direct measurement of acetylcholine is extremely difficult. Moreover, its primary metabolite, choline, also acts as its precursor (along with a coenzyme), thus adding confusion to studies involving measurement of acetylcholine metabolic products. The activity of acetylcholine, however, can be estimated by indirectly inhibiting acetylcholine esterase, the enzyme that degrades acetylcholine, by treatment with physostigmine (Janowski et al., 1972). The administration of this compound resulted in changes of mood in the direction of depression, although manic bouts could be elicted as well. Inasmuch as acetylcholine and catecholamines may act in a balanced fashion, these data support the contention that some forms of depression may reflect the interaction of different neurotransmitters, including acetylcholine.

Depression and Prior Stress History

Stress as an Antecedent of Depression Without question, it is exceedingly difficult to assess experimentally the relationship between stress and depression. Because human subjects cannot be stressed within an experimental setting, at least not to the extent that the stress induces depression, a limited number of approaches are open. The first approach is the retrospective evaluation of stress among depressed and non-depressed people. As we have said, this approach is burdened with experimental problems, and the data that are derived must be scrupulously evaluated. (For an analysis focusing on assumptions and methodological strategies, see Costello, pp. 93–124, this volume.) A second approach is that of awaiting natural catastrophes in which a high incidence of depression might be expected. Understandably, in many of these instances one can expect less than full cooperation from subjects. A third method involves the evaluation of individuals in clinical settings to determine whether a given stress will induce depression at a rate above that expected in the general population (e.g., among subjects entering hospital for elective surgery). This approach, of course, suffers because of the numerous uncontrolled variables that may be encountered (e.g., age factors, prior surgical history, nature of the surgery, nature of the illness prompting the surgery, personality variables associated with the people who seek the surgery, as in the case of cosmetic surgery). Finally, one could attempt to simulate depression by invoking stress in a laboratory situation. It is dubious, however, whether the behaviors seen in such instances actually reflect naturally occurring depressions. Despite the problems associated with each of these approaches, some studies have evaluated stress and its relationship to depression under well-controlled conditions. While these experiments must be carefully scrutinized (and the reader is advised to consult the original sources), it seems that they have enjoyed some degree of success.

Before reviewing the stress-depression literature several additional caveats must be introduced. We have said that the effectiveness of a stressor may vary among individuals. Indeed, a given stressor (e.g., divorce) which may represent a traumatic stress to one individual may prove to be a blessing to a second individual. So, if stress is defined in a narrow context, it should not be surprising to find only a limited relationship with depression.

SEPARATION STRESS Several studies have evaluated the incidence of separation in depressed populations relative to that observed in other clinical populations or to the population at large. The incidence of separation prior to hospitalization has been observed to be greater than that seen in nondepressed hospital populations (Sethi, 1964) or the general population (see Paykel, 1973). Likewise, the incidence of separation was greater among suicide attempters than among nonsuicidal psychiatric patients (Levi et al., 1966). Clayton, Halikas, and Maurice (1972) found that 35% of bereaved persons (the bereaved population being 109) exhibited depressive symptoms within 1 month of separation. In contrast to these reports, however, other investigators failed to find a relationship between stress of separation and subsequent depression (Forrest, Fraser, & Priest, 1965; Hudgens et al., 1967). Moreover, Hudgens, Robins, and deLong (1970) questioned the validity of self-disclosure of stress experiences because disagreement exists between patient information concerning a stressor and that provided by an informant.

Several comments of a general nature concerning separation and depression should be added. First, it is important to define the nature of the separation specifically. In this respect, Briscoe and Smith (1975) found that the symptomatology of hospitalized unipolar depressives were not entirely congruent. That is, although their samples were all diagnosed as unipolar depressives, the bereaved subjects seemed to form a group that was distinguishable from the remaining subjects. They exhibited fewer prior episodes of depression and fewer first-degree relatives suffering either depression or some other psychiatric disorder. Of primary importance is the fact that the divorced and the bereaved people both suffered different types of symptoms. One cannot be entirely sure of the source of these differences, but, as we later see, factors such as control over stress and feelings of guilt may have contributed. At any rate, these data suggest questions about whether separation can be considered in a unitary fashion.

To summarize thus far, some evidence suggests that stress in the form of separation may be aligned with depression. However, it should be borne in mind that separation alone does not lead to depression in most people. Accordingly, other factors must be considered in determining the affective response to separation. Furthermore, in some proportion of cases, particularly those in which separation does not involve death of a close relation (e.g., divorce), the depression may provoke separation rather than separation provoking depression.

The effects of stress, such as separation, of course, also affect syndromes other than depression. It has been shown by Holmes and Rahe and their associates (Holmes & Rahe, 1967; Holmes & Masuda, 1973, 1974; Rahe, 1968, 1974; Rahe & Paasikivi, 1971) that stress is associated with several illnesses of a physiological and psychological nature, including cardiac arrest and inguinal hernia among many others. Moreover, evidence derived from human and animal work has shown that stress may promote the development and growth of transplanted tumors as well as carcinogen-induced tumors (see Sklar & Anisman, 1979, and the review by Fox, 1978). As such, it is probably incorrect to assume that the effect of stress on depression (assuming it represents one point on a continuum of physiological illnesses) is due solely to the cognitive effects of stress (e.g., guilt).

LIFE STRESS OTHER THAN SEPARATION Inasmuch as separation appears to be one of the most severe life stresses (Holmes & Rahe, 1967; Rahe, 1968), it is not surprising that it is among the most effective stimuli in eliciting depression. By no means, however, is this form of stress unique in its capacity to promote affective illnesses. Indeed, several of the studies that reported separation to be associated with depression also indicated that other life stresses preceded hospitalization (these stresses included social isolation, interpersonal discord, illness in the family, personal illness, and departure from a dwelling) (Forrest et al., 1965; Paykel, 1973, 1974; Paykel et al., 1969). Again, it is not certain to what extent these stressors precipitated the depression or were consequences of the depression. It has been shown, however, that certain types of stress (e.g., those involving "exits," such as the death of a relative or a child leaving home) were more predictive of depression than stress involving "entrances," (e.g., a new person in the household, marriage [Paykel, 1974; Paykel, Prusoff, & Uhlenhuth, 1971]).

In a retrospective analysis of factors related to depression, Leff, Roatch, and Bunney (1970) found that depression was preceded by an average of four major life-stress events. Moreover, the apparent precipitating factors in an endogenous and nonendogenous group of depressives could not be differentiated from one another, thus supporting the contentions made by Goodwin and Bunney (1973) concerning the similarities between the two forms of depression. Using a factor analysis in which the ratings of depression (conducted by an independent rater) were made blind as to life-stress events, Paykel, Prusoff, and Klerman (1971) also found some degree of relationship between life-stress events and depression. The problems inherent in retrospective studies notwithstanding, when these results are coupled with other data reported by Paykel and his associates (Paykel, 1973, 1974; Paykel et al., 1969, 1971), a strong case for an association between stress and depression appears.

Sensitization to Stress Despite the data indicating that stress may be a precipitating factor for depression, Paykel (1973, 1974) has indicated that it would be naive to assume that depression would occur simply as a result of exposure to traumatic stress. Personality variables, genetic predisposition, and prior stress history could be expected to influence the depressionogenic effects of an acute stress (Akiskal & McKinney, 1973, 1974), and, indeed, data are available that support such a contention. With respect to prior stress history, some evidence indicates that early life trauma may sensitize the individual to stress of a similar nature (see Akiskal & McKinney, 1975; Heinicke, 1973, for reviews; see also Beck, Sethi, & Tuthill, 1963; Dennehy, 1966; Heinicke, 1973; Hill, 1969; Greer, 1964; Munro, 1966).

Broad-scale Stress A number of investigators have made use of the life-stress scale developed by Holmes and Rahe (1967). This procedure assigns numerical values to a series of 43 life events which require "social readjustment." On this scale, "death of a spouse" is scored as 100, "divorce" as 73, and other stresses such as "trouble with boss" and "minor violation of the law" receive scores of 23 and 11, respectively. The severity of life stress is categorized as mild (150–199 points), moderate (220–299 points), and severe (300+ points). Implicit in this scaling procedure is the assumption that the effectiveness of life-stress events are dependent on the number and nature of the stress. In effect, the life stress of "marriage separation," "trouble with boss," and "minor violation of the law" are equal to "death of spouse."

This procedure is, at first blush, less than compelling! Certainly, in terms of life stress it is unreasonable to assume that this equation is valid. Nevertheless, it is equally unlikely that depression would only be expected after a single traumatic event. Rather, given a sufficiently great number of stressors of less severity, one might expect depressive episodes to occur. However, the symptomatology that might be expected in these instances might differ in several respects.

Paykel et al. (1969) have, in fact, observed that certain types of stress events are most likely to precede depressive episodes. These can be broadly classified into three groupings: marital difficulties, including increased arguments or separation; deaths and illnesses; and work changes. Furthermore, these investigators found that the incidence of depression was not necessarily related to the extent of life change or readjustment but was rather more closely aligned to the assumed undesirability of life events. To our knowledge, experiments have not compared directly the influence of a single traumatic event to the effect of multiple undesirable events of lesser magnitude. Using a cluster-analysis technique, Paykel (1971) was able to define four main groupings of depressed persons—psychotic, anxious, hostile, and young depressive with personality disorder. The stress score was found to be lowest in the anxious group of depressives, suggesting that perhaps the incidence of major traumas was fewer in this category. The data presentation does not allow for a re-analysis of the relationship between stress type and depressive symptomatology. It would prove interesting, however, if the depressive symptomatology could be classified in terms of the nature of the life-stress events encountered. As we see in ensuing sections, recent theoretical models of depression have concentrated less on the severity of the stress per se and more on the attribution of the stress experience together with expectation of subsequent outcomes.

Most of the experiments described thus far have considered stress in terms of the "social readjustment" following a given experience or set of experiences. Modifications of this approach have appeared insofar as the role of "exits" and "entrances" differentially influence depression despite their similarity or difference on a scale of social readjustment. More recently, further modifications of this scaling procedure have been offered, with particular reference not only to the social readjustment required but also to the pleasantness-unpleasantness of a given experience (Lewinsohn & Amenson, 1978). The unpleasantness of an event, rather than the social readjustment per se, has been shown to be the better discriminator of depression. A similar finding was obtained by Vinokur and Selzer (1975) in evaluating the desirability or undesirability of life events. These findings by no means provide major difficulties for the life-stress events schedule proposed by Holmes and Rahe. Rather, they simply add to the discriminability and precision of the Holmes and Rahe procedure.

Stress, Cognitive Changes, and Depression

Although traumatic stress seems to play a prominent role in the induction of the depressive symptomatology among some individuals, recent formulations of the depressive syndrome have paid increasingly greater attention to the role of coping processes in determining the consequences of stress. That is, when faced with aversive stimuli, the organism attempts in some way to cope with these stimuli. The extent of the perceived stress may reflect not so much the quality or quantity of applied stress as the organism's ability to limit the impact of the stress effectively. Thus, depression might ensue when the organism becomes aware that it cannot eliminate the aversive stimulation.

Several theoretical models of depressions have considered coping factors as critical in determining the effects of stress. Bibring (1953), for instance, postulated that depression resulted when the ego became cognizant of its helplessness to achieve its aspirations. Similarly, Schmale (1973) has indicated that depression may be a consequence of helplessness and hopelessness (the former refers to the belief that aid from others is not forthcoming; the latter refers to the belief that attempts to modify environmental events must invariably meet with failure). A formulation of this type brings to bear an important characteristic to the stress-depression concept, namely, that stress might be best considered in terms of aspirations, or expectancies, and the individual's ability to meet these aspirations.

Beck (1967) offered a formal proposition, encompassing and extending the stress-depression models. According to his formulation, depression is associated with a cognitive triad of negative conceptions concerning the person's own adequacy. That is, the person has a negative perception of self, negative views of past experiences, and negative expectations of the future. Not only have there been and do there remain insurmountable barriers to achieving certain goals, but the person is also pessimistic of future improvements.

A position not unlike that proposed by Beck was postulated by Seligman and his associates (Abramson, Seligman, & Teasdale, 1978; Miller, Seligman, & Kurlander, 1975; see also Miller & Seligman, pp. 149–178, this volume). According to this hypothesis, cognitive changes, based on previous stress experiences, are the primary sources for the negative perceptions and affect that characterize the depressed person. That is, experience with uncontrollable events, or events perceived as uncontrollable, results in learning that one is "helpless" in determining one's own destiny. These negative perceptions come to engender the depressed symptomatology.

The helplessness formulation as described by Seligman has undergone considerable modification since its initial inception (see Abramson et al., 1978; Miller & Seligman, pp. 149–178, this volume). These variations of the hypothesis are thought to account for individual differences in response to uncontrollable stress as well as the time course for individual variations in the time course for depression. As Miller and Seligman indicate in Chapter 6, helplessness is not simply considered a consequence of failure, it results from a person's attributions of failure and subsequent expectations concerning performance.

It is not our intent to make a critical evaluation of the helplessness hypothesis. Several investigators have provided in-depth criticisms of the helplessness hypothesis, and the reader should consult these reviews (Costello, 1978; Depue & Monroe, 1978; Wortman & Dintzer, 1978).[2] It should be added, however, that the helplessness hypothesis, like other cognitive-learning formulations, has not dealt with several issues pertinent to an understanding of depression. First, such formulations have not considered the neurochemical consequences of stress and their similarity to neurochemical correlates of depression (see Anisman, 1978; Anisman & Sklar, 1979; Weiss, Glazer, & Pohorecky, 1976). Similarly, the helplessness position does not address itself to the therapeutic success achieved by pharmacological treatments. Finally, in a more general context, reports relating cognitive deficits and helplessness have consistently ignored the fact that symptom and etiology are not one and the same. The empirical investigations of depression have shown that feelings of helplessness and hopelessness are associated with the affective illness. That is, these factors are *symptoms* of depression. Yet, the helplessness hypothesis assumes that these negative perceptions are *causative* (etiological) factors for depression. There is, in fact, little reason to believe that the depressive syndrome derives from these cognitive factors. It is equally, or more likely either that the helplessness and hopelessness are products of the depression or that perhaps these cognitive factors exacerbate depression once present.

In agreement with cognitive interpretations, it is our contention that stress may be a precipitating factor of depression. Moreover, factors such as expectancy and attribution of failure, as well as numerous other organismic and environmental factors, may determine the way in which stress influences a person. However, in light of the proliferation of evidence implicating a role for neurochemical mechanisms in subserving depression, it is appropriate to consider the relationship between stress and depression in the context of neurochemical processes. The ensuing section provides the reader with a brief survey of the literature pertaining to the conditions under which stress provokes amine changes and their nature. We then integrate the stress-neurochemistry and depression-neurochemistry literature, with the aim of clarifying the role of stress in precipitating and augmenting clinical depression.

Stress-Induced Neurochemical Changes

Effects of Acutely Applied Stress within a Perspective of Adaptation Processes When faced with a stressor, the organism will probably take a course of action in order to diminish or eliminate the severity of the stress. The organism may attempt to remove itself from the vicinity of the stressor or to remove the stressor from its vicinity. Concurrently, we might expect several physiological changes which would aid the organism in meeting environmental demands. Among other things, stress of moderate severity has been shown to result in an increase in the synthesis and utili-

[2]*Editor's note:* In addition to S. Miller and M. E. P. Seligman's account of the reformulated helplessness model in this volume, the reader may wish to consult M. E. P. Seligman's comments on several points of criticism: Seligman, M. E. P., Comment and integration. *Journal of Abnormal Psychology,* 1978, *87,* 165–179.

zation of brain neurotransmitters, to enhance secretion of pituitary hormones, and to influence immune functioning.

It has been reported that moderate stress results in an increase in synthesis of NE, DA, and 5-HT. If the stress is sufficiently severe, depletion of NE will occur in several brain regions, including the brainstem, hypothalamus, hippocampus, and frontal cortical region (see Anisman, 1978; Stone, 1975; Weiss, Glazer, & Pohorecky, 1976, for reviews). Such effects have been reported following a variety of stressors and have been reported in several infrahuman species (see Anisman 1978; Stone, 1975). The duration of the depletion varies as a function of the severity of the stress, although depletions of only a few hours are most common (e.g., Maynert & Levi, 1964; Barchas & Freedman, 1963). It has been suggested that during severe stress the rate of amine utilization increases greatly and will eventually exceed its synthesis, ultimately resulting in the depletion (Welch & Welch, 1970).

The hypothesis that stress results in increased NE utilization has derived support from several different types of analyses. For example, the reduction of NE induced by inhibiting catecholamine synthesis (through tyrosine hydroxylase inhibition) is accentuated by stressors such as footshock and restraint (Corrodi, Fux, & Hokfelt, 1968; Korf, Aghajanian, & Roth, 1973a, b). Indeed, such an effect is noted even when the stress itself does not produce the amine depletion (e.g., Korf, 1976). A second source of evidence descends from experiments showing that metabolites of NE (e.g., normetanephrine and MHPG) are increased by stress exposure (Stolk, Conner, Levine & Barchas, 1974; Stone, 1975b). Finally, it has been demonstrated that stress increased the disappearance of exogenously administered ^{3}H-NE (Thierry, 1973; Thierry et al., 1968; Thierry, Blanc, & Glowinski, 1970, 1971).

As in the case of utilization, stress has been shown to increase NE synthesis. For example, it has been shown that footshock or restraint will increase ^{3}H-NE formed from the precursors ^{3}H-tyrosine or ^{3}H-DA (Huszti & Kenessey, 1976; Thierry, 1973; Thierry et al., 1968, 1970, 1971). Likewise, cold stress was shown to increase ^{14}C-NE synthesized from ^{14}C-tyrosine (Gordon et al., 1966). It is interesting in this respect, that both moderate and severe stress resulted in depletion of exogenously administered ^{3}H-NE or ^{3}H-NE newly formed from ^{3}H-tyrosine. However, only the intense stress resulted in the disappearance of previously stored ^{3}H-NE (Thierry et al., 1970, 1971). Given this, it has been suggested that moderate stress results in the release of NE from the functional storage pools, whereas severe stress results in NE release from both the functional and main storage pools.

The neurochemical changes promoted by stress are not restricted to NE. It has been shown that activity of 5-HT neurons are influenced by various forms of stress. As in the case of NE, stress will augment the 5-HT depletion following inhibition of tryptophan hydroxylase (see Thierry, 1973). Moreover, levels of 5-hydroxyindoleacetic acid, the metabolite of 5-HT, are increased after stress exposure (Bliss, Thatcher, & Ailion, 1972; Ladisch, 1974). Not unexpectedly, stress also increases the rate at which ^{3}H-5-HT disappears (Thierry, 1973; Thierry et al., 1968a, b). In contrast to effects on NE neurons, the increased disappearance rate of the labeled transmitter is increased after severe stress but is unaffected by moderate intensity stress. In effect, although stress increased the utilization of 5-HT, the stress severity necessary to provoke such an effect was greater than that which elicited increased NE utilization.

With respect to the effects of stress on DA neuronal activity, the available data are less decisive. For example, areas rich in DA (e.g., substantia nigra) do not appear to be greatly affected by stress (e.g., Thierry et al., 1976). Moreover, the effects of stress on DA levels after administration of a tyrosine hydroxylase inhibitor are contradictory (see Brown, Snider, & Carlson, 1974; Otto & Paalzow, 1975). Finally, although stress will increase ^{3}H-DA formed from ^{3}H-tyrosine, this increase may reflect DA activity within NE neurons (see Thierry et al., 1968a, b). In contrast to these reports, however, a different picture emerges when assays are performed on discrete brain regions, such as the arcuate nucleus of the hypothalamus or the nucleus accumbens. Specifically, stress will increase DA turnover in the nucleus accumbens (Thierry et al., 1976) and will result in depletion of DA in the arcuate nucleus (Kobayashi et al., 1976). Inasmuch as the arcuate nucleus comprises only a small portion of the hypothalamus, it is not particularly surprising that analyses of the entire hypothalamus reveal no such effect. This point is emphasized by the fact that some hypothalamic nuclei show increased DA levels after stress exposure.

Finally, turning to the effects of stress on levels of ACh, there exists a relative paucity of published data. Nevertheless, the few studies that have been published have indicated that stress increases levels of this transmitter (e.g., Karczmar, Scudder, & Richardson, 1973; Saito et al., 1976) or produce an initial decline of ACh followed by an increase in levels (Zajaczkowska, 1975). The increase of ACh levels is apparent approximately 40 minutes after termination of the stress session. Given the long delay in the occurrence of the ACh increase, it is difficult to say whether the change reflects a direct effect of stress on ACh neuron activity or a secondary (compensatory) reaction to the monoamine changes evoked by the stress.

Coping with Stress and Neurochemical Change Whether or not stress will result in depletion of brain NE is dependent on several experiential and organismic variables. Of particular interest is the finding that control over stress is a primary determinant for the NE depletion after stress exposure. In a particularly intriguing series of experiments, Weiss and his associates (Weiss, Stone, & Harrell, 1970; Weiss et al., 1975; Weiss, Glazer, & Pohorecky, 1976) observed that exposure to escapable footshock resulted in an increase of NE in several brain regions. However, an identical amount of shock, applied in a yoked paradigm, resulted in a depletion of brain NE. Anisman, Pizzino, and Sklar (1980) have similarly found that NE depletion varies as a function of the organism's ability to control shock offset (see Figure 7-4). Weiss et al. (1976) suggested that the effects of stress and failure to cope with stress on brain NE were not due to motoric factors associated with the shock treatment. Specifically, NE depletion was not evident regardless of whether shock could be terminated by active responses or passive responses. Depletion of NE, however, occurred in rats that received yoked inescapable shock. It seems that the animal's

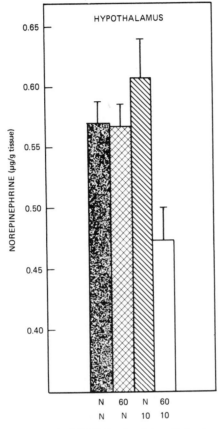

Fig. 7-1. Mean (± S.E.M) levels of hypothalamic norepinephrine among mice exposed to no shock treatment (stippled bar), 60 shocks of 150 μA followed by no treatment 24-hr later (cross-hatched bar), 10 inescapable shocks prior to decapitation (hatched bar), or 60 shocks followed 24-hr later by exposure to 10 shocks (white bar). Note that the stress reexposure resulted in norepinephrine depletion although the effects of 60 shocks were absent 24-hr after the initial stress session, and 10 shocks alone did not influence levels of the amine. (Modified from Anisman & Sklar, 1979.)

ability to cope with stress was the primary determinant for the stress-induced amine changes.

Interesting data congruent with these results have been reported by Stolk et al. (1974). These investigators found that the NE changes provoked by stress were absent if rats were allowed to fight with one another during shock exposure. Moreover, the extent of the NE changes and of the metabolites of NE was related to the number of fighting bouts the animals engaged in. Although it is not certain, it is likely that fighting acted as a coping response, thereby modifying the nature of the neurochemical changes.

Two independent views can be formulated to account for the differential effects of escapable and inescapable shock. We have seen that amine depletion occurs after inescapable shock because utilization exceeds synthesis of the amine. Thus, one assumption might be that utilization will only exceed synthesis once animals have learned that they are unable to influence shock offset (i.e., when animals learn that they are helpless). The other view might hold that stress ordinarily results in increased synthesis and utilization of amines. Under conditions of sufficiently severe stress, the utilization will exceed the synthesis of amines. That is, the burden of coping with environmental insults is initially placed on physiological processes. If the animal finds some behavioral means of coping with stress (e.g., escape or fight), then the burden of coping is not fully placed on the physiological system and hence utilization rates decrease. The difference between the two views, of course, is that the former attributes the depletion to cognitive abilities on the part of the organism (i.e., "I am helpless"); the latter view assumes that the differences between inescapable and escapable treatments is not so much that one set of animals learns that it is helpless, but that the other group learns that it has some method of coping with stress.

Irrespective of the mechanism involved, it appears fairly certain that control over stress is critically important in determining whether or not an amine depletion will occur. Anisman, Pizzino, and Sklar (1980) indicated that prior exposure to controllable shock influences the changes of NE levels that occur upon subsequent exposure to uncontrollable shock. Specifically, as seen in Figure 7-3, exposing mice to 60 inescapable shocks (6-sec duration, 150A) results in NE depletion in the hypothalamus, as well as in the hippocampus and cortex. Amine depletion in the hippocampus and cortex was prevented by exposing the mice to 30 escapable shocks 24 hours earlier. In effect, exposure to controllable shock "immunizes" animals against NE depletion, just as it immunizes against performance deficits (see Maier & Seligman, 1976).

Whether or not the effects of stress on the activity of DA neurons is determined by coping factors remains to be determined. In light of the few studies evaluating stress effects on DA in discrete hypothalamic nuclei, it is not surprising to find that coping processes have not yet been evaluated in this respect.

In the case of ACh, no single experiment has been conducted with the express purpose of evaluating the role of coping factors in determining changes influenced by stress. Nevertheless, there are some indications that coping processes largely influence the nature of ACh changes that occur. For example, Karczmar et al. (1973) reported increased levels of ACh after inescapable shock, whereas no such increase was evident after escapable shock. Because the experiments were not conducted to evaluate the role of coping factors specifically, the amount of shock the animals received was not identical in the two conditions, and these data must be interpreted cautiously. Saito et al. (1976) observed that NE and ACh levels were not markedly affected following avoidance training. However, after cold water immersion NE was reduced and levels of ACh increased. Again, it is not possible to discern to what extent coping was primarily responsible for the effects observed; however, these data provide preliminary evidence to suggest the importance of control-

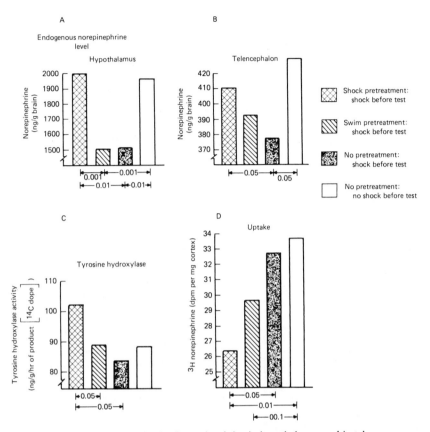

Fig. 7-2. Mean levels of norepinephrine in hypothalamus and in telencephalon, tyrosine hydroxylase activity, and rate of norepinephrine uptake among rats given an acute stress session (stippled bars), the acute stress preceded by 14 successive inescapable shock sessions (cross-hatched bars), the acute stress preceded by 14 successive sessions of swim stress (hatched bars), or no stress (white bars). Note that levels of NE are not depleted among rats that received the chronic shock reexposure treatment. In addition, tyrosine hydroxylase activity is increased and NE reuptake rate is reduced. (From Weiss et al., 1975.)

ability in modulating neurochemical activity. Finally, Aprison et al. (1968) and Aprison and Hingtgen (1970) reported that a decline of performance in a Sidman avoidance task was accompanied by increased levels of brain ACh. Of course, it can be argued that the ACh change precedes the performance deterioration. Nevertheless, these data again suggest a relationship between ACh levels and the organism's ability to cope with stress.

Stress Reexposure and Neurochemical Changes The neurochemical changes induced by stress have been shown to vary as a function of the organism's prior stress history. Specifically, it has been shown that if animals had previously been exposed to stress, the extent of the neurochemical changes observed upon stress reexposure are magnified. Keim and Sigg (1976) demonstrated that stress applied over 5 successive days resulted in increasingly greater depletions of brain NE. Interestingly, the levels of NE, in independent groups determined prior to the successive stress session, became increasingly greater immediately prior to stress application. In effect, 24 hours after stress, exposure levels of NE exceed control values but decline very dramatically upon stress inception. In the same fashion, Anisman and Sklar (1979) reported that footshock (60 shocks at 150 μA at 1-min intervals) stress will reduce hypothalamic NE by about 25%. Within 24 hours, levels of NE may be

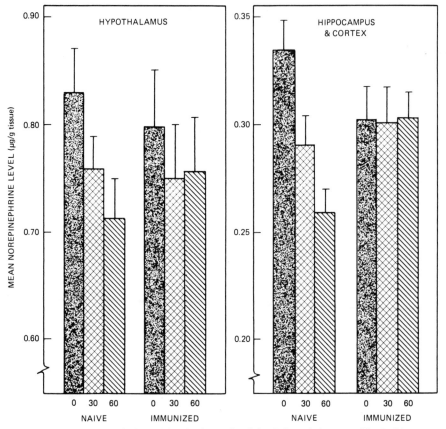

Fig. 7-3. Mean ($\pm$ S.E.M) levels of norepinephrine in hypothalamus and in the hippocampus and cortex as a function of prior escape training (naive versus immunized) and inescapable shock treatment (0, 30, or 60 shocks of 150 μA, 6 sec duration). (From Anisman, Pizzino, & Sklar, 1980.)

slightly elevated. However, if mice are reexposed to even a moderate amount of stress (10 shocks at 150 μA), which itself is ineffective in modifying NE, a profound depletion of the amine is observed (see Figure 7-1). More recently, Cassens, Kuruc, Orsulak, and Schildkraut (1979) found that a CS previously paired with shock would, upon subsequent presentation, increase NE utilization (as measured by increased MHPG levels). Finally, with respect to ACh changes, Hingtgen et al. (1976) found that a CS paired with shock in a CER paradigm subsequently came to produce increases of ACh levels. Similar effects of the CS on NE, DA, and 5-HT were not evident.

Regardless of whether the NE and ACh changes are due to conditioning or sensitization, it is of practical importance to recognize that stress effects on neurotransmitter activity, although transient, may have long-term repercussions, given that the organism is reexposed to a stressor or a cue that had been paired with an aversive stimulus. This not only applies to the recent finding that stress may influence the response to drug treatments even after very long intervals following stress exposure (Antelman et al., 1978), but also to the possibility that relatively innocuous stresses may have very profound effects at relatively long intervals following an initial stress experience, thereby influencing affective states.

Neurochemical Changes After Chronic Stress Exposure Although a single stress session may result in a pronounced depletion of brain NE, Weiss et al. (1976) reported that the depletion was absent if rats had previously been exposed to the stress over 15 successive days. As seen in Figure 7-2, the reuptake of NE was reduced in the chronic-stress group, and in addition, the activity of tyrosine hydroxylase was increased. Thierry et al. (1968b) similarly observed increased turnover of NE after repeated stress, and this effect persisted for at least 24 hours after the termination of the last stress experience. Adaptation to stress will not only occur when repeated stress is used, but also when animals are exposed to a single protracted stress session. Thus, Kvetnansky et al. (1976) found that a single session of restraint stress that lasted 20–60 minutes produced a reduction of brain NE. However, after 180 minutes of restraint stress, the depletion was not evident. Moreover, tyrosine hydroxylase activity and dopamine-β-hydroxylase activity were increased after the long stress session. The adaptation effect has been reported to occur to a variety of different stressors, including noise and flashing lights (Huttunen, 1971; Pare & Livingston, 1970; Buckley, 1973).

To summarize, it seems that after chronic stress several adaptive changes occur in order to meet environmental demands. Not only is utilization reduced, but, in addition, synthesis of the amine is increased. Once released, the amine remains in the synaptic cleft for longer periods, assuring increased effectiveness.

Organismic Variables It is well known that factors such as housing condition will have profound effects on neurochemical activity, as well as on response to drug treatments (see Brain, 1975, for a review). Following isolation, the excitability of the animal is increased and the incidence of fighting is greatly augmented. Several inves-

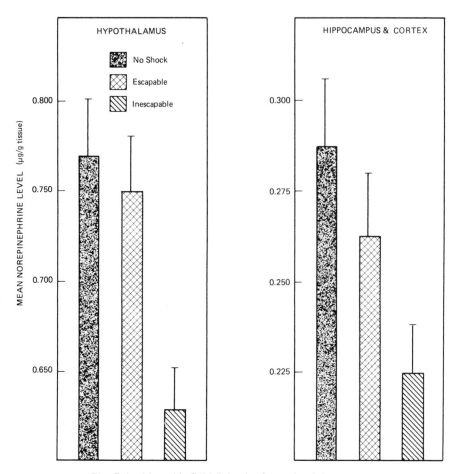

Fig. 7-4. Mean (± S.E.M) levels of norepinephrine in hypothalamus and in the hippocampus and cortex among mice exposed to 60 escapable shocks (150 μA, 6.2 sec average duration), yoked inescapable shock, or no shock. (From Anisman, Pizzino, & Sklar, 1980.)

tigators have observed that the depletion of NE after tyrosine hydroxylase inhibition is decreased among mice housed in isolation (e.g., Modigh, 1976; Welch & Welch, 1970), suggesting reduced turnover of the amine. Interestingly, after stress exposure that ordinarily increases NE levels, the depletion ordinarily induced by tyrosine hydroxylase inhibition is slightly antagonized among group-housed mice. In contrast, among isolated mice the drug-induced depletion is exaggerated (Welch & Welch, 1970). It seems that experiential factors may influence the organism's ability to deal effectively with stressors by modifying the basal rate of amine synthesis and metabolism.

In addition to experiential variables, data reported by Ritter & Pelzer (1978) revealed that turnover of NE is dependent on the age of the animal. That is, stress results in more pronounced NE depletion among senescent rats than among mature adults. Moreover, the amine depletion induced by stress persists for a considerably longer duration among the older animals. It appears that the ability of the organism to cope will be dependent on the age of the animal. With decreased synthesis and utilization of NE among older animals, stress more readily provoked depletion of NE, thus encouraging failure in a task that may reflect the coping abilities of the animals.

Finally, in discussing the effects of stress on neurochemical activity it is important to consider the effects noted across different strains of animals within a species. It is known that strain differences occur in levels and turnover of various neurotransmitters (Ebel et al., 1973; Eleftheriou, 1974; Tunnicliff et al., 1973) and their associated enzymes (Ciaranello et al., 1972; Ebel et al., 1973). Moreover, it has been shown that housing conditions will differentially influence NE turnover among different strains of mice (Goldberg et al., 1973). Several investigators have also reported that the stress effects on uptake of catecholamines will vary between different strains of mice (Hendley et al., 1973; Moisset et al., 1975) and rats (Ray & Barrett, 1975).

Stress as an Antecedent of Depression: A Reformulation

Although we have discounted the role of cognitive factors in the precipitation of depression, we have not dismissed them. To be sure, cognitive factors may enter into the depressive symptomatology. For instance, in the already depressed person feelings of helplessness and hopelessness may serve to sustain the illness and even to increase the depth of depression. Indeed, even if one were to make a strong argument in favor of a neurochemically based explanation of helplessness, one could not dismiss the possibility that cognitive processes serve to enhance the neurochemical changes (see Post & Goodwin, 1973). Indeed, the position could be entertained that the neurochemical changes are a direct result of the cognitive factors, rather than the cognitive changes following from neurochemical variations.

In accepting a causal relationship between stress and depression, several factors must be recognized from the outset. Some of these have been mentioned earlier, but they warrant repetition. There is no reason to believe that all persons will react to stress in a similar fashion. Thus, a stressor that is viewed in a particular manner by one person may be viewed entirely differently by another. Moreover, whether or not the stress is one with negative consequences may depend on a variety of factors, including genetic, experiential, and organismic ones. Finally, given that stress produces a variety of neurochemical changes, and, further, that individuals are differentially sensitive to drugs that affect different neurotransmitter systems, it might be expected that stress will influence affective states through a variety of different mechanisms.

The relationship between stress and depression, as we view it, stems from the literature concerning the neurochemical concomitants of stress and the presumed association between depression and neurochemical events. As we have said, depression is assumed to be related to both depletion of brain norepinephrine and/or serotonin, and, in addition, some evidence suggests the involvement of acetylcholine. There is no reason to believe that any one of these exclusively mediates the depressive symptomatology. Rather, these neurotransmitters may act in combination in the induction of the depressive state. The particular transmitter(s) involved will presumably also contribute to the nature of the symptoms displayed by the person. Moreover, the choice of treatment should reflect the nature of the neurochemical mechanisms underlying the depression.

In considering the role of stress in producing the affective state, it will be recalled that uncontrollable stress may result in the depletion of brain NE, DA, and 5-HT and produce an increase of ACh. It follows, then, that given a sufficiently traumatic stress these neurochemical events may lead to the depressive symptomatology. Inasmuch as DA is affected by stress, and this transmitter has been implicated in motoric functioning, it is not unreasonable to assume that retarded forms of depression may be related to depletion of this transmitter. Indeed, this hypothesis is buoyed by the fact that L-DOPA influences this form of depression, at least insofar as it reduces the retarded motor responding associated with the affective state.[3]

Given the vast individual differences in response to stress, it must be considered that a variety of experiential and personality factors should be related to our definition of stress and coping. As such, the formulations of Abramson et al. (1978) may apply to the stress-depression axis. That is, among people who believe that control over stress is not possible, the probability of neurochemical depletion is increased. Furthermore, the generalizability of these expectancies will determine whether the neurochemical changes are restricted to particular situations or whether they will occur across a broad range of events (expectancies associated with failure are being defined here as a stress). If the attribution derived from the expectancy is that the person is responsible for failure (the "personal helplessness" of Abramson et al.), then one might expect associated guilt feelings. These cognitive factors could represent a stress, which could exacerbate the neurochemical changes, which could promote the depression. In effect, to a limited extent we agree with some of the postulations of Seligman and of Abramson (see also Miller & Seligman, pp. 149–178, this

---

[3]It is interesting that the behavioral deficits introduced by inescapable shock are eliminated by L-DOPA (see Anisman & Sklar, 1979; Anisman et al., 1979). In light of the limited effectiveness of L-DOPA in the treatment of depression, these data challenge the contention that the "helplessness effect" among infrahuman animals is an adequate model of depression.

volume). Our proposition and theirs differ in the main over whether attributions and expectancies directly influence the affective state or whether these cognitive factors provoke neurochemical changes, which in turn precipitate the depression.

The two positions assume similar stress-depression relationships in some situations but not in others. First, the neurochemical view assumes pharmacological treatments to be an effective aid in alleviating or reducing depression. This does not mean that this treatment alone will suffice; certainly, the source for the neurochemical changes (i.e., the stress) must be eliminated before total remission will be forthcoming. In contrast to this view, the cognitive hypotheses assume that the most effective treatment would be one that modifies the individual's control over life events. To be sure, we do not exclude this as a treatment for depression. However, by treating first the neurochemical pathology, the individual may be more receptive to the behavioral-cognitive type of treatment.

A second difference between the two views stems from the fact that the neurochemical hypothesis assumes that the effects of stress are not only dependent on personality characteristics but also evolve from the endogenous neurochemical state of the organism. In a sense, depression is viewed as an illness, just as most other physical maladies. That is, the depression reflects inabilities or deficiencies of a physical system. Thus, two individuals with similar personality characteristics and similar stress histories may display different affective states if it is assumed that the neurochemical system of one person is better able to adapt or to accommodate the environmental insults. In this respect, the deficit in one person may reflect norepinephrine activity; in a second, 5-HT activity; and in yet a third, a combination of both.

This discussion has been concerned primarily with the effect of a single acute stress. An additional set of factors must be considered when chronic stress is applied to the individual. Chronic stress not only refers to the repeated application of stress, but also to a single protracted stress (e.g., a loved one dying or a protracted business failure). The animal literature indicates that the NE depletion which occurs after acute stress is not apparent after repeated stress or after a single stress session of long duration. It appears that adaptive mechanisms, in the form of increased enzyme activity and blocked reuptake, assure that amine levels will be available in sufficient concentrations to deal with the stress. However, the possibility cannot be ignored that just as different strains of mice might be differentially susceptible to the depletion, strains might also differ with respect to the ability of accommodating with chronic stress. Extending this logic to the human model, the difference between the short-lived depression and the depression that lingers might be a reflection of the organism's ability to adapt to the environmental insults through neurochemical compensation. This notion, of course, is purely speculative. However, if correct, it adds another dimension to the factors that must be considered in assessing the stress-depression topography.

Finally, the organism's stress history may determine the nature and extent of neurochemical changes, and, hence, the depth of depression induced by stress exposure. The animal literature has indicated that if animals are exposed to stress, subsequent reexposure may induce very rapid and pronounced depletions of norepinephrine. With respect to the human model, the possibility exists that if the organism is exposed to traumatic stress, reintroduction to stress, even a fairly innocuous one, may promote NE depletion and may elicit the depressive symptomatology. It is not clear at this time whether the reexposure effects of stress in rats and mice occur only under conditions where the two stresses are the same, or whether the effect will occur across divergent types of stress. If the latter holds true, the possibility should be entertained that the initial stress results in sensitization of mechanisms responsible for the NE depletion, or that cognitive factors associated with a stress experience subsequently come to act as a stimulus for the NE depletion. At present, limited data exist concerning the effects of stress exposure on subsequent stress reactions in humans, at least with reference to depression. As we have said, there is some evidence that early separation may be associated with increased affective illness in later life. Whether this is a direct result of the early stress or an effect due to stress exposure in adulthood is not clear.

Concluding Remarks

We have argued that neurochemical factors may be one important mechanism that underlies depressive illness. Furthermore, in some individuals these neurochemical changes may be invoked by stress. Whether or not stress results in depression depends not only on stress severity but also on the organism's ability to cope with the stress. In this respect, personal attributions as well as individual characteristics may determine whether or not subsequent depression will occur. Similarly, the effectiveness of stress in producing a given neurochemical change will depend largely on the adaptability of neuronal systems activated by stress. Moreover, the organism's ability to cope with stress determines whether neurochemical changes will occur. In addition, prior stress experiences may augment the neurochemical changes ordinarily produced by a given stress experience.

References

Abramson, L. Y., Seligman, M. E. P., & Teasdale, J. D. Learned helplessness in humans: Critique and reformulation. *Journal of Abnormal Psychology*, 1978, *87*, 49–74.

Akiskal, H. S., & McKinney, W. T. Depressive disorders: Toward a unified hypothesis. *Science*, 1973, *183*, 20–29

Akiskal, H. S., & McKinney, W. T. Overview of recent research in depression. Integration of ten conceptual models into a comprehensive clinical frame. *Archives of General Psychology*, 1975, *32*, 285–305.

Anisman, H. Neurochemical changes elicited by stress: Behavioral correlates. In H. Anisman & G. Bignami (Eds.), *Psychopharmacology of aversively motivated behavior*. New York: Plenum, 1978.

Anisman, H., & Sklar, L. S. Catecholamine depletion upon reexposure to stress: mediation of the escape deficits produced by inescapable shock. *Journal of Comparative and Psychological Psychology,* 1979, *93,* 610–625.

Anisman, H., deCatanzaro, D., & Remington, G. Escape performance following exposure to inescapable shock: Deficits in motor response maintenance. *Journal of Experimental Psychology: Animal Behavior Processes,* 1978, *4,* 197–218.

Anisman, H., Remington, G., & Sklar, L. S. Effects of inescapable shock on subsequent escape performance: Catecholaminergic and cholinergic mediation of response initiation and maintenance. *Psychopharmacology,* 1979, *61,* 107–124.

Anisman, H., Pizzino, A., & Sklar, L. S. Coping with stress, norepinephrine depletion and escape performance. *Brain Research,* 1980, in press.

Anisman, H., Grimmer, L., Irwin, J., Remington, G., & Sklar, L. S. Escape performance after inescapable shock in selectively bred lines of mice: Response maintenance and catecholamine activity. *Journal of Comparative and Physiological Psychology,* 1979, *93,* 229–241.

Antelman, S. M., & Caggiula, A. R. Norepinephrine-dopamine interactions and behavior. *Science,* 1977, *195,* 646–652.

Antelman, S. M., Eichler, A. J., Black, C. A., & McCloskey, G. Long lasting influence of stress on the behavioral effects of amphetamine and haloperidol. *Society for the Neurosciences,* 1978, *4,* 485. (Abstract)

Aprison, M. H., & Hingtgen, J. N. Evidence of a central cholinergic mechanism functioning during drug-induced excitation in avoidance behavior. In E. Heilbronn & A. Winter (Eds.), *Drugs and Cholinergic Mechanisms in the CNS.* Stockholm: Forsvarets Forsckning-sanstalt, 1970.

Aprison, M. H., Kariya, T., Hingtgen, J. N., & Toru, M. Neurochemical correlates of behavior: Changes in acetylcholine, norepinephrine and 5-hydroxytryptamine concentrations in several discrete brain areas of the rat during behavioral excitation. *Journal of Neurochemistry,* 1968, *15,* 1131–1139.

Ashcroft, G. W., Blackburn, I. M., Eccelston, D., Glen, A. I. M., Hartley, W., Kinlock, N. E., Lonergen, M., Murray, L. G., & Pullar, I. A. Changes on recovery in the concentrations of tryptophan and the biogenic amine metabolites in the cerebrospinal fluid of patients with affective illness. *Physiological Medicine,* 1973, *3,* 319–325.

Baldessarini, R. J. The basis for amine hypotheses in affective disorders. *Archives of General Psychiatry,* 1975, *32,* 1087–1093.

Barchas, J. D., & Freedman, D. X. Brain amines: response to physiological stress. *Biochemical Pharmacology,* 1963, *12,* 1232–1235.

Beck, A. *Depression: Clinical, experimental and theoretical aspects.* New York: Harper & Row, 1967.

Beck, A., Sethi, B., & Tuthill, R. Childhood bereavement and adult depression. *Archives of General Psychiatry,* 1963, *9,* 295–302.

Beckmann, H., & Goodwin, F. K. Antidepressant response to tricyclics and urinary MHPG in unipolar patients. *Archives of General Psychiatry,* 1975, *32,* 17–21.

Beckmann, H., St. Laurent, J., & Goodwin, F. K. The effect of lithium on urinary MHPG in unipolar and bipolar depressed patients. *Psychopharmacologia,* 1975, *42,* 277–282.

Bertillson, L., Asberg, M., & Thorun, P. Differential effect of clomipramine and nortriptyline on metabolites of serotonin and noradrenaline in the cerebro-spinal fluid of depressed patients. *European Journal of Clinical Pharmacology,* 1974, *7,* 365–368.

Beskow, J., Gottfries, C. G., Roos, B. E., & Winoblad, B. Determination of monoamine and monoamine metabolites in the human brain: postmortem studies in a group of suicides and in a control group. *Acta Psychiatrica Scandinavica,* 1976, *53,* 7–20.

Bibring, E. The mechanism of depression. In P. Greenacre (Ed.), *Affective disorders.* New York: International Universities Press, 1965.

Birkmayer, W., & Riederer, P. Biochemical post-mortem findings in depressed patients. *Journal of Neuronal Transmission.* 1975, *37,* 95-109.

Bliss, E. L., Thatcher, W., & Ailion, J. Relationship of stress to brain serotonin and 5-hydroxymdole-acetic acid. *Journal of Psychiatric Research*, 1972, *9*, 71–80.

Bond, P. A., Jenner, F. A., and Sampson, G. A. Daily variations of the urine content of 3-methoxy-4-hydroxyphenylglycol in two manic-depressive patients. *Psychological Medicine*, 1972, *2*, 81–85.

Bourne, H. R., Bunney, W. E., Colburn, R. W., Davis, J. M., Davis, N. J., Shaw, D. M., & Coppen, A. J. Noradrenaline, 5-hydroxytryptamine and 5-hydroxyindoleacetriacid in hindbrain of suicidal patients. *Lancet*, 1968, *2*, 805–808.

Bowers, M. B., Jr., Heninger, G. R., & Gerbode, F. Cerebral spinal fluid 5-hydroxyindoleaceticacid and homovanillic acid in psychiatric patients. *International Journal of Neuropharmacology*, 1969, *8*, 255–262.

Brain, P. What does individual housing mean to a mouse? *Life Sciences*, 1975, *16*, 187–200.

Briscoe, C. W., & Smith, J. B. Depression in bereavement and divorce. *Archives of General Psychiatry*, 1975, *32*, 439–443.

Brown, R. M., Snider, S. R., Carlsson, A. Changes in biogenic amine synthesis and turnover induced by hypoxia and/or foot shock stress. II. The central nervous system. *Journal of Neural Transmission*, 1974, *35*, 293–305.

Buckley, J. P. Biochemical and physiological effects of intermittent neurogenic stress. In S. Nemeth (Ed.), *Hormones, metabolism and stress*. Bratislava: Publishing house of the Slovak Academy of Sciences, 1973.

Bunney, W. E. Current status of research in catecholamine theories of affective disorders. *Psychopharmacology Communications*, 1975, *1*, 599–610.

Bunney, W. E., Jr., & Davis, G. M. Norepinephrine in depressive reactions: A review. *Archives of General Psychiatry*, 1965, *13*, 483–494.

Bunney, W. E., Jr., Goodwin, F. K., & Murphy, D. L. The "switch process" in manic-depressive illness. III. Theoretical implications. *Archives of General Psychiatry*, 1972, *27*, 312–317.

Bunney, W. E., Jr., Murphy, D. L., & Goodwin, F. K. The switch process from depression to mania: Relationship to drugs which alter brain amines. *Lancet*, 1970, *1*, 1022–1027.

Carpenter, W. T., & Bunney, W. E. Adrenal cortical activity in depressive illness. *American Journal of Psychiatry*, 1971, *128*, 31–40.

Carroll, B., & Davies, B. Clinical associations of 11-hydroxycorticoid suppression and non-suppression in severe depressive illnesses., *British Medical Journal*, 1970, *1*, 789.

Carroll, B. J., Curtis, G. C., & Mendels, J. Neuroendocrine regulation in depression 1: Limbic system adrenal cortical dysfunction. *Archives of General Psychiatry*, 1976, *33*, 1039–1044.

Carroll, B. J., Curtis, G. C., & Mendels, J. Neuroendocrine regulation in depression. 2: Discrimination of depressed from nondepressed patients. *Archives of General Psychiatry*, 1976, *33*, 1051–1057.

Cassens, G., Kuruc, A., Orsulak, P. J., & Schildkraut, J. J. Conditioning of stress-induced alternations of norepinephrine metabolism in rat brain: Studies in progress. Paper presented at 9th Annual Meeting of Society for Neuroscience, Atlanta, Georgia, 1979.

Ciaranello, R. D., Barchas, R., Kessler, S., & Barchas, J. D. Catecholamines: Strain differences in biosynthetic enzyme activity in mice. *Life Sciences*, 1972, *11*, 565–577.

Clayton, P., Halikas, J., & Maurice, W. The depression of widowhood. *British Journal of Psychiatry*, 1972, *120*, 71–77.

Cohn, C. K., Dunner, D. L., & Axelrod, J. Reduced catechol-O-methyl-transferase activity in the red blood cells of women with primary affective disorder. *Science*, 1970, *170*, 1232–1324.

Coppen, A., Shaw, D., Hersberg, B., & Maggs, R. Tryptophan in the treatment of depression. *Lancet*, 1967, *2*, 1178–1180.

Corrodi, H., Fuxe, K., & Hokfelt, T. The effect of immobilization stress on the activity of central monoamine neurons. *Life Science*, 1968, *7*, 107–112.

Costello, C. G. A critical review of Seligman's laboratory experiments on learned helplessness and depression in humans. *Journal of Abnormal Psychology*, 1978, *87*, 21–31.

Davies, B., Carroll, B. J., & Mowbray, R. M. *Depressive illness: Some research studies*. Springfield, Ill.: Charles C Thomas, 1972.

Dennehy, C. Childhood bereavement and psychiatric illness. *British Journal of Psychiatry*, 1966, *112*, 1049–1069.

Depue, R. A., & Monroe, S. M. The unipolar-bipolar distinction in the depressive disorders. *Psychological Bulletin*, 1978, *85*, 1001–1029.

Dunner, D. L., & Goodwin, F. K. Effect of 1-tryptophan on brain serotonin metabolism in depressed patients. *Archives of General Psychiatry*, 1972, *26*, 364–366.

Dunner, D. L., Cohn, C. K., Gershon, E. S., & Goodwin, F. K. Differential catechol-O-methyl-transferase activity in unipolar and bipolar affective illness. *Archives of General Psychiatry*, 1971, *25*, 348–353.

Ebel, A., Hermetet, J. C., & Mandel, P. Comparative study of acetylcholinesterase and choline acetyltransferase enzyme activity in brain of DBA and C57 mice. *Nature, New Biology*, 1973, *242*, 56–57.

Eleftheriou, B. E. Genetic analysis of hypothalamic retention of [3H] corticosterone in two inbred strains of mice. *Brain Research*, 1974, *69*, 77–82.

Fawcett, J., Maas, J. W., & Dekirmenjian, H. Depression and MHPG excretion. *Archives of General Psychiatry*, 1972, *26*, 246–251.

Fleming, O., & Seagor, J. P. Incidence of depressive symptoms in users of oral contraceptives. *British Journal of Psychiatry*, 1978, *132*, 431–440.

Forrest, A. D., Fraser, R. H., & Priest, R. G. Environmental factors in depressive illness. *British Journal of Psychiatry*, 1965, *111*, 243–253.

Fox, B. H. Premorbid psychological factors as related to cancer incidence. *Journal of Behavioral Medicine*, 1978, *1*, 45–133.

Fraser, A., Pandy, G. N., & Mendels, J. Metabolism tryptophan in depressive disease. *Archives of General Psychiatry*, 1973, *29*, 528–535.

Gershon, E. S. The search for genetic markers in affective disorders. In M. A. Lipton, A. DiMascio, & K. F. Killam (Eds.), *Psychopharmacology: A generation of progress*, New York: Raven Press, 1978.

Gibbons, J. L. Cortisol secretion note in depressive illness. *Archives of General Psychiatry*, 1964, *10*, 572–575.

Goldberg, M. E., Insalaco, J. R., Hefner, M. A., & Salama, A. I. Effect of prolonged isolation on learning, biogenicfemine turnover and aggressive behaviour in three strains of mice. *Neuropharmacology*, 1973, *12*, 1049–1058.

Goodwin, F. K. & Bunney, W. E. Psychobiological aspects of stress and affective illness. In J. P. Scott & E. C. Senay (Eds.), *Separation and depression: Clinical and research aspects*, Washington: AAAS, 1973.

Goodwin, F., & Bunney, W. E., Jr. A psychobiological approach to affective illness. *Psychiatric Annals*, 1973, *3*, 19–53.

Goodwin, F. K., & Post, R. M. Cerebro-spinal fluid amine metabolites in affective illness. *Journal of Psychiatric Research*, 1974, *10*, 320.

Goodwin, F. K., & Post, R. M. Cerebrospinal fluid amine metabolites in effective illness and schizophrenia: clinical and pharmacological studies. *Psychopharmacology Communications*, 1975, *1*, 641–653.

Gordon, E. K., & Oliver, J. 3-Methoxy-4-hydroxyphenylethylene glycol in human cerebrospinal fluid. *Clinical Chim Acta*, 1971, *35*, 145–150.

Gordon, R., Spector, S., Sjoerdsma, A., & Udenfriend, S. Increased synthesis of norepinephrine and epinephrine in the intact rat during exercise and exposure to cold. *Journal of Pharmacology and Experimental Therapeutics*, 1966, *153*(3), 440–447.

Gottfries, C. G., Oreland, D. L., & Wibeig, A. Brain levels on monoamine oxidase in depression. *Lancet*, 1975, *2*, 360.

Greenspan, K., Schildkraut, J. J., Gordon, E. K., Levy, B., & Durell, J. Catecholamine metabolism in affective disorders. II. Norepinephrine, normetanephrine, epinephrine, metanephrine and UMA excretion in hypomanic patients. *Archives of General Psychiatry*, 1969, *21*, 710–716.

Greenspan, K., Schildkraut, J. J., Gordon, E. K., Baer, L., Aranoff, M. S., & Durell, J. Catecholamine metabolism in affective disorders. III. MHPG and other catecholamine metabolites in patients treated with lithium carbonate. *Journal of Psychiatric Research*, 1970, *7*, 171–183.

Greer, S. The relationship between parental loss and attempted suicide: A control study. *British Journal of Psychiatry*, 1964, *110*, 698–705.

Gregory, I. Studies of parental deprivation in psychiatric patients. *American Journal of Psychiatry*, 1958, *115*, 432–442.

Heinicke, C. Parental deprivation in early childhood. In J. Scotland & E. Senay (Eds.), *Separation and depression: Clinical and research aspects*, Washington: AAAS, 1973.

Hendley, E. D., Moisset, B., & Welch, B. C. Catecholamine uptake in cerebral cortex: Adaptive change induced by fighting. *Science*, 1973, *180*, 1050–1052.

Hill, O. The association of childhood bereavement with suicidal attempt in depressive illness. *British Journal of Psychiatry*, 1969, *115*, 301–304.

Hingtgen, J. N., Smith, J. E., Shea, P. A., Aprison, M. H., & Gaff, T. M. Cholinergic changes during conditioned suppression in rats. *Science*, 1976, *193*, 332–334.

Hoffer, M. A., Wolfe, C. T., Friedman, S. B., & Mason, J. W. Bereavement, part I. 17 hydro-corticosteroid excretion rates of parents following death of their children from leukemia. *Psychosomatic Medicine*, 1972, *34*, 481–491.

Hoffer, M. A., Wolfe, C. T., Freedman, S. B., & Mason, J. W. Bereavement, part 2: Observation on the process of mourning in relation to adrenocortical function. *Psychosomatic Medicine*, 1972, *34*, 492–504.

Holmes, T. S., & Holmes, T. H. Short-term intrusions into the life style routine. *Journal of Psychosomatic Research*, 1970, *14*, 121–132.

Holmes, T. H., & Masuda, M. Life change and illness susceptibility. In B. S. Dohrenwend & B. P. Dohrenwend (Eds.), *Stressful life events: Their nature and effects*. New York: Wiley, 1974.

Holmes, T. H., & Rahe, R. H. The social readjustment scale. *Journal of Psychosomatic Research*, 1967, *11*, 213–218.

Holmes, T. H., & Masuda, M. Life change and illness susceptibility In J. P. Scott & E. C. Senay (Eds.), *Separation and depression: Clinical and research aspects*. Washington: AAAS, 1973.

Hudgens, R. W. Personal catastrophe and depression. In B. S. Dohrenwend & B. P. Dohrenwend (Eds.), *Stressful Life Events: Their Nature and Effects*. New York: Wiley, 1974.

Hudgens, R., Morrison, J., & Barchha, R. Life events and onset of primary effective disorders. *Archives of General Psychiatry*, 1976, *16*, 134–145.

Hudgens, R. W., Robins, E., & Delong, W. B. The reporting of recent stress in the lives of psychiatric patients. *British Journal of Psychiatry*, 1970, *117*, 635–643.

Huszti, Z. & Kenessey, A. ^{3}H-tyrosine incorporation into proteins and catecholamines in immobilized rats. In E. Usdin, R. Kvetnansky, & I. J. Kopin (Eds.), *Catecholamine and stress*. New York: Pergamon Press, 1976.

Huttunen, M. O. Persistent alteration of turnover of brain noradrenaline in the offspring of rats subjected to stress during pregnancy. *Nature*, 1971, *230*, 53–55.

Iversen, S. D. Brain dopamine systems and behavior. In L. L. Iversen, S. D. Iversen, & S. H. Snyder (Eds.), *Handbook of psychopharmacology* (Vol. 8). New York: Plenum, 1977.

Janowsky, D., El-Yousef, K., Davis, M., & Sekerke, H. J. A cholinergic-adrenergic hypothesis of mania and depression. *Lancet*, 1972, *2*, 632–635.

Jones, F. D., Maas, J. W., Dekirmenjian, H., & Fawcett, J. Urinary catecholamine metabolites during behavioral changes in a patient with manic-depressive cycles. *Science*, 1973, *179*, 300–302.

Karczmar, A. G., Scudder, C. L. & Richardson, D. L. Interdisciplinary approach to the study of behavior in related mice types. In S. Ehrenpreis & I. J. Kopin (Eds.), *Chemical approaches to brain function*. New York: Academic Press, 1973.

Katz, M. M., & Hirschfeld, R. M. A. Phenomenology and classification of depression. In M. A. Lipton, A. DiMascio, & K. F. Killam (Eds.), *Psychopharmacology: A generation of progress*. New York: Raven Press, 1978.

Kaye, M. B. Oral contraceptives in depression. *Journal of the American Medical Association,* 1963, *522,* 186.

Keim, K. L., & Sigg, E. B. Physiological and biochemical concomitants of restraint stress in rats. *Pharmacology Biochemistry & Behavior,* 1976, *4,* 289–297.

Kelly, P. H. Drug-induced motor behavior. In L. L. Iversen, S. D. Iversen, & S. H. Snyder (Eds.), *Handbook of psycho-pharmacology* (Vol. 8). New York: Plenum, 1977.

Klaiber, E. L., Broverman, D. M., Vogel, W., Kobayashi, Y., & Moriarty, D. Effect of estrogen therapy on plasma MAO activity and EEG during responses of depressed women. *American Journal of Psychiatry,* 1972, *128,* 42–48.

Kobayashi, R. M., Palkovits, M., Kizer, J. S., Jacobwitz, D. M. & Kopin, I. J. Selective alterations of catecholamines and tyrosine hydroxylase activity in the hypothalamus following acute and chronic stress. In E. Usdin, R. Kvetnansky, & I. J. Kopin (Eds.), *Catecholamines and Stress.* New York: Pergamon Press, 1976, 29–38.

Korf, J. Locus coeruleus, noradrenaline metabolism and stress. In E. Usdin, R. Kvetnansky, & I. J. Kopin (Eds.), *Catecholamines and stress.* New York: Pergamon Press, 1976, 105–111.

Korf, J., Aghajanian, G. K., & Roth, R. H. Stimulation and destruction of the locus coeruleus: Opposite effects on 3-methoxy-4-hydroxyphenylglycol sulfate levels in the rat cerebral cortex. *European Journal of Pharmacology,* 1973, *21,* 305–310.

Korf, J., Aghajanian, G. K., & Roth, R. H. Increased turnover of norepinephrine in the rat cerebral cortex during stress. Role of the locus coeruleus. *Neuropharmacology,* 1973, *12,* 933–938.

Kupfer, D. J., & Detre, T. P. Tricychic and monoamine-oxidase-inhibitor antidepressants: Clinical use. In L. L. Iversen, S. D. Iversen, & S. H. Snyder (Eds.), *Handbook of psychopharmacology* (Vol. 14). New York: Plenum, 1978.

Kvetnansky, R., Mitro, A., Palkovits, M., Brownstein, M., Torda, T., Vigas, M., and Mikulaj, L. Catecholamines in individual hypothalamic nuclei in stressed rats. In E. Usdin, R. Kvetnansky, & I. J. Kopin (Eds.), *Catecholamines and stress.* New York: Pergamon Press, 1976.

Ladisch, W. Effect of stress upon serotonin metabolism in various regions of the rat brain. *Arzheim Forschung,* 1974, *24,* 1025–1027.

Landoni, G., & Ciompi, L. Etudes statistique sur l'aage de prédilection des troubles depressif's l'evolution psychotrique. *Tome,* 1971, *36,* 583–605.

Leff, M. J., Roatch, J. F., & Bunney, W. E. Environmental factors preceding the onset of severe depressions. *Psychiatry,* 1970, *33,* 298–311.

Levi, L. D., Fales, C. H., Stein, M., & Sharp, V. H. Separation and attempted suicide. *Archives of General Psychiatry,* 1966, *15,* 158–165.

Lewinsohn, P. M., & Amenson, C. S. Some relations between pleasant and unpleasant mood-related events and depression. *Journal of Abnormal Psychology,* 1978, *87,* 644–654.

Lloyd, K. G., Farley, I. J., Deck, G. H. N., & Hornykiewicz, O. Serotonin and 5-hydroxyindoleacetic acid in discrete areas of the brain stem of suicide victims and control patients. *Advances in Biochemistry and Psychopharmacology,* 1974, *11,* 387–397.

Maas, J. W., Fawcett, J. A., & Dekirmenjian, H. Catecholamine metabolism, depressive illness, and drug response. *Archives of General Psychiatry,* 1970, *26,* 252–261.

Maas, J. W., Dekirmenjian, H., & Jones, F. The identification of depressed patients who have a disorder of norepinephrine metabolism and/or disposition. In E. Usdin & S. Snyder (Eds.), *Frontiers of catecholamine research.* New York: Pergamon Press, 1973, 1091–1096.

Maas, J. W., Dekirmenjian, H., Garver, D., Redman, D. E., & Landis, D. H. Excretion of catecholamine metabolites following intraventricular injection of 6-hydroxydopamine in the inacaca speciosa. *European Journal of Pharmacology,* 1973, *23,* 121–130.

Maier, S. F., & Seligman, M. E. P. Learned helplessness: Theory and evidence. *Journal of Experimental Psychology: General,* 1976, *105,* 3–46.

Maier, S. F., Seligman, M. E. P., & Solomon, R. L. Pavlovian fear conditioning and learned helplessness. In B. A. Campbell & R. M. Church (Eds.), *Punishment.* New York: Appleton-Century-Crofts, 1969, 229–343.

Malek-Ahmadi, P., & Behrmann, P. J. Depressive syndrome induced by oral contraceptives. *Disease of the Nervous System,* 1976, 406–408.

Maynert, E. W., & Levi, R. Stress-induced release of brain norepinephrine and its inhibition by drugs. *Journal of Pharmacological and Experimental Therapeutics,* 1964, *143,* 90–95.

McLure, D. J. The role of dopamine in depression. *Canadian Psychiatric Association Journal,* 1973, *18,* 309–312.

Mendels, J., Fraser, A., Fitzgerald, B. G., Ramsay, T. A., & Stokes, J. W. Biogenic amine metabolites in cerebrospinal fluid in depressed and manic patients. *Science,* 1972, *175,* 1380–1382.

Miller, W. R., Seligman, M. E. P., & Kurlander, H. M. Learned helplessness, depression and anxiety. *Journal of Nervous and Mental Disease,* 1975, *61,* 347–357.

Modigh, K. Influence of social stress on brain catecholamine mechanisms. In E. Usdin, R. Kvetnansky, & I. J. Kopin (Eds.), *Catecholamines and stress.* New York: Pergamon Press, 1976, 17–28.

Moisset, T. B., Hendley, E. D., Welch, B. L. Norepinephrine uptake by cerebral synaptosomes of mouse: Strain differences. *Brain Research,* 1975, *92,* 157–164.

Moses, S. G., & Robins, E. Regional distribution of norepinephrine and dopamine in brains of depressive suicides and alcoholic suicides. *Psychopharmacological Communications,* 1975, *1,* 327–337.

Munro, A. Parental deprivation in depressive patients. *British Journal of Psychiatry,* 1966, *112,* 443–457.

Murphy, D. L. Amine precursors, amines and false neurotransmitters in depressed patients. *American Journal of Psychiatry,* 1972, *129,* 141–148.

Murphy, D. L., & Costa, J. L. Utilization of cellular studies of neurotransmitter-related enzymes and transport processes in man for the investigation of biological factors in behavioral disorders. In J. Mendels (Ed.), *Recent biological studies of depressive illness.* New York: Spectrum Books, 1975.

Murphy, D. L., Goodwin, F. K., & Bunney, W. E. A reevaluation of biogenic amines in manic and depressive states. *Hospital Practice,* 1972, *7,* 85.

Murphy, D. L., & Weiss, R. Reduced monoamine oxidase activity in blood platelets from bipolar depressed patients. *American Journal of Psychiatry,* 1972, *128,* 35–41.

Murphy, D. L., Campbell, I., Costa, J. L. Current status of the indoleamine hypothesis of the affective disorders. In M. A. Lipton, A. DiMascio, & K. F. Killam (Eds.), *Psychopharmacology: A generation of progress.* New York: Raven Press, 1978.

Otto, U., & Paalzow, L. Effect of stress on the pharmacokinetics of sodium salicylate and quinidine sulphate in rats. *Acta Pharmacologia et Toxicol,* 1975, *36,* 415–426.

Papeschi, R., & McLure, D. J. Homovanillic acid and 5-hydroxyendoleacetic acid in cerebro-spinal fluid in depressed patients. *Archives General of Psychiatry,* 1971, *25,* 355–358.

Pare, C. M. B., Yeung, D. P. H., Price, K., & Stacey, R. S. 5-hydroxytryptamine in brainstem, hypothalamus and caudate nucleus of controls and patients committing suicide by coal-gas poisoning. *Lancet,* 1969, *2,* 133–135.

Paykel, E. S. Life events and acute depression. In J. P. Scott & E. C. Senay (Eds.), *Separation and depression: Clinical and research aspects.* Washington: AAAS, 1973.

Paykel, E. S. Life stress and psychiatric disorder. In B. S. Dohrenwend & B. P. Dohrenwend (Eds.), *Stressful life events: Their nature and effects.* New York: Wiley, 1974.

Paykel, E. S., Myers, J. K., & Dienelt, M. N. Life events and depression. *Archives of General Psychiatry,* 1970, *21,* 753–760.

Paykel, E. S., Prusoff, B. A., & Uhlenhuth, E. H. Scaling of life events. *Archives of General Psychiatry,* 1971, *25,* 340–347.

Paykel, E. S., Myers, J. K., Dienelt, M. N., Kleman, G. L., Lindenthal, J. J., & Pepper, M. P. Life events and depression. *Archives of General Psychiatry,* 1969, *21,* 753–760.

Post, R. M., & Goodwin, F. K. Simulated behavior states: An approach to specificity in psychobiological research. *Biological Psychiatry,* 1973, *7,* 237–254.

Post, R. M., & Goodwin, F. K. Approaches to brain amines in psychiatric patients: A reevaluation of cerebrospinal fluid studies. In L. L. Iversen, S. D. Iversen, & S. H. Snyder (Eds.), *Handbook of psychopharmacology.* New York: Plenum, 1978.

Post, R. M., Gordon, E. K., Goodwin, F. K., & Bunney, W. E., Jr. Central norepinephrine metabolism in affective illness: MHPG in the cerebrospinal fluid. *Science, 1973, 179,* 1002–1003.

Post, R. M., Kotin, J. K., Goodwin, F. K., & Gordon, E. K. Psychomotor activity and cerebrospinal fluid amine metabolites in affective illness. *American Journal of Psychiatry, 1973, 130,* 67.

Prange, A. J., Wilson, I. C., & Rabon, A. M. Enhancement of imipramine antidepressant activity by thyroid hormone. *American Journal of Psychiatry, 1969, 126,* 457–469.

Rahe, R. H. Life change patterns surrounding illness experience. *Journal of Psychosomatic Research,* 1968, *11,* 341.

Rahe, R. H. The pathway between subjects' recent life changes and their near-future illness reports: Representative results and methodological issues. In B. S. Dohrenwend & B. P. Dohrenwend (Eds.), *Stressful Life Events: Their Nature and Effects.* New York: Wiley, 1974.

Rahe, R. H., & Paasikivi, J. Psychosocial factors and myocardial infarction. II. An outpatient study in Sweden. *Journal of Psychosomatic Research,* 1971, *15,* 33–39.

Ray, O. S., & Barrett, R. J. Behavioral, pharmacological and biochemical analysis of genetic differences in rats. *Behavioral Biology,* 1975, *15,* 391–417.

Ritters, S., & Pelzer, N. L. Magnitude of stress-induced brain norepinephrine depletion varies with age. *Brain Research,* 1978, *152,* 170.

Robinson, D. S., Davis, J. M., Nies, A., Colbern, R. W., Davis, J. N., Bourne, H. R., Bunney, W. E., Shaw, D. M., & Coppen, A. J. Aging, monoamines and monoamine oxidose levels. *Lancet,* 1972, *1,* 290–292.

Roos, B. E., & Sjostrom, R. 5-hydroxyindoleacetic acid and homoranilic acid levels in the cerebro-spinal fluid after probenicid application in patients with manic-depressive psychosis. *Journal of Clinical Pharmacy,* 1969, *1,* 153–155.

Saito, H., Morita, A., Miyazaki, I., & Takagi, K. Comparison of the effects of various stresses on biogenic amines in the central nervous system and animal symptoms. In E. Usdin, R. Kvetnansky, & I. J. Kopin (Eds.), *Catecholamines and stress,* 1976, 95–103.

Sachar, E. J., & Coppen, A. J. Biological aspects of affective psychoses. In G. E. Gaull (Ed.), *Biology of brain dysfunction.* New York: Plenum, 1975.

Sachar, E. J., Helsman, L., Fukushima, D. K., & Gallagher, T. F. Cortesol production in depressive illness: A clinical and biochemical clarification. *Archives of General Psychiatry,* 1970, *23,* 289–298.

Schildkraut, J. J. The catecholamine hypothesis of affective disorders: A review of supporting evidence. *American Journal of Psychiatry.* 1965. *122,* 509–522.

Schildkraut, J. J. Biogenic amines and affective disorders. *Annual Review of Medicine,* 1974, *25,* 338–348.

Schildkraut, J. J. Biochemical criteria for classifying depressive disorders and predicting responses to pharmacotherapy; preliminary findings from studies of norepinephrine metabolism. *Pharmacopsychiatry,* 1974, *7,* 98–105.

Schildkraut, J. J. Current status of the catecholamine hypothesis of affective disorders. In M. A. Lipton, A. DiMascio, & K. F. Killam (Eds.), *Psychopharmacology: A generation of progress.* New York: Raven Press, 1978.

Schildkraut, R., Chandra, O., Osswald, M., Ruther, E., Baarfüsser, B., & Matussek, N. Growth hormone release during sleep and with thermal stimulation in depressed patients. *Neuropsychology,* 1975, *1,* 70–79.

Schildkraut J. J., Keeler, B. A., Grob, E. L., Kantrowich, J., & Hartmann, E. MHPG excretion on clinical classification in depression. *Lancet,* 1973, *1,* 1251–1252.

Schmale, A. H. Adaptive role of depression in health and disease. In J. P. Scott & E. C. Senay (Eds.), *Separation and depression: Clinical and research aspects.* Washington: AAAS, 1973.

Sebens, J. B., & Korf, J. Cyclic AMP in cerebro-spinal fluid, accumulation following probenicid and brogenic amines. *Experimental Neurology,* 1975, *46,* 333–344.

Seligman, M. E. P. *Helplessness: On depression, development and death.* San Francisco: Freeman, 1975.

Sethi, B. B. Relationship of separation to depression. *Archives on Psychiatry*, 1964, *10*, 486–496.

Shaw, D. M., Kemps, F. E., & Ecclestone, E. J. 5-hydroxytryptamine in hind brain of depressive suicides. *British Journal of Psychiatry*, 1967, *113*, 1407–1411.

Shopsin, B., Wilk, S., Gershon, S., Davis, K., & Suhl, M. Cerebrospinal fluid MHPG. *Archives of General Psychiatry*, 1973, *28*, 230–233.

Shulman, R., Griffith, J., Dewold, P. Catechol-O-methyltransferase activity in patients with depressive illness and anxiety state. *British Journal of Psychiatry*, 1978, *132*, 133–137.

Sinanam, J., Keating, A. M. B., Beckett, P. G. S., & Love, W. C. Urinary cyclic AMP in endogenous and neurotic depression. *British Journal of Psychiatry*, 1975, *126*, 49–55.

Sklar, L. S., & Anisman, H. Stress and coping factors influence tumor growth. *Science*, 1979, *205*, 513–515.

Slater, S., & Both, M. *Mayer Gross Clinical Psychiatry*. Baltimore: Williams & Wilkins, 1969.

Stolk, J. M., Conner, R. L., Levine, S., & Barchas, J. P. Brain norepinephrine metabolism and shock induced fighting behavior in rats: Differential effects of shock and fighting on the neurochemical response to a common footshock stimulus. *Journal of Pharmacology and Experimental Therapeutics*, 1974, *190*, 193–209.

Stone, E. A. Stress and catecholamine. In A. J. Friedhoff (Ed.), *Catecholamines and behavior* (Vol. II). New York: Plenum, 1975.

Stone, E. A. Effect of stress sulfated glycol metabolites of brain norepinephrine. *Life Sciences*, 1975, *16*, 1725–1730.

Sulser, F. Functional aspects of the norepinephrine receptor coupled adenylate cyclase system in the limbic forebrain and its modification by drugs which precipitate or alleviate depression: molecular approaches to an understanding of affective disorders. *Pharmakopsychia Neuropsychopharmako*, 1978, *11*(1), 43–52.

Takahashi, R., Condo, H., & Keto, N. Effect of 1-5-hydroxytryptophan on brain monoamine metabolism and evaluation of its clinical effect in depressed patients. *Journal of Psychiatric Research*, 1975, *12*, 177–187.

Takahashi, R., Utina, H., Mashiyama, Y., Kurihama, M., Otsuka, T., Nakamura, T., & Konamura, H. Tyrosine metabolism in manic depressive illness. *Life Sciences*, 1968, *7*, 1219–1231.

Thierry, A. M. Effects of stress on the metabolism of serotonin and norepinephrine in the central nervous system of the rat. In S. Nemeth (Ed.), *Hormones, metabolism and stress: Recent progress and perspectives*. Bratislava: Publishing house of the Slovak Academy of Sciences, 1973.

Thierry, A. M., Blanc, G., & Glowinski, J. Preferential utilization of newly synthesized norepinephrine in the brain stem of stressed rats. *European Journal of Pharmacology*, 1970, *10*, 139.

Thierry, A. M., Blanc, G., & Glowinski, J. Effect of stress on the disposition of catecholamines localized in various intraneuronal storage forms in the brain stem of the rat. *Journal of Neurochemistry*, 1971, *18*, 449–461.

Thierry, A. M., Fekete, M., & Glowinski, J. Effects of stress on the metabolism of noradrenaline, dopamine and and serotonin (5-HT) in the central nervous system of the rat. II. Modifications of serotonin metabolism. *European Journal of Pharmacology*, 1968, *4*, 384–389.

Thierry, A. M., Javoy, F., Glowinski, J., & Kety, S. S. Effects of stress on the metabolism of norepinephrine, dopamine, and serotonin in the central nervous system of the rat. *Journal of Pharmacological and Experimental Therapeutics*, 1968, *163*, 163–171.

Thierry, A. M., Tassin, J. P., Blanc, G., & Glowinski, J. Selective activation of nesocortical DA system by stress. *Nature*, 1976, *263*, 242–244.

Tunnicliff, G., Wimer, C. C., & Wimer, R. E. Relationships between neurotransmitter metabolism and behavior in seven inbred strains of mice. *Brain Research*, 1973, *61*, 428–434.

Van Praag, H. M. Toward the biochemical typology of depression. *Pharmacopsychiatry*, 1974, *7*, 281–292.

Van Praag, H. M. Toward a biochemical classification of depression. In E. Costa, G. L. Gessa, & M. Sandler (Eds.), *Serotonin new vistas: Biochemistry and behavioral and clinical studies*. New York: Raven Press, 1974, 357–368.

Van Praag, H. M. *Psychotropic drugs: A guideline for the practicing physician.* New York: Brunner/ Mazel, 1978.

Van Praag, H. M. Amine hypotheses of affective disorders. In L. L. Iversen, S. D. Iversen, & S. H. Synder (Eds.), *Handbook of Psychopharmacology* (Vol. 13). New York: Plenum, 1978.

Van Praag, H. M., Korf, J., & Puite, J. 5-Hydroxyindoleacetic acid levels in the cerebro-spinal fluid of depressive patients treated with probenicid. *Nature,* London, 1970, *225,* 1259–1260.

Van Praag, H. M., & Korf, J. Retarded depression and dopamine metabolism. *Psychopharmacologia,* 1971, *19,* 199–203.

Van Praag, H. M., & Korf, J. Endogenous depression with and without disturbances in 5-hydroxytrypt- amine metabolism: A biochemical classification? *Psychopharmacologia,* 1971, *19,* 148–152.

Van Praag, H. M., & Korf, J. Control monoamine deficiency in depression: Causative or secondary phenomenon. *Pharmakopsychiatr Neuropsychopharma,* 1975, *8,* 332–326.

Van Praag, H. M., Korf, J., Dols, L. C. W., & Schut, T. A pilot study of the predictive value of the probenicid test and application of 5-hydroxytryptophan as an antidepressant. *Psycharmacologia,* 1972, *25,* 14–21.

Van Scheijen, J. D., Van Praag, H. M., & Korf, J. A controlled study comparing nomifensive and clomipromine in unipolar depression using probenicid techniques. *British Journal of Clinical Phar- macology,* 1977, *4,* 1795–1845.

Vinokur, A., & Zelzer, M. L. Desirable and undesirable life events: Their relationship to stress and mental distress. *Journal of Personality and Social Psychology,* 1975, *32,* 329–337.

Walinder, J., Scott, A., Nagy, A., Carlson, A., & Roos, B. E. Potentiation of antidepressant action of clomipramine by tryptophan. *Lancet,* 1975, *1,* 984.

Weiss, B. L., Kupfer, D. J., Foster, F. G., & Delgado, J. Psychomotor activity, sleep and biogenic amine metabolites in depression. *Biological Psychiatry,* 1974, *9,* 45–54.

Weiss, J. M., & Glazer, H. I. Effects of acute exposure to stressors on subsequent avoidance-escape behavior. *Psychosomatic Medicine,* 1975, *37,* 499–521.

Weiss, J. M., Stone, E. A., & Harrell, N. Coping behavior and brain norepinephrine level in rats. *Jour- nal of Comparative and Physiological Psychology,* 1970, *72,* 153–160.

Weiss, J. M., Glazer, H. I., Pohorecky, L. A., Brick, J., & Miller, N. E. Effects of chronic exposure to stressors on avoidance-escape behavior and on brain norepinephrine. *Psychosomatic Medicine,* 1975, *37,* 522–534.

Weiss, J. M., Glazer, H. I., & Pohorecky, L. A. Coping behavior and neurochemical changes: An alter- native explanation for the original "learned helplessness" experiments. In G. Serban & A. Kling (Eds.), *Animal models in human psychobiology.* New York: Plenum, 1976.

Welch, B. L., & Welch, A. S. Control of brain catecholamines and serotonin during acute stress and after d-amph by natural inhibition of monoamine oxidase: An hypothesis. In E. Costa & S. Gar- antini, (Eds.), *Amphetamines and related compounds.* New York: Raven Press, 1970.

Whybrow, P. C., Coppen, A., Prange, A. J., Noguera, R., & Bailey, J. E. Thyroid function and the response to Liothyronine in depression. *Archives of General Psychiatry,* 1972, *26,* 242–245.

Wilk, S., Shopsin, B., Gershon, S., & Suhl, M. CSF levels of M.H.P.G. in affective disorders. *Nature,* London, 1972, *235,* 440–441.

Winokur, G., Clayton, P. J., & Reich, T. *Manic depressive illness.* St. Louis: Mosby, 1969.

Winokur, G. Mania and depression: Family studies and genetics in relation to treatment. In M. A. Lipton, A. DiMascio, & K. F. Killam (Eds.), *Psychopharmacology: A generation of progress.* New York: Raven Press, 1978.

Wise, R. A. Catecholamine theories of reward: A critical review. *Brain Research,* 1978, *152,* 215–247.

Wortman, C. B., & Dintzer, L. Is an attributional analysis of the learned helplessness phenomenon viable? A critique of the Abramson-Seligman-Teasdale reformulation. *Journal of Abnormal Psy- chology,* 1978, *87,* 75–90.

Zajaczkowska, M. N. Acetylcholine content in the central and peripheral nervous sytem and its syn- thesis in the rat brain during stress and post-stress exhaustion. *Acta Physiologica Polska,* 1975, *26,* 493–497.

Chapter 8

Cognition, Emotion, and Motivation: The Doctoring of Humpty-Dumpty*

RICHARD S. LAZARUS, JAMES C. COYNE,

and SUSAN FOLKMAN

University of California
Berkeley, California

The importance of cognitive processes in human adaptation is now generally accepted, and the cognitive orientation has experienced such a general resurgence in psychology that it has even been referred to as a "cognitive revolution" (Dember, 1974). Yet, "campaigners for a 'cognitive movement' can hardly afford to slacken their efforts now that their candidates have ostensibly assumed office" (Mahoney, 1977a, p. 6). They have campaign promises to keep or apologies to make as they confront the basic problems of psychology from their special perspective. Undoubtedly, extreme ideological positions will have to be softened or abandoned as cognitive theorists come to terms with important areas of inquiry they have previously ignored.

During the nineteenth century, it was fashionable to separate cognition (reason) from emotion (passion) and motivation (will or volition). Few would still seriously subscribe to the view that the three are distinct and fundamental faculties capable

*Writing of this paper was supported in part by a research grant from the National Institute on Aging (AG 00799).

of independent development, but their reintegration—the doctoring of the shattered Humpty-Dumpty—has proven to be a frustrating problem for a succession of theoretical frameworks.[1] Too often the problem has been settled with the accession of one of the three, the banishment of another, and a denial of any data that might embarrass this arrangement. Emotion has been assimilated into drive, motivation and emotion denuded of thought or taken over altogether by cognition. The "organism" that emerges from such conceptualizations is inevitably fragmented and incomplete. Furthermore, if the distinctions among the three concepts have been drawn too sharply and reified, so too has the distinction between the person to whom are ascribed the thoughts, emotions, and motives, and the environment to which that person responds.

Our objective here is to struggle with the perennial problem of the interdependence of thoughts, emotions, and motivations, and their involvement in the person's ongoing relationship to the environment. In doing so, we give our main attention to cognition and emotion and touch motivation only lightly. In addition, we address the implications of our speculation for the study and treatment of psychopathology, an arena too in which the effects of a cognitive resurgence are being felt (Mahoney, 1977b).

Although we shall raise doubts throughout about the tendency to separate and reify the cognitive, motivational, and emotional, this is also a good moment to affirm two ideas that are central to our perspective. First, there is no way to understand emotion without reference to the way a person construes or cognizes his/her relationship with the environment and, indeed, with the particular environmental context of the moment. Thus, we argue that cognitive activity has a pivotal significance for an emotional reaction. Second, as we have elsewhere (e.g., Coyne & Lazarus, in press; Lazarus, 1980; Lazarus & Launier, 1978), we also make a case that how a person acts and reacts, whether adaptively or maladaptively, can only be understood from a transactional metatheoretical framework. In developing our arguments, it is best to begin with a brief history of our current outlook.

The Background of Our Present Thinking

Since the sixties, the work of Richard S. Lazarus and his coworkers has been characterized by two main themes. First, the quality and intensity of an emotional reaction are determined by *cognitive appraisal* processes, that is, the person's continually reevaluated judgments about the significance of demands and constraints in ongoing transactions with the environment and about the options for meeting them. Second, cognitive appraisal processes underlie *coping* activities which, in turn, continually

---

[1]Since writing this we have come across a related quote from Riegel (1979) concerning faculty psychology and modern experimental psychology. He writes:

But not even all the King's horses and all the King's men could put Humpty-Dumpty together again, and thus, experimentalists were bound to fail in their attempts of putting meaning back into their psychology from which they had eliminated it so radically. Meaning is not something that can be added later to the system analyzed; rather, it is the most fundamental topic (p. 3).

shape the emotional reaction by altering in various ways the meanings of ongoing relationships between the person and the environment, that is, by affecting appraisal itself via *reappraisal*. This emphasis on the pivotal significance of cognition in emotion and adaptation stemmed from a sense that its role had been understated in traditional drive-oriented views, and also from a belief that cognitive appraisal often represents a critical juncture in the person-environment transaction (Coyne & Lazarus, in press). We frequently apply the term "causal" to cognition in discussing its role in emotional response and adaptation in general. In doing so, however, we intend a rather restricted meaning. We do not mean that cognition is a separate force or entity acting on emotional and adaptational processes; we consider cognition an integral part of them. Instead, we are calling attention to the vital necessity of invoking cognitive concepts in understanding how people come to respond in the manner that they do.

The research of the Lazarus group has progressed from laboratory studies of cognitive mediation, to stressful films, to the more naturalistic study of coping with anticipated surgery (Cohen & Lazarus, 1973), and, most recently, to a large-scale attempt to describe stress and coping processes over the course of a year in a sample of normal middle-aged adults (Coyne & Lazarus, in press, Note 1). This current study focuses on the flux and flow of the relationship of men and women to their environments by examining major life changes, minor daily hassles and uplifts, cognitive appraisals of stressful episodes, coping processes, patterns of emotion, and adaptational outcomes. This shift in attention to natural settings and everyday life reflects a growing conviction that the most important theoretical issues are refractory to laboratory-derived data (Lazarus, 1980; Lazarus & Launier, 1978).

The early film studies generated substantial data in support of the notion that how a person appraises and copes with an environment can have an important bearing on emotional and adaptational outcomes. The findings also challenged prevailing conceptions of emotion as motivator or drive and called attention to limitations inherent in the treatment of emotion as an antecedent variable. Given our current interest in the relationships among cognition, emotion, and motivation, it would be useful to return briefly to some of these studies, to examine how the relationship between cognition and emotion was construed, and to contrast this with the then dominant view. After that, we note some disturbing tendencies of cognitive theorists to fall prey to the same conceptual traps that characterized earlier views of emotion as drive or motivator, that is, as a causal antecedent of cognition and behavior.

Motion pictures were chosen as a source of stress because they did not depend on deception but relied on the natural tendency of people to react emotionally while watching others have a damaging experience (Lazarus et al., 1962). In some of the studies, situational manipulations designed to influence the subject's appraisal of the film events predictably raised or lowered the level of emotional disturbance, as measured by self-report and autonomic indicators, while the film was being watched. Further analyses of the results of these and additional studies revealed that the effectiveness of these manipulations depended in part on the personality of the subjects (see Lazarus, Averill, & Opton, 1970, for a review). One study (Koriat et al., 1972) examined self-generated rather than situationally induced modes of emotional control. Subjects were instructed to detach themselves from the emotional impact of a film showing woodshop accidents or to involve themselves more fully, but in neither case were they given explicit instructions as to how to do this. It was found that people could indeed modulate their emotional states volitionally, as measured by self-report and heart rate.

These demonstrations that cognitive coping strategies could dampen or eliminate emotional response encouraged rejection of the then prevailing view of coping as the *result* of emotion. In the revised view, coping is treated not as a consequence but as having causal significance in the emotional response and as an integral component of that response. Emotions, from this perspective, are better regarded as a reflection of a person's ongoing appraisal of information with respect to its significance for well-being, rather than as being merely fortuitously conditioned to physical stimuli.

The focus on person and environmental antecedents of cognitive and self-regulatory processes opens up a multidirectional diversity in the theoretical handling of emotion. Treating emotion as a dependent variable, describable in terms of a set of self-report, behavioral, and physiological measures, also calls attention to discrepancies among measures of the same concept and to more general issues inherent in the study of the topography of emotional response.

Still, the legitimacy of emotion as an antecedent variable too should not be totally rejected. There is, after all, an extensive body of older work showing the disruptive effects of emotion on cognitive functioning (e.g., Basowitz et al., 1955; Child & Waterhouse, 1953; Sarason, 1972; Sarason, Mandler, & Craighill, 1952; see also Lazarus, 1966; Lazarus, Deese, & Osler, 1952, for reviews and analysis). Particularly in the latest work of the Lazarus group, care has been taken to note that in adaptation there is constant interplay between cognitive appraisals, emotion, subsequent information-processing, reappraisals, and so on (Folkman, Schaefer, & Lazarus, 1979). For the purpose of hypothesis-testing or theoretical explanation, one can intervene in this sequence, designating one phase as an antecedent condition, and then examine its consequences (Coyne & Lazarus, in press). For example, one can induce a positive mood state in a group of subjects and observe resulting differences in cognitive processes (Isen et al., 1978) or look first at commitments and observe their impact on thought and fantasy (Klinger, 1975).

At the same time, we must remain cognizant of the arbitrariness of the sequence that is observed, i.e., that it is relative to one's point of entry into the process. With alternative punctuations of the sequence, other, even reversed, "causal" patterns can be observed. For instance, the effects of cognitive processes on mood can also be studied by having subjects attend to negatively or positively valued aspects of themselves and then assessing their mood states (Teasdale & Fogarty, 1979). The major hazard, however, lies in our tendency to reify the *direction* of this relationship as going always one way or the other.

A second hazard is to treat emotion and cognition as theoretically and empirically *separable.* If one conceptualizes these manipulations of emotion and cognition as one might a cue stick driving one of two billiard balls (cognition or emotion) into the other, one can generate all sorts of insoluble questions about how emotion can influence cognition, vice versa, or even about emotionless thought or thoughtless emotion. Our conceptual past history has frequently had us do just this. Taking their distinctiveness too seriously (as separate and independent billiard balls), one is left unprepared for the many circumstances in which emotion and cognition have the same referents and are neither theoretically nor empirically separable.

For example, anger refers not only to a disturbed physiological, subjective, and behavioral state but also to cognitions about a hostile environmental agent. Fear involves not only actions (or impulses) of avoidance or flight but also an appraisal of a dangerous environmental agent which is the object of the fear. These emotions, cognitions, and impulses or actions are often best treated as interdependent and totally *fused* aspects of the person's relationship with the environment. This does not mean these aspects are *always* fused. There can be attack without anger and anger without attack, or avoidance without fear and fear without avoidance. When there is this type of separation in life, it is because of some special additional process such as inhibition or defensive reappraisal. But the *full* experience of anger and fear includes at least three fused elements: the impulse to act, the cognitive appraisal of a relationship with the environment, and the physiological and subjective disturbance which defines these emotional states (Lazarus, 1966).

Whether or not it is done with a cognizance of these problems, the separation of cognition and emotion and the designation of one as causal antecedent and the other as consequence is an important directive in the organization of theory and research that has far-reaching consequences. We should explore, therefore, what has happened in theory and research in the recent past when emotion was reified as an antecedent condition of cognition and action.

Emotion as Antecedent

At the time of the original film studies (1960–1971), theoretical treatments of emotions focused almost exclusively on changes in behavior as a consequence of emotion. Attention was directed to emotion's arousing or motivational functions, and its substantive qualities and determinants were largely ignored. Emotion was generally fused (and sometimes confounded) with concepts of drive and activation (e.g., Duffy, 1934, 1962; Lindsley, 1951). Even later conceptualizations of emotion advertised as cognitive were not fully cognitive but emphasized a process of cognitive labeling of a diffuse state of activation (Schachter, 1966). Therefore, Schachter's two-factor theory (emphasizing both activation and cognitive labeling) seems to hold to the core concept of drive activation, this being a necessary element in emotion. As a result, cognitive processes seem weakened as causal elements by being treated largely as labeling rather than a full process of appraisal of the significance for one's well-being of a social encounter.

We have argued that there is nothing inherently illogical or improper in treating emotion provisionally as an antecedent to some behavior of interest. Yet theorizing in this vein has been plagued by recurring problems (Lazarus, 1968). It became dominated by a set of five rather consistent imbalances and distortions.

1. Conceptualization of emotion as a drive, antecedent, or even as an intervening variable, directed attention away from its own determinants and, in particular, from any consideration of cognitive and motivational processes mediating between a stimulus situation and the observed reactions. The association between emotion and stimulus conditions was assumed to be acquired fortuitously, as a result of simple contiguity and drive reduction or reinforcement. Subsequent evocation of an emotion by these conditions was assumed to be automatic. Any sense of emotion as a *relational* or *meaning-centered* concept that could be concerned with the significance of a person's ongoing transactions with the environment was lost. Empirical questions as to the person and environmental variables that might influence these judgments (or appraisal processes)—and therefore the observed pattern of emotional response—were simply not articulated in theoretical analysis.

Over many years, a large variety of studies were designed to examine the effects of emotional arousal on laboratory task performance. Many of these studies were based on some variant of the Yerkes-Dodson Law (1908), suggesting an inverted U-shaped relationship between arousal and performance. Much research also emphasized the tendency of high arousal to interfere with the subject's ability to deal with task requirements (Child & Waterhouse, 1953; Easterbrook, 1959; Sarason, Mandler, & Craighill, 1952). Other such studies had a Hullian basis and, while also conceptualizing emotion as nonspecific arousal, attempted to delineate a systematic relationship between performance, drive, and habit strength (Spence & Farber, 1954; Spence & Spence, 1966). For example, to manipulate emotion or drive as an independent variable, subjects were given an ostensibly solvable task which was not in fact solvable. It was assumed that experimenter-induced failure would automatically induce emotional arousal or drive. Little attention was given to the constellation of experimental demands and personal variables (e.g., motives, beliefs) that might make failure threatening or to the cognitive processes involved in making the judgment that something important enough to create emotion was at stake for the experimental subject.

Conceptions of emotion as an antecedent condition involved more than a downplaying of the antecedents of emotion itself. Consistently and uncritically applied, a concentration on the consequences of emotion ultimately led to a default in the form of the theoretical judgment that the psychological processes mediating the emotional reaction were insignificant or even nonexistent.

2. Conceptualizations of emotion as an antecedent also downplayed questions of its measurement, focusing instead on limited aspects of concomitant and subsequent behavior. A variety of types of information can be used to infer the quality and intensity of emotional response. In conjunction with eliciting conditions, researchers can employ measures of physiological response, self-reported cognitions and feelings, and

the patterning of behavior (e.g., avoidance, attack, facial expression). Yet, as Lazarus (1968) and others have noted, there is substantial lack of agreement among alternative indices of emotion:

> No single response component is capable of producing adequate inferences about any internal state, be it an emotion or some other conceptual entity. Motoric-expressive cues are unreliable because people wear masks. Self-report fails for similar reasons, and is also confounded with response sets, self-justifications, etc. Physiological changes can also be produced by conditions of nonemotional relevance (p. 204).

The patterning of response indices of emotion presents both theoretical and methodological challenges. Theoretically, it raises the possibility of identifying distinct emotional states with specific patterns of measurement (Lazarus, Kanner, & Folkman, 1980). Methodologically, however, one is faced with the need for multiple measures and a way of explaining discrepancies among them. Conception of emotion as an antecedent condition ignored these important and complex issues. Instead, limited performance measures were assumed to reflect the effects of emotion as a unidimensional state of arousal. The possibility that different patterns of emotion—as assessed by self-report and physiological or alternative behavioral measures—might be associated with divergent performance impairments was not raised. Conceivably, a subject might perform poorly following a failure induction as a concomitant of being angry, anxious, depressed, bored, or simply indifferent. However, an equally logical possibility is that different patterns of emotion, say, anger as opposed to depression, both generated by failure induction, could have different performance outcomes, for example, different degrees of impairment or even similar impairment achieved in quite different ways. With only simple performance and emotion state measures, however, such possibilities could not be explored.

The lack of attention to the substantive characteristics of emotions by drive-related or activation conceptions reduced emotion to a narrow, unidimensional construct, an undifferentiated state of drive or arousal rather than a rich panoply of experiences, somatic patterns, and action patterns. Studies of experimenter-induced failure construed the subject's emotional state variously and vaguely as being frustrated, stressed, anxious, or simply aroused (Brown & Farber, 1951). No need for a choice among these possible labels, nor any sense of loss at not speaking of anger, fear, guilt, sadness-depression, jealousy, disgust, or some combination or sequence of them. The great importance attached to the drive or motivational properties of emotion led to the virtual disappearance of emotion as a substantive topic in psychology journals. Aspects of emotion that were not readily accommodated in these terms were neglected, as were positive emotions such as joy, love, and elation. Psychology suffered a severe form of tunnel vision.

3. Conceptualization of emotion as antecedent to behavior came to imply that it had a causal status with respect to the very behavior that served as its referent. Webb (1948) proposed explicitly that "emotion be defined as an inferred concept which

results in a change in the organism's behavior" (p. 332). In too literally accepting the notion that it *results* in the behavior change, a false explanatory power was granted to the concept of emotion. If one accepts a causal status for an inferred variable, one ceases to look for further explanations of the behavior change in antecedent conditions. Yet emotion was a concept abstracted from the very behavior for which it was being proffered as a cause. As such, it begged rather than provided an explanation. The legerdemain by which emotion passed from a description of a psychological and physiological state or process to an explanation of behavior took a number of forms.

One common approach was to administer a measure of emotionality such as the Manifest Anxiety Scale (Taylor, 1953) and relate subjects' scores to their performance on some laboratory task. The most parsimonious description of such a procedure is that a self-report measure is being correlated with concurrent behavior; one is examining the concordance of two alternative indices of anxiety. However, if one conceptually detaches the performance measure from the self-reported anxiety score, one can be easily led to accept that the anxiety score explains the observed difference in performance, a seemingly more profound observation than a simple correlation. When such explanations were presented, they were typically bolstered by references to presumed neurochemical events, yet little empirical support for this was available. Even if it had been, neurochemical data would only have provided a further dimension to emotion as an inferred organismic state, not a complete explanation for concomitant behavior.

Another variation of the tautological use of emotion as an explanation can be found in the experimental manipulation of emotional arousal itself, such as experimenter-induced failure. The effectiveness of the manipulation is usually judged by whether the subject's performance is impaired. When impairment was observed in such studies, it was taken as evidence of emotional arousal (e.g., anxiety), which in turn was invoked to explain the impairment.

Still a third variant has been to substitute the term "anxiety" for the superordinate term "emotion," and psychology soon seemed to be saying that anxiety was a dominant causal factor both in psychopathology (e.g., Dollard & Miller, 1950) and in positive adaptation (e.g., Davis, 1944). Anxiety became the "prime" emotion for all behavior. If any other emotions existed, for example, sadness-depression, anger, or guilt, they were downplayed as intervening factors in adaptation and maladaptation or relegated to somewhat esoteric work such as efforts to distinguish between guilt and shame (Ausubel, 1955), to psychoanalysis, or to other disciplines such as anthropology. And virtually no attention was paid to what might be called positively toned emotions (Lazarus et al., 1980). The person, in this scheme, seems to become an anxiety-reducing machine, and anxiety reduction can serve him or her well (as in successful ambition) or badly (as in psychopathology).

4. With emotion thus conceptually detached from antecedent person and environment variables, mediating psychological processes, and even the differences in behavior it was intended to explain, doubts could be raised about the concept's scientific

status. Some called for its elimination. Duffy (1941, 1962) argued, for example, that the concept was worse than useless. Duffy (1941) noted that the features of behavior for which emotion was invoked as an explanation were features of *all* behavior:

All responses, not merely "emotional" responses, occur as adjustment to stimulating conditions. All responses, not merely emotional responses, occur at some particular energy level. All responses manifest discrimination, or response to relationships (p. 292).

In a highly influential paper, Brown and Farber (1951) also rejected emotion as a substantive concept suitable for scientific study. "Emotion is not a *thing* in the simple, naive sense that a chair or table is a thing" (p. 466). Even if scientific study does not require that a phenomenon be a "thing," Brown and Farber did raise legitimate questions about the particularly truncated concepts of emotion that emerged from its treatment as an antecedent variable. As Peters (1963) described it, theorists "had been erroneously led to treating emotion as a separate category or part of behavior, a force and an agent" (p. 438).

Problems associated with emotion as antecedent can be summarized in various ways. Such a conception offers little improvement over folk or naive psychological conceptions of emotion as a force seizing or overwhelming the person. However consistent with the phenomenology of emotion such explanations may be, they really do not extend our knowledge of the determinants of emotion, and they are tautological at best. When it is detached from antecedent conditions and used to explain its own behavioral referents, emotion becomes an intervening variable without true explanatory power.

Refocusing on emotion as a *consequence,* one can open issues of its measurable antecedents and the substantive features of the behavior pattern to which it refers. A *cognitive* conception of emotion as consequence emphasizes the active processing of information inherent in an emotional reaction, and suggests attention to both person and environmental variables affecting such processes. A cognitive orientation to emotion reestablishes a linkage between emotion and its antecedents—not just environmental conditions, but the various determinants of the individual's orientation to them.

One can legitimately speak of the cognitive determinants of emotion, but herein also lies the potential for conceptual mischief. Cognition, like emotion, is an inferred variable, and it can similarly be abused by making it an antecedent condition detached from its own measurable antecedents and then employing it as the explanation for its sole referent. Like emotion, cognition can be treated as an elusive inner "thing" rather than a relational process. Instead of clarifying the structure of the person's transactions with the environment, the construct can be employed in a way that leaves the person lost in thought. Examples abound in the current cognitive literature.

Cognition Über Alles

The triumph of cognition over both emotion and motivation as explanatory concepts has been both dramatic and thorough. Pervin (Note 1) has documented and qualified this with reference to changes in the *Psychological Abstracts* and the *Annual Review of Psychology*. By 1978, the number of entries in *Psychological Abstracts* listed in association with cognition had four times the number listed under the concept of emotion and ten times those under motivation. The concept of drive, which had often subsumed emotion in the past, was missing from the index for the first time in 1965, and although it reappeared in 1968, it was again missing for the period 1972–1978. Cognition had not even been a chapter heading in the *Annual Review* before 1966, but by 1978 the number of subheadings under it exceeded the combined total under emotion and motivation.

Yet now that cognition is in ascendancy, clear signs indicate that the cognitive orientation is in danger of not fulfilling its promise to provide an understanding of the whole person as a "cognitive, conative, affective, biological and social individual" (McKeachie, 1976; cited in Pervin, Note 1) in transaction with the environment. The particular illustration we present below has not been chosen because it is in any way exceptional. Rather, it is all too representative of dominant trends.

Self-Statement and Emotion A number of cognitive theorists, including Ellis (1962) and Beck (1976), postulate that thoughts, or self-statements, are responsible for both normal and abnormal states of elation and depression. Some cognitive therapists such as Ellis treat people with affective disorders by direct attempts to alter their thought contents. A major body of supportive evidence for a simple unicausal relationship between thought and emotion comes from studies employing the Velten (1968) mood-induction procedure. In the typical study, subjects read aloud a long list of statements that describe themselves as experiencing either a state of elation or a state of depression, with the explicit instructions that the experimenter wishes to see if "a person can talk himself into a mood" and that subjects will find it easy to do so. Usually, a control group also reads an equally long series of affectively neutral statements, and all groups perform on laboratory tasks and complete self-report mood measures. Writers citing these studies generally argue that they demonstrate that what people tell themselves determines their mood or emotional response.

Rogers and Craighead (1977) and Buchwald, Strack, and Coyne (in press) have carefully reviewed the procedures and patterns of results in those studies, and they conclude that only weak and inconsistent support for the effectiveness of the mood-induction procedure is provided. Following a mood induction, differences in self-reported mood are typically significant and in the right direction. However, for performance measures, even when there are significant differences between the group receiving a depression induction and the group receiving an elation induction, these groups frequently do not differ significantly from a control group. Furthermore, Buchwald et al. (in press) noted shortcomings in previous efforts to examine the role of demand characteristics in the induction procedure. Subjects receiving the mood-induction procedure have typically received stronger demands to act elated or depressed and more information about how to do this than groups designed to control for demand characteristics. Buchwald et al. (in press) found that when differences in procedures were corrected, the hypothesis that the mood induction's apparent effects were entirely due to demand characteristics could not be rejected.

Empirical results aside, it is instructive to examine the model of thought and emotion that is involved, namely, that simply reading statements of self-reference is sufficient to change a person's emotional state. No importance is attached to whether the person believes the statements to be true or whether the statements are discrepant with assessment of autonomic feedback or other aspects of the subject's context. It is assumed that the subject can and does think in a manner isomorphic with the stimulus self-statements, but other cognitive processes, particularly critical ones or those involving evaluative processes, are ignored. The manner in which the self-statements are assumed to "grip" the subject is similar in many respects to the way earlier models treated emotion. The unicausal relationship between cognition and emotion is reversed, but the conceptual pitfalls are the same. Once again, mediational processes are reduced to inferential entities that interact like colliding billiard balls.

Whither Motivation?

As a concept, motivation has gotten its major impetus in psychology from the need to explain what pushed a quiescent, equilibrated organism into action. The obvious answer was a motivating force of some kind, which in the heyday of Freud and of associative learning theory—both based on the theme of tension-reduction and reinforcement—was conceptualized as drive (see Hull, 1943; Spence, 1956, 1958). All behavior represented efforts to reduce tension, and behavior that seemed to deviate from the principle (e.g., altruism, ambition) was viewed as merely a necessary detour. The main sources of drive energy were tissue needs or instincts, but other, acquired, drives became conditioned to these through chance reinforcement, that is, by virtue of their success in producing tension-reduction. Because many forms of human activity seemed as likely to add tension as to subtract it, Allport (1937) introduced his concept of functional autonomy, and Dollard and Miller (1950) argued that even neurotic or maladaptive behaviors (e.g., defenses) were learned and survived because they reduced anxiety (a form of tension) and that they persisted because the person never discovered that the threatening outcomes producing the anxiety were unrealistic.

We all know that what seemed like an elegant edifice—drive and simple reinforcement theory—passed out of favor because it had to be shored up constantly by costly qualifications and the gradual addition of necessary complications in the form of mediating processes such as cognition. This is not the place to detail this interesting history in which several major personages, among them McClelland, Harlow, Klein, and White, played important roles. At the same time, arousal theorists (e.g., Duffy,

1941, 1962; Lindsley, 1951; and Malmo, 1959), who contributed to the appeal of the drive concept by bringing together three key strands into a single arousal dimension, namely, physiological arousal, behavioral activation, and drive, were slowly losing ground to evidence of autonomic (physiological) specificity (Lacey, 1967; Lazarus, 1966; Mason et al., 1976; Shapiro, Tursky, & Schwartz, 1970). The fall of logical positivism as an ideological basis for an elegant theory also contributed to the demise of drive formulations.

Although there had been abundant treatments of motivation from a more cognitive point of view (e.g., Kelly, 1955; Murray, 1938), George Klein and Robert White managed to remain within the drive framework while modifying it in a cognitive direction. White's (1959) beautifully constructed argument that the infant is normally far less involved in feeding or obtaining oral stimulation than in examining and manipulating the environment (effectance motivation) was very influential in turning psychology away from a strictly drive formulation. And writing within the ego psychology tradition, Klein (1970) infused the concept of drive with cognitive activity, redefining it more or less as follows:

It seems more economical to . . . think of drive as a construct which refers, on the one hand, to the "relating" process—the meaning—around which selected behavior and memories are organized; and in terms of which goal-sets, anticipations and expectations develop, and on the other hand, to those processes which accommodate this relational activity to reality. In this way drive is defined solely in terms of behavior and thought products. . . .

Klein's concept of drive is obviously no longer drive in the Freudian or associative learning sense; while retaining its instinctual or tissue basis (primary or viscerogenic), it has been shifted toward means-ends and goal-related thought. Drive is now suffused with cognitive activity.

This shift away from tissue tensions and toward thought brought with it a corresponding shift away from a conceptualization of the person as normally quiescent and passive to one that is constantly active in seeking stimulation, in having an effect on the environment, in exploring and understanding, in interpreting itself, an organism for whom quiescence and homeostasis are foreign. Activity, per se, need no longer be explained (see also Piaget, 1952). As Miller, Galanter, and Pribram (1960,) put it:

Plans are executed because people are alive. This is not a facetious statement, for so long as people are behaving, *some* plan or other must be executed. The question thus moves from why *Plans* are executed to a concern for which plans are executed (p. 62).

But in the fervor to move away from the old-fashioned concept of drive and toward the role of thought, we must not forget that the the answer to Miller et al.'s question must still lie partly in motivational concepts. "Which plans are executed" depends on personal agendas on the basis of which transactions with the environment are evaluated. To be benefited and thus to feel good, or to be harmed, threatened, or challenged, means to have some personal stake in an outcome; the more significant the stake, the greater the potential for harm, threat, or challenge, or for a positive emotion in the case of a favorable outcome. In lower animals, the stakes are mainly physical safety, survival, and comfort; in humans, they involve long-range goals and commitments and are largely symbolic. No matter how difficult the task of conceptualizing motivational concepts and understanding their developmental course, operation, and behavioral consequences, not to mention their interrelationships with thought and emotion, a motivational concept cannot be abandoned in the effort to understand stress and adaptation.

The term "commitment" illustrates what we are saying very well because it is a motivational concept heavily infused with cognitive processes. A commitment is a statement of what is important to the person (see Wrubel, Benner, & Lazarus, in press), and it can be defined at many levels of abstraction. For example, one can be committed to an ideal, such as parenting, or to a specific goal, such as having three children. Klinger (1977) has described the importance of commitments in people's lives, explaining depression as a process of disengagement from commitments. What is important to a person parallels the idea of stakes in our earlier discussion of harm, threat, and challenge. Without some such concept it would not be possible to understand the emotional response to a transaction.

Commitment illustrates the way cognition and emotion fuse in real life. To understand a commitment requires knowledge about its cognitive referent—i.e., commitment to what?—and also about the strength with which it is held and the contexts in which it is relevant. The meaning and significance of stressful events and how they unfold is also carried by the concept of commitment because this meaning includes what and how much can be gained, lost, or endangered, as well as how much must be expended to prevent or live with the loss. It also implies a sense of other commitments that might remain to take up the slack. The meaning and significance of an encounter from a motivational standpoint is expressed in the kind and intensity of emotion experienced—relief, exultation, or guilt at escaping loss, anger, or depression, for example.

Why isn't it enough to say that motivation is a form of cognition and hence subsumable under the concept of cognition? Because we know that people hold to commitments with greater or lesser fervor; because striving occurs not merely in a directional sense but also with greater or lesser intensity and persistence; because some commitments never turn off as do short-term goal-oriented behaviors; in short, because commitments are a special form of thought characterized by something that might be called arousal. Yet, because committed people are not always aroused, even when they are in pursuit of their commitments, it is not enough to say that motivation, therefore, can be subsumed under emotion or arousal. Their fervor is indeed related to emotion, often even fused with it, but as much in a dispositional sense as directly evident. Motivation does not reduce to emotion, though when it is most clearly in evidence the two concepts are very apt to be conjoined.

Although we cannot here fully resolve this problem of the lack of parallelism among the concepts of thought, emotion, and motivation—indeed, with so much having been written on the concept of motivation, it would be arrogant to try in a few paragraphs—we are still firm in our assertion that it is not fruitful or even possible to speak of one without reference to the other in the natural context of human behavior. The shattered egg does not serve us, conceptually, because its pieces have no life as separable identities. We must try somehow to keep Humpty-Dumpty intact. In the final portions of this paper, we consider the implications of this position for our understanding of psychopathology and its treatment.

Implications for Psychopathology

The emergence of the cognitive-behavioral perspective in psychology is particularly evident in the study and treatment of psychopathology, bringing with it renewed interest in cognitive activity as an explanation of dysfunctional patterns of living and coping. This trend is very evident in current clinical work on depression, and it is instructive to consider what we have said above, using depression—traditionally viewed as an affective disorder—as an exemplar for psychopathology in general. Similar analyses could also be made for other disorders.

Much of the large body of research and theory examining the cognitive aspects of depression has given prior causal status to cognition, thereby subordinating the behavioral, emotional, and motivational aspects. A number of studies indicate, for example, that cognitive-behavioral psychotherapy is effective with depression, perhaps even more so than traditional drug treatment (Rush et al., 1977; Shaw, 1977), though one must always be wary not to ignore the possibility of endogenous or biochemical forms of depression for which drugs might be particularly suitable.

This growing literature seems to present a compelling case for the cognitive viewpoint. However, a careful examination of the claims that are being made suggests a basic confusion between what can be empirically demonstrated and what is likely to be untestable ideology. Specifically, elaborate descriptions of the cognitive features of depression do not in themselves establish a prior causal role for cognition; neither does the apparent effectiveness of psychotherapy that is labeled "cognitive" or "cognitive-behavioral."

Beck and Rush (1978) have reviewed much of the research examining cognitive features of depression. They conceptualize the disorder in terms of cognitive distortions

that induce the individual to regard himself, his experience, and his future in an idiosyncratic manner. The content . . . revolves around the themes of loss and deprivation and is reflected in the patient's systematic bias against himself (p. 36).

These distortions dominate information-processing in depression. Depressed persons make arbitrary inferences, overgeneralize, and selectively abstract from their experience in a way that magnifies their faults and minimizes their strengths and accomplishments. These cognitive distortions maintain depressed persons' existing negative schema of themselves and their past, present, and future. Depressed persons see themselves as deficient, inadequate, and unworthy. They find validation for this in their interpretation of their past and present situations, and they expect the future to confront them with exorbitant demands and insuperable obstacles.

The wide range of data that Beck and Rush (1978) cite in support of this interpretation include studies of the dream content of depressed patients; the results of story completion and focused fantasy tests; and differences between depressed and nondepressed persons in measures of self-concept, selective recall, generalized expectancies, and specific expectancies of success or failure in games of skill and chance. The typical study of cognitive aspects of depression involves the selection of depressed and nondepressed subjects on the basis of a self-report measure of depression and administration of some stimulus to elicit evidence of cognitive processes. For example, subjects might be asked to generate outcomes for incomplete stories in which the protagonist faces the possibility of some loss or gain. It should be noted that although a variety of statistics can be employed to analyze the resultant data, the basic design is correlational in nature. Causal inferences cannot therefore be easily evaluated.

Because of their purported cognitive distortions, depressed persons are generally considered unreliable in their reports about themselves and their situations. Their self-reports are viewed as reflecting their negative biases rather than actual occurrences. People *in general* also have difficulty reporting on cognitive processes, and the reports that are obtained frequently do not accurately reflect controlling conditions or predict subsequent behaviors (Nisbett & Wilson, 1977). Given these limitations, it is notable that the one type of self-report in which depressed people are treated as "expert witnesses" is the report of inner processes. Many of the studies of cognitive aspects of depression are little more than correlations of measures of depression with such reports. It is assumed that depressed people cannot give an adequate accounting of themselves or of their past, present, or future, but that they can readily and accurately make reports on inner processes that prove problematic for people in general.

Second, the causal priority assigned to cognition in depression has generally precluded consideration of motivational variables. Essentially, the self-reports of depressives involve complaints of inefficiency, ineffectiveness, bad luck, and other adversity. In many contexts, such complaints can be instrumental in leading to relief from demands and responsibility and even the avoidance of experiences in which failure or rejection is likely. The hypothesis that the self-reports of depressed persons have instrumental value (a motivational function) is empirically testable. One might, for example, vary the expected consequences of a self-report and determine whether the reports that are obtained vary. A positive finding, however, would not deny a role for cognition in depression. It might also only demonstrate some limitations on self-reports as pure indicators of cognitive processes. However, a rigid adherence to cognition as causal antecedent to depression and an uncritical acceptance of the validity of self-report have prematurely closed this issue in the current depression literature.

Also prematurely closed is whether depressed persons are faced with negative responses to their behavior and therefore are getting feedback consistent with their complaints. Coyne (1976a) examined the basis for the stereotypic complaint of depressed persons that they are socially rejected. He found that depressed people induced anxiety, depression, and hostility in others, and that, presumably in consequence, they were rejected socially. Yet the direct feedback they obtained was confusing. Coyne (1976b) argued that depressed people are aversive to others but their obvious distress inhibits direct confrontation. The negative response they receive is therefore diffuse and ambiguous in its referents, so that depressed persons are led to broad negative generalizations about themselves.

A series of studies has recently suggested that depressed persons might be "sadder but wiser" than nondepressed persons, a conclusion offered by Alloy and Abramson (1979), who found that depressed persons were more accurate in their judgments of the contingencies between their behavior and its outcomes than the nondepressed. Lewinsohn, Mischel, Chaplin, and Barton (1980) obtained related findings in a social situation. Their depressed group perceived themselves more negatively than did the nondepressed, but this negative perception was actually consistent with the perceptions of others that, indeed, the depressed persons were actually less socially competent. In effect, depressed persons were realistic in their self-perceptions as indicated by agreement with others. Nondepressed persons, however, viewed themselves more positively than did observers, so that their view of themselves could be said to be unrealistically positive. Nelson and Craighead (1977) observed depressed persons to be surprisingly accurate in their recall of feedback. On the other hand, Buchwald (1977) found that depressed persons recalled fewer successes in a learning task than actually occurred. Consistent with the view that depressed persons are sadder but wiser, Mischel (1979) has expressed doubt that unrealistic self-appraisal is the basic ingredient of depression and even questioned whether realism is the crux of appropriate affect.

Expecting to do well and feeling good may . . . encourage one to attend selectively to one's other assets and positive attributes, at the risk of generating an illusory glow (p. 752).

Considering the many studies purporting to demonstrate cognitive distortions associated with depression, there is a real paucity of studies examining the information available to depressed persons in their ongoing transactions with their typical environments. Coyne (1976b) has argued that the failure to consider the role of feedback from the environment will lead an observer to overemphasize the causal role of the inner processes of a depressive at the expense of the social context and the person-environment transaction. In effect, the uncritically held assumption that cognition is solely an activity in the head has distracted researchers and theorists from examining the depressive's involvement with the world. Mischel (1979) makes a similar point in suggesting we place the concept of "cognitive structure" in the interaction between the existing beliefs of the observer and the characteristics of the observed environment rather than simply placing it in the head of the observer.

Depressive symptomatology can be viewed from a behavioral, emotional, or motivational perspective in addition to a cognitive one. Depression can be described from the perspective of a deficit in adaptive (behavioral) resources accompanied by an excess of depressive complaints, whining, or avoidant behaviors. Depression can also be viewed as a persistence of negative mood (emotional) such that the pleasure associated with normal activities is not experienced and negative experiences are amplified. This emphasis calls attention to variables controlling mood and the need to determine the kinds of experiences that can disrupt this state. One can also emphasize the abulia, or "paralysis of will" (motivational), that characterizes depressed persons. One is thereby led to consider how it is that depressed persons have lost a purpose or direction to their behavior and what conditions would motivate a resumption of normal activities.

These alternative perspectives simply represent different facets of the same phenomenon, depression, all of which are genuine. These referents are often reinterpretations of the same observation from behavioral, emotional, or motivational perspectives. The adoption of any of these perspectives does not deny a critical role for cognition but only highlights a set of different considerations. In a strict sense, one cannot legitimately assign a unicausal status or priority to cognition or, for that matter, to behavior, motivation, or emotion. Depressive behavior, negative mood, low motivation, and cognitions of unworthiness, failure, and loss occur together as fused aspects of the same psychological event. Theoretical assertions that one aspect is an antecedent of the others in any absolute or unidirectional sense is more a matter of ideology than a testable proposition.

Implications for Treatment

In contrast to theory and research on depression generated from the cognitive perspective, the psychotherapeutic interventions associated with it seem flexible and eclectic, making use of a wide range of variables. Cognitive therapy for depression is usually much more than simply trying to change the depressed person's thoughts or assumptions. Consistent with this, Beck's (1976) approach to therapy has been criticized by Ellis (1977) for being too action-oriented and for downplaying "philosophic persuasion." Beck's approach does involve identification of the cognitions that figure in a given depressed person's symptoms, but then behavioral tasks are assigned that provide feedback capable of refuting these maladaptive attitudes. Rather than conceptualizing depression in terms of rigid cognitive structures, Beck's therapeutic interventions implicitly assume that depressed persons will reappraise themselves and their situations if they can only engage the environment in a way that produces inconsistent feedback.

The challenge is to circumvent the depressed person's complaints and to structure a task so that it is failure-proof. If depressed persons find that their coping is effective in a number of contexts, their appraisals will fall into agreement. Presumably, the person's depression has persisted only because such coping efforts have not been attempted in a way that appropriate outcomes were assured. Beck's therapy approach involves explicit structured homework assignments to break this pattern. Additionally, Beck's approach does not ignore affective and motivational considerations. Depressed persons may find a narrower range of activities as pleasurable or meaningful, but there are nonetheless activities that provide both enjoyment and a sense of purposeful accomplishment. Beck's "mastery and pleasure" therapy attempts to identify such specific activities and encourage them.

Studies thus far seem to indicate that cognitive-behavioral therapy is effective in the treatment of depression, even with patients whose pattern of symptomatology would suggest an "endogenous" label and a strong biological component. Cognitive-behavioral therapy for depression is truly cognitive in that it exploits the assumptions that people are not stimulus-bound but that they actively process information about their ongoing transactions with the environment and are therefore responsive to feedback. The depressed person is not treated as the hapless victim of inaccessible inner events, but rather as a person whose maladaptive view of the world, sadness, and lack of motivation are in a mutually maintaining relationship with an inept way of engaging the world. Cognitive-behavior therapy attempts to interdict this pattern at a number of junctures.

If one looks beyond what is said about the causes and nature of depression to what is actually being done in cognitive-behavioral therapy, the seeds of a broader transactional cognitive perspective can be found. The therapeutic approach assumes that people are thoughtful and potentially self-reflective, but also conative, affective, biological, and social beings. Cognitive theorists and researchers would do well to go beyond their narrow ideology to examine the intricate relationships among cognition, emotion, motivation, and behavior that are implicated in the process of therapeutic change.

A doctrinaire adherence to a theoretical sequence in which cognition is the sole antecedent condition has led researchers to focus narrowly on the description of cognitive distortions. As objects of study, the depressed person then becomes utterly detached from the environment, from bodily feedback, and from the goals, projects, commitments, and emotions that organize or disorganize his or her behavior. More than a description of cognitive distortions is needed. A comprehensive cognitive perspective on depression requires a description of how depressed persons appraise their ongoing relationship with their environment, how they cope, how they reappraise the results of this, and how motivational and affective variables and processes also shape these transactions.

Concluding Remarks

The concepts of cognition, motivation, and emotion emphasize different but related aspects of the person's transactions. The cognitive revolution has righted some excesses and imbalances in previous theory and research. It called attention to the usefulness of the assumption that people not only process and appraise information about the nature of their relationship to the environment, they also can exert considerable control over it. The importance of this point should not, however, distract us from the perspectives on the person-environment relationship provided by the concepts of emotion and motivation.

Emotion organizes our awareness that cognition and behavior are embodied, and that measures of the state of this body, whether physiological or subjective feelings, provide important information about the state of the person-environment relationship. Motivation emphasizes that people have goals, plans, projects, and commitments that organize the person-environment relationship. Apparent inconsistencies in the person's behavior can be explained potentially with reference to their relevance to these motivational considerations. Furthermore, motivational variables set the terms for the way a person construes transactions by identifying the stakes and payoffs that influence cognitive processes, action impulses, and the emotional response.

Thoughts, emotions, and motives are inferred from observations of the person, and we have noted how they often have the same referents. How we partition these concepts and punctuate theoretical sequences is often a matter of theoretical and methodological convenience. Yet we cannot lose sight of the fact that cognition, motivation, and emotion are inferential processes, not entities, each with a separate and independent existence. For purposes of conceptual analysis, it is appropriate to distinguish among them. However, we must realize that in nature, that is, in the actual phenomena of human experience and action, they are usually fused and difficult to separate. To speak of such fusion is not a matter of conceptual sloppiness but a recognition of the necessity of putting the pieces back together into an organized whole.

In his classic work, Ryle (1949) warned of the insolubility of certain theoretical questions about the relations among presumed inner entities. If cognition and emotion, for example, are separate entities in relation to each other, one has to establish some tie between them. But one cannot conceptualize this tie as either cognitive or emotional without disturbing their status as separate entities. The solution, of course, is that *people* think and respond emotionally, rather than endure passively the interaction of thoughts and emotion.

It is this point, i.e., that activity and involvement with the environment characterize people rather than detached fragments of them, that might allow the cognitive perspective to reintegrate the person, as McKeachie (1976) proposed in his A.P.A. presidential address. To focus on cognitions, motives, and emotions as separable entities, linked in strict, one-way causal sequences, is to continue the conceptual confusion of the past and to seriously distort their operation in the natural course of living. The pieces of poor Humpty-Dumpty cannot be allowed to lie separately and lifelessly on the ground, and however awesome the synthetic task, they must surely be put back together again.

References

Alloy, L. B., & Abramson, L. Y. Judgment of contingency in depressed and nondepressed students: Sadder but wiser? *Journal of Experimental Psychology: General,* in press.

Allport, G. W. *Personality: A psychological interpretation.* New York: Holt, 1937.

Ausubel, D. P. Relationships between shame and guilt in the socializing process. *Psychological Review,* 1955, *62,* 378–390.

Basowitz, H., Persky, H., Korchin, S. J., & Grinker, R. R. *Anxiety and stress.* New York: McGraw-Hill, 1955.

Beck, A. T. *Cognitive therapy and the emotional disorders.* New York: International Universities Press, 1976.

Beck, A. T., & Rush, A. J. Cognitive approaches to depression and suicide. In G. Serbin (Ed.), *Cognitive defects in the development of mental illness.* New York: Brunner/Mazel, 1978.

Brown, J., & Farber, I. E. Emotions conceptualized as intervening variables—with suggestions toward a theory of frustration. *Psychological Bulletin,* 1951, *48,* 465–495.

Buchwald, A. M. Depressive mood and estimates of reinforcement frequency. *Journal of Abnormal Psychology,* 1977, *86,* 443–446.

Buchwald, A. M., Strack, S., & Coyne, J. C. Demand characteristics and the Velten Procedure. *Journal of Consulting and Clinical Psychology,* in press.

Child, I. L., & Waterhouse, I. K., Frustration and the quality of performance: II. A theoretical statement. *Psychological Review,* 1953, *60,* 127–139.

Cohen, F., & Lazarus, R. S. Active coping processes, coping dispositions, and recovery from surgery. *Psychosomatic Medicine,* 1973, *35,* 375–389.

Cole, C. S., & Coyne, J. C. Situational specificity of laboratory-induced "learned helplessness." *Journal of Abnormal Psychology,* 1977, *86,* 615–623.

Coyne, J. C. Depression and the response of others. *Journal of Abnormal Psychology,* 1976, *85,* 186–193. (a)

Coyne, J. C. Toward an interactional description of depression. *Psychiatry,* 1976, *39,* 28–40. (b)

Coyne, J. C., & Lazarus, R. S. Cognition, stress, and coping: A transactional perspective. In I. L. Kutash & L. B. Schlesinger (Eds.), *Pressure point: Perspectives on stress and anxiety.* San Francisco: Jossey-Bass, in press.

Coyne, J. C., & Lazarus, R. S. The ipsative-normative framework for the longitudinal study of stress. Paper presented at the 87th Annual Convention of the American Psychological Association, New York, September, 1979.

Davis, A. Socialization and adolescent personality. *Yearbook of the National Society for the Study of Education,* 1944, *43,* Part I, 198–216.

Dember, W. N. Motivation and the cognitive revolution. *American Psychologist,* 1974, *29,* 161–168.

Dollard, J., & Miller, N. E. *Personality and psychotherapy.* New York: McGraw-Hill, 1950.

Duffy, E. Emotion: An example of the need for reorientation in psychology. *Psychological Review,* 1934, *41,* 184–198.

Duffy, E. An explanation of emotional phenomena without the use of the concept of "emotion." *Journal of General Psychology,* 1941, *25,* 283–293.

Duffy, E. *Activation and behavior.* New York: Wiley, 1962.

Ellis, A. *Reason and emotion in psychotherapy.* New York: Lyle Stuart, 1962.

Ellis, A. Review of cognitive therapy and the emotional disorders by A. T. Beck. *Behavior Therapy.* 1977, *8,* 295–296.

Folkman, S., Schaefer, C., & Lazarus, R. S. Cognitive processes as mediators of stress and coping. In V. Hamilton & D. M. Warburton (Eds.), *Human stress and cognition: An information-processing approach.* New York: Wiley, 1979, pp. 265–298.

Hull, C. L. *Principles of behavior.* New York: Appleton-Century-Crofts, 1943.

Isen, A. M., Shalker, T. E., Clark, M., & Karp, L. Affect, accessibility of material in memory and behavior: A cognitive loop? *Journal of Personality and Social Psychology,* 1978, *36*(1), 1–12.

Kelly, G. A. *The psychology of personal constructs.* New York: Norton, 1955 (2 volumes).

Klein, G. S. *Perception, motives and personality.* New York: Knopf, 1970.

Klinger, E. Consequences of commitment to and disengagement from incentives. *Psychological Review,* 1975, *82,* 1–25.

Klinger, E. *Meaning and void.* Minneapolis: University of Minnesota Press, 1977.

Koriat, A., Melkman, R., Averill, J. R., & Lazarus, R. S. The self-control of emotional reactions to a stressful film. *Journal of Personality,* 1972, *21,* 25–29.

Lacey, J. I. Somatic response patterning and stress: Some revisions of activation theory in psychological stress. In M. H. Appley & R. Trumbull (Eds.), *Psychological stress.* New York: Appleton-Century-Crofts, 1967.

Lazarus, R. S. *Psychological stress and the coping process.* New York: McGraw-Hill, 1966.

Lazarus, R. S. Emotions and adaptation: Conceptual and empirical relations. In W. J. Arnold (Ed.), *Nebraska Symposium on Motivation.* Lincoln: University of Nebraska Press, 1968.

Lazarus, R. S. The stress and coping paradigm. In C. Eisdorfer, D. Cohen, A. Kleinman, & P. Maxim (Eds.), *Theoretical bases for psychopathology.* New York: Spectrum, 1980.

Lazarus, R. S. The costs and benefits of denial. In S. Breznitz (Ed.), *Denial of stress.* New York: International Universities Press, in press.

Lazarus, R. S., Averill, J. R., & Opton, E. M., Jr. Toward a cognitive theory of emotions. In M. Arnold (Ed.), *Feelings and emotions.* New York: Academic Press, 1970, pp. 207–232.

Lazarus, R. S., Deese, J., & Osler, S. F. The effects of psychological stress upon performance. *Psychological Bulletin,* 1952, *49,* 293–317.

Lazarus, R. S., Kanner, A. D., & Folkman, S. Emotions: A cognitive-phenomenological analysis. In R. Plutchik & H. Kellerman (Eds.), *Theories of emotion.* New York: Academic Press, 1980.

Lazarus, R. S., & Launier, R. Stress-related transactions between person and environment. In L. A. Pervin & M. Lewis (Eds.), *Perspectives in interactional psychology.* New York: Plenum, 1978.

Lazarus, R. S., Speisman, J. C., Mordkoff, A. M., & Davison, L. A. A laboratory study of psychological stress produced by a motion picture film. *Psychological Monographs,* 1962, *76* (34, Whole No. 553).

Lewinsohn, P. M., Mischel, W., Chaplin, W., & Barton, R. Social competence and depression: The role of illusory self-perceptions? *Journal of Abnormal Psychology,* 1980, *89*(2), 203–212.

Lindsley, D. B. Emotions. In S. S. Stevens (Ed.), *Handbook of experimental psychology.* New York: Wiley, 1951.

Mahoney, M. J. Cognitive therapy and research: A question of questions. *Cognitive Therapy and Research,* 1977, *1,* 5–17. (a)

Mahoney, M. J. Reflections on the cognitive learning trend in psychotherapy. *American Psychologist,* 1977, *32,* 5–13. (b)

Malmo, R. B. Activation: A neuropsychological dimension. *Psychological Review,* 1959, *66,* 367–386.

Mason, J. W., Maher, J. T., Hartley, L. H., Mougey, E., Perlow, M. J., & Jones, L. G. Selectivity of corticosteroid and catecholamine response to various natural stimuli. In G. Serban (Ed.), *Psychopathology of human adaptation.* New York: Plenum, 1976, pp. 147–171.

McKeachie, W. J. Psychology in America's bicentennial year. *American Psychologist,* 1976, *31,* 819–833.

Miller, G. A., Galanter, E. H., & Pribram, K. *Plans and the structure of behavior.* New York: Holt, 1960.

Mischel, W. On the interface of cognition and personality. *American Psychologist,* 1979, *34,* 740–754.

Murray, H. A. *Exploration in personality.* New York: Oxford University Press, 1938.

Nelson, R. E., & Craighead, W. E. Selective recall of positive and negative feedback, self-control behaviors, and depression. *Journal of Abnormal Psychology,* 1977, *86,* 379–388.

Pervin, L. A. Are we leaving humans buried in conscious thought?: The cognitive revolution, and what it leaves out. Unpublished manuscript, 1979, Princeton University, Princeton, New Jersey.

Peters, H. N. Affect and emotion. In M. H. Marx (Ed.), *Theories in contemporary psychology.* New York: Macmillan, 1963, pp. 435–454.

Riegel, K. F. *Foundations of dialectical psychology.* New York: Academic Press, 1979.

Rogers, T., & Craighead, W. E. Physiological responses to self-statements: The effects of statement valence and discrepancy. *Cognitive Therapy and Research,* 1977, *1,* 99–120.

Rush, A. J., Beck, A. T., Kovacs, M., & Hollon, S. Comparative efficacy of cognitive therapy and imipramine in the treatment of depressed outpatients. *Cognitive Therapy and Research,* 1977, *1,* 17–37.

Ryle, G. *The concept of mind.* London: Hutchinson, 1949.

Sarason, I. G. Experimental approaches to test anxiety: Attention and the uses of information. In C. D. Spielberger (Ed.), *Anxiety: Current trends in theory and research* (Vol. 2). New York: Academic Press, 1972.

Sarason, S. B., Mandler, G., & Craighill, P. C. The effect of differential instructions on anxiety and learning. *Journal of Abnormal and Social Psychology,* 1952, *47,* 561–565.

Schachter, S. The interaction of cognitive and physiological determinants of emotional state. In C. D. Spielberger (Ed.), *Anxiety and behavior.* New York: Academic Press, 1966.

Shapiro, D., Tursky, B., & Schwartz, G. E. Differentiation of heart rate and blood pressure in man by operant conditioning. *Psychosomatic Medicine,* 1970, *32,* 417–423.

Shaw, B. F. A comparison of cognitive therapy and behavior therapy in the treatment of depression. *Journal of Consulting and Clinical Psychology,* 1977, *45,* 543–551.

Spence, J. A., & Spence, K. W. The motivational components of manifest anxiety: Drive and drive stimuli. In C. D. Spielberger (Ed.), *Anxiety and behavior.* New York: Academic Press, 1966.

Spence, K. W. *Behavior theory and conditioning.* New Haven: Yale University Press, 1956.

Spence, K. W. A theory of emotionally based drive (D) and its relation to performance in simple learning situations. *American Psychologist,* 1958, *13,* 131–141.

Spence, K. W., & Farber, I. E. The relation of anxiety to differential eyelid conditioning. *Journal of Experimental Psychology,* 1954, *47,* 127–134.

Taylor, J. A. A personality scale of manifest anxiety. *Journal of Abnormal and Social Psychology,* 1953, *48,* 285–290.

Teasdale, J. D., & Fogarty, S. J. Differential effects of induced mood on retrieval of pleasant and unpleasant events from episodic memory. *Journal of Abnormal Psychology,* 1979, *88,* 248–257.

Velten, E. A laboratory task for induction of mood states. *Behavioral Research and Therapy,* 1968, *6,* 473–482.

Webb, W. B. Motivational theory of emotions. *Psychological Review,* 1948, *55,* 329–335.

White, R. W. Motivation reconsidered: The concept of competence. *Psychological Review,* 1959, *66,* 297–333.

Wrubel, J., Benner, P., & Lazarus, R. S. Social competence from the perspective of stress and coping. In J. Wine & M. Smye (Eds.), *Social competence.* New York: Guilford, in press.

Yerkes, R. M., & Dodson, J. D. The relation of strength stimulus to rapidity of habit formation. *Journal of Comparative Neurological Psychology,* 1908, *18,* 459–482.

Chapter 9

On Decisional Processes Instigated By Threat: Some Possible Implications For Stress-Related Deviance*

R. W. J. NEUFELD

University of Western Ontario
London, Ontario

Just as the number of publications on anxiety mushroomed with the advent of the Taylor Manifest Anxiety Scale (Taylor, 1953), in the last few years studies on correlations between stress and a number of disorders have proliferated with the advent of life-event scales (e.g., Holmes & Masuda, 1974). Psychiatric disorders have not been exempt, several studies having reported their connection to increased frequencies of stressful life experiences (e.g., Hudgens, 1974; Paykel, 1974; for evaluative reviews, see chapters by Costello and by Spring & Coons, pp. 93–124 and 13–54, this volume; also Rabkin, 1980). Since the relations between stressful events and psychological disorder have been correlational—the preponderance of such events for patients are compared to the preponderance among nonpatients typically using retrospective surveys—it is possible that incipient psychopathology may potentially con-

*Studies on psychological stress carried out by the author, including those originally reported here, were supported by Grant 410-78-0568-R1 from the Social Sciences and Humanities Research Council of Canada. The research on schizophrenia and preparation of this manuscript were supported by Grant MA5028 from the Medical Research Council of Canada.

tribute to higher frequency of stressful experiences rather than the reverse.[1] Unfortunately, relatively few studies have been directed toward the question of why stress should generate symptoms of psychopathology. If the primary direction of influence is from the domain of stress to that of psychopathology, then it is conceivable that constituent processes mediating the effects of stress should intervene between these two domains. Theory and research directed to such processes may add substantially to our knowledge about these sets of relations.

In the absence of work on mediating events, some researchers investigating the biology of stress (e.g., Anisman, 1978; also Anisman & LaPierre, pp. 218–239, this volume; Goodwin & Bunney, 1973) have dissected the effects of stress on neurotransmittor amines in animals and, in turn, taken into account neurotransmittor correlates of affective disorders ("depression," "mania," and "hypomania"). The systematic analyses of stress, on the one hand, and correlates of certain syndromes, on the other, have provided some leads as to possible links between these two domains.

As mentioned, this work has been directed toward *biological* aspects of both stress and the selected disorders. Thus far, the literatures on the psychological aspects of stress and such disorders have not been as extensively integrated. This absence is a bit surprising because those working largely from a biological perspective have themselves pointed to the potential importance of cognitive-behavioral transactions with stressful events (Akiskal & McKinney, 1975; Anisman, 1978; Goodwin & Bunney, 1973). Akiskal and McKinney (1975) have noted the roles played by "cognitive schemata" and the severity of "psychosocial stressors" in effecting certain neurological events central to their hypotheses on depression. Goodwin and Bunney have referred to "prephysiologically significant" levels of stress occurring before substantial shifts in amine neurotransmittors take place. Similarly, Anisman (1978) cites cognitive variables—meaning the apparent cognizance of escape possibilities—as playing a role in moderating changes in amine (norepinephrine) levels among stressed animals. Accounts such as these suggest a "buffer zone" which may intervene between stressor onset and physiological events correlated with selected[2] disorders. Allowing for the time being that such a buffer zone is tenable, it is possible that this may be an area where findings on the psychology of stress and coping have potentially important implications for psychopathology.

Elucidation of the interface between stress and psychopathology from the perspective of cognitive-behavioral factors may take a worthwhile cue from the preceding approaches. The examination of overlap between biochemical effects of stress and biochemical correlates of psychopathology suggests a parallel analysis: examination of cognitive-behavioral aspects of stress in conjunction with cognitive-behavioral deficits in psychopathology.

---

[1]It is also possible that the direction of influence is two-way, or that any correlation between stressful experiences and psychiatric symptoms is attributable only to their mutual correlation with a third factor such as socioeconomic status.

[2]Goodwin and Bunney (1973) have interpreted clinical studies as indicating that catecholamine imbalance may be more closely related to "manic" and "hypomanic" symptoms than to "depression."

The following discussion adopts this perspective in developing possible links between stress and certain aspects of abnormal behavior. Emphasis is placed on events which are both undesirable and imminent (rather than ongoing). In other words, anticipated stressful occurrences (threats) form the main subject matter. As a result, potential roles of predictive judgments and decisional operations in negotiating with expected stress are considered in detail.

First, a sample of predictive assessments which may be involved in such transactions is outlined; later, a tentative schema of decision-related factors having to do with undertaking counterstress activities is presented. Implications of the latter schema for stress-relevant aspects of selected disorders are then discussed. Finally, some boundaries of the present formulations are outlined.

Situations with Potential Stress, Control over Their Confrontation, and Forms of Cognitive Deficit

In this section we want to illustrate some of the decisional factors implicated in deliberations about future stress. To motivate the discussion, we first present a scenario consisting of a person facing several potentially stressful situations, some being avoidable and some not. This example brings up a number of considerations.

One of these consists of the degree to which entry into any one of the situations is optional; in other words, can the person elect to enter into one or another situation, or is entry not controllable? Second, if entry is controllable, what factors might be involved in decisions surrounding it?

In this example, each hypothetical situation has a number of aspects that must be taken into account. For example, if a situation involved entering a social gathering, one aspect might be the possibility of an innocuous interchange with a friend; a second might be an interchange with someone who is particularly abrasive. Other aspects could also be taken into account. Each of these situational aspects has several subjective estimates attached to it: there is a certain likelihood of the aspect occurring; there is a certain likelihood of stress, given its occurrence; and the anticipated stress associated with the aspect of the situation has its own degree of expected severity. If such estimates of the constituent aspects making up the situation at large were sufficiently undesirable when considered together, the situation may be avoided in favor of an alternative one, such as staying home or attending a different event.

The assessment of a situational aspect can be considered in decision-theoretical terms as follows. Because both "likelihood of event occurrence" and "undesirability of the event" are implicated in this example, the evaluation of a given aspect can be translated into "expectancy" terminology:

The expected stress associated with a given situational aspect [E(stress)/situational aspect] is the subjective probability that the aspect will arise [P(situational aspect)], multiplied by the probability of stress, should the situational aspect arise (P(stress/

situational aspect), multiplied, finally, by the anticipated severity of stress[3] associated with the aspect under consideration [(stress impact)]. Using the terms in square brackets:

E(stress)/situational aspect $=$ P(situational aspect) P(stress/situational aspect) (stress impact).

At this point, it should be mentioned that the above formulation involves the "expectancy" portion of anticipated stress only. As such, consideration of possible stress instigated by the assessment process itself is temporarily put aside. However, certain aspects of stress associated with the demands of the judgment process receive some attention later in this chapter. In addition, the format of the preceding equation is somewhat idealistic in the following sense. It is based on subjective expected utility theory (Edwards, 1955) which requires a rather stringent set of assumptions about the relationships between values of probability and "cost" (in this case, "stress impact") (see Payne, 1973). In most cases of betting or economic predictions, the assumptions may not be tenable (Slovic, Fischoff, & Lichtenstein, 1977). As we see later in this chapter, they appear to be equally suspect in the area of stress-related judgments. Nevertheless, the formulation above can serve a useful purpose. It permits an estimation of the information which can potentially enter into judgments—which indeed should enter into such judgments—according to mathematical expectancy theory. As such, the formulation can be used to identify the amount of potentially relevant information bearing on the desirability (or undesirability) of alternative situations. Whether or not persons actually employ the relevant information in the manner defined is another matter (and considered in more detail later).

The amount of potential information formulated this way can vary substantially according to the number of options available to the individual. Consider the following components of "control," viewed for the time being as avoidability of the entities under consideration. The first component is whether or not situations can be avoided; the second is whether or not their constituent aspects can be avoided. In Table 9-1, several combinations of these components are listed in the first column. The middle column contains the relevant terms of the corresponding judgments, and the third column indicates the objects of these judgments. The list of combinations by no means exhausts the total number of combinations available (e.g., in a given set of circumstances, "situational aspects" may be controllable in one "situation" but not another). Furthermore, the list is restricted to circumstances where situation and aspects are "mutually exclusive" and "independent" meaning that: (1) if one situation or aspect is confronted, the remainder, at least for the time being, are not; and (2) the probability value for one aspect does not affect the probability value for

---

[3]In terms of formal "expectancy" theory, the sum of cross products consisting of each possible amount of stress which may emerge in the aspect under consideration, multiplied by the corresponding probability of that amount occurring, should be included; however, for illustrative purposes, violating this requirement by including only one value (say, the maximum anticipated level of stress) does not appear to be serious when considering the gain in simplicity of presentation.

Table 9-1 **Nature of Judgmental Estimates and Number of Estimates as a Function of Control Avoidability**

CIRCUMSTANCES OF CONTROL	RELEVANT JUDGMENTAL INFORMATION	OBJECTS OF JUDGMENT AND TOTAL NUMBER OF JUDGMENTS TO BE MADE (IN SQUARE BRACKETS)
A. Control over situation entry and control over situation aspect	P (stress/situational aspect) (stress impact)	Each relevant*situation aspect of each situation [(number of situations) $\times$ (number of relevant situational aspects)]
B. Control over situation entry but no control over situation aspect; each aspect arises according to (subjective) prior probabilities**	P (situational aspect) P (stress/situational aspect) (stress impact)	Each relevant aspect of each situation [(number of situations) $\times$ (number of relevant situational aspects)]
C. Control over situation entry but no control over situation aspect; aspect is arbitrarily assigned	P (stress/assigned situational aspect) (stress impact)	Single assigned aspect of each situation (number of situations)
D. No control over situation entry, but control over situation aspect	P (stress/situational aspect) (stress impact)	Each relevant aspect of single assigned situation (number of relevant situational aspects)
E. No control over situation entry and no control over situation aspect; aspect arises according to subjective prior probabilities	P (situational aspect) P (stress/situational aspect) (stress impact)	Each relevant aspect of single assigned situation (number of relevant situational aspects)
F. No control over situation entry and no control over situation aspect; aspect is arbitrarily assigned	P (stress/assigned situational aspect) (stress impact)	Single assigned aspect of single assigned situation (1)

Note: Terms of the middle column are defined in the formula for E (stress/situational aspect) in the text. The number of situations and their relevant aspects are considered to be constant across A through F; for convenience, circumstances of uncontrollable situation entry where the subjective probability of confrontation invokes subjective prior probability values of situation occurrence, are omitted.

*The term "relevant" refers to those situational aspects where both P (stress/situational aspect) as well as (stress impact) exceed 0.

**See text for explanation.

another. For convenience, the number of aspects per situation is left constant. This latter condition, while clearly artificial, permits the same inferences as would be drawn if situations had differing numbers of relevant aspects. It also allows matters to be simplified by dispensing with mathematical summation notation. Of course, it goes without saying that situations which in reality would have relatively few relevant aspects to consider would require correspondingly fewer judgments than those with more aspects. As a final qualification, note that the term *prior probability* refers to one's subjective estimate that a situational aspect will arise as in the usual course of events (e.g., one's estimate of its past probability of occurrence).

Having made these qualifying statements, we can now turn to an examination of Table 9-1. Several observations are in order. First, as one proceeds from circumstances where situation entry is under the individual's control to those where it is not (control over situation aspects momentarily held constant), there is a marked decline in the number of judgments that might be undertaken. Consider, for example, contrasts of the square-bracketed numbers in the third column for the following pairs of circumstances: A versus D, B versus E, and C versus F. Similarly, moving from circumstances which permit control over selection of relevant situation aspects to those which do not (control over situation entry held momentarily constant), a decline in the number of possible judgments occurs. Consider, for example, circumstances A versus C, and D versus F.

With the entry of prior probabilities, an increase in the information appropriate to a given judgment, though not necessarily the number of judgments, can occur as control over situational aspects is decreased; for example, compare the middle column for circumstances A and B, and for D and E. On the other hand, when prior probabilities become appropriate and control is kept constant, both the amount of information per judgment and the number of judgments can increase: C versus B and F versus E. Overall, controllability as depicted in Table 9-1 leads to increased demands on the synthesizing of information. This trend appears most dramatically when comparing circumstances A (or B) to F.

Further consideration of Table 9-1 suggests two main components of judgmental behavior which may have a bearing on cognitive deficit in psychopathology. The first involves the content of the judgments; in other words, given that predictive estimates occur, what form do they take? This component relates to the values taken on by the respective probability and "stress-impact" terms of Table 9-1. A propensity toward expecting negative outcomes could express itself in terms of higher probability and/or stressor-impact values. This type of expectation has been linked to "clinical anxiety," (e.g., Beck, Laude, & Bonehart, 1974); to "clinical levels of depression" (Beck, 1967, 1974); as well as, under certain circumstances, to "compulsive neuroses" (Carr, 1974). However, it should be noted that each of these sets of correlates between negative expectations and clinical syndromes has been based more on clinical observations and case studies than on formal investigations.

The second component involves the "availability" of predictive judgments, regardless of their content. Requirements in the way of information processing include the formulation of the judgments and then their combination into an integrated assessment. In some instances, the predictive judgments may be less attainable because of constraints emanating from external conditions in which the judgments must take place (e.g., in unfamiliar situations where the relevant aspects cannot be discerned; and/or where situational aspects are unfamiliar, and probability and stress impact values cannot be formulated). However, our primary focus is on other sources of reduced availability of judgments, specifically, those sources stemming from lessened capacity of an individual to process the necessary information.

Referring once again to Table 9-1, persons with lower processing ability may perform less adequately in at least four contingents of the types of judgmental assessments under consideration. The first of these is the initial detection of control options. The inequalities among the circumstances depicted in column 1 of Table 9-1 would be meaningless if the control options (or lack of options) characterizing each case were undetected.

A second source of difficulty entails one's access to the information entering into the respective judgments represented by the middle column of Table 9-1. The constituents of such access appear to be (1) identification of salient characteristics of the objects of prediction and (2) memory of past events and conveyed information associated with these characteristics (see Estes, 1976). For example, one may be considering a new job situation. Suppose one aspect of the situation consists of facing a reprimand from one's superior. The subjective probability that this event will occur—P (situational aspect)—may depend on the salient characteristics of the job milieu (e.g., the observed tolerance versus intolerance of mistakes made by one's coworkers) in conjunction with the interpretation of these characteristics according to past experience. Apart from its probability of occurrence, the event of facing a reprimand may be submitted to one's memory so as to ascertain certain accompanying properties: the subjective probability and the impact values of stress—values of P (stress-situational aspect) and stress impact, respectively.

To the degree that the relevant characteristics of the situation cannot be discerned or that the relevant information surrounding them is unavailable in memory, the judgments would be undermined. Deficits in cognitive abilities underlying either of these components would be expected to detract from these judgments.

A third source of potential difficulty involves the load placed on the processing system in terms of the number of judgments to be made. As we have already said in reference to Table 9-1, these vary considerably over the various sets of circumstances depicted there. Where requirements are increased, individuals less able to undertake a larger number of judgments would be expected to perform more poorly.

A fourth source of difficulty involves the synthesis of the formulated judgments. Formal "mathematical expectancy theory" requires that the products appearing in the middle column of Table 9-1 for a given set of circumstances be summed. The number of such products to be summed is stated in the corresponding row of the third column. However, it is doubtful that subjects actually combine individual judgments through the summing of cross products (see Payne, 1973). Regardless of the specific means whereby judgments are combined, as their number increases, the demands on synthesizing processes, in whatever form they take, also increase. Deficiencies in operations involving information combination would be expected to interfere with performance, especially under circumstances with heavy demands of this sort.

Columns 2 and 3 of Table 9-1 suggest the types and numbers of judgments inherent in various circumstances of electability in situations and situation aspects. There are likely to be wide differences in the degree to which actual judgments conform to the presented configurations. Departures from these configurations are likely to occur among normal subjects (as studies in the next section suggest). More severe departures would be expected from those suffering cognitive deficits associated with psychopathology.

The most pronounced effects of deficiencies in carrying out and synthesizing constituent judgments should occur under those circumstances where processing demands are greatest; in other words, under such circumstances, departure from the appropriate judgment operations would be most apparent. (As we saw, according to Table 9-1 the greater processing demands may often accompany stimulus constellations where control [avoidability] of situations and/or situational aspects are also greater.)

According to studies of cognitive operations among psychiatric patients, there is good reason to suggest that certain syndromes of psychopathology may increase susceptibility to stress under circumstances where the types of processing operations enumerated above are called for. Because of their association with deficits in such operations, perhaps the most prominent syndromes to be implicated are the categories of schizophrenia (see Broga & Neufeld, 1981). A survey of the literature on cognitive performance among these patients suggests a number of deficits which may lead to shortcomings in the types of judgments outlined here. Delineating which specific deficits hamper which specific processing operations would seem a worthwhile pursuit, but one requiring extensive treatment well beyond the scope of this chapter.

Before leaving this topic, we should mention that "processing inefficiency" has also been found among patients with "depressive illnesses." Cognitive deficit among these patients has often been associated with bias in the content of predictions, the bias being viewed as one of greater expected stress, or increased "pessimism" about important areas of one's functioning (see Shaw, pp. 125–146, this volume). However, deficits in the efficiency of judgmental performance have been found in the form of general retardation on intellectual tests (Payne & Hewlett, 1960). More recently, using paradigms assessing the components of "information processing," depressed patients have been found to share certain deficits with those classified as "schizophrenic" (Hemsley & Zawada, 1976; Russell & Beekhuis, 1976), while other deficits appear to be unique among "depressives" (compare Byrne, 1976, to Koh, Szoc, & Peterson, 1977; Marusarz & Koh, 1980; Neufeld, 1977; Russell, Considine, & Knight, 1977; Checkosky, cited in Sternberg, 1975; Wishner, Stein, & Paestrel, 1978).

These observations and inferences drawn from Table 9-1 far from exhaust those available. However, the framework presented there is essentially a tentative "working" one, that is, it is based on a logical rather than empirical analysis of informational dimensions and circumstances of "control." Hence, the observations and inferences are somewhat speculative, and, as such, they should be treated with due caution. Considering these limitations, enumeration of all possible inferences is certainly not in order.

Nevertheless, tentative frameworks such as these have been found useful in research on psychopathology in the past (see Maher, 1970). They can serve the positive purpose of integrating extant findings and generating new tests. If viewed with a healthy skepticism, they can serve the negative purpose of preventing their being taken at face value prematurely.

The types of formal arithmetic models put forth as "objectively appropriate" forms of information derivation and combination may not accurately describe what subjects do in reality. Varying degrees of departure from "ideal" modes of information processing certainly exist. According to the literature on predictive judgments, it seems unlikely that normal subjects implement information in the "orthodox manner" couched in these models.

While the studies do not in themselves bear directly on processing among patient samples, they are nevertheless presented in some detail for these reasons. First, they provide examples of how research in the experimental analysis of cognitive processes might be applied to predictive appraisals of stress. Second, because they assess the judgmental strategies used by normals, including certain inaccuracies implied by these strategies, the studies carry some interest in their own right. Third, in suggesting the types of processes which may be involved in predictive judgments among normals, they indicate subject matter for research among abnormal samples; the resulting questions are of the form, "How do the processes identified among normals operate differently among pathological populations?"

Predictive Judgments of Stress

The aim of this section is threefold: first, to present a general description of the main avenues of research on cognitive processes involved in predictive behaviors; second, to draw out possible implications for predictions surrounding the anticipation of stress; and third, to present data bearing on the extension of predictive processes in general to predictions surrounding stress in specific.

Examination of the literature on predictive judgments reveals two semi-independent approaches to this topic. The first is based on a branch of learning theory devoted to "associative models of memory" (see Estes, 1975, 1976, 1977). The second is based on the analysis of "predictive heuristics," referring to inferential properties surrounding the objects of prediction—properties which may enter into these judgments inappropriately (Kahneman & Tversky, 1973).

The approach based on associative models of memory places emphasis on those aspects of prediction which depend on the frequencies of events. In this case, attention is directed toward discrete events (e.g., winning versus losing outcomes among competitors). The cumulative frequencies of occurrences of these events in recent experience are examined with respect to the roles they play in predictions. One concern has been to compare the frequency of one type of outcome (e.g., winning) to that of the opposite type with respect to its influence on predictions (e.g., predicting the winner of a match between two competitors). In examining the comparative influence of the alternate types of events under various conditions, a number of inferences have been drawn about the way frequency information is involved in such judgments. These inferences have surrounded two main operations: (1) the manner in which subjects arrange relative frequencies of each type of event or category in memory; and (2) the manner in which these memorial representations are brought forward for ensuing predictions. The research procedures and interpretations of findings from this approach are considered quite thoroughly because they provide fertile examples of work on cognitive processes which can be extended to stress-related predictions. In addition, the extensions as presented later, require considerable methodological detail to point out required paradigm changes in the transition to stress investigations.

The basic paradigm in a sequence of studies on these questions has been as follows. Subjects are presented with pairs of stimuli putatively representing two competing political candidates, or two commercial products. They are told that opinion polls have been conducted on each item and that the results are to be presented by successively pitting one against the other and showing which was the winner. Accordingly, a marker indicates the item in each pair preferred over the other. After a substantial number of such presentations ("information" trials), subjects are once again presented with pairs of the earlier items (though mainly in combinations different from before) but are now asked to predict the winning item on the present occasion ("judgment trials").

During the information trials, some items are presented more often than others. Unequal frequency of occurrence permits several advantages in studying the parameters of interest. For example, as one proceeds from item to item, the number of victories accumulated by each can be kept independent of the number of losses accumulated. In other words, a coefficient of correlation calculated between values of "total wins" and "total losses" across the various items can be maintained at 0; if frequencies of appearance were kept equal across the items, the correlation between total win and total loss values would inevitably be -1.

A second advantage is that total frequencies of either wins or losses can be kept from correlating perfectly with "contingent probability," the latter term referring to the probability that an item will win, given its appearance. Contingent probability is most easily calculated as the proportion of an item's appearances which were winning occasions. Two items can have identical cumulative frequencies of victories but unequal contingent probabilities as follows. Suppose item A was presented 50 times and was preferred to its competitor 20 times. The contingent probability of item A would be .40. Item B, on the other hand, may have been presented only 25 times, but with a contingent probability of .80, it would have accumulated the same number of wins as item A.

The inferences made available by these advantages will become apparent as we discuss the findings from the experiments and their implications for frequency information in predictive judgments. Results from each study indicated that subjects used certain categories of information at the expense of other equally relevant categories. The category most influential in predictive judgments was that of winning outcomes, while the frequencies of losing outcomes were relatively incidental to these judgments.

Because of this imbalance in influence, several consequences were forthcoming. Because use of the contingent probability required essentially an even focus on both types of outcome, contingent-probability values were less highly correlated with the judgment configurations than were those of the winning-outcome frequencies. Second, because calculation of the absolute *frequency of occurrence* of a given item requires consideration of both winning and losing outcomes, subjects were evidently insensitive to variation in this variable. Third, and somewhat redundantly, subjects based their judgments on total-win-frequency values regardless of how these values came about. Subjects did not distinguish between those items accumulating numerous wins by virtue of comparatively large contingent-probability values from those accumulating numerous wins simply because they appeared more often.

The third consequence represents the principal source of judgmental error as revealed in these experiments. Where one item has a higher contingent probability than a second, it should be predicted as the winner over the second. However, if the second item has appeared more often and thereby accumulated more wins than the first, subjects will erroneously tend to select the second item as the winner.

Implications for memorial processes involved in the use of frequency data were drawn as follows. First, the types of judgments and their integration into the main dependent variables should be considered. During each judgment trial, the subject was required to make a discrete prediction as to which item of the presented pair would be the winner. The proportion of aggregate judgments where the first item in the pair was picked over the second formed the datum of principal interest. The proportion for each pair of items was based primarily on the ratio of total wins for the first to total wins for the second. Estes (1976) suggested that subjects behaved as though winning occasions for each item were attended to and encoded; later, on being called to predict the winning item, memory scanning may have taken the form of probing for memory traces associated with each item in the pair. The relative number of times the first item would be picked over the second item would then be proportional to the preponderance of memorial "win traces" for the first item as compared to the second.

In this approach to investigating predictions, the objects of judgment were essentially "content free" in the sense that letters of the alphabet were used to stand for hypothetical competitors. The only meaningful information available to the subjects was the past frequencies of the alternate types of outcomes. Thus, the role of categorical memory in predictive behaviors could be examined without interference from other factors such as characteristics of the objects of prediction. Subjects were restricted to categorical frequencies, and this specific aspect of judgment could be studied in isolation.

In contrast, studies carried out on "predictive heuristics" have left the content of the object of prediction free to vary (see Kahneman & Tversky, 1973). Examination has centered on how dimensions of content are brought into play and how they replace the appropriate statistical data for predictions. For example, subjects may be asked to judge how likely it is that a personality description of a hypothetical student fits someone in science versus someone in liberal arts. Here, one can use such statistical properties as the preponderance of each category of student on campus ("base rates"), the contingent probability that, given a student from faculty "X," the present personality description would be obtained, and so on. Instead of using the appropriate combinations of statistical data, judges have tended to base their inferences on the characteristics of the judged objects themselves. Illustrations of such characteristics include the similarity between the judged object and the predicted event (e.g., the similarity between the personality description referred to in the example and the student stereotype associated with each faculty); the feasibility of the object of prediction causing the predicted event (e.g., the feasibility of certain personality traits "causing" one to enroll in faculty "X"); the salience of associations between the object and the predicted event in memory; and so on.

The "predictive-heuristic" approach to this topic can be compared to the "categorical-memory" approach in the following way. The categorical-memory approach concentrates on errors in the use of statistical (frequency) information in terms of its incorrect combination; the predictive-heuristic approach concentrates on errors in terms of the replacement of statistical information with dimensions of content. Each approach unveils potentially important processes involved in predictive operations, and each can be used to uncover aspects of judgmental behavior surrounding predictions of stress.

First, we should consider some of the modifications in research paradigms necessary for examining categorical-frequency aspects of stress predictions. One of these changes involves the number of stimuli judged at one time. In the paradigm where the subject predicted whether a given item would win, the item needed a competitor so that stimuli had to be presented in pairs. However, in predicting whether or not a stimulus will produce an "undesirable event," the stimulus can be judged singly.

Second, judgments involved in stress predictions are not necessarily discrete as they were in the case of the win-lose paradigm. Instead, degrees of likelihood are possible; a person may be more apt to assess the *probability* of an undesirable occurrence than to make an all-or-none assessment.

Third, the categories of outcomes are different. They should involve events which differ in stressor properties; for example, one category of outcome might consist of physically aversive events while another consists of benign events.

With paradigm changes such as these, changes in the influences of categorical frequencies may also shift. For example, consider the number of category frequencies potentially entering into a comparison between two stimuli in the earlier paradigm. An even balance of attention to each type of outcome would require consideration of four protocols at a time, the winning and losing frequencies of each item in the pair. Subjects may be inclined to "economize" on the amount of information taken into account by reducing the number of protocols by one-half—the two winning records only. On the other hand, when dealing with one stimulus at a time, as in stress-related predictions, only two protocols of events are relevant: the stimulus record of undesirable outcomes and its record of benign outcomes. Since there are fewer sets of frequencies to deal with at the outset, judges may be more inclined to take due account of each one. Furthermore, since the types of events involved in such cases are more personally relevant (in the sense that they happen to the judge himself or herself rather than to some hypothetical entity), there is added reason to suggest that judges may give balanced attention to the alternative types of outcome.

On the other hand, if, as we suggested, probability rather than all-or-none judgments were undertaken, each assessment might be more demanding. Estes (1976) has suggested that a single probability judgment may result from a series of covert all-or-none predictions. As such, increased economy in the way of a diminished number of outcome protocols may be offset by increased complexity of probability assessments.

All in all, the operation of categorical frequency information in stress-related predictions appears to require empirical data to help answer some of these questions. Herzog and Neufeld (Note 1) carried out a study where the paradigmatic changes for stress predictions were undertaken. The task was presented in the guise of market research, with the question of interest putatively directed to how individuals evaluated audio equipment (electrical resistors of varying quality). Each "resistor" (eight in all) was designated by its own upper-case letter which appeared on a screen during each of its "test trials."

If, on a given trial, the resistor "failed," a 1-sec burst of 100 or 110 db SPL white noise (each level having been found to elicit consistent ratings of "stress" according to preliminary scaling) would be delivered through headphones; if the resistor "held," a corresponding period of silence, accompanied by a green light above the screen, would occur instead. Subjects were later required to make judgments about the probability of noise occurring to each upper-case letter (judgment trials). After these judgment trials, several additional estimates pertaining to other stimulus properties were obtained.

During the test trials, the upper-case letters did not appear the same number of times. The inequality allowed the total frequency of "noise" occurrences to be imperfectly correlated with the contingent probability values; it also permitted a correlation between the frequencies of noise and silence to be 0. Hence, as in the previous work on win-loss records and prediction, the contribution of each of the latter two types of information could be isolated. Finally, to increase the salience of certain types of outcome, one-third (40) of the subjects pronounced "silence" after each silent outcome; one-third pronounced "noise" after each noise outcome; and one-third pronounced neither type of outcome.

Results from this experiment were as follows. The judged probabilities of noise, averaged over all subjects in the experiment, correlated .98 with the frequencies of noise; conversely, the judgments correlated only −.15 with the frequencies of silence. This imbalance suggested that the contingent probabilities, which required both types of events to be taken into account, would not be weighted as heavily as the frequency of noise. The actual correlation was .80. According to analysis of variance, the pattern of judgments remained constant across the different conditions of pronounciation.[4]

As mentioned earlier, several additional judgments were made. Two of these were obtained for the following reason. The influence of a particular type of outcome would seem to require a subject both to register it in memory during test trials and to scan its memorial representation during the predictive judgments. The influence of one type of outcome may be degraded because it is not scanned at the time of prediction rather than because it has not been registered when it occurred. Therefore, subjects were requested to estimate the frequency of noise and the frequency of silence. The mean judged frequency of noise correlated .97 with the actual frequency of noise, and .01 with the actual frequency of silence. However, the mean judged frequency of silence also correlated substantially with the actual frequency of noise, $r = -.97$, but trivially with the actual frequency of silence, $r = -.05$. Finally, judgments of subjective stress associated with each item followed the same pattern as those of the probability judgment just described.

It is fairly apparent from these data that earlier findings on the operation of categorical frequencies in the prediction of innocuous events generalized with little modification to stress-related predictions. The generalization occurred despite the several changes in the experimental task outlined earlier. The main difference in results from previous findings pertained to the effects of outcome pronunciation. Estes (1976) found that when the occurrences of initially degraded outcomes (losses) were pronounced, and the initially enhanced outcomes (wins) were not, the influence of the first increased appreciably. However, the pronunciation conditions made little difference to the configuration of present results.

All in all, it is apparent that essentially the only information entering into the predictive and other judgments was noise frequency. It was suspected that a subject might probe his/her memory for two types of traces associated with the stimulus at hand: those of a "stimulus-noise" format and those of a "stimulus-silence" format.

---

[4]Because the contingent probability values were correlated moderately with the frequency of each type of outcome, "part correlations" were also computed. Here, the correlations between the judgments and the contingent-probability and outcome frequencies were obtained after the correlations between the contingent-probability and outcome frequencies had first been removed. The part correlation between the judgments and the frequency of noise was .42; that between the judgments and the frequency of silence was −.22; and the part correlation between the judgments and the contingent probabilities was .013. Correlations carried out on individual subject data, rather than on the collapsed data, produced similar results. However, as expected, the average correlation for the responses taken individually were lower. For example, that between the judgments and the frequency of noise was reduced from .98 to .82.

The proportion of traces of a "stimulus-noise" variety might then be used as the basis of one's estimate. Instead, the data suggested that predictions for the various stimuli were determined more or less exclusively by their relative densities of "stimulus-noise" traces.

Interpretation of these results has leaned rather heavily on the concept of "retention of selected categorical frequencies in memory." However, before leaving these data, an alternative—and in some ways simpler—interpretation should be mentioned: despite the variation in frequencies of appearance of the several items (some items differing in this regard by a factor of 3.6), throughout their judgments subjects may still have assumed that the items occurred equally often. (After the experimental session, subjects seldom remarked that some items were presented more often than others.) If so, the inaccurate aspects of these judgments may have reflected not so much the unavailability of certain earlier event categories in memory as the operation of the false assumption of equal frequency of item appearance which allowed subjects to regard these earlier event categories as informationally redundant and to neglect them.

The preceding study pertained to the operation of categorical frequencies in stress-related predictive judgments. An additional study was carried out from the perspective of the "predictive heuristic" approach to forecasting events. In this study, several hypothetical incidents were presented to several groups in questionnaire form. Unlike the previous study, the objects of judgment varied considerably in content (see the 15 incidents listed in Table 9-2). One group of 30 undergraduates rank-ordered the incidents according to the likelihood that each would produce stress according to the following instructions:

In the following task, we would like you to make some judgments about stress. Stress is usually described by people as occurring in the following situations:

where there is potential embarrassment or threat associated with interpersonal relations;

where there is the very real risk of physical danger;

where the situation is new or strange;

where there is the real possibility of pain;

where there is a risk of failure at something important;

where there is the threat of punishment because of some offense or some incomplete task.

This is what we are referring to as stress, and it is what we would like you to make judgments about. In front of you, there is a selection of situations. You are to make judgments about what would happen if you encountered them. Specifically, we want you to assess the likelihood that stress would occur in each. Your task is to rank the situations from highest to lowest according to the *likelihood that they would produce stress* upon *future* encounter. The situation ranked highest would have the highest likelihood of producing it, and the situation ranked lowest would have the least likelihood of producing it.

Table 9-2 **Hypothetical Incidents, Mean Rank Predictive Responses, and Mean Rank Scale Values**

		SITUATION SCALE VALUES			
Incident	PREDICTIVE RESPONSES	SIMILARITY TO "TYPICAL STRESS-INDUCING SITUATION"	STRESSFUL PROPORTION OF PAST ENCOUNTERS	TOTAL NUMBER OF PAST STRESSFUL ENCOUNTERS	TOTAL NUMBER OF PAST NONSTRESSFUL ENCOUNTERS
1. Having just been returned an examination paper with one of the lowest marks in the class	4.50	4.13	5.40	7.29	11.30
2. Doing poorly on a final examination with a low average going into the examination	3.50	3.27	4.07	6.53	11.10
3. Sailing in a boat on rough waters with an inexperienced friend	6.17	6.83	8.03	9.30	10.20
4. While on a hike, having ventured onto a high mountainside	4.87	6.07	6.97	9.03	10.03
5. Taking an automobile trip on a freeway during a holiday weekend	10.56	10.43	10.03	8.67	6.17
6. Chatting with some friends about a weekend social event	14.27	13.37	13.0	10.63	3.00
7. Giving an oral presentation before a large class	5.3	4.47	4.03	5.03	10.40
8. Being able to follow the professor's points during a lecture	11.43	10.63	10.133	8.0	5.67
9. Getting exactly the questions expected on an examination	11.3	11.67	10.07	9.3	5.47
10. Halfway through a trip in a jumbo jet and being told by the captain to fasten seat belts and extinguish cigarettes because of an unexpected emergency	3.97	4.07	5.13	9.23	10.77
11. Discussing television with some classmates during a break between classes	14.13	14.1	14.03	10.533	3.67

Table 9-2 Hypothetical Incidents, Mean Rank Predictive Responses, and Mean Rank Scale Values
(*Continued*)

| | | SITUATION SCALE VALUES | | | |
Incident	PREDICTIVE RESPONSES	SIMILARITY TO "TYPICAL STRESS-INDUCING SITUATION"	STRESSFUL PROPORTION OF PAST ENCOUNTERS	TOTAL NUMBER OF PAST STRESSFUL ENCOUNTERS	TOTAL NUMBER OF PAST NONSTRESSFUL ENCOUNTERS
12. Starting a new summer job	7.27	8.27	6.63	7.33	7.80
13. Taking a blood test at the doctor's office	9.83	9.50	9.17	9.00	6.50
14. Waiting for the insertion of a needle during a dental appointment	6.90	7.63	6.30	6.10	8.77
15. Waiting for your paper while the professor hands back an examination	6.00	5.57	6.37	4.00	9.17

Now please arrange the situations according to their ranks from highest to lowest. Are there any questions?

The referent description of stress was designed to incorporate the factors common to several multivariate analyses of subjective reports (Ekehammar, Magnusson, & Ricklander, 1974; Endler & Okada, 1970; Magnusson & Ekehammar, 1975; Neufeld, 1978).

Four other groups were given similar instructions but were asked to judge other properties of the incidents. One group was asked to rank-order the incidents in terms of their similarity to the "typical stressful situation." This group provided data on the "representativeness" heuristic, the one considered most appropriate from among the several heuristics studied so far (see Tversky & Kahneman, 1978). One of the remaining three groups judged the proportion of times that past encounters with each incident were stressful, another group judged the absolute number of past stressful encounters with each incident, and the last group judged the absolute number of benign encounters with each incident. The last two sets of judgments reflected certain aspects of categorical-frequency information, with the second last group providing estimates of the frequencies of stressful encounters, and the last group providing estimates of the frequencies of benign encounters. Although categorical-frequency and inferential heuristic approaches to predictive behavior have seldom been studied in combination, it is conceivable that scaled frequency values may provide information additional to the scaled heuristic values. Of course, the relationship of the scaled frequency values to actual past frequencies cannot be ascertained; as noted in the preceding experiment, the judged values may be nonveridical with "real" values. Nonetheless, at least the scale values permit an estimate of how the "cognitive representation" of the frequency dimensions enter into the predictive judgments.

The correlations of the average rank orders for the predictive judgments with those of the respective dimensions were as follows: .98 with similarity between the judged incidents and "typically stressful incidents"; .96 with proportion of prior encounters judged as entailing stress; .58 with total number of past stressful encounters; and −.99 with total number of prior nonstressful encounters. Clearly, the "representativeness heuristic" adequately described the predictions, as did the scale values for the stressful portions of past encounters and (inversely) the number of benign past encounters. The lower correlation for the number of past stressful encounters suggested that subjects were somewhat sensitive to the fact that the more dangerous incidents seldom occurred.

Pursuing this observation for a moment, several relationships of interest can be educed. First, if in assessing the total frequency of stressful contacts, subjects implicitly multiplied the total frequencies of encounter by the stressful portions (representing contingent probabilities) of past encounters in the appropriate way, then the following results should hold. When a partial correlation coefficient is computed between the predictive judgments and the judged number of stressful contacts, with the "contingent probability" values partialed out of each, the resulting coefficient should be negative (ostensibly reflecting the sensitivity of judges to the fact that the more stressful or dangerous incidents occur less often). The obtained partial correlation was −.541, a change of −1.12 from the intact correlation. In contrast, the partial correlation between the contingent probabilities and the predictive judgments, with the total frequencies of stressful encounters partialed out, was .95, a change of −.01.

From this set of correlations, one is tempted to suggest that the judgments generally conformed to the appropriate statistical rules: the contingent probability values—the appropriate statistical information—appear to have described the predictive assessments adequately. However, it was possible that subjects were in fact using the "representativeness heuristic" and that the apparent influence of the contingent probability values was fortuitous by virtue of its correlation of .97 with the representativeness heuristic. If judgments followed the representativeness heuristic rather than the contingent probabilities, then among a subset of incidents where the two dimensions were imperfectly correlated, the predictions should be more closely related to the former dimension. Exclusion of the six lowest-ranking incidents on the predictive-judgment scale (which were also the lowest-ranking incidents on the other two scales) led to a correlation between the two dimensions of .76. In turn, the correlation of the predictive judgments with the mean similarity ranks was .93, while their correlation with contingent probability judgments was .62. With variance associated with the contingent probability dimension partialed out, the correlation between the predictions and the similarity values was .90. On the other hand, with the latter values partialed out, the correlation between the contingent probability and predictive judgments was −.39.

From this configuration, it appears that the judgments of similarity between the incident and the "typically stressful incident" characterized the predictions of stress more closely than the contingent probability values. Because of the weight placed on "similarity," it seems that the "cost" component—in this case, the "stress-impact component"—of the expected cost (expected stress) formula was more prominent than the contingent probability of stress, given the incident's occurrence.

These two experiments addressed themselves to the roles of categorical-frequency information and dimensions of content (predictive heuristics) in stress-relevant predictions. In each case, inaccuracies in judgment emerged when results were held up to formal statistical requirements.

Regarding categorical-frequency information, judges tended to relegate their judgments to the frequency of aversive events (bursts of loud noise). The respective contributions of (1) contingent probabilities and (2) frequencies of appearance to the frequencies of aversive events were not separated.

This lack of separation meant incorporating information on the relative frequency of occurrence of the stimulus item when it had in fact already occurred. Nevertheless, certain occasions of judgment suggest that the influence of the judgmental object's frequency of occurrence[5] may be quite in order and that its fortuitous inclusion in judgments may be desirable.

For example, consider the circumstances presented in Table 9-1. Both B and E circumstances implicate the prior probabilities[6] of the objects of judgment, while the remainder do not. View, for a moment, the letter-resistor items of the first experiment in the preceding section as standing for "relevant aspects" of the "laboratory situation."

If a subject were judging situational aspects the way he/she were judging the letter-resistor items in the first experiment, the information on frequency of appearance would be appropriately included in the circumstances B and E. On the other hand, bringing the same information into judgments about the individual aspects where their probabilities of occurrence were not at issue—circumstances where they were determined either by the individual ("controllable") or by external constraints ("assigned")—would result in considerably greater risk of inaccuracy.

---

[5]Subjective and objective frequencies of occurrence are not separated here because the actual values (objective frequencies) and the values inferred from the judgmental data (subjective frequencies) were similar.

[6]In discussing the occurrences of stimulus items, reference has been made to relative frequencies of occurrence among the stimuli rather than their relative "prior probabilities." The prior probability of an aspect of some situation is the following function of its frequency of occurrence:

$$\frac{[\text{frequency of occurrence of the situational aspect}]}{[\text{sum of frequencies of occurrences of all relevant aspects of the situation}]}$$

Within a given situation, the prior probabilities are proportional to the frequencies of occurrence because the denominator of the ratio above is constant. However, the proportionality is maintained *across situations* only if the denominator continues to remain constant—in effect, if prior probabilities of situations are fixed (see note to Table 9-1).

The artificial features of the laboratory context necessarily limit the degree to which the results from these experiments can be generalized. Nevertheless, as the results currently stand, they point up potentially important considerations when evaluating judgment strategies: considerations involving the nature of the strategies themselves in conjunction with the circumstances in which they occur.

Before leaving this section and discussing possible implications for psychopathology, one or two more observations should be made. The preceding sections have dealt with two prominent approaches to predictions of future events. Little can be said at this time about the comparative roles played by processes revealed by these two approaches. The degree to which one or the other type of information is invoked may depend largely on the context of judgment. For example, on occasions where the object(s) of judgment are relatively "content-free," or where characteristics necessary for drawing "heuristic" inferences are not discernible, the influence of category-frequency information may be greater. Conversely, the importance of predictive heuristic information may be greater where category-frequency information is not available but where the characteristics of the judged object(s) are somewhat rich in their "heuristic inferences."

Information Entering into Stress-Relevant Judgments and Cognitive Deficits in Psychopathology

Earlier in this chapter, two components of judgment formulations having potential implications for psychopathology were (1) the content of judgments, meaning the "optimism" versus "pessimism" of expectations and (2) the "availability" of judgments, meaning the efficiency with which expectations were formed. With respect to the literature on cognitive deficit, several studies have had rather direct relevance to the categorical-frequency and inferential-heuristic aspects of prediction.

Several of these studies have been done on the memory of "depressed" subjects for desirable versus undesirable events. Note that inasmuch as undergraduates' (Buchwald, 1977; Kuiper, 1978; Nelson & Craighead, 1977), hospital volunteers (Wener & Rehm, 1975) or psychiatric outpatients (De Monbreun & Craighead, 1977) were the participants, each of these experiments was done on subjects with more or less "depressive affect" rather than those with extant disabling behavior patterns. Memory performance was examined as a function of where the subjects scored on psychometric scales for depression (e.g., the BDI; Beck et al., 1977).

In each study, the "stressor outcome" was failure on a given trial of a laboratory task and the benign outcome was success. In two studies (Kuiper, 1978; Wener & Rehm, 1975), subjects tried to identify the correct meanings of words, while in another (DeMonbreun & Craighead, 1977), they were required to detect the closest associate to an earlier nonsense syllable from an array of 5 syllables. In each task, the alternatives were equally viable, but "correct" versus "incorrect" feedback was given according to a prespecified schedule.

Invariably, subjects higher on the depression scales remembered significantly fewer "correct" trials. In another study, Buchwald (1977) correlated depression-scale scores with underestimation of correct performance rates (on a digit-word paired-associate test); analyses correcting for actual performance rates led to significant correlations among females and the combined sample, but not among males.

One study examined recall of frequencies of both desirable (success) and undesirable (failure) outcome categories (Nelson & Craighead, 1977). Similar to the experiments by DeMonbreun and Craighead (1977), subjects were required to identify an earlier nonsense syllable from an array of 5 syllables, "correct performance" feedback again being arbitrarily assigned. For subjects in a "reinforcement" condition, the salience of successful outcomes was enhanced through adding a 5-cent increment to an initial credit of $2. Those in a "punishment" condition had 5 cents removed for each "failure." Otherwise, the conditions were identical. Results indicated that subjects with higher depression-scale scores recalled fewer successful outcomes but more failures than did those with lower scores.

These studies revealed relatively consistent differences in categorical memory among subjects differing in depressive affect. Whether or not these differences express themselves in predictive behaviors remains unanswered. In the study by Buchwald (1977), predictive judgments were obtained and found to correlate .94 with recall judgments; however, the two judgments were obtained immediately adjacent to one another.

In each of these investigations, the frequencies of desirable and undesirable outcomes were interdependent—one was the complement of the other. Therefore, it could not be ascertained whether subjects effectively utilized one type of outcome only. For example, it was possible that subjects' estimates of desirable outcomes were an inverse function of undesirable outcomes (as was suggested earlier by the study of Herzog & Neufeld, Note 1). If so, enhanced emphasis of undesirable outcomes on the part of those with higher scale scores may have been at the root of the obtained differences.[7,8]

Turning to predictive heuristics, the study just reported suggested that similarity between a judged incident and one's conceptual stressor prototype determined normals' predicted likelihoods of stress. Two studies (Neufeld, 1975, 1976) examined

---

[7]If group differences resulted from unequal sensitivity to one type of outcome only, then the amount of deficit in recalling successes should parallel the amount of excess in recalling failures. An analysis of Nelson and Craighead's (1977) data directed toward this question indicated that the one difference was not significantly greater than the other, $F_{(1/48)} < 1$. Of course, while this analysis increases the tenability of the influence of a single outcome somewhat, it says nothing of which outcome might be involved. Nor does it contradict the possibility that both outcomes were involved but that subjects with depressed affect were less sensitive to successful outcomes and more sensitive to failures by equal amounts.

[8]Whether reported judgmental differences associated with "depressive affect" center on *proportions* versus single-outcome frequencies assumes possible importance in the following sense. The format of these judgmental differences may change little; however, the "level" at which they operate toward a given stimulus context may change considerably. Judgmental values may, in general, be quite high for a stimulus context encountered comparatively often because the critical associations would have had a greater chance to accumulate, even if their *proportion* were relatively low. Furthermore, judgment-modifying manipulations would be appropriately deployed away from the outcome with weak influence in favor of the one with strong influence.

the performance of "schizophrenic" subjects in carrying out similarity assessments. The objects of judgment were verbal descriptors of affect and personality. Therefore, deficits inferred from these results may not generalize to stress-related similarity assessments. Instead, they should be considered as suggesting where deficits in the latter area may lie.

One study (Neufeld, 1976) examined whether or not the dimensions of meaning underlying global similarity judgments of the affect and personality descriptors were available in the repertoires of schizophrenics. When the individual dimensions (essentially, those of the Semantic Differential) were specified to the patients and the task involved rating the descriptors according to their dimensional locations, performance was indistinguishable from that of normals. On the other hand, when the task called for implementing more than one dimension at a time in identifying the overall similarity between one item and the next, the schizophrenics were significantly less efficient than normals. Those classified as "paranoid schizophrenic" were most deficient in this regard (Neufeld, 1975; 1976).

The dimensions of similarity used here were different from those entering into stress-relevant judgments (see the description of stress in the instructions to the earlier experiment). Stress-relevant dimensions may or may not be available in the repertoires of schizophrenics the way the preceding dimensions of affect and personality descriptors appeared to be. On the other hand, the processes required to implement constituent dimensions into global similarity assessments may not change for different types of dimensions. If not, schizophrenics' (especially paranoids') assessments of similarity with respect to stress may falter in the area of these processes.

Decisional Processes and Counterstress Activity

In this section, we turn from general considerations of stress demands on predictive judgments to a somewhat specific stress-related dimension of psychopathology. This dimension consists of the propensity versus the reticence to engage in counterstress activity. The dimension can be illustrated by referring to two types of deviance: behaviors associated with "depression" and behaviors classified as "compulsions."

The relevant "symptom of depression" is that of a disinclination to carry out some available response, even though doing so might change events in one's immediate environment (see Eastman, 1976). In the case of compulsions, the relevant symptom is an elevated propensity to engage in activities (usually of a stereotyped form) despite their having little or no material effect on the events to which they are directed (see Rachman, 1976).

The following schema devolves from an analysis of the propensity-versus-reticence dimension in the light of possible decisional processes instigated by threat. The schema was designed to accord with findings on decisional processes in conjunction with findings of deviant behavior related to this dimension. However, "corroboration" of the schema awaits future research, and some of its testable implications are presented later.

Before embarking on the formulation itself, some preliminary comments on the term "counterstress activity" are in order. In their review of the role of activity in attenuating stress, Gal and Lazarus (1975) noted two categories of activity functions: (1) "threat-related," referring to those activities which are directed toward the likelihood and/or impact of impending events, and (2) "non-threat-related activities" which, among other functions, might serve to distract the individual from impending events. Our emphasis here is on the first category. Restricting our frame of reference in this way is in keeping with the preceding illustrations where "activity deficit" was considered as abstinence from responding when external events might be affected and "activity excess" was considered in terms of the opposite combination.

Furthermore, covert as well as overt activities can fall into this category. Strategies such as scanning alternative courses of action, planning a selected course of action, and so on, meet the criterion for being directed toward probability and stress-impact properties of the threatening circumstances.

Finally, since focus is on anticipatory phases of stress transactions, the phrase "propensity toward counterstress activity" is taken to mean "inclination" or "preparedness to act." Consequences for counterstress activity per se might be manifest in such parameters as latency, "effusiveness," and "perseverance" of activity.

The main construct of this schema is that of "stress expectancy," denoted E(stress). Since counterstress activity is at issue, two expectancy values are necessary: one representing expected stress, given counterstress activity, denoted E(stress)/counterstress activity;[9] the other representing expected stress, given no counterstress activity, denoted E(stress)/no counterstress activity.

Before proceeding further, it should be pointed out that the construct of "expected stress" is adapted from subjective-expected-utility approaches to other areas of decisional operations (see Edwards, 1955). However, the derivation of expectancy values in terms of summed subjective probability-utility products is not implied in the present adaptation. As we said earlier, in gambling and economic judgments, subjects' performance seems to violate this derivation. According to the studies reported in this chapter, this derivation may not be appropriate in the case of stress predictions either.

With this qualification in mind, the topic of propensity to engage in counterstress activity can be considered in greater detail. From a decision-theoretical perspective, this factor can be represented by a contrast between the values, E (stress)/counterstress activity, and E (stress)/no counterstress activity. A straightforward method of quantifying this contrast is to construct a ratio:

$$\frac{E \text{ (stress)/counterstress activity}}{E \text{ (stress)/no counterstress activity}}$$

The propensity to engage in counterstress activity would be expected to vary inversely with the size of the ratio.

---

[9] Note that there could be one expectancy value for each type of viable activity (e.g., escape, attempting somehow to neutralize the potential stressor by preparing to act directly on it, and so on). Restricting the present development to a single activity affords greater manageability of presentation without detracting from the principal points.

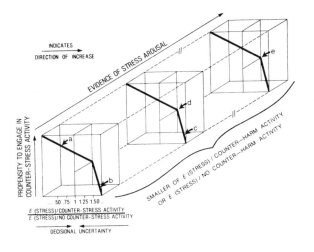

Fig. 9-1.

In Figure 9-1, the ratio is seen to vary along the horizontal axis of each three-dimensional segment. The vertical axis of each segment represents the propensity to engage in counterstress activity. Elevation of the thick lines appearing in the midst of the segments, as numerical values of the ratio decrease, represents the above relationship.

While attempts to specify the terms entering into the expectancy values, or their modes of combination, would be premature, certain components appear to warrant future consideration. With respect to the numerator of the ratio above, components additional to event likelihood and/or stress impact include the following: the amount of personal investment required by the counterstress activity and the possible "frustrating effects" of unsuccessful activity (see Gray, 1971).

Another construct incorporated into the present schema is "stress arousal." Empirical indicators of this construct have typically taken the form of physiological—usually autonomic—activity, subjective reports of disturbance, and disrupted performance on psychomotor and cognitive-perceptual tasks (see McGrath, 1970). The integration of this construct into the preceding ratio is discussed below.

First, note that anticipatory stress arousal is considered to be a positive function of stress expectancy. Several studies can be cited to illustrate this relationship. Subjects have been presented with probability values purportedly representing the likelihood of impending electric shock. When anticipatory stress arousal has been measured shortly after the information has been given, it has paralleled the differences in the conveyed probabilities (Grings & Sukonek, 1971; Niemela, 1969; Ohman, Bjorkstrand, & Ellstrom, 1973). On the other hand, when more time has been allowed to pass, the correspondence between the conveyed probabilities and the stress arousal measures either has been lessened or has disappeared (see Monat, Averill, & Lazarus, 1972). A factor diminishing this correspondence may have been reduced veridicality of subjects' expected values with the conveyed values due to reappraisal during the longer intervals (see Koriat, Melkman, Averill, & Lazarus, 1972). When the conveyed probabilities have been presented in a relatively "salient" manner (having subjects draw cards, where .05, .50, or .95 of the deck would supposedly lead to shock) as opposed to simply informing the subject about the putative probabilities, measures of stress arousal once again paralleled the conveyed probabilities (Gaines, Smith, & Skolnik, 1977) despite the longer intervals. The more salient form of presentation may have lessened the opportunity for the reappraisal referred to above.

Returning to the expectancy portion of stress arousal and the preceding ratio, the following observations are forthcoming. First, the main influence on stress arousal should emanate from either the numerator or the denominator, whichever is smaller. This inference depends on the operation of two factors in these decisional transactions: first, that individuals are somewhat cognizant of the alternative expectancy values, and, second, that they are inclined to adopt the option associated with the lesser value. Accordingly, anticipatory stress arousal is more likely to be influenced by the expectancy value associated with the option to be "put into effect." The higher expectancy value may be substantial but comparatively inconsequential by virtue of its emanating from the option to be disgarded. In Figure 9-1, stress arousal is represented by the third (depth) dimension. The three segments depict differing values of the ratio's smaller term.

If anticipatory stress arousal is primarily a function of the smaller term in the ratio, the following pattern of covariation between counterstress activity and stress arousal is implied. First, note that because the first is represented in ratio form, it can remain invariant despite changes in its constituent values. Consider increases in the numerator according to arbitrary units of 1, 2, and 3. Commensurate increases in the denominator of 2, 4, and 6 maintain the same ratio value of .5. However, because the smaller term increases, evidence of stress arousal should also increase. Hence, the three segments in Figure 9-1 indicate increased stress arousal while sharing similar ratio values on their horizontal axes. For example, positions (b) and (c) are the foremost and middle segments represent comparable propensities to engage in counterstress activity but unequal stress arousal. Furthermore, within each segment the propensity toward counterstress activity varies while the smaller of the two terms—and its corresponding stress arousal—remains fixed. An example is provided by positions (a) and (b) on the foremost segment.

There is some increase in stress arousal within each segment as the ratio approaches 1 (by way of the values of the larger term approaching that of the smaller term). As the expectancy values become more similar, decisional difficulty (uncertainty) increases and is regarded as a source of incremental stress arousal. On the right-hand side of each segment, the increase accompanies elevation in the propensity to engage in counterstress activity, while on the left-hand side, it accompanies a decreased propensity. For example, this difference is seen as one proceeds toward the middle of the foremost segment from positions (b) and (a) respectively.

The operation of the schema can be illustrated by considering changes in the main constructs corresponding to the changes in location represented by the lower-case letters. Focusing on the foremost segment, note that to the left of the ratio value of 1, the numerator is the smaller term, but to the right, the denominator is the smaller of the two. However, in each case the values of the smaller terms are identical. Position (a) contrasts position (b) with respect to propensity to engage in counterstress activity, but stress arousal remains approximately equal for the two positions. Movement from (b) to (c) has already been discussed as involving a change in stress arousal only. Shifts from (c) to (d) and (c) to (e) indicate some contrasting effects of changes in the larger versus the smaller of the two terms in the ratio.

Let (c) stand for an example ratio of, say, 1.5, obtained with arbitrary values of 3 divided by 2. If the numerator were to approach the denominator until it reached 2, position (d) would be obtained. Here, the propensity to engage in counterstress activity would have increased, and so would stress arousal due to greater decisional uncertainty. In contrast to this change in position, moving from (c) to (e) implies an increase in the denominator from 2 to 3. Now the smaller of the two terms has increased, requiring a change in the location of the segment. Within the segment itself, further increase in stress arousal has accompanied heightened decisional uncertainty. As was the case with movement from (c) to (d), the propensity to engage in counterstress activity has increased in this instance as well.

Limitations and Boundaries of the Present Schema

While one of the main components of the present schema is the ratio of expected stress, given counterstress activities, to expected stress, given no counterstress activities, the use of this ratio as a unifying construct in its own right is highly limited. Rather, utility is derived from its suggestion of external correlates of abnormal expectancy values. Second, the empirical consequences accruing to its relationship to other constructs in the schema are potentially informative.

Difficulties with the ratio per se center on exclusive reliance on subjective report for its measurement. Although subjective expected utilities have been found to covary with certain behaviors in past studies (Mausner & Platt, 1971), as have measures of "expected self efficacy" (Bandura, 1977), their use as predictors is questionable for the following reasons. In these cases, both the predictor and predicted variables consist of subjects' responses. As such, the variables may simply represent two different measures of the same construct: propensity versus reluctance to act. Subjective expectancy values may merely be indirect self-descriptions of behaviors which subjects know are in the offing. In contrast, despite their failures to account for human decisional processes adequately, objective expected utilitary approaches (see Edwards, 1955) have at least afforded independent estimates of the predictor variable by arriving at probability and utility values as objective properties of situational factors external to the subject.

As mentioned, one of the uses of the presently formulated ratio lies in its implications for possible antecedents of abnormal stress-expectancy values. First, abnormalities in the direction of reticence—corresponding to expectancy-ratio values of 1 or greater—are considered. Two forms of deficit in predictive judgments suggest themselves as possible sources.

The first consists of deficits which inflate the numerator (or deflate the denominator) of the ratio. Evidence of deviations in categorical memory performance among those with "depressive affect" illustrate the form of deficit referred to here.

The second form is that of inefficiency in formulating expectancy values—that is, deficits which reduce accessibility to these values. Carrying out predictive judgments depends on information-processing operations of the variety discussed earlier. Reduced ability to carry out these operations would interfere with the formulation of expectancy values. Because formulation of these values would be deficient, so would formulation of the *inequality* in expectancy values (i.e., values corresponding to ratings less than 1) associated with the propensity to engage in counterstress activity.

Examples of this form of deficit have been suggested in relation to schizophrenia (e.g., their reduced ability to carry out multidimensional similarity judgments resembling those involved in certain types of stress predictions). Based on analysis of inefficiency in cognitive tasks among those classified as "clinically depressed" (Russell & Beekhuis, 1976), similar suggestions may be forthcoming with regard to these patients.

With respect to abnormalities in propensity toward counterstress activities (e.g., compulsions), relatively little data on decision processes have become available. However, hypotheses conforming to an inflated denominator of the present ratio have been put forth (Carr, 1974). Studies directed toward abnormalities in expectancy values favoring "excessive" counterstress activity may prove informative. Because deficiency in formulating expectancy values should detract from the type of imbalance in these values associated with such excessive activity (for reasons suggested above), studies on processing inefficiency, as opposed to biased processing, among these patients may prove less promising.

A second set of empirical implications of the present schema obtains from the relationships among its constituent constructs. Since the propensity to engage in counterstress activity[10] is represented by the expectancy ratio, while anticipatory stress arousal is determined partly by the lesser term of the ratio and partly by decisional uncertainty, the following consequences are suggested. Where the ratio is maintained at a constant value despite being formed from different numerators and denominators (e.g., [arbitrary] values of ½, ¾, ⅝, etc.), the propensity to engage in counterstress activity should remain relatively fixed. On the other hand, because the lesser term of the ratio varies in this case, so should evidence of stress arousal.

Note that the opposite combination—constancy in stress arousal amidst changes in the propensity to engage in counterstress activity—does not necessarily hold. Reference to any one of the three segments of Figure 9-1 should help to make this point. Changes in the lesser term of the expectancy ratio are associated with changes in stress arousal. Allow for a moment the former to remain constant, and consider the

---

[10]Detectable consequences on such parameters as latency, effusiveness, and perseverance of ensuing counterstress activity may be restricted to ratios less than 1 because ratios exceeding 1 purportedly express "negative propensity" toward counterstress activity.

effects of changes in the larger term of the expectancy ratio. Both the propensity to engage in counterstress activity and decisional uncertainty are affected, stress arousal varying with decisional uncertainty. However, the change in decisional uncertainty is bidirectional as one proceeds across the range of ratio values, whereas the change in the propensity to undertake counterstress activity is unidirectional.

Although the preceding sets of relations are somewhat complex, certain rather straightforward properties can be seen to emerge. One of these properties is that the propensity to engage in counterstress activity is semi-independent of stress arousal. A study illustrating part of this semi-independence has been carried out by Gatchel and Proctor (1976; see also Gatchel, McKinney, & Koebernick, 1977). One group of subjects underwent a series of trials where attempts to escape aversive tones had no effect on their termination, a second group could execute a response which stopped the tone, and a final group simply experienced the tones with no effort to escape. Several behavioral measures as well as skin conductance and heart-rate responses surrounding these trials were monitored continuously. Two of the scores derived from skin conductance were tonic conductance levels and spontaneous electrodermal responses. The former index has been thought to reflect "task involvement" while the latter has been more closely associated with "emotional stress" (see Kilpatrick, 1971). Subjects experiencing inescapable noise produced lower tonic conductance levels but more frequent spontaneous electrodermal responses compared to those who could escape. Viewing "task involvement" as a propensity toward counterstress activity and "emotional stress" as the present schema's "stress arousal," the present combinations appear to have occurred: (1) "high propensity toward counterstress activity" and "low stress arousal"; and (2) "low propensity toward counterstress activity" and "high arousal." These combinations parallel positions (a) and (c) of Figure 9-1, respectively. However, combinations of high propensity and high arousal and of low propensity and low arousal were not obtained (nor were they sought) in this study.

Concluding Remarks

The approach to stress-related aspects of deviance taken in the present chapter can be described with reference to the following sequence:

$$A \longrightarrow B \longrightarrow C$$

where A stands for the stress-related circumstances facing the individual; C stands for judgments about impending events; B stands for processes involved in arriving at these judgments; and the arrows represent transitions from one component to the next.

Two types of abnormalities in C have been specified: (1) distortion in the form taken on by C, and (2) reduced accessability to C. In turn, the following deficits in B have been underscored: (1) bias in the processing of information (e.g., accentuation of "negative properties"), and (2) inefficiency in carrying out the processes specified by B.

In assessing B, judgments have been examined among normals. Upon identifying some of the component processes of B (e.g., categorical-frequency and inferential-heuristic aspects of prediction), inferences have been drawn about judgmental aspects of stress-related deviance. Unfortunately, many of these inferences remain "indirect" in the following sense.

Studies which have focused on processes resembling those of B, but not necessarily processes involved in stress-related judgments per se, have been used to estimate probable deficits in the latter. Clearly, more studies comparing patients to controls on processes directly related to B are necessary before firm conclusions can be drawn. Experimental ingenuity will be called for in striking an optimal compromise between ethical constraints and relevance of obtained results to these specific processes.

References

Akiskal, H. S., McKinney, W. T. Overview of recent research on depression. *Archives of General Psychiatry*, 1975, *32*, 285–305.

Anisman, H. Neurochemical changes elicited by stress. In H. Anisman & G. Bigam (Eds.), *Psychopharmacology of aversively motivated behavior*. New York: Plenum, 1978.

Bandura, A. Self efficacy: Toward a unifying theory of behavioral change. *Psychological Review*, 1977, *84*, 191–215.

Beck, A. T. *Depression: Clinical, experimental and theoretical aspects*. New York: Harper & Row, 1967.

Beck, A. T., Ward, C. H., Mendelson, M., Mock, J., & Erbaugh, J. An inventory for measuring depression. *Archives of General Psychiatry*, 1961, *4*, 561–571.

Beck, A. T. The development of depression: A cognitive model. In R. J. Friedman & M. M. Katz (Eds.), *The psychology of depression: Contemporary theory and research*. New York: Winston-Wiley, 1974.

Beck, A. T., Laude, R., & Bonehart, M. Ideational components of anxiety neurosis. *Archives of General Psychiatry*, 1974, *31*, 319–325.

Broga, M. J., & Neufeld, R. W. J. Evaluation of information sequential aspects of schizophrenic performance. I: Framework & current findings. *Journal of Nervous & Mental Disease*, 1981 (in press).

Buchwald, A. M. Depressive mood and estimates of reinforcement frequency. *Journal of Abnormal Psychology*, 1977, *86*, 443–446.

Byrne, D. G. Vigilance and arousal in depressive states. *British Journal of Social and Clinical Psychology*, 1976, *15*, 267–274.

Carr, A. T. Compulsive neurosis: A review of the literature. *Psychological Bulletin*, 1974, *81*, 311–318.

DeMonbreun, B. G., & Craighead, W. E. Distortion of perception and recall of positive and neutral feedback in depression. *Cognitive Therapy and Research*, 1977, *4*, 311–329.

Edwards, W. The prediction of decisions among bets. *Journal of Experimental Psychology*, 1955, *50*, 201–214.

Estes, W. K. Structural aspects of associative models for memory. In C. N. Cofer (Ed.), *The structure of human memory*. San Francisco: Freeman, 1975.

Estes, W. K. The cognitive side of probability learning. *Psychological Review*, 1976, *83*, 37–64.

Estes, W. K. Some functions of memory in probability and choice behavior. In G. H. Bower (Ed.), *The psychology of learning and motivation* (Vol. 10). New York: Academic Press, 1977.

Gaines, L. B., Smith, B. D., & Skolnick, B. Psychological differentiation, event uncertainty, and heart rate. *Journal of Human Stress*, 1977, *3*, 11–25.

Gal, R. G., & Lazarus, R. S. The role of activity in anticipating and confronting stressful situations. *Journal of Human Stress,* 1975, *4,* 4–20.

Gatchel, R., & Proctor, J. D. Physiological correlates of learned helplessness in man. *Journal of Abnormal Psychology,* 1976, *85,* 27–34.

Gatchel, R. J., McKinney, M. E., & Koebernick, L. F. Learned helplessness, depression, and psychophysiological responding. *Psychophysiology,* 1977, *14,* 25–31.

Goodwin, F. K., & Bunney, W. E. Psychobiological aspects of stress and affective illness. In J. P. Scott & E. C. Senay (Eds.), *Separation and depression.* Baltimore: King Printing Company, 1973.

Gray, J. *The psychology of fear and stress.* New York: McGraw-Hill, 1971.

Grings, W. W., & Sukoneck, H. I. Prediction probability as a determiner of anticipatory and preparatory electrodermal behavior. *Journal of Experimental Psychology,* 1971, *91,* 310–317.

Hemsley, D. L., & Zawada, S. "Filtering" and the cognitive deficit in schizophrenia. *British Journal of Psychiatry,* 1976, *128,* 456–461.

Herzog, H., & Neufeld, R. W. J. Acquisition of probabilities in anticipatory appraisals of stress. *Research Bulletin #486,* Department of Psychology, University of Western Ontario, London, Ontario, 1978, ISSN 0316-4675; ISBN 0-7714-0112-4.

Holmes, T. H. & Masada, M. Life change and illness susceptibility. In B. S. Dohrenwend & B. P. Dohrenwend (Eds.), *Stressful life events: Their nature and effects.* New York: Wiley, 1974.

Hudgens, R. W. Personal catastrophe and depression: A consideration of the subject with respect to medically ill adolescents and a requiem for retrospective life-event studies. In B. S. Dohrenwend and B. P. Dohrenwend (Eds.), *Stressful life events: Their nature and effects.* New York: Wiley, 1974.

Kahneman, D., & Tversky, A. On the psychology of prediction. *Psychological Review,* 1973, *80,* 237–251.

Kilpatrick, D. Differential responsiveness of two electrodermal indices to psychological stress and performance of a complex cognitive task. *Psychophysiology,* 1972, 9, 218–226.

Koh, S., Szoc, R., & Peterson, R. Short-term memory scanning in schizophrenic young adults. *Journal of Abormal Psychology,* 1977, *86,* 451–460.

Koriat, A., Melkman, R., Averill, J. R., & Lazarus, R. S. The self-control of emotional reaction to a stressful film. *Journal of Personality,* 1972, *40,* 601–609.

Kuiper, N. A. Depression and causal attributions for success and failure. *Journal of Personality and Social Psychology,* 1978, *36,* 236–246.

Lacey, J. I. Somatic response patterning and stress. Some revisions of activation theory. In M. Appley & R. Trumbull (Eds.), *Psychological stress: Issues and research.* New York: Appleton-Century-Crofts, 1967.

Maher, B. Introduction to research in psychopathology. New York: McGraw Hill, 1970.

Marusarz, T. Z., & Koh, S. D. Contextual effects on short-term memory retrieval of schizophrenic young adults. *Journal of Abnormal Psychology,* 1980, *89,* 683–696.

Mausner, B., & Platt, E. S. *Smoking: A behavioral analysis.* New York: Pergamon Press, 1971.

McGrath, J. E. Settings, measures and themes: An integrative review of some research on social-psychological factors in stress. In J. E. McGrath (Ed.), *Social and psychological factors in stress.* New York: Holt, 1970.

Monat, A., Averill, J. R., & Lazarus, R. S. Anticipatory stress and coping reactions under various conditions of uncertainty. *Journal of Personality and Social Psychology,* 1972, *24,* 237–253.

Nelson, R. E., & Craighead, W. E. Selective recall of positive and negative feedback, self control behaviors, and depression. *Journal of Abnormal Psychology,* 1977, *86,* 379–388.

Neufeld, R. W. J. A multidimensional scaling analysis of schizophrenics and normals perception of verbal similarity. *Journal of Abnormal Psychology,* 1975, *84,* 498–507.

Neufeld, R. W. J. Simultaneous processing of multiple stimulus dimensions among paranoid and nonparanoid schizophrenics. *Multivariate Behavioral Research,* 1976, *4,* 425–442.

Neufeld, R. W. J. Components of processing deficit among paranoid and nonparanoid schizophrenics. *Journal of Abnormal Psychology,* 1977, *86,* 60–64.

Neufeld, R. W. J. Verdicality of cognitive mapping of stressor effects: Sex differences. *Journal of Personality*, 1978, *46*, 623–644.

Nieemla, P. Electrodermal response as a function of quantified threat. *Scandinavian Journal of Psychology* 1964, *10*, 49–56.

Ohman, A., Bjorkstrand, P., & Ellstrom P. Effect of explicit trial-by-trial information about shock probability in long interstimulus interval GSR conditioning. *Journal of Experimental Psychology*, 1973, *98*, 145–151.

Paykel, E. S. Life stress and psychiatric disorder: Applications of the clinical approach. In B. S. Dohrenwend and B. P. Dohrenwend (Eds.), *Stressful life events: Their nature and effects*. New York: Wiley, 1974.

Payne, J. W. Alternative approaches to decision making under risk: Moment versus dimensions. *Psychological Bulletin*, 1973, *80*, 439–453.

Rabkin, J. Stressful life events and schizophrenia: A review of the research literature. *Psychological Bulletin*, 1980, *87*, 408–425.

Rachman, S. The modification of obsessions: A new formulation. *Behavior Research and Therapy*, 1976, *14*, 437–443.

Roessler, R. Personality, psychophysiology and performance. *Psychophysiology*, 1973, *10*, 315–327.

Russell, P. & Beekhuis, M. Organization in memory: A comparison of psychotics and normals. *Journal of Abnormal Psychology*, 1976, *85*, 527–534.

Russell, P. N., Consedine, C. E., & Knight, R. G. Visual and memory search by process schizophrenics. *Journal of Abnormal Psychology*, 1980, *89*, 109–114.

Slovic, P., Fischoff, B., & Lichtenstein, S. Behavioral decision theory. *Annual Review of Psychology*, 1977, *28*, 1–39.

Sternberg, S. Memory scanning: New findings and current controversies. In D. Deutsh, J. Deutsh, Eds., *Short-term memory*. New York: Academic Press, 1975.

Suboski, M. C., Brace, T. G. Jarrold, L. A., Teller, K. J., & Dieter, R. Interstimulus interval and time estimation in ratings of signaled shock aversiveness. *Journal of Experimental Psychology*, 1972, *96*, 406–415.

Taylor, J. A. A personality scale for manifest anxiety. *Journal of Abnormal and Social Psychology*, 1953, *48*, 285–290.

Wener, A. E., & Rehm, L. Depressive Affect: A test of behavioral hypotheses. *Journal of Abnormal Psychology*, 1975, *84*, 221–237.

Wishner, J., Stein, M. K., & Paestrel, A. L. Stages of information processing in schizophrenia: Sternberg's paridigm. In L. C. Wynne. R. L. Cromwell & S. Matthyse (Eds.), *The nature of schizophrenia: New approaches to research and treatment*. New York: Wiley, 1978.

Part IV

TREATMENT INTERVENTIONS DIRECTED TOWARD STRESS-RELEVANT PORTIONS OF DISTURBED BEHAVIOR AND EXPERIENCE

Chapter 10

Biological Treatment of Stress-Related Disorders

WALTER B. ESSMAN

Queens College
of the City University of New York
Flushing, N.Y.

The sources, nature, and variety of responses to stress comprise an encyclopedic body of variables, disciplines, and empirical findings; as such, some aspects of this broad inclusive topic may find common ground in a variety of biological approaches that have been employed to define changes in such responses. These changes, whether behavioral, neurological, physiological, biochemical, or endocrine, have largely emerged from one broad biological approach to the treatment of stress-related disorders—the use of psychotropic drugs. Certainly psychopharmacotherapy does not represent the only biological approach to stress-derived disorders, but it probably does constitute the most frequently utilized and possibly the most thoroughly studied of these approaches. Stress has been viewed as a vital sign for which one of the treatment goals may include the directed application of psychopharmacological agents, a course of action implying that the signs or symptoms under treatment represent the consequences of stress (Cooper, 1979). It is the purpose of this chapter to consider some of the psychopharmacological and related biological parameters with which the consequences of stress have been shown to interact and

273

to deal with several aspects of these interactions as they concern several *systemic* interactions in animals and man.

It has been noted that several stress-induced effects on task performance have similar effects in animals and man. Such stress effects may be derived from conflict and social environmental restrictions (Perry, 1975), or they may derive more directly from high arousal states (Williams, 1975). The characteristic responses considered have broadly included perseverative behavior and response variability, both of which may account for impaired performance. It has been observed (Valdman, 1976) that stress-induced impairment of performance may be reduced or abolished in human beings by a variety of pharmacological agents administered either before or after the stress event. Differences in the efficacy of a given pharmocological agent, however, appear to depend not only on the nature of the stress situation, its duration, and the accompanying functional alterations, but also on the age of the subject being stressed and its responsiveness to the given pharmacological agent.

Because of age-related differences in the development of central mechanisms mediating drug response, and the effects of stress on such systems, as well as peripheral mechanisms concerning the integrity of the hepatic microsomal system for drug metabolism, some attention to age factors in stress-drug interactions appears warranted. Some issues appear particularly relevant to this relationship, notably the administration of psychoactive compounds to the pregnant female subjected to many sources of stress. It is well known, for example, that phenothiazines, sometimes used in pregnancy as antiemetics, induce fetal hepatic enzyme systems. Thus, a potential source of difference in drug effect during the perinatal and possibly the prenatal period may be provided—either by maternal drug treatment or by stress-induced corticosteroid excess. It is therefore relevant to the present discussion to observe how some age factors can function in stress-drug interactions.

Age Factors in Stress and Drug Effects

The perinatal period, particularly, represents a time when stress effects can be assessed developmentally. It has been shown, for example, that daily intraperitoneal injection of saline during the first 12 postnatal days could constitute a potent stress (Barrett & Stockham, 1963; Hodges & Mitchley, 1970). Such stress, however, was shown to confer a later increase in body size, greater seminal vesicle weight, and increased serum levels of potassium and corticosterone (Erdösová et al., 1975). Corticosterone levels increased during the perinatal period in injection-stressed animals but also appeared to induce a state of postnatal "stress-nonresponsiveness" (Denenberg & Zarrow, 1970; Zarrow et al., 1970) wherein the susceptibility to stress was apparently decreased as a result of the effects of perinatal stress. In 4-day-old rats, the administration of diazepam, a minor tranquilizer of the benzodiazepine class, reduced the level of plasma corticosterone that was elevated by the injection of saline or polyethylene glycol, but this index of stress was still elevated above the level for uninjected (unstressed) animals. This finding suggests that even a single intraperitoneal injection to a young rat, even though the contents administered are presumably stress-attenuating, can produce a change correlated well with stress (Erdösová et al., 1977). It is of interest to observe that for injection-stressed animals, circulating plasma corticosterone levels are indistinguishable from nonstressed levels if diazepam is administered (Bassett & Caincross, 1974; Lahti & Barsuhn, 1975). It is difficult to compare stress effects among perinatal, young adult, adult, and geriatric groups, but it does appear that those stimuli that are highly stressful in the early age groups (e.g., intraperitoneal injection) are minimally, if at all, stressful in older animals (where a change from baseline, prediazepam-administration corticosterone level is taken as an index of stress effect). Similarly, the antistress effects of an agent such as diazepam appear to be more effective, utilizing the same index, in the older age group.

The response or symptoms may, however, differ in an elderly group, even where the source of the stress is the same. The common factors such as the secretion of thyroid and corticosteroid hormones which occur with stress can affect many other factors, such as carbohydrate turnover, lipid synthesis, calcium and magnesium disposition, heart rate, peripheral vascular resistance, and salt and water metabolism. Not only are such "stress responses" altered in the elderly (Davison, 1978), the effects of such systemic changes may well be more prominent or tolerated less well, particularly in the presence of common systemic diseases—another potential source of still other stress effects.

One notable site where this relationship is highly relevant is the myocardium—tissue which is notable for its increased susceptibility to insult with advancing age. The effects of stress on cardiac function appear quite directly related to the change in disposition of norepinephrine (nerve terminal release or adrenal release) produced by stress. In adult rats, immobilization stress significantly decreased the norepinephrine content of the heart (Martinez-Sierra et al., 1978). A number of psychoactive drugs were examined in relation to this cardiac change, and it was observed that pargyline, a monoamine oxidase (MAO) inhibitor, and imipramine, another MAO inhibitor and tricyclic antidepressant compound, prevented the stress-induced decrease in cardiac norepinephrine. This effect on the stress-induced change in cardiac norepinephrine content was not altered by other psychoactive agents such as chlorpromazine or lithium chloride. The latter agents, unlike the former, do not possess any MAO-inhibiting properties, which may, to some extent, relate to the significance of the interaction of specific drugs with the stress-induced changes in cardiac norepinephrine. The norepinephrine normally released by stress would not be deaminated in the presence of an MAO inhibitor; the latter would also effect a ganglionic blockade as the level of norepinephrine increased with reduced deamination.

Hypoxia as a cause of MAO inhibition leads to increased cardiac norepinephrine levels, and this effect can be further augmented with stress. Hypoxia and increased beta adrenergic receptor activity appear to be stress-related causative factors in the etiology of myocardial infarction and in the supraventricular and ventricular arrhythmias associated with such injury. In a related respect, it has been observed that MAO activity increases with aging (Robinson, 1975), so that conditions such as stress may cause a greater loss of myocardial catecholamine and, potentially, a greater likelihood of myocardial injury.

Developmentally, the adrenal medulla is an important site as well as target organ for the stress response. The chromaffin cells, the locus of sympathomimetic amine activity, have been noted as early as in the 27mm human fetus, when the adrenal cortex is invaded by these cells; the presence of pressor amines, consisting mainly of norepinephrine and epinephrine, has been recognized in the 70mm fetus. These catecholamines are actually dehydroxylated phenolic compounds that are formed from the oxidation of the amino acid, tyrosine, to form 3, 4-dihydrophenylalanine (dopa); 3, 4-dihydroxyphenylethylamine (dopamine) is then formed by decarboxylation with the enzyme dopa decarboxylase. The side chain of dopamine is hydroxylated to form norepinephrine. Within the chromaffin granules of the adrenal medulla, phenylethanolamine-N-methyltransferase methylates norepinephrine to form epinephrine. The latter two sympathetic amines appear to be particularly relevant to stress-drug interactions.

The Sympathoadrenal Medullary System in Stress: Interactions with Drugs

Genetic differences and/or a genetically conferred predisposition to behavioral differences may also be reflected in sympathoadrenal medullary activity during stress. This system is highly responsive to stressful stimuli. Levels of epinephrine and norepinephrine in the plasma of spontaneously hypertensive (BP $= 126 \pm 2$ heart rate $= 322 \pm 10$) rats were significantly higher under basal conditions, and catecholamine levels were greatest in this strain in response to foot-shock stress (McCarty & Kopin, 1978). Increased catecholamine responsiveness was also observed in a strain of stroke-prone hypertensive rats, suggesting that a genetic predisposition to hypertension is positively related to an increased responsiveness of the sympathoadrenal medullary system to stress. This interesting finding raises several questions relevant to drug effects on such responsiveness to stress and also, as we saw in the preceding section, to the relationship between adrenal catecholamine responsiveness and cardiac function. The cardiac action of glycosides such as ouabain appears to be related to the availability of catecholamines (Cession-Fossion, 1966; Tanz & Marcus, 1966), and ouabain-induced cardiac arrhythmias may be related to the release of catecholamines from the myocardium or from the adrenal (Nadeau & DeChamplain, 1973). The release or reuptake of catecholamines may also be altered by ouabain (Seifen, 1974a, 1974b). The production of cardiac arrhythmias by stress resembles the cardiac rhythm disturbances produced by ouabain. The benzodiazepine, diazepam, significantly increases adrenal catecholamine release, augments the catecholamine release produced by electrical or immobilization stress in rats, and results in a higher incidence of ventricular arrhythmias (Gascon, 1977).

The release of adrenal catecholamines by stress provides one vehicle through which plasma glucose levels may be elevated by increased gluconeogenesis. A post-stress diabetic response has also been demonstrated in restrained, cold-exposed rats (Vargas et al., 1974); in this instance, glucose uptake was apparently inhibited by a stress-mediated substance localized in the plasma, α_2 = inhibitor (Vargas et al., 1970). Restraint stress in rats has been shown to produce hyperglycemia which may be potentiated by the hyperglycemic effects of chlorpromazine (Vargas & Kawada, 1976). Although hyperglycemia produced by chlorpromazine is probably mediated by a reduction in insulin secretion (Ammon et al., 1973), it is apparent that this major tranquilizer can potentiate at least one effect of acute stress, the production of hyperglycemia. The interaction very likely occurs centrally as do other drug-stress interactions that influence adrenal output. This central location may well be the case for corticosteroids in stress and their release regulation by centrally active compounds, particularly those which directly or indirectly alter the release of adrenocorticotropic hormone (ACTH). Stress-induced ACTH release has been associated with decreased brain norepinephrine content and increased turnover (Van Loon, 1974). Several tranquilizer drugs which inhibit an increase in brain norepinephrine turnover prevent stress from producing an increase in plasma corticosterone concentration (Nasmyth, 1955; Lidbrink et al., 1972). Restraint stress produces a rise in plasma corticosterone concentrations in rats, apparently correlated with stress-induced ACTH release and the above-mentioned cerebral catecholamine changes. The pretreatment of restraint-stressed rats with either diazepam, desmethylimipramine, haloperidol, or phenobarbital diminished the rise in corticosterone (Keim & Sigg, 1977). In this instance, diazepam also reduced the stress-induced reduction of hypothalamic norepinephrine level.

In the rat brain, a major metabolite (that is, a product of metabolic conversion) of norepinephrine is 3-methoxy-4-hydroxyphenylethylenglycol (MOPEG-SO$_4$), apparently a good index of brain norepinephrine turnover and status. Stress (forced swimming in cold water) increased the ratio of MOPEG-SO$_4$/norepinephrine to 0.62, suggesting an increase of neuronal impulse flow and norepinephrine release (Bareggi et al., 1978). Not only norepinephrine content and turnover, but the status of other putative neurotransmitters (substances involved in the continuity of neural information transfer) such as dopamine and serotonin are also affected by stress (Bliss et al., 1968; Morgan et al., 1975; Palkovits et al., 1975; Yuwiler, 1979). As such, it is reasonable that cyclic nucleotides which serve as intracellular messengers to mediate neurotransmitter effects may also be influenced by stress and by pharmacological agents utilized in the stress response. For example, cyclic guanosine 3, 5′ = monophosphate (cGMP) levels in the mouse brain were elevated by stress, but cyclic adenosine 3, 5′-monophosphate levels (cAMP) were unaffected (Dinnendahl, 1975). A number of psychotropic agents have also been shown to affect cGMP level in the brain, including neurotropic agents such as amphetamine, reserpine, chlorpromazine, diazepam, and dopaminergic agents (Ferrendelli et al., 1972; Mao, 1975; Opmeer et al., 1976). The rise in brain cGMP level produced in mice by forced cold-water swimming or immobilization stress was attenuated by prestress administration of centrally depressant drugs such as reserpine, chlorpromazine, haloperidol, diazepam, and pentobarbital (Dinnendahl & Gumulka, 1977). These findings suggest no consistent role for neurotransmitter mediation of the cGMP effect, except perhaps for dopamine or γ = aminobutyric acid (GABA) which are involved in the stress-induced elevation of brain cGMP level.

Because a number of psychoactive agents affect appetite, food intake, and satiety, it is reasonable to expect that such drugs in their interaction with stress or its consequences may also modify appetitive behavior. Generally speaking, central nervous system stimulants such as the amphetamines, strychnine, and methyl xanthines, reduce appetite and decrease food consumption. Differences in the potentially reinforcing effects of food or food consumption in or following the stress situation can certainly contribute to altered drug.

Stress, Appetitive Behavior, and Drug Effects

The effects of stress on appetitive behavior have been reflected in hyperphagia (excessive food intake) developed in rats following tail-pinch stimulation (Antelman & Szechtman, 1975; Roland & Antelman, 1976). Psychotropic drugs that act as dopamine antagonists (suppressants of dopaminergic activity) interfere with the development of such stress-induced hyperphagia (Antelman et al., 1975). Several psychoactive agents have been examined for their effects on stress-induced hyperphagia in rats (Wallach et al., 1977). Prestress treatment with amphetamine, chlorpheniramine diethylpropion, fenfluramine, methamphetamine, morphine, chlorpromazine, and haloperidol decreased hyperphagia, and this is consistent with the clinical observation that these agents are anorexigens. The hyperphagic response was increased by benzodiazepines. Inasmuch as the latter agents appear more relevant for GABA system (Bowden 1979) whereas the former seem more specific for catecholamines, some potential central relationship to stress-induced food intake may be suggested. It is also apparent that stress factors inherent in the anorexogenic properties of adulterated foods or fluids, although modifying consumption, still maintain appropriate adiposity (Peck, 1978).

Another physiological response that has been observed with stress and effected with restraint stress is hyperthermia. The production of hyperthermia with apomorphine appears to be dependent on the concomitant production of stress. Apomorphine with foot shock or restraint produced hyperthermia in the rabbit (Snow & Horita, 1977); diazepam or haloperidol, which decrease the response of the rabbit to stress, also abolished apomorphine-induced hyperthermia. Motor activity is also affected by stress: reduced locomotion has been observed when open field behavior was tested in bright light (Donovick & Wakeman, 1969; Williams, 1971) or following electric shock (Pinel & Mucha, 1973). These data have been interpreted as a stress-induced inhibition of exploratory behavior. The administration of lithium chloride, which has been shown to reduce responsiveness to environmental change (Johnson, 1972), significantly reduced rearing behavior of stressed rats in an open field (Gray et al.,

1976). Locomotor activity was also reduced to a greater extent by lithium in stressed as compared with nonstressed animals.

It has been shown that electroshock stress increases brain protein kinase activity (Holmes et al., 1977), a reflection of the nonspecific activity of cAMP; the latter has, in some studies (Daly, 1975; Delapez et al., 1975; Lust et al., 1976), been shown to be elevated after stress. Lithium chloride has been shown to produce small, but significant, increases in the stress-stimulated activity of brain protein kinase in rats (Holmes el al., 1977). This finding may be of interest in view of the stress-related elevation of cAMP, but not cGMP noted earlier (Dinnendahl, 1975), and the expectation that agents which reduce central stimulation should increase cAMP or increase cGMP. The effects of lithium chloride are interesting in this regard, and possibly specific to the stressor stimulus as well as the poststress response. In any case, further studies are necessary to define the interaction of stress with lithium salts.

Another class of stress-inducing stimuli appear to have an intensity-based relationship to locomotor activity. Noise is one stressor (Davies, 1968) which, at 70–90 db, increases locomotor activity in rats if presented continuously but decreases such activity if presented discontinuously (Cox & Lee, 1976). Viloxazine, an antidepressant drug, was shown to augment locomotor activity in continuous noise stress and to decrease locomotion with discontinuous noise stress. The changes in locomotion depending on the continuity or noncontinuity of the stress probably reflect differences in adaptive behavior. An increased level of motor behavior as part of the pattern of agitated behavior observed in hospitalized psychiatric patients is quite characteristic in the response to stress observed in geriatric populations. A comparison of the effects of tiparide, a substituted benzamide tranquilizer, and meprobamate, a muscle relaxant with sedative properties, showed that the former compound produced significantly greater benefit in the reduction of stress-induced motor agitation, verbal and motor agitation, and aggressive behavior (Peyramond, 1978).

One agent that has been considered as possibly interactive with stress is marijuana. This agent has vasoactive, cardiotropic, and steroidogenic effects and, in addition, enhances the response of the sympathoadrenal system to stress (Horowitz & Nersasian, 1978). The nature of the interaction of marijuana with the stress response depends heavily on the central effects of this agent. The behavioral response of rats to cannabis and tetrahydrocannabinols can be altered by such stressors as morphine withdrawal, hunger, and cold (Carlini & Gonzales, 1972; Carlini et al., 1972), and an increased incidence of adverse responses to stress have been noted in human marijuana users (Talbott & Teague, 1969). Mild sedation and minimal hypothermia have been observed in response to Δ^8-tetrahydrocannabinol (Δ^8-THC) in unstressed rats, yet in stressed rats (isolation-housed and food-deprived) the drug produced marked hyperreactivity, immobility, and hypothermia (Maclean & Littleton, 1977). The combination of stress with THC produces increased uptake of dopamine by the striatum, and this may represent the mechanism whereby the behavioral effects of stress are enhanced by THC. The deprivation of REM sleep in rats is another stress state that affects the response of cannabis upon one consequence of such stress-aggressive behavior. It has been suggested that REM-sleep deprivation produces a dopamine receptor supersensitivity (Carlini et al., 1976; Tufik et al., 1977). Turnover in brain dopamine (a catecholamine neurotransmitter) was decreased by a marijuana extract in rats deprived of REM sleep but not in unstressed rats (Carlini et al., 1977).

Several of those same psychotropic agents that modify or interact with stress-induced changes in appetitive behavior play an important role in the process of nociception—particularly insofar as this may constitute a basis for stress, be modified by stress, or affect the consequence of stress action on pain-related behavior.

Stress, Pain, and the Effects of Drugs

It is important that a basis for a potentially significant interaction between stress and drug effects resides in the use of drugs which may possess some analgesic properties. Some of the effects mediated centrally by stress parallel some of the conditions wherein direct central stimuli have been utilized; as such, there has been some suggestion that components of stress-related behaviors may affect those central mechanisms whereby the response to nociceptive stimuli is regulated. A significant analgesia has been noted after selective brain stimulation in animals (Reynolds, 1969; Meyer & Liebeskind, 1974; Oliveras et al., 1974; Oliveras et al., 1975; Soper, 1976) and in man (Adams, 1976; Hosobuchi et al., 1977; Richardson & Akil, 1977). The production of analgesia by such brain stimulation has been shown to be associated with the release of morphine-like peptides in the brain (Akil et al., 1976). Painful stimulation has also been shown to produce pain relief in experimental conditions (Parsons & Goetzl, 1975) and in clinical circumstances (Travell & Rinzler, 1952). A prolonged relief from pain by the administration of a brief, intense transcutaneous shock has also been documented (Melzack, 1975).

Analgesia, as measured by several methods, was shown to occur from exposure of rats to several stressful conditions (Hayes et al., 1978). It is perhaps appropriate to note that the opiate receptor antagonist, naloxone, did not modify the stress-induced analgesia, suggesting that the effect is not mediated by a stress-directed activation of brain opiate receptors or the release of an analgesic peptide. In other studies (Amir & Amit, 1978), however, with the use of immobilization stress, naloxone given before stress reversed the effect on pain-motivated behavior. These results have suggested that immobilization stress-induced changes in pain-related behavior may occur as a consequence of activation, by stress, of an endogenous opiate-like receptor system. In other studies, several interesting differences between the response to stressful, painful stimulation and the action of analgesic drugs in stressed and nonstressed mice were examined (Kita et al., 1976). In general, stressed mice showed a greater response to painful stimulation and had a greater analgesic effect than nonstressed mice when given such agents as aminopyrine or morphine. This phenomenon might also be explained in terms of a synergistic effect on the analgesic effect of the drug produced by stress-induced activation of central opiate-like receptors. A relationship of the stress response to brain stimulation is further supported by data linking both to the hypothalamo-pituitary adrenal axis (Hartmann et al., 1974), although certain stressors, such as ether anesthesia, which releases ACTH, apparently do not produce a postanesthesic analgesis or involve central opiate receptors (Hayes et al., 1978).

The reciprocation between stress and the neuroendocrine system has offered an important basis on which psychoactive drug effects have been elaborated. The next section of this chapter treats several issues relevant to these relationships.

Stress, Hormones, and Drug Effects

Nonspecific stress effects have been shown to involve other trophic substances in the hypothalamic-pituitary axis which have also been related to more specific drug effects. For example, cold-exposure stress has been shown to increase the release of thyroid-stimulating hormone (TSH) from the anterior pituitary—probably due to an activation of the central noradrenergic system which regulates rodent TSH secretion (Krulich et al., 1977). Cold-stress-induced increases in TSH secretion were blocked by agents that depleted norepinephrine, such as diethyldithiocarbamic acid (DDC) or blocked α-adrenergic receptors, such as phenoxybenzamine. Stress imposed by maintenance of continuous lighting caused an elevation of TSH level measured both in the serum (22.46 $\pm$ 4.79 ng/ml to 34.45 $\pm$ 5.45 ng/ml) and in the pituitary (17.92 $\pm$ 4.61 μg/ng to 24.56 $\pm$ 4.06 μg/ng) of male rats (Simiomescu et al., 1978). Treatment with chlorpromazine further increased the TSH levels after light stress. Other pituitary hormones were also affected by light stress as well as by chlorpromazine. Growth hormone secretion was increased by this stress, but in this case chlorpromazine blocked the stress-induced release. Chlorpromazine further caused an increased prolactin secretion but had only a minimal effect on the change in pituitary prolactin level caused by stress (Simionescu, et al., 1978).

The effects of stress on androgens has been given some attention, particularly with a view toward the possibility that androgens may exert psychotropic effects (Herrmann & Beach, 1976). One aspect of this issue concerns potential androgen deficits in depression—the latter commonly associated with stress, at least within clinical observations (for a review of depression and "loss" as a source of stress, see Costello, pp. 93–124, this volume). Adrenal androgen activity, assessed by the urinary level of the metabolites, 11-deoxy-17-oxysteroids was lower in depressed females and returned to within a normal range after recovery from depression (Ferguson et al., 1964) after treatment with electroconvulsive shock. The measurement of plasma testosterone levels in acutely stressed men after 23 weeks of intensive military training revealed significantly lower levels after stress than before or during a nonstressed period (Kreuz et al., 1972). A prolonged decrement in plasma testosterone level has also been observed in subjects following the stress of major surgery (Matsumoto et al., 1970). It has also been observed that in young men there is a positive correlation between plasma testosterone levels and aggressiveness (Persky et al., 1971). This finding, taken in the context of stress-induced reduction of testosterone level and aggressive behavior in animal studies and testosterone-induced aggressiveness in animals, supports the interrelationship of stress, testosterone activity, and aggressiveness. It has been shown that isolation stress will produce aggressive behavior in rodents, that this may be modified by a number of drugs (Valzelli, 1967), and that this is associated with several brain metabolic changes (Valzelli, 1973). As part of this stress-induced aggressive behavior pattern, ACTH release stimulates adrenal testosterone synthesis; conditions which reduce such stress-induced aggressive behavior, such as alloxan diabetes, also serve to reduce adrenocortical testosterone synthesis (Essman, 1979). Drug effects on the relationship between stress-induced aggressive behavior and testosterone synthesis have also been examined. Isolation stress increased adrenocortical testosterone synthesis in male mice, and these male mice also develop aggressive behavior. Isolation-stressed female mice do not become aggressive unless they are treated with testosterone (Essman et al., 1973). Testosterone synthesis as well as stress-induced aggressive behavior in rodents are affected by several benzodiazepine derivatives. Of those compounds examined, diazepam and N-demethyldiazepam inhibited testosterone synthesis only in the male adrenal cortex but increased 17-β-estradiol synthesis in both male and female gonadal tissue. The synthesis of this estrogen was increased in testicular tissue by medazepam, nitrazepam, and chlordiazepoxide (Essman, 1978). Alterations in stress-induced aggressive behavior by benzodiazepines might be dependent on decreased testosterone synthesis—either or both of which would predictably attenuate such a stress response.

Observations concerning the peripheral adrenergic system in stress behavior have already been made. It is also relevant to observe that central catecholamines serve both as modulators and as indices of stress-drug interactions. The final section of this chapter presents a brief overview of some of the issues.

Central Catecholamines, Stress, and Drug Action

Another well-documented response to a variety of stressors is the development of gastric lesions in animals and man. Such gastric ulceration has been induced by immobilization stress (Essman & Frisone, 1965) and is potentiated under such conditions by isolation stress (Essman, 1966). It has been further shown that other stress-related variables such as food deprivation and gastric emptying affect relevant factors in the etiology of gastric ulcerogenesis, such as gastric pH, and the distribution of biologically active gastric amines (Essman et al., 1971). It is reasonable to expect that psychoactive agents affect and interact with the consequences of stress in contributing to gastric ulceration. Certainly the central nervous system has been given an important role in the regulation of gastrointestinal functions (Feldman et al., 1961; Fennegan & Puiggari, 1966). Further support for the central regulation of stress-induced ulceration derives from pharmacological studies; in rats, fusaric acid, a dopamine β-hydroxylase inhibitor prevented stress-induced ulcers (Osumi et al., 1973; Hidaka et al., 1974). The role of central catecholamines in stress-induced gastric ulceration has been examined in rats with bilateral destruction of the ventral bundles, the norepinephrine regulatory inputs into the hypothalamus (Osumi et al., 1977). It was observed that restraint stress decreased the norepinephrine concentration in the hypothalamus and cerebral cortex and that this change was inhibited by the ventral bundles lesion. Tetrabenazine, which releases catecholamines centrally, and aggravates stress-induced ulceration (Osumi et al., 1973), enhanced the stress-induced decrease in brain norepinephrine and aggravated the gastric ulceration; the effects of tetrabenazine, however, were completely blocked in animals with lesions of the ventral bundles. These findings support the role of hypothalamic norepinephrine release, via the ventral bundles, in the mediation of stress-induced gastric ulceration as well as in the proulcerogenic effect of tetrabenazine.

In human beings, stress-induced anxiety states have been approached therapeutically on the basis of presumed adrenergic hyperactivity, and β-adrenergic receptor blockade has been considered as one approach (Turner, 1976). Several studies have failed to demonstrate any significant effects on anxiety states with high doses of the β-adrenergic blocker, propranalol (Lader & Tyrer, 1972; Ogle et al., 1976). The β-adrenergic blocker exyprenolol exerted several significant effects on measures of task-induced stress in normal human subjects (Farhoumand et al., 1977); these included a fall in pulse rate and blood pressure, a decrease in critical flicker frequency, and decreased alertness.

Concluding Remarks

It is apparent that just as the sources of stress in animals and man are varied, complex, and often indirect, the consequences of stress are geometrically derived with multiple variables and intricate governing mechanisms. The intricate manner in which the responses to stress interact with pharmacological agents represents an important but singular approach to the biological treatment of stress-related disorders. The emphasis here has been on the drug-stress response interaction rather than on a documentation of stress responses or a survey of the psychopharmacopae. In treating this subject from the viewpoint of an interaction, the most relevant psychotropic agents and the more common responses to stress have been included. The level of the stress response differs, depending on the focus of its biological analysis. Similarly, the level of drug effect relevant to that response elucidates different potential mechanisms which underlie the stress response and which bear on its interaction with specific drugs and classes of psychoactive agents.

References

Adams, J. E. Naloxone reversal of analgesia produced by brain stimulation in the human. *Pain,* 1976, *2,* 161–166.

Akil, H., Watson, S., & Barchas, J. Increase in opiate-like factors upon analgetic electrical stimulation in rat brain. *Neuroscience Abstracts,* 1976, *2,* 563.

Amir, S., & Amit, Z. Endogenous opioid ligands may mediate stress-induced changes in the affective properties of pain related behavior in rats. *Life Sciences*, 1978, *23*, 1143–1152.

Ammon, H. P. T., Orci L., & Steinke, J. Effect of chlorpromazine (CPZ) on insulin release "in vivo" and "in vitro" in the rat. *Journal of Pharmacology and Experimental Therapy*, 1973, *187*, 423–429.

Antelman, S. M., & Szechtman, H. Tail-pinch induces eating in sated rats which appears to depend on nigrostriatal dopamine. *Science*, 1975, *189*, 731–733.

Antelman, S. M., Szechtman, P. C., & Fisher, A. E. Tail-pinch-induced eating, gnawing and licking behavior in rats: Dependence on the nigrostriatal dopamine system. *Brain Research*, 1975, *99*, 319–337.

Bareggi, S. R., Markey, K., & Paoletti, R. Effects of amphetamine, electrical stimulation and stress on endogenous mopeg-so$_4$ levels in rat brain. *Pharmacological Research Communications*, 1978, *10*, No. 1, 65–73.

Barrett, A. M., & Stockham, M. A. The effect of housing conditions and simple experimental procedures upon the corticosterone level in the plasma of rats. *Journal of Endocrinology*, 1963, *26*, 97–105.

Bassett, J. R., & Caincross, K. D. Effects of psychoactive drugs on responses of the rat to aversive stimulation. *Archives Internationale Pharmacodyname et Therapie*, 1974, *212*, 221–229.

Bliss, E. L., Ailion, J., & Zwanziger, J. Metabolism of norepinephrine, serotonin and dopamine in rat brain with stress. *Journal of Pharmacology and Experimental Therapeutics*, 1968, *164*, 122–134.

Bowden, C. L. Recent advances in the benzodiazepines. *Texas Medicine*, 1979, *75*, 51–54.

Carlini, E. A., & Gonzales, C. Aggressive behaviour induced by marihuana compounds and amphetamine in rats previously made dependent on morphine. *Experientia*, 1972, *28*, 542.

Carlini, E. A., Hamoui, A., & Märtz, R. M. W. Factors influencing the aggressiveness elicited by marihuana in food deprived rats. *British Journal of Pharmacology*, 1972, *44*, 794.

Carlini, E. A., Lindsey, J., & Tufik, S. Environmental and drug interference with effects of marihuana. *Annals of N.Y. Academy of Science*, 1976, *281*, 229–242.

Carlini, E. A., Lindsey, C. J., & Tufik, S. Cannabis catecholamines, rapid eye movement, sleep and aggressive behaviour. *British Journal of Pharmacology*, 1977, *61*, 371–379.

Cession-Fossion, A. Effets adrénergiques généraux de la oubaïne. *Journal of Physiology, (Paris)*, 1966, *58*, 489–490.

Cooper, T. (Ed.). The consequences of stress (Vol. 1). Bloomfield, N.J.: *Health Learning Systems*, 1979.

Costello, C. G. Loss as a source of stress in psychopathology. In R. W. J. Neufeld (Ed.), *Psychological Stress and Psychopathology*. New York: McGraw-Hill, 1981.

Cox, T., and Lee, J. Noise stress and effects of viloxazine (vivaian), a new antidepressant, on open field activity in rats. *Pharmacology, Biochemistry and Behavior*, 1976, *4*, 729–730.

Daly, J. Rise of cyclic nucleotides in the nervous system. In L. L. Iversen. S. D. Iversen, & S. H. Snyder, (Eds.), *Handbook of psychopharmacology V*. New York: Plenum, 1975.

Davies, D. R. Physiological and psychological effects of exposure to high intensity noise. *Applied Acoustics*, 1968, *1*, 218–233.

Davison, W. Stress in the elderly. *Physiotherapy*, 1978, *64*, No. 4, 113–115.

Delapez, R. L., Dickman, S. R., & Grosser, B. I. Effects of stress on rat brain adenosine 3′, 5′-monophosphate in vivo. *Brain Research*, 1975, *85*, 171–175.

Denenberg, V. H., & Zarrow, M. X. Infantile stimulation, adult behavior and adrenocortical activity. In S. Kazda & V. H. Denenberg (Eds.), *Postnatal development of phenotype*. Prague: Academia, 1970.

Dinnendahl, V. Effects of stress on mouse brain cyclic nucleotide levels in vivo. *Brain Research*, 1975, *100*, 716–719.

Dinnendahl, V., & Gumulka, S. W. Stress-induced alterations of cyclic nucleotide levels in brain: effects of centrally acting drugs. *Psychopharmacology*, 1977, *52*, 243–249.

Donovick, P. J., & Wakeman, K. S. Open field luminance and septal hyperemotionality. *Animal Behavior*, 1969, *17*, 186–190.

Erdösová, R., Jakoubek, B., & Kraus, M. Effect of stress and diazepam treatment during infancy on the corticosterone regulation and androgenic activity in adult male rats. *Experientia*, 1975, *31*, 62–63.

Erdösová, R., Kraus, M., & Rehulka, J. Corticosterone synthesis and serum levels at the end of the perinatal period. A study of the effects of stress, diazepam and polyethylene glycol treatments. *Physiologia Bohemoslovaca*, 1977, *26*, 297–302.

Essman, W. B. Isolation-induced facilitation of gastric ulcerogenesis in mice. *Journal of Psychosomatic Research*, 1966, *10*, 183–188.

Essman, W. B. Benzodiazepines and aggressive behavior. *Modern Problems in Pharmacopsychology*, 1978, *13*, 13–28.

Essman, W. B. Neurochemical changes in aggressive behavior. In J. Obiols, C. Ballus, E. G. Monclus, & J. Pujol (Eds.), *Biological Psychiatry Today*. Amsterdam: Elsevier/North-Holland, 1979.

Essman, W. B., Essman, S. G., & Golod, M. I. Metabolic contributions to gastric ulcerogenesis in mice. *Physiological Behavior*, 1971, *7*, 509–516.

Essman, W. B., & Frisone, J. D. Stress-induced gastric lesions in mice. *Psychological Report*, 1965, *16*, 941–946.

Essman, W. B., Heldman, E., Valzelli, L., & Malick, J. Attenuation of isolation-induced aggressive behaviors and testosterone synthesis in mice by electroconvulsive shock. *Federation Proceedings*, 1973, *32*, 384.

Farhoumand, N., Harrison, J., & Wadsworth, J. Controlled comparison of a single high dose of oxprenolol with lorazepam on stress-induced physiological changes and on some psychophysiological variables. *British Journal of Clinical Pharmacology*, 1977, *4*, 402P.

Feldman, S., Birbaum, D., & Behar, A. Gastric secretion and acute gastroduodenal lesions following hypothalamic and preoptic stimulation. *Journal of Neurosurgery*, 1961, *18*, 661.

Fennegan, F. M. & Puiggari, M. J. Hypothalamic and amygdaloid influence on gastric motility in dogs. *Journal of Neurosurgery*, 1966, *24*, 497.

Ferguson, H. C., Bartram, A. C. G., Fowlie, H. C., Cathro, D. M., Birhall, K., & Mitchell, F. L. A preliminary investigation of steroid excretion in depressed patients before and after electro-convulsive therapy. *Acta Endocrinologica*, 1964, *47*, 58–68.

Ferrendelli, J. A., Kinscherf, D. A., & Kipnis, D. M. Effects of amphetamine, chlorpromazine and reserpine on cyclic GMP and cyclic AMP levels in mouse cerebellum. *Biochemical & Biophysical Research Communications*, 1972, *46*, 2114–2120.

Gascon, A. L. Effect of acute stress and ouabain administration on adrenal catecholamine content and cardiac function of rats pretreated with diazepam. *Canadian Journal of Physiology and Pharmacology*, 1977, *55*, 65–71.

Gray, P., Solomon, J., Dunphy, M., Carr, F., & Hession, M. Effects of lithium on open field behavior in "stressed" and "unstressed" rats. *Psychopharmacology*, 1976, *48*, 277–281.

Hartmann, G., Fekete, M., & Lissak, K. Self-stimulation and adrenocortical activity in young rats. *Acta Physiologica Academiae Scientiarum Hungaricae, Tomus*, 1974, *45* (3–4), 297–303.

Hayes, R. L., Bennett, G. J., Newlon, P. G., & Mayer, D. J. Behavioral and physiological studies of non-narcotic analgesia in the rat elicited by certain environmental stimuli. *Brain Research*, 1978, *155*, 69–90.

Herrmann, W. M., & Beach, R. C. Psychotropic effects of androgens: a review of clinical observations and new human experimental findings. *Pharmakopsychiatrie*, 1976, *9*, 205–219.

Hidaka, H., Hara, F., Harada, N., Hashizume, Y., & Yano, M. Selective inhibition of dopamine β-hydroxylase in the peripheral tissues by 5-dimethyldithiocarbamylpicolinic acid; its effect on stress-induced ulcer, ethanol-induced sleep and blood pressure. *Journal of Pharmacology and Experimental Therapeutics*, 1974, *191*, 384.

Hodges, J. R., & Mitchley, S. The effect of "training" on the release of corticotrophin in response to minor stressful procedures in the rat. *Journal of Endocrinology*, 1970, *47*, 253–254.

Holmes, H., Rodnight, R., & Kapoor, R. Effects of electroshock and drugs administered in vivo on protein kinase activity in rat brain. *Pharmacology, Biochemistry and Behavior*, 1977, *6*, 415–419.

Horowitz, L. G. & Nersasian, R. R. A review of marijuana in relation to stress-response mechanisms in the dental patient. *Journal of American Dental Association,* 1978, *96,* 983–986.

Hosobuchi, Y., Adams, J. E., & Linchitz, R. Pain relief by electrical stimulation of the central gray matter in humans and its reversal by naloxone. *Science,* 1977, *197,* 183–186.

Johnson, F. N. Chlorpromazine and lithium: Effects on stimulus significance. *Disorders of the Nervous System,* 1972, *33,* 235–241.

Keim, K. L., & Sigg. E. B. Plasma corticosterone and brain catecholamines in stress: Effect of psychotropic drugs. *Pharmacology, Biochemistry and Behavior,* 1977, *6,* 79–85.

Kita, T., Hata, T., & Yoneda, R. Analgesic effect of neurotropin in mice and comparison of analgesic effect of some drugs on SART-STRESS mice and normal mice. *Folia Pharmacologica Japon,* 1976, *72,* 573–584.

Kreuz, L. E., Rose, R. M., & Jennings, J. R. Suppression of plasma testosterone levels and psychological stress. *Archives of General Psychiatry,* 1972, *26,* 479–482.

Krulich, A., Giachetti, A., Marchlewska-Koj, A., Hefco, E., & Jameson, H. E. On the role of the central noradrenergic and dopaminergic systems in the regulation of TSH secretion in the rat. *Endocrinology,* 1977, *100,* 496–505.

Lader, M. H., & Turner, P. J. Central and peripheral effects of propranolol and sotalol in normal human subjects. *British Journal of Pharmacology,* 1972, *45,* 557–560.

Lahti, R. A. & Barsuhn, C. The effect of various doses of minor tranquilizers on plasma corticosteroids in stressed rats. *Research Communications in Chemistry, Pathology and Pharmacology,* 1975, *11,* 595–603.

Lidbrink, P., Corrodi, H., Fuxe, K., & Olson, L. Barbiturates and meprobamate: decreases in catecholamine turnover of central dopamine and noradrenaline neuronal system and the influence of immobilization stress. *Brain Research,* 1972, *45,* 507–524.

Lust, W. D., Goldberg, N. D., & Passonneau, J. V. Cyclic nucleotides in murine brain: The temporal relationship of changes induced in adenosine 3', 5'-monophosphate and guanosine 3', 5'-monophosphate following maximal electroshock or decapitation. *Journal of Neurochemistry,* 1976, *26,* 5–10.

Maclean, K. I., & Littleton, J. M. Environmental stress as a factor in the response of rat brain catecholamine metabolism to Δ^8-tetrahydrocannabinol. *European Journal of Pharmacology,* 1977, *41,* 171–182.

Mao, C. C., Guidotti, A., & Costa, E. Inhibition by diazepam of the tremor and the increase of cerebellar cGMP content elicited by harmaline. *Brain Research,* 1975, *83,* 516–519.

Martinez-Sierra, R., Andres-Trellas, F., & Herrero, C. V. Close relation between hypothalamic and cardiac norepinephrine during stress and its role in acute myocardial infarction disrhythmias. *Experientia,* 1978, *34,* 1611–1613.

Matsumoto, K., Takeyasu, K., Mizutani, S. Hamanaka, Y. Ha., & Uozumi, T. Plasma testosterone levels following surgical stress in male patients. *Acta Endocrinologia,* 1970, *65,* 11–17.

Mayer, D. J., & Liebeskind, J. C. Pain reduction by focal electrical stimulation of the brain: An anatomical and behavioral analysis. *Brain Research,* 1974, *68,* 73–93.

McCarty, R., & Kopin, I. J. Sympatho-adrenal medullary activity and behavior during exposure to footshock stress: A comparison of seven rat strains. *Physiology and Behavior,* 1978, *21,* 567–572.

Melzack, R. Prolonged relief of pain by brief, intense transcutaneous somatic stimulation. *Pain,* 1975, *1,* 357–373.

Morgan, W. W., Rudeen, P. K., & Pfeil, K. A. Effect of immobilization stress on serotonin content and turnover in regions of the rat brain. *Life Sciences,* 1975, *17,* 143–150.

Nadeau, R. & DeChamplain, J. Comparative effect of 6-hydroxydopamine and reserpine on ouabain toxicity in the rat. *Life Sciences,* 1973, *13,* 1753–1761.

Nasmyth, P. A. The effect of chlorpromazine on adrenocortical activity in stress. *British Journal of Pharmacology,* 1955, *10,* 336–339.

Ogle, C. W., Turner, P., & Markomihelakis, H. The effects of high doses of oxprenolol and of propranolol on pursuit rotor performance, reaction time and critical flicker frequency. *Psychopharmacologia (Berl.)*, 1976, *46*, 295–299.

Oliveras, J. L., Besson, J. M., Guilbaud, G., & Liebeskind, J. C. Behavioral and electrophysiological evidence of pain inhibition from midbrain stimulation in the cat. *Experimental Brain Research*, 1974, *20*, 32–44.

Oliveras, J. L., Redjemi, F., Guilbaud, G., & Besson, J. M. Analgesia induced by electrical stimulation of the inferior centralis nucleus of the raphe in the cat. *Pain*, 1975, *1*, 139–144.

Opmeer, F. A., Gumulka, S. W., Dinnendahl, V., & Schönhöfer, P. S. Effects of stimulatory and depressant drugs on cyclic guanosine 3′, 5′-monophosphate and adenosine 3′, 5′-monophosphate levels in mouse brain. *Nanyn-Schmiedeberg's Archives of Pharmacology*, 1976, *292*, 259–265.

Osumi, Y., Muramatsu, I., & Fujiwara, M. The effects of destruction of noradrenergic ascending ventral bundles and tetrabenazine on formation of stress-induced gastric ulcer. *European Journal of Pharmacology*, 1977, *41*, 47–51.

Osumi, Y., Takaori, S., & Fujiwara, M. Preventive effect of fusaric acid, a dopamine β-hydroxylase inhibitor, on the gastric ulceration induced by water immersion stress in rats. *Japanese Journal of Pharmacology*, 1973, *23*, 904.

Palkovits, M., Kobayashi, R. M., Kizer, J. S., Jacobowitz, D. M., & Kopin, I. J. Effects of stress on catecholamines and tyrosine hydroxylase activity of indivual hypothalamic nuclei. *Neuroendocrinology*, 1975, *18*, 144–153.

Parsons, C. M., & Goetzl, F. R. Effect of induced pain on pain threshold. *Proceedings of Society of Experimental Biology (N.Y.)*, 1975, *60*, 327–329.

Peck, J. W. Rats drinking quinine- or caffeine-adulterated water defend lean body weights against caloric and osmotic stress. *Physiology and Behavior*, 1978, *21*, 599–607.

Perry, G. Aspects of stress in man and animals. *Proceedings of Royal Society of Medicine*, 1975, *68*, 423–425.

Persky, H., Smith, K. D., & Basu, G. K. Relation of psychologic measures of aggression and hostility to testosterone production in man. *Psychosomatic Medicine*, 1971, *33*, 265–277.

Peyramond, A. Etude comparative croisée de l'action du tiapride (*) et du méprobomate sur les états d'agitation. *Semaine Hospital, Paris*, 1978, *54*, 542–545.

Pinel, J. P. J., & Mucha, R. F. Activity and reactivity in rats at various intervals after footshock. *Canadian Journal of Psychology*, 1973, *27*, 112–118.

Reynolds, D. V. Surgery in the rat during electrical analgesia induced by focal brain stimulation. *Science*, 1969, *164*, 444–445.

Richardson, D. E., & Akil, H. Pain reduction by electrical brain stimulation in man. Part 2: Chronic self-administration in the periventricular gray matter. *Journal of Neurosurgery*, 1977, *47*, 184–194.

Robinson, D. S. Changes in monoamine oxidase and monoamines with human development and aging. *Federal Proceedings*, 1975, *34*, 103–107.

Roland, N. E., & Antelman, S. M. Stress-induced hyperphagia and obesity in rats: A possible model for understanding human obesity. *Science*, 1976, *191*, 310–312.

Seifen, E. Evidence for participation of catecholamine in cardiac action of ouabain; positive chronotropic effect. *British Journal of Pharmacology*, 1974, *51*, 481–490. (a)

Seifen, E. Evidence for participation of catecholamine in cardiac action of ouabain; release of catecholamines. *European Journal of Pharmacology*, 1974, *26*, 115–118. (b)

Simionescu, L., Oprescu, M., & Dimitriu, V. The action of chlorpromazine upon the serum and hypophyseal variations of growth hormone, prolactin and TSH in the male adult rat under continuous-lighting stress. *Revue Roumaine Medicine and Endocrinology*, 1978, *16*, 15–21.

Snow, A. E., & Horita, A. Preliminary studies on the effect of electric foot shock stress on apomorphine induced hyperthermia. *Proceedings of the Western Pharmacological Society*, 1977, *20*, 281–286.

Soper, W. Y. Effects of analgesic midbrain stimulation on reflex withdrawal and thermal escape in the rat. *Journal of Comparative and Physiological Psychology,* 1976, *90,* 91–101.

Talbott, J. A., & Teague, J. W. Marihuana psychosis. *Journal of the American Medical Association,* 1969, *210,* 299.

Tanz, R. D., & Marcus, S. M. Influence of endogenous cardiac catecholamine depletion on the force and rate of isolated heart preparations and their response to ouabain. *Journal of Pharmacology and Experimental Therapeutics,* 1966, *151,* 38–45.

Travell, J., & Rinzler, S. H. The myofascial genesis of pain. *Postgraduate Medical Journal,* 1952, *11,* 425–434.

Tufik, S., Lindsey, C. J., & Carlini, E. A. Does REM sleep deprivation procedure induce dopamine receptor supersensitivity. *Pharmacology,* 1978, *16,* 98–105.

Turner, P. Beta-adrenoceptor blockade in hyperthyroidism and anxiety. *Proceedings of the Royal Society of Medicine,* 1976, *69,* 375–377.

Valdman, A. V. Pharmacologic aspects of the problems of emotional stress. *Patologi Fisiologi Eksperimental Toksikologi (Moscow),* 1976, *5,* 3–10.

Valzelli, L. Drugs and aggressiveness. *Advances in Pharmacology,* 1967, *5,* 79–108.

Valzelli, L. The "isolation syndrome" in mice. *Psychopharmacologia,* 1973, *31,* 305–320.

Van Loon, G. R. Brain catecholamines in the regulation of ACTH secretion. In *Recent Studies of Hypothalamic Function.* Basal: Karger, 1974.

Vargas, L., Bronfman, M., & Foradori, A. Identification of the alpha$_2$-glucose inhibitor with alpha$_2$-glycoprotein. *Excerpta Medical International Congress,* 1970, Series No. 209, 182 (Abstract).

Vargas, L., Bronfman, M., & Kawada, M. E. Stress, insulin antagonist and transient diabetes mellitus in the rat. *Hormonal and Metabolic Research,* 1974, *6,* 275–280.

Vargas, I., & Kawada, M. E. Adrenal and liver participation in the rat's post-stress response. *Hormonal and Metabolic Research,* 1976, *8,* 383–388.

Wallach, M. B., Dawber, M., McMahon, M., & Rogers, C. A new anorexigen assay: Stress-induced hyperphagia in rats. *Pharmacolocy, Biochemistry and Behavior,* 1977, *6,* 529–531.

Williams, D. I. Maze exploration in the rat under different levels of illumination. *Animal Behavior,* 1971, *19,* 365–367.

Williams, D. I. Aspects of stress in man and animals. *Proceedings of the Royal Society of Medicine,* 1975, *68,* 425–427.

Yuwiler, A. Stress and serotonin. In W. B. Essman (Ed.), *Serotonin in health and disease. V. Clinical correlations.* Englewood Cliffs, N.J.: Spectrum Books 1979.

Zarrow, M. X., Philpott, J. E., & Denenberg, V. H. Responsiveness of the adrenal gland of the neonatal rat. In S. Kazda & V. H. Denenberg (Eds.), *Postnatal development of phenotype.* Prague: Academia, 1970.

Chapter 11

Stress, Coping, and Disease:
A Cognitive-Behavioral Perspective

DONALD MEICHENBAUM   *DENNIS TURK*

University of Waterloo   *Yale University*
Waterloo, Ontario   *New Haven, Connecticut*

The literature on the relationship between stress and disease has been examined recently by a number of reviewers (e.g., Antonovsky, 1978; Cohen, 1979; Lipowski, 1977; Rabkin & Struening, 1976; Weiner, 1977). In fact, an issue (June, 1979) of the *Journal of Human Stress* was devoted entirely to this topic. Several themes emerge in these reviews of the literature that provide a framework for appreciating the potential contributions of a cognitive-behavioral approach in clarifying the relationship between stress, coping, and disease. We examine these emerging themes by discussing first the concepts of disease and stress and then the nature of coping.

A major feature of this chapter is a description of the recent attempts to develop assessment procedures to measure more adequately the role that cognitive factors play in both stress and disease. These assessment procedures are summarized under the rubric of *cognitive ethology*. We believe that cognitive ethology techniques can do for the study of cognitive processes in stress what radioimmunoassay techniques have done for the study of endocrine processes in stress. As the respective methodologies of radioimmunoassay and cognitive ethology develop, we will be able to describe more adequately the complex relationship between stress and psychopathology. Thus, the present chapter highlights the needed advances in measurement required to assess cognitions. Finally, we conclude with a discussion of treatment implications and a description of a cognitive-behavioral approach of stress inoculation that has been used in the prevention and treatment of stress-related disorders.

Concept of Disease

A brief examination of the nature and changing incidence of disease sets the stage for a discussion of the cognitive-behavioral approach. In earlier times, illness was thought to result from the presence of a single pathogenic agent—toxin, germ, endocrine imbalance, vitamin or nutritional deficiency. New knowledge, however, has increased the recognition that the etiology of poor health is multidetermined. Moreover, recent immunological research, as reviewed by Thomas (1978), has shown that in most instances infectious disease is due to the misreading of signals between an invading agent or pathogen and the host. It is often the organism's own bodily reactions or defense mechanisms that cause the disease (analogous to Selye's [1978] description of the diseases of adaptation). Thomas provides several examples of where the disease and resultant death of an organism is due to its own immunological system's overreaction.

This view of infectious disease as the misreading of signals between the invader and the host has interesting implications. For the signals to be misread, they must first be read. This appears to explain why certain diseases are specific to certain forms of life and not to others. We believe that the appraisal of an event, whether it is an invading pathogen or a threatening stressor, and the individual's appraisal of his or her coping resources play a central role in determining the occurrence of stress and disease.

A second set of observations about disease involves the increasing recognition that disease patterns in Western countries have shifted dramatically in the last century. As Jonas (1978) has noted, in 1900 the leading causes of death tended to be infectious disease; by midcentury, however, they had become chronic diseases. For example, in 1968 the likelihood of dying from an infectious disease was one-sixth what it was in 1900, but the death rate from heart disease had increased 268 percent. Current predictions are that over 80 percent of the male children born this year will eventually die of chronic disease. The nature of the problem is further highlighted by Haggerty (1977), who stated:

One's lifestyle, including patterns of eating, exercise, drinking, coping with stress, and use of tobacco and drugs, together with environmental hazards, are the major known modifiable causes of illness in America today.

Thus, any comprehensive attempt to engender health and reduce illness will have to consider each of the factors that Haggerty has implicated. In recent years (see

Meichenbaum, 1977, 1979; Turk, 1979) cognitive-behavioral techniques have been used to modify several of these causes of illness (e.g., smoking, obesity, coping with stress).

The final set of observations on the concept of disease that has implications for a cognitive-behavioral approach is the need to distinguish between illness and illness behavior. Mechanic (1978) has noted that illness behavior involves three components: (1) attentiveness to physical or mental symptoms; (2) processes affecting how symptoms are defined and accorded significance; and (3) the extent to which help is sought, life routines altered, and so on. The course and outcome of a disease depend not only on the physical and psychological state of the patient, but also on the ways clinical staff, family, employers, and friends react to the situation. The form and magnitude of illness are products of both subjective experience and social definitions, as well as the severity and quality of actual symptoms and physical incapacity. Cognitive behavioral assessment and interventions are intimately concerned with such subjective experience and social definitions.

One theme here is that illness should be viewed as both multifaceted and multidetermined. In fact, a number of authors (e.g., Cassel, 1976; Dodge & Martin 1970; Syme 1967, 1974) have argued that psychological stress may be an etiological factor in almost all diseases and especially in chronic diseases. According to Rabkin and Struening (1976), illness onset is generally associated with a number of factors, including:

The presence of stressful environmental conditions, perceptions by the individual that such conditions are stressful, the relative ability to cope with or adapt to these conditions, genetic predisposition to a disease and the presence of a disease agent (p. 1014).

In summary, three themes pervade the literature, namely, the increasing prevalence and incidence of chronic diseases; the expression and definition of such diseases in terms of the social and cultural definitions; and the multidetermined nature of disease. In this chapter, we explore the implications for intervention of these three themes. Let us now turn our attention to the concepts of stress and coping.

The Concept of Stress

In 1936, Hans Selyé articulated his concept of stress as the "general adaptation syndrome," a set of nonspecific physiological reactions to any noxious environmental event. This formulation was largely responsible for popularizing the concept of stress in medicine. Since then, there has been a good deal of debate on the definition of stress. Some have viewed stress as referring to those factors or stimuli, usually external to the organism, which demand some response or change in behavior (e.g., Holmes & Rahe, 1967). Another view of stress refers to the response of the person when placed in a threatening or challenging environment (e.g., Selye, 1978). On the one hand, stress is referred to as a condition of the environment; on the other, stress is referred to as changes provoked in the organism.

In contrast, the model of stress that most readily fits the cognitive-behavioral perspective is a *transactional model,* as described by Lazarus and his colleagues (Lazarus & Cohen, 1977; Lazarus & Launier, 1978; Roskies & Lazarus, 1979) and by Mason (1975). The transactional model highlights the nature of the (mis)fit between the organism and the environmental demands. The discrepancy between the demands impinging on an organism, whether those demands are internal or external, whether challenges or goals, and the way the person perceives his potential responses to these demands constitute stress. Within a transactional model, it is the person's own perception of the stressfulness of the event and the appraisal of one's ability to cope that ultimately defines stress. Thus, how the organism interprets an environmental stimulus and the resources for responding to the demand and not the stimulus or response per se determines the stressfulness of the stimulus.

The Concept of Coping

Within such a transactional model of stress one must immediately consider the nature of the coping processes, for coping is the other side of the coin from stress. Since physical and environmental demands are ubiquitous, what distinguishes one person from another is the ability to cope. It is the nature of the coping process and not the demands per se that determine the occurrence and extent of disease. Roskies and Lazarus (1979) have noted that coping is not simply a response to an event that has happened, but instead is an active process in shaping what has happened and what will happen. In short, a transactional model is established whereby the person is both the recipient and perpetrator of stress, whereby one's coping is a reaction to demands and also a shaper of the stress experience.

Zubin and Spring (1977), who have adopted a transactional model of stress, speculate on the extent to which life stressors (a la Holmes & Rahe, 1967) really do occur as random happenstances. With the exception of natural calamities such as floods and earthquakes, it may be that a person's choice of lifestyle contributes to the likelihood of encountering demanding events. Zubin and Spring speculate that it may be possible to identify "stress-prone" patterns of living, just as one might discuss "accident-prone" people. A case in point is the relationship between Type A personalities and coronary heart disease.

Thus, central to both the concepts of stress and coping as a transactional process is the notion that the person filters stimulus information and that the resulting appraisal determines whether the situation is evaluated as relevant, threatening, challenging, or whatever. Cognitive-behavioral modification has a unique contribution to make to both the assessment of and the intervention in these cognitive processes.

It is important to recognize that coping with stress is not limited to intrapsychic cognitive processes. For example, Lazarus and Launier (1978) define coping "as efforts, both action oriented and intrapsychic to manage (i.e., master, tolerate, reduce, minimize) environmental and internal demands and conflicts which tax or exceed a person's resources." In some instances, an adequate coping response may be to change the situation for the better, if we can, or to escape from an intolerable one. In other situations, where we cannot alter or avoid the situation, we may use what Lazarus and Launier call palliative modes of coping (i.e., methods of responding that make us feel better in the face of threat or harm without resolution of the problem per se). Under certain conditions such responses as intellectualizing, maintaining detachment, or avoiding thinking about certain matters, may indeed represent the most appropriate means of coping. Successful coping in a given situation will not always involve active mastery of one's environment.

Pearlin and Schooler (1978) pointed out that the protective function of coping behavior can be exercised in three ways: "by eliminating or modifying conditions giving rise to problems; by perceptually controlling the meaning of experience in a manner that neutralizes its problematic character; and by keeping the emotional consequences of problems within manageable bounds" (p. 2). Any stress-management training program will have to be sensitive to the variety of different aspects of the coping process. This sensitivity is apparent in the following set of guidelines for teaching coping responses.

Guidelines for Teaching Coping Responses

Exactly how do we learn to cope with problems and with stress? At present, the acquisition of coping responses seems to be quite haphazard and indirect. Such skills are not developed with conscious intent but seem to arise unwittingly in the course of living. We seem to learn to cope by "osmosis," by imitating the adaptive and maladaptive coping models available in our culture. Instead, let us consider what a training approach designed explicitly to teach effective coping responses on a preventive and treatment basis should include.

In developing such stress-management training procedures, it is necessary to consider what factors might contribute to less than optimal handling of the situation. One needs to conduct a task analysis of the different situational demands and then consider the intrapersonal and interpersonal component skills required for competent responding. A detailed discussion of how to conduct such a behavior-analytic analysis is beyond our scope here (see Turk, 1980), but at least two points should be noted. First, people must have adequate skills within their repertoire, and, second, they must produce these skills when the situation demands them. Both are necessary. An approach to training effective responding, therefore, requires attention both to the needed skills and to the factors that contribute to the facilitation or inhibition of producing these skills. These interfering factors may include such processes as the person's attributions, expectations, self-statements, images, current concerns, and so on, as well as the person's physical status at the time (e.g., fatigue, poor health). In short, it is important that the person not only possess the skills necessary to confront a given task, but, equally crucially, one must possess the belief in one's capacity to accomplish the task and the motivation to exert the effort to accomplish the task. Bandura's (1977) writings on the importance of the concept of self-efficacy also highlight the important role of such cognitive processes in coping with stress.

Any guidelines for teaching coping techniques must thus take into consideration the great diversity of person and situational factors. Coping devices are complex, and they need to be flexible. In fact, flexibility of coping styles seems to be the key to adaptation. Coping devices used successfully in one situation may be unsuccessful in another situation or even in the same situation at another time.

Consistent with a call for flexibility is the need for any training technique to be sensitive to individual differences and cultural differences. In particular, any stress-management program must pay particular heed to the important role of cognitive factors in the coping process.

A final guideline for a stress-training program is the need to expose the person to graded instances of stress. The actual exposure, during training, to less threatening stressful events should have a beneficial effect in consolidating stress-management skills and in fostering both a sense of control and self-efficacy. The notion of providing a person with a prospective defence against stress is in some respects analogous to immunization against attitude change and, of course, medical inoculation against disease. The general underlying principle in these two situations is that a person's resistance is enhanced by exposure to a stimulus that is strong enough to challenge the defenses without being so powerful as to overcome them. Graded exposure to a variety of interpersonal and intrapersonal stressors should enhance one's coping ability. By insuring that the person has a variety of different coping responses and by exposing him/her to a host of different graded stressors, he/she should develop a generalized sense of efficacy and competence in coping with stress.

The importance of such graded preexposure in a stress-training program is illustrated by the work of Epstein (1967) who compared the anxiety levels of inexperienced and experienced parachutists. Epstein found that novice parachutists tend toward an all-or-none variety of controlling levels of arousal, whereas experienced parachutists use compensatory coping responses at low intensities of arousal. Epstein believes that the ability to tolerate stress is acquired through *inoculations* with increasing amounts of stress. With experience, the nature of the parachutists' coping response changed due to exposure.

The possibility of helping individuals to become stress-resistant was also noted by Orne (1965), who wrote:

One way of enabling an individual to become resistant to a stress is to allow him to have appropriate prior experience with the stimulus involved. The biological notion of immunization provides such a model. If an individual is given the opportunity to deal with a stimulus that is mildly stressful and he is able to do so successfully (mastering it in a psychological sense) he will tend to be able to tolerate similar stimuli of somewhat greater intensity in the future. . . . It would seem that one can markedly affect

an individual's tolerance of stress by manipulating his beliefs about his own performance in the situation ... and his feelings that he can control his own behavior (pp.
315–316).

Cognitive Ethology

A central feature of the concepts of disease, stress, and coping that have been
offered is the important role of cognitive processes. In order to describe the complex
relationship between such cognitive processes and emotion, and between behavior
and disease, it is necessary to assess these cognitive processes more adequately. Meichenbaum and Butler (1980) have described a variety of possible cognitive assessment procedures under the heading of *cognitive ethology*. Like the ethologist who
follows the pattern of overt behavior (e.g., the interaction of a female bird and its
young), noting fixed action patterns, looking for releasing stimuli, and the like, we
wish to develop procedures to capture the flow of cognitions as evident in coping
processes. Perhaps a more appropriate example is the ethologically oriented investigator who studies the developmental relationship between a mother and her child.
This researcher develops a category system for mother behaviors and a category system for child behaviors, then examines the transactional and interactional nature of
these respective streams of behavior in an analysis of sequential probabilities in the
mother-child matrix. We propose that a similar strategy may be helpful in studying
the interaction between stress (coping) and disease (physiological processes).

Imagine being able to map the flow of ideation as evident in coping processes and
the accompanying flow of endocrinological changes that may contribute to the occurrence of disease. Clearly, other streams of behavior may be important to assess as
well, but, for the purpose of this presentation, let us focus on the cognitive stream.

The assessment of the stream of consciousness or the concern with introspection
has a long history that we will not consider at this time (see Pope & Singer, 1978).
Our focus instead will be to describe some of the techniques that have been employed
to assess the different patterns of cognition in the coping process (see Meichenbaum
& Butler, 1980, for a more detailed account).

Cognitive ethology is our term for the variety of measurement techniques that are
employed to describe the content, frequency, and patterning of cognitions (self-statements, images, appraisals, expectancies). Cognitive ethology requires the development of an armamentarium of techniques (interviews, pre- and postperformance
questionnaires, think-aloud protocols, videotape reconstruction procedures, thought
sampling, and so on) to assess the person's cognitive processes and cognitive
structures.

Each of the cognitive ethology assessment procedures depend on the person's self-
report, and we recognize the pitfalls and dangers of using such accounts. We would
argue that multiple assessment procedures must be used on the same target population in order to trace the changes in ideation related to the course of the disorder.
Thus, by using cross-sectional, longitudinal, and mixed-sectional designs, and by

using multiple forms of assessment, we can begin to trace the changes in ideation over the course of an illness. If a similar pattern of ideation emerges across populations and across measurement approaches, we can begin to have some "faith" that a fixed-action pattern, releasing stimuli, and so forth, have been identified for a given maladaptive process.

That such a task may prove worthwhile was noted by Meichenbaum and Butler (1980), who reviewed the effect of cognitive factors and performance across populations and tasks. They noted a growing convergence of theory and research on the influential role of *self-referent negative thought* in psychological functioning. Although the research on people under stress was conducted from a number of different perspectives, a similar pattern of ideation seems to be evident, namely, inadequate performance is accompanied by negative self-referent ideation. Such self-referent ideation refers to the person's penchant to become excessively preoccupied with one's own personal deficiencies; to cognize potential difficulties as more formidable than they really are; and to judge oneself inefficacious in coping with environmental demands. A common pattern of ideation (perhaps, using the ethology analogy, one could describe it as a kind of fixed-action pattern) seems evident across a variety of stressful situations. Inadequate performance is accompanied by a style of thinking in which the person is: (1) self-oriented rather than task-oriented, which serves to deflect attention from the task at hand, and (2) negative rather than positive, which serves to inhibit motivation. Such self-referent ideation seems to have an automatic, stereotyped "run-on" character. The effect of such ideation is to produce arousal and impair performance by diverting attention from the task to self-evaluative concerns. More specifically, the thinking processes of stressed persons who perform inadequately have some of the following characteristics:

1. Worrying about one's performance, including how well others are doing as compared with oneself.

2. Ruminating too long and fruitlessly over alternative responses.

3. Being preoccupied with bodily reactions associated with arousal.

4. Ruminating about possible consequences of doing poorly on the task or in the situation; overconcern with social disapproval, loss of status or esteem, punishment, damage to one's self-concept.

5. Thoughts and feelings of inadequacy, including active self-criticism or self-condemnation, considering oneself as worthless.

This pattern of self-referent ideation has been evident in such varied stressful settings as taking an examination (Hollandsworth et al., 1979); responding to social challenges (Schwartz & Gottman, 1976; Smye, 1977); handling angry feelings (Novaco, 1975); performing in athletic competition (Mahoney & Avener, 1977; O'Hara, 1977); and producing creative responses on tests of divergent thinking (Henshaw, 1978). More relevant to our concerns here, similar negative self-referent ideation has also been found to interfere with performance in such situations as tolerating pain (Genest, Turk, & Meichenbaum, 1978), undergoing catheterization (Kendall et al., 1979), and tolerating cancer (Weisman & Sobel, 1979). What is important to recognize is that this similar pattern of debilitating self-referent ideation is evident across varied populations and tasks even though markedly different assessment procedures were used, including interviews, think-aloud samples, post-performance questionnaires, and so forth.

Perhaps an example from a recent study will further illustrate the potential richness of such a cognitive ethology assessment approach. In a recent doctoral dissertation, Lewandowski (1979) compared the thinking styles of Type A (coronary-prone people who have an aggressive, pressured life-style) versus Type B (converse of Type A) businesspeople. The subjects were asked to perform a coding task under time pressure and were asked to list their thoughts immediately after the task. Table 11-1 illustrates the types of thoughts offered respectively by Type A and B people. A comparison of the self-statements offered by Type A and B subjects in Table 11-1 validates the differences reported by others.

Table 11-1   **The Listing of Statements Made by Type A and B Men.
(Taken from Lewandowski, 1979).**

QUESTION: WHAT THOUGHTS OR IDEAS OCCURRED TO YOU WHILE YOU WERE WORKING ON THIS TASK?
WHAT DID YOU FIND YOURSELF SAYING TO YOURSELF?

Type A Respondents (N = 8)

1. Well, I'm an achiever so I tried harder. I suspected it might be a fake.

2. Get better, Joe. I tried to memorize them.

3. I got self-critical—come on, you can go faster. You should be able to do it.

4. You're kidding. I can't believe it. I'm getting frustrated now. No.

5. Hey, buddy, improve. I couldn't imagine how to move faster except eye reactions—quicker pick up.

6. I've developed tests so I got angry. What's this damn instrument for?

7. I should be developing the number-symbol relationship. Why the hell am I going slower. Push.

8. I'm not too concerned with accuracy. I tried to memorize them. He's trying to create a stress so ignore it.

Type B Respondents (N = 8)

1. I figured I'd go as good as I could anyway—besides, it's probably related to age and I'm not as young as I used to be.

2. I got uptight. Hey, you're getting keyed up—back off, relax. I tried to put my mind in limbo and did get better at the end.

3. Nothing. I'm usually slow. I'm more interested in being right than breaking any speed records.

4. I tried to keep my mind open—not let the "slower" get me down. I tried to relax—to get set for the next round instead of getting nervous about feeling I'm below norm.

5. I thought about should I memorize this? Then I thought he's not telling me the truth.

6. I'm slower than average. Time is not my asset.

7. I know I'm not the fastest clerical worker in the world, probably slower than most.

8. I already know I'm not fast at this kind of thing.

A further comment concerning such self-report data is worth making, namely, that one cannot be sure that Lewandowski's subjects actually engaged in such thoughts during the coding task or whether the self-statements reported represent postperformance rationalizations or what they thought were socially desired responses. The subjects' thoughts may reflect what Tversky and Kahneman (1973) characterize as "availability heuristics" (i.e., the person's a priori theories about his or her cognitive processes in the situation). Thus, one may raise a question concerning the interpretation or explanation to be offered for the subjects' self-report of their cognitions. But it is clear that substantial individual differences are evident in the report of one's cognitive processes and that these differential reports have important relationships to behavior and disease. This is most evident when we compare those who cope well with those who falter in performance when stressed (see Meichenbaum et al., 1979).

In contrast to those who performed inadequately in stress-engendering situations, persons who have a strong sense of efficacy use their skills competently in meeting the demands of the situation and even seem spurred on by obstacles. Meichenbaum et al. (1979) have noted that in evaluative situations a common pattern of thinking processes (which they characterize as a failure to adopt a problem-solving set) contributes to inadequate performance on a variety of tasks. Similarly, Turk (1980) noted such a deficient problem-solving set in patients who adapted less adequately to chronic illness.

So far, we have described two major styles of thinking, namely, self-referent ideation that interferes with performance and self-efficacious, problem-solving-oriented thinking that enhances performance. A third style has been described in the literature, and the usefulness of this style depends on the situational demands, namely, the style of denial (Weisman, 1979). In some situations little or nothing can be done, and in such situations there may be value in the use of denial, intellectualization, maintaining detachment, and even deceiving oneself in order to feel better and maintain hope and a sense of self-worth. Lazarus (1979) has reviewed the evidence that denial interferes with coping situations where constructive action is possible (i.e., where a problem-focused mode of thinking would help). However, in situations that permit little or nothing to be done, the use of emotion-reducing modes of thinking such as denial seems beneficial. Denial may be especially appropriate in circumstances where there is a built-in likelihood of a favorable outcome. If the stress is likely to abate on its own, then the person has little to lose from not attending to it.

In short, what is being proposed is a provocative hypothesis that we can develop assessment procedures to trace the flow of ideation as people cope with stress and that this analysis will yield meaningful, consistent profiles across populations, situations, and assessment methods. The identification of such consistenices may be of particular value in developing prevention and intervention approaches to stress management. In the same way that the endocrinologist is looking for profiles of endocrine reactions, the cognitive ethologist is searching to explicate patterns of thought. Much work is required since one must go beyond the mere labeling of a form of thinking. Take denial, for example. What is being denied? One's internal feeling? External events? How does this denial change over time? Do subjects know that they are denying? Do they choose not to think about some area?

Moreover, the cognitive ethology analysis must go beyond the specific pattern of ideation or the internal dialogue to consider the person's meaning system, current concerns, and hidden agendas that give rise to specific internal dialogues (see Meichenbaum & Butler, 1979, and Turk, 1980, for discussions of the role of these meaning systems). For purposes of illustration, consider the observation that high-test-anxious persons who must deal with an evaluative stressful situation have similar patterns of self-referent thought (internal dialogue) in testing situations, but they may have them for entirely different reasons. The content of negative self-referent ideation has been found to be the same for high-anxiety people in evaluation situations (a kind of final common pathway of similar patterns of ideation is evident, if one uses the neurological analogy), but a variety of different concerns or meanings influence their behaviors and thoughts in such situations. These might center around: (1) concerns about loss of control, fears of being overwhelmed by arousal; (2) concerns about the esteem of authority figures and/or peers; (3) concerns that success might jeopardize social relations with members of the opposite sex; and (4) concerns with success. That such varied concerns may have a direct effect on physiological functioning is illustrated in a study by Mahl (1949), who examined students' reactions to an impending college examination. Mahl found that two of his eight subjects did not show the expected increase in secretion of hydrochloric acid. For different reasons, these two nonresponders deviated from the rest of the group, one because his expectations did not go beyond attaining a C, the other because he had already been accepted by a medical school.

It seems that psychological stress does *not* occur without the person facing a threat of failure or loss, yet the meaning of failure and loss in part depends on personal and social values and the acceptance of cultural definitions of what is valuable. It is being proposed that intimately involved in the nature of coping and in the course of a disease are both a person's internal dialogue and meaning system. It is now time to consider the implications for treatment of the several observations that have been offered on disease, stress, coping, and the role of cognitive processes.

An Overview of Stress-Inoculation Training

In recent years, a cognitive-behavioral training procedure, stress inoculation, has been developed for both the prevention and treatment of stress disorders. The stress-inoculation coping skills training procedure has been successfully applied to a number of different populations. These include clients with speech anxiety (Goldfried, in press; Meichenbaum, Gilmore, & Fedoravicius, 1971), test anxiety (Holroyd, 1976; Meichenbaum, 1972), persistent avoidant fears (Meichenbaum, 1977), anger management (Novaco, 1975), interpersonal anxiety (Glass, Gottman, & Shmurack, 1976), rape victims (Vernonen & Kilpatrick, 1979), alcoholism (Chaney, O'Leary, Marlatt, 1978; Sanchez-Craig, 1975), burn patients (Wernick, 1979), and laboratory and clinical pain (Holroyd, 1980; Levendusky & Pankratz, 1975; Rybstein-Blinchik & Gresiak, 1977; and Turk, 1976, 1977). The stress inoculation training regimen has recently been extended *on a preventive* basis to nonclinical populations including surgical patients (Langer, Janis & Wolfer, 1975), patients undergoing cardiac catheterization (Kendall et al., 1979), law enforcement officers (Novaco, 1979), and Type A managers (Roskies et al., in press). Stress-inoculation training manuals have been written for a variety of disorders including anger management (Novaco, 1978), pain (Turk, Meichenbaum, & Genest, in press), as well as other disorders (see Meichenbaum, 1979, for a list of published and unpublished manuals).

The present space only permits an overview of the stress-inoculation approach. A more detailed account of the procedures is offered by Meichenbaum and Jaremko (1980).

Operationally, stress-inoculation training involves three phases. The first phase, educational in nature, is designed to provide the person in lay terms with a means of understanding the nature of stressful reactions: in essence, a "theory" of stress and a framework for the training to be offered. From this conceptual framework, a number of behavioral and cognitive coping skills are offered for the person to rehearse during the second phase of training. This training is designed to enhance the person's repertoire of coping skills and to encourage flexibility. During the third phase, the person is given an opportunity to practice personally relevant and self-selected coping skills while he is exposed to a variety of stressors. Let us consider each of these phases in a bit more detail.

Phase I: Conceptualization and Translation The first phase of stress-inoculation training is designed to provide the participant with a framework for understanding the nature of his response in stress encounters. Clients are asked to describe a situation in which they experience stress and then to relive this situation by means of imagery. The imagery procedure permits them to replay the thoughts and feelings that preceded, accompanied, and followed the stress episode. This imagery procedure helps to convey the degree to which people contribute to their own reactions, revealing the transactional nature of both stress encounters and the coping process. People not only react to a problematic situation but also help to change that situation, for better or worse.

Stress inoculation involves exposing the person to preparatory information that describes what it will be like to experience possible negative consequences of a chosen course of action. Such preparatory information functions as a form of inoculation by enabling the person to develop effective reassurances and coping mechanisms. Stress tolerance is enhanced by providing the person with warnings in advance about what to expect together with sufficient reassurances. As part of the education phase, the trainer reflects that the person's stress may be viewed as consisting of various phases, such as preparing for a stressor, confronting or handling a stressor, possibly being overwhelmed by a stressor, and, finally, a period of subsequent reflection on whether the conflict or stress was resolved and, if so, how. In this way the stress situation is divided into manageable elements. The trainer also provides clients with some conceptualization of their reaction in terms of (1) how they can learn to control the level of physiological arousal by means of mental and physical relaxation; (2) how they can substitute positive coping strategies for negative self-referent ideation; and (3) how they can engage in graded task exposure to practice coping skills systematically.

Several important points have to be noted about this initial educational phase. First, it is *not* didactic. The trainer does not lecture. Rather, information is conveyed in a Socratic dialogue in which participants are encouraged to offer their own ideas of events that do or do not fit the evolving conceptualization. One objective of this educational phase is to help the participants to view their presenting problems and reactions in a more differentiated manner.

In short, the educational phase of stress-inoculation training attempts to help clients reconceptualize their problems, to change what they say to themselves about the presenting problem or initial stress reaction. Such a *translation* process evolves in the course of training and follows from the type of questions the trainer asks, the kinds of tests administered, the homework assigned, as well as the explicit rationale offered.

In fact, the scientific validity of the particular conceptualization offered is less important than its face validity. The content of the educational phase can be readily adapted to the particular population (e.g., anger control in parents or police officers, anxious clients, pain patients).

Phase II: Acquisition and Rehearsal The second phase of stress-inoculation training encourages participants to employ whatever adaptive coping techniques they already possess and to provide a variety of other direct-action and cognitive coping technqiues. Direct-action modes include such activities as changing the environment in some way, arranging for escape routes, learning physical and mental relaxation skills and communication skills. Another important direct-action mode of coping involves developing and using one's social networks and support systems.

The cognitive coping modes include training in the fundamentals of problem solving (e.g., problem definition, anticipation of consequences, evaluating feedback), altering appraisals, attributions, and self-labels, shifting attention, imagery rehearsal, and so forth. The teaching of such cognitive coping skills is made possible if one views such processes as sets of statements and images (or internal dialogue) that people say or imagine to themselves. One can then help modify the participants' internal dialogues by having them become aware of, self-monitor, and change the negative, anxiety-engendering, self-defeating self-statements and images they experience during stress encounters.

In collaboration with the trainer, participants can generate sets of coping self-statements or strategems that encourage them to assess the situation; anticipate and evaluate what might happen and what has to be done; postpone action and possibly relabel arousal; "psych" themselves up; tolerate frustration; and, in some situations, even deceive themselves to maintain hope and a sense of self-worth.

One purpose of the cognitive skills training is to have the participants develop a problem-solving, task-oriented set, thinking of each stressful situation as a problem to be solved, with accompanying response alternatives, rather than viewing the stressor as a provocation or threat. One important by-product of cognitive skills training is that generalization is built into the regimen. After training, a participant's recognition of his/her own maladaptive behaviors, feelings, or thoughts, or even the reactions of others, now becomes a cue to use the coping skills that were modeled, discussed, and rehearsed in training. Participants' recognition of their own behavior can then act as reminders to employ adaptive coping responses. Stress-inoculation training teaches participants to attend to early warning signs, and this heightened awareness leads to the use of adaptive coping behavior.

Phase III: Application and Practice The final phase of the stress-inoculation training is designed to provide participants with an opportunity to try out their skills and to employ them with both laboratory and real-life stressors. The application phase is designed to enhance a sense of self-efficacy. In order to achieve this, the participants are viewed as fellow scientists who are experimenting in finding the best set of coping techniques (in a sort of cafeteria selection) to use in different situations. The specific set of graded stressors used in training can be tailored to the participants' needs. Both ego-threatening and pain-threatening laboratory stressors (e.g., stress films, failure experiences, unpredictable electric shock) could be included. Such techniques as imagery and behavioral rehearsal, role playing, modeling films where the models illustrate the needed cognitive and behavioral coping skills, real-life behavioral assignments that become increasingly demanding, and other tools from the armamentarium of cognitive-behavioral modification research could be employed in the application training. In conducting such application training, it is important to bridge the gap between what is required in the real-life stress transactions and in the simulated training situations. The application and practice phase of stress-inoculation training emphasizes that participants must not only possess the skills necessary to handle a given circumstance, they must also possess a belief in their capacities to accomplish this task, or what Bandura (1977) calls "efficacy expectancies."

Concluding Remarks

The stress-inoculation training includes the following components:

1. Teaching the person the role that cognitions and emotions play in engendering and potentiating stress.

2. Training in the self-monitoring of maladaptive thoughts, images and feelings, and behaviors.

3. Training in the fundamentals of problem solving (e.g., problem definition, anticipation of consequences, evaluating feedback).

4. Modeling and rehearsal of effective cognitive strategems, attention-focusing skills, and positive self-evaluation.

5. Training in specific, direct-action coping skills such as relaxation, communication skills, and the development and use of social networks.

6. Real-life behavioral assignments that become increasingly demanding.

The studies of the relative efficacy of stress-inoculation training are encouraging (see Meichenbaum & Jaremko, 1980), but much more empirical information is required to demonstrate the full value of such an approach. In short, the cognitive-behavioral stress-inoculation approach is designed to affect how physical and mental symptoms are appraised and the nature of the coping processes that are employed. For how one appraises symptoms and copes affects the course of disease.

References

Antonovsky, A. *Health, stress and coping.* San Francisco: Jossey-Bass, 1979.

Bandura, A. Self-efficacy: Towards a unifying theory of behavioral change. *Psychological Review,* 1977, *84,* 191–215.

Bandura, A. Self-efficacy: An integrative construct. Unpublished manuscript, Stanford University, 1979.

Cassel, J. The contribution of the social environment to host resistance. *American Journal of Epilimology,* 1976, *104,* 107–123.

Chaney, E., O'Leary, M., & Marlatt, G. Skill training with alcoholics. *Journal of Consulting and Clinical Psychology,* 1978, *46,* 1092–1104.

Cohen, F. Personality, stress and development of physical illness. In G. Stone, F. Cohen, & N. Adler (Eds.), *Health psychology: A handbook.* San Francisco: Jossey-Bass, 1979.

Dodge, D., & Martin, W. *Social stress and chronic illness: Mortality patterns in industrial society.* Notre Dame, Ind.: University of Notre Dame Press, 1970.

Epstein, S. Toward a unified theory of anxiety. In B. Maher (Ed.), *Progress in experimental personality research* (Vol. 4). New York: Academic Press, 1967.

Genest, M., Turk, D., & Meichenbaum, D. A cognitive behavioral approach to the management of pain. Paper presented at the meeting of the Association for the Advancement of Behavior Therapy, Atlanta, Georgia, 1977.

Glass, C., Gottman, J. & Shmurack, S. Response acquisition and cognitive self-statements modification approaches to dating skill training. *Journal of Counseling Psychology,* 1976, *23,* 520–526.

Goldfried, M. Anxiety reduction through cognitive-behavioral intervention. In P. Kendall and S. Hollon (Eds.), *Cognitive-behavioral interventions: Theory, research, and procedures.* New York: Academic Press, in press.

Haggerty, K. Changing lifestyles to improve health. *Preventive Medicine,* 1977, *6,* 276–289.

Henshaw, D. A cognitive analysis of creative problem-solving. Unpublished doctoral dissertation, University of Waterloo, 1978.

Hollandsworth, J., Galeski, L., Kirkland, K., Jones, G., & Van Norman, L. An analysis of the nature and effects of test anxiety: Cognitive, behavioral and physiological components. *Cognitive Therapy and Research,* 1979, *3,* 165–180.

Holmes, T., & Rahe, R. The social readjustment rating scale. *Journal of Psychosometric Research,* 1967, *11,* 213–218.

Holroyd, D. Cognition and desensitization in the group treatment of test anxiety. *Journal of Consulting and Clinical Psychology,* 1976, *44,* 991–1001.

Holroyd, K. Stress, coping, and the treatment of stress. In J. McNamara (Ed.), *Behavioral approaches to medicine: Application and analysis.* New York: Plenum, 1980.

Jonas, S. *Medical mystery: The training of doctors in the United States.* New York: Norton, 1978.

Kendall, P., Williams, L., Pechacek, T., Graham, C., Shisslak, C., & Herzoff, N. Cognitive-behavioral and patient education in catheterization procedures. *Journal of Consulting and Clinical Psychology,* 1979, *47,* 49–58.

Langer, E., Janis, I. & Wolfer, J. Reduction of psychological stress in surgical patients. *Journal of Experimental Social Psychology*, 1975, *11*, 155–165.

Lazarus, R. The power of positive thinking; or, was Norman Vincent Peale right? Paper presented at the conference on "The effectiveness and cost of denial," held in Haifa, Israel, 1979.

Lazarus, R., & Cohen, J. Environmental stress. In I. Altman & J. Wohlwill (Eds.), *Human behavior and environment* (Vol. 2). New York: Plenum, 1977.

Lazarus, R., & Launier, R. Stress-related transactions between person and environment. In L. Pervin and M. Lewis (Eds.), *Perspectives in interactional psychology*. New York: Plenum, 1978.

Levendusky, P., & Pankrantz, L. Self-control techniques as an alternative to pain medication. *Journal of Abnormal Psychology*, 1975, *84*, 165–169.

Lewandowski, A. An investigation of the cognitive and attitudinal correlates of the coronary prone behavior pattern. Unpublished doctoral dissertation, University of Waterloo, Waterloo, Ontario, 1979.

Lipowski, Z. Psychosomatic medicine in the seventies: An overview. *American Journal of Psychiatry*, 1977, *184*, 233–244.

Mahl, G. Anxiety, HCL secretion and peptic ulcer etiology. *Psychosomatic Medicine*, 1949, *11*, 30–44.

Mahoney, M., & Avener, M. Psychology of the elite athlete: An exploratory study. *Cognitive Therapy and Research*, 1977, *1*, 135–142.

Mason, J. Specificity in the organization of neuroendocrine response profiles. In P. Seeman and J. Brown (Eds.), *Frontiers in neurology and neuroscience research*. Toronto, Ontario: University of Toronto Press, 1974. First International Symposium of the Neuroscience Institute.

Mason, J. A historical view of the stress field: Part I. *Journal of Human Stress*, 1975, *1*, 6–12.

Mechanic, D. Effects of psychological distress on perceptions of physical health and use of medical and psychiatric facilities. *Journal of Human Stress*, 1978, *4*, 26–32.

Meichenbaum, D. Cognitive modification of test anxious college students. *Journal of Consulting and Clinical Psychology*, 1972, *39*, 370–380.

Meichenbaum, C. *Cognitive-behavior modification: An integrative approach*. New York: Plenum, 1977.

Meichenbaum, D. *Cognitive-behavior modification newsletter*. Unpublished manuscript, University of Waterloo, 1979.

Meichenbaum, D., & Butler, L. Toward a conceptual model for the treatment of test anxiety: Implications for research and treatment. In I. Sarason (Ed.), *Test Anxiety: Theory research and applications*. Hillsdale, N.J.: Lawrence Erlbaum Publishers, 1979.

Meichenbaum, D., & Butler, L. Cognitive ethology. Assessing the streams of cognition and emotion. In K. Blankstein, P. Pliner, & J. Polivy (Eds.), *Advances in the study of communication and affect: Assessment and modification of emotional behavior* (Vol. 6). New York: Plenum, 1979.

Meichenbaum, D., Henshaw, D., & Himel, N. Coping with stress as a problem-solving process. In W. Krohne and L. Laux (Eds.), *Achievement, stress and anxiety*, Washington, D.C.: Hemisphere, 1979.

Meichenbaum, D., Gilmore, J. & Fedoravicius, A. Group insight vs. group desensitization in treating speech anxiety. *Journal of Consulting Clinical Psychology*, 1971, *36*, 410–421.

Meichenbaum, D., & Jaremko, M. *Stress prevention and management: A cognitive-behavioral approach*. New York: Plenum, 1980.

Novaco, R. *Anger control: The development and evaluation of an experimental treatment*. Lexington, Mass.: D.C. Heath, 1975.

Novaco, R. A stress-inoculation approach to anger management in the training of law enforcement officers. *American Journal of Community Psychology*, 1977, *5*, 327–346.

Novaco, R. Anger and coping with stress: Cognitive behavioral interventions. In J. Foreyt and D. Rathjen (Eds.), *Cognitive behavior therapy: Research and applications*. New York: Plenum, 1978.

O'Hara, T. A comparison of the biofeedback and cognitive stress reduction methods in competitive motor performance using personality variables as moderators. Unpublished doctoral dissertation, University of Ottawa, 1977.

Orne, M. Psychological factors maximizing resistance to stress with special reference to hypnosis. In S. Klausner (Ed.), *The quest for self-control.* New York: Free Press, 1965.

Pearlin, L., & Schooler, C. The structure of coping. *Journal of Health and Social Behavior,* 1978, *18,* 2–21.

Rabkin, J. & Struening, E. Life events, stress and illness. *Science,* 1976, *194,* 1013–1020.

Roskies, E. Considerations in developing a treatment program for the coronary-prone (Type A) behavior pattern. In P. Davidson (Ed.), *Behavioral medicine: Changing health life styles.* New York: Brunner/Mazel, 1979.

Roskies, E., & Lazarus, R. Coping theory and the teaching of coping skills. In P. Davidson (Ed.), *Behavioral medicine: Changing health life styles.* New York: Brunner/Mazel, in press.

Roskies, E., Spevack, M. Surkis, A., Cohen, C., & Gilman, S. Changing the coronary-prone (Type A) behavior pattern in a non-clinical population. *Journal of Behavioral Medicine,* in press.

Rybstein-Blinchik, E., & Gresiak, R. Treatment of chronic pain. Paper presented at the meeting of the Association for the Advancement of Behavior Therapy, Chicago, December, 1977.

Sanchez-Craig, M. A self-control strategy for drinking tendencies. *Ontario Psychologist,* 1975, *7,* 25–29.

Schwartz, R., & Gottman, J. Toward a task analysis of assertive behavior. *Journal of Consulting and Clinical Psychology,* 1976, *44,* 910–920.

Selye, H. *The stress of life* (2nd ed.). New York: McGraw-Hill, 1978.

Smye, M. Verbal, cognitive and behavioral correlates of social anxiety. Unpublished doctoral dissertation, University of Toronto, 1977.

Syme, S. Implications and future prospects. In S. Syme and L. Reeder (Eds.), *Social stress and cardiovascular disease. Milbank Memorial Fund Quarterly,* 1967, *45,* 175–180.

Syme, S. Social and psychological risk factors in coronary heart disease. *Modern Concepts of Cardiovascular Diseases,* 1975, *14,* 17–21.

Thomas, L. Nature of disease. *The New Yorker,* January, 1978.

Turk, D. Cognitive control of pain: A skills training approach for the treatment of pain. Unpublished master's thesis, University of Waterloo, 1976.

Turk, D. An expanded skills training approach for the treatment of experimentally induced pain. Unpublished doctoral dissertation, University of Waterloo, 1977.

Turk, D. Cognitive learning approaches: Applications in health care. In D. Doleys, R. Meredith, and A. Ciminero (Eds.), *Behavioral psychology in medicine: Assessment and treatment strategies.* New York: Wiley, 1979.

Turk, D. Factors influencing the adaptive process with chronic illness: Implications for intervention. In I. Sarason and C. Spielberger (Eds.), *Stress and anxiety* (Vol. 7). Washington, D.C.: Halstead Press, 1980.

Turk, D., Meichenbaum, D., & Genest, M. *Pain: A cognitive-behavioral treatment approach.* New York: Guilford Press, in press.

Tverskey, A., & Kahnemann, D. Availability: A heuristic for judging frequency and probability. *Cognitive Psychology,* 1973, *5,* 207–232.

Vernonen, L., & Kilpatrick, D. Stress-inoculation training as a treatment for victims of rape. Paper presented at the Southeastern Psychological Association, New Orleans, March, 1979.

Weiner, H. *Psychobiology and human disease.* New York: American Elsevier, 1977.

Weisman, A. *Coping with cancer.* New York: McGraw-Hill, 1979.

Weisman, A., & Sobel, H. Coping with cancer through self-instruction: A hypothesis. *Journal of Human Stress,* 1979, *5,* 3–8.

Wernick, R. Stress-inoculation training for burn patients. Paper presented at the Southeastern Psychological Association, New Orleans, March, 1979.

Zubin, J., & Spring, B. Vulnerability—a new view of schizophrenia. *Journal of Abnormal Psychology,* 1977, *86,* 103–126.

Chapter 12

Psychophysiological Factors in the Treatment of the Stress of Pain: Biofeedback

BARTON A. JESSUP

Regina Mental Health Clinic
Regina, Saskatchewan

Pain is estimated to incapacitate 40 million people for at least 1 to 3 days annually in the United States. The financial cost alone of this suffering is about $50 billion, consisting 90% of lost productivity and 10% of direct health care costs (J. Bonica, in Boeckh, 1979). Pain is thus one of the most pervasive and costly of all stress phenomena. Over the past decade biofeedback (FB) has joined other numerous procedures designed to alleviate pain.

This chapter examines applied and basic research on FB control of pain. Theoretical issues are also outlined. Let the reader be warned at the outset: this is a topic more worthwhile in its linking of behavioral and physiological domains than in its proof of treatment efficacy. Even an author optimistic enough to have called FB a "major new therapeutic approach" included the disclaimer, "There have been some disappointments, reconsiderations, and retreats from early enthusiasm" (Fuller, 1978, p. 47). Other researchers have been more cautious. Miller (1978, p. 396) noted, "Therapeutic applications of FB already have too high a ratio of uncontrolled pilot studies." Merskey (1978, p. 40) also called for more controlled research on various FB treatments for pain and emphasized, "They must all be shown to be better than powerful suggestion." Finally, some psychophysiologists (Venables & Christie, 1975) have not been persuaded at all by the claims of biofeedback:

A lot of material is available on this controversial area which lies between solid work which unfortunately seems to have been not wholly repeatable, and a fashionable quackery with less than desirable ethical connotations (p. vi).

What Is Biofeedback?

In biofeedback with humans, one (or occasionally more) of an individual's physiological processes are measured and "fed back" to him as a tone, meter, or light display. Biofeedback is fairly easily described in operational terms. Typically, the subject reclines in a comfortable chair. Appropriate electrodes or other transducers are attached. Electronic equipment connected to the transducers alters the raw physiological signals from the body to operate devices that present a representation of the physiological activity. The subject observes a moving meter, changing light display, or varying sound that very accurately indicates on a moment-to-moment basis the physiological process of interest. Thus, a usually unnoticed physiological response is presented to the person as a sensory stimulus.

The operational definition of FB varies somewhat from study to study. Usually, subjects are told that changes in one direction are desired, such as decreasing an electromyogram (EMG) level in the case of muscle contraction headache (e.g., Budzynski, Stoyva, & Adler, 1970). However, the need to indicate the desired direction of change, or even the physiological parameter under measurement has been questioned (e.g. Blanchard et al., 1974; Shapiro, Schwartz, & Tursky, 1972). Another procedural difference is the use of continuous analogue feedback versus discrete binary feedback (Lang & Twentyman, 1974). Some researchers have added reinforcers such as money or viewing attractive slides to the correct knowledge of results (Shapiro, Tursky, & Schwartz, 1970). Operationally, FB consists of a family of similar procedures, having as their common element the individual's observation of a sensory representation of his/her on-going physiological processes.

In practice, a bald operational definition may be sufficient, but historically the theoretical description of FB has been contentious. Early observations of "voluntary" control of autonomic functions such as heart rate were largely overlooked (e.g., Tarchanoff, 1885) until they were reprinted in the Aldine publishing company's annual review *Biofeedback and Self-Control,* 1972 (Shapiro et al., 1973). Other early work included the use of EMG feedback to treat maladaptive chronic muscle tension (Whatmore & Kohli, 1968) and to aid in neuromuscular rehabilitation (Marinacci & Horande, 1960). These early EMG researchers thought of FB essentially as "training" or trial-and-error learning.

The key theoretical issue in biofeedback arose with attempts to condition operantly changes in physiological processes controlled by the autonomic nervous system

(ANS). Previously, the ANS was thought to learn only by classical Pavlovian conditioning, whereas the voluntary musculature, through central nervous system mediation, could also learn by operant conditioning (Skinner, 1938). The explosion of research on FB (currently totalling about 1000 publications) began with attempts to demonstrate operant conditioning of the ANS (Katkin & Murray, 1968; Kimmel, 1967; Miller, 1969; Miller & DiCara 1967). Initial findings were very encouraging, but by 1972 Miller reported a decrease in the amount of effect observed in FB studies over a 5-year period (Miller, 1972).

A key theoretical issue, then, is whether or not FB is operant conditioning, particularly of the ANS. Alternative conceptualizations include operant conditioning of voluntarily (CNS) controlled processes that affect ANS functions, such as respiration (Black, 1966). Biofeedback has also been conceptualized as identification of cognitions that affect ANS phenomena (Lazarus, 1975) and as a placebo effect (Jessup, under review). Agreement on a universally acceptable theoretical definition of FB has not yet been reached. Clarification of this issue continues (Keefe & Gardner, 1979).

The Pain Response

Debate concerning the specific benefit of FB treatment of pain is also related to the complex nature of the pain experience (Beecher, 1959; Liebeskind & Paul, 1977; Melzack, 1973; Merskey & Spear, 1967; Sternbach, 1974). Pain is more than a simple sensation: a gamut of cultural (Zborowski, 1969), environmental (Fordyce, Fowler, & DeLateur, 1968), and psychological (Sternbach, 1968) factors influence the "reaction" of pain (Beecher, 1957). These factors interact with physiological processes to produce pain as it is experienced. Accordingly, pain treatment can be effective by acting on one or more of several factors. Identification and measurement of the factors influenced by FB treatments is central to much of the best FB work with pain.

Physiological Correlates of Pain Used in Biofeedback

Muscle Contraction Headache When pain is treated by FB, physiological correlates are added to an already complex phenomenon. The use of FB to treat pain is based on certain models of the pathophysiology of pain. These models are themselves currently under research and are still far from irrefutably supported. Rather, depending upon the skepticism of the investigator, their acceptance varies from medical diagnosis to "assumptions" (Turk, Meichenbaum, & Berman, 1979) or "contentious research issue" (Jessup, Neufeld, & Merskey, 1980).

The models of the physiological processes underlying muscle contraction (MC) headache and migraine pain are the most cogent to FB research because over 75% of FB pain studies investigate headache. The current model of MC headache is that the pain is due to the sustained contraction of muscles around the head and neck.

The muscles most frequently implicated are the frontallis under the forehead and the occipitalis at the lower back of the scalp. The process by which chronic muscle contraction develops at the head is as yet unresolved (Bakal, 1975). Standard references on the topic suggest that the sustained contraction is a response to psychological stress (Friedman et al., 1962; Dalessio, 1972).

The research linking muscle contraction headache to muscle contraction is generally supportive of the model, although the main early source of support for the muscle-contraction model of MC headache is Sainsbury and Gibson (1954) who found that resting frontalis EMG levels were higher in MC headache sufferers than in nonsufferers. This finding has more recently been replicated by Hutchings and Reinking (1976). Also tangentially supporting the muscle-contraction model was Rodbard's (1970) finding that ischemia plus sustained muscle contraction in the fingers caused pain. However, sustained contraction alone was not painful.

More recent work appears to be in keeping with the model, but certain features of the studies suggest that their support is somewhat restricted. During FB sessions in a study by Haynes, Griffin, Mooney, and Parise (1975), 10 subjects had headaches while in the lab. Although the mean frontalis EMG for this group was 28% higher during headaches, some subjects did not show higher EMG with reported head pain. Conceivably this finding may indicate that not all MC headaches primarily involve the frontalis. McKenzie, Ehrisman, Montgomery, and Barnes (1974) found that frontalis and neck EMG did not reliably covary in MC headache sufferers.

Two studies did pre-experimental EMG assessments of their participants to discover the tensest head muscle for use as the FB parameter. Peck and Kraft (1977) found that the tensest muscle EMG declined 51% during FB training, while headache "density" (rated intensity × duration) decreased 54%. Tensest muscle EMG and density correlated .57. Philips (1977) reported a mean correlation of .7 between each session's baseline EMG from the tensest muscle and reported headache intensity. Reeves (1976) also reported a similar correlation, but its meaningfulness is weakened by his observation of a 33% decrease in headache density during preliminary cognitive skills training that was not accompanied by any change in EMG levels.

Clear support for the muscle contraction basis of MC headache is sometimes impossible to separate from treatment effects. For example, Budzynski, Stoyra, Adler, and Mullaney (1973) reported a .9 correlation between frontalis EMG and headache intensity during a FB training program, compared to a nonsignificant −.05 correlation in a pseudo-FB group. Philips (1977) calculated 11 correlations between headache intensity and tensest muscle EMG, based on the individual data of 11 subjects taken over the treatment period. These correlations confound any effect of treatment with spontaneous fluctuation in headache pain and EMG level. That is, both the treatment and EMG level may contribute to the reported pain, but their relative effects cannot be separated. Consequently, EMG-pain intensity correlations *during treatment* can not be used to clarify the pathophysiology of MC headaches.

Even with the various constraints on unambiguous interpretation of data relating to MC headache to increased EMG levels at the head, the muscle-contraction model does at least seem plausible. The use of muscle tension at the head as a feedback parameter for the FB treatment of MC headache appears to be defensibly grounded in current knowledge.

Migraine The second most frequent form of FB pain treatment is the use of skin temperature feedback for migraine, initiated by Sargent, Walters, and Green (1973). The etiology of migraine pain is somewhat complex. Psychological, biochemical, and efferent and afferent nerve tracts appear to be involved. The currently dominant model of migraine holds that migraine pain is due to dilation and hyperpermeability of extracranial and intracranial arteries. The hyperpermeability of the arteries allows an edema containing pain-threshold-reducing neurotransmitters to form around the artery, and it is thus related mainly to biochemical features of the migraine process. The role of cranial vasodilation is probably more cogent to FB procedures. The painful phase of migraine is associated with arterial dilation. In about one quarter, and perhaps all, migraine sufferers, a brief phase of vasoconstriction precedes the dilation (Bakal & Kagonov, 1977; Dalessio, 1972). The mechanism that initiates the dilation cycle is not yet clear. Neural and humoral factors have been suggested (Sicuteri, 1972).

Sargent et al. (1973) conceptualized migraine as a stress syndrome, characterized by excessive sympathetic nervous system arousal. Because the vascular beds of the fingers are almost entirely under the vasoconstrictive control of the sympathetic nervous system, finger temperature was seen as a one-variable index of sympathetic arousal. As sympathetic arousal increased, finger blood-flow, and hence temperature, decreased. When sympathetic arousal decreased, finger temperature increased due to passive dilation of blood vessels released from active constriction caused by sympathetic stimulation. Therefore, Sargent et al. (1973) suggested that training migraine sufferers to warm their hands should help them to reduce excessive sympathetic arousal, and hence their migraines.

The sympathetic-arousal model of migraine faces certain complications that render it less than entirely satisfactory. First of all, sympathetic vasoconstrictive fibers also innervate the cranial arteries (Pick, 1970). Therefore, reduction of sympathetic arousal could also cause cerebral vasodilation, the very phenomenon that the treatment is attempting to alleviate. This criticism is nullified though, if one argues that the painful dilatory phase of migraine is a reaction to initial vasoconstrictive ischemia. Such a position is certainly defensible, because reflexive vasodilation to ischemia is one control mechanism of cerebral blood flow (Dalessio, 1974). Handwarming feedback would then make sense as a procedure designed to prevent the initial sympathetic-mediated vasoconstrictive phase of migraine, thereby precluding the painful, reflexive dilatory phase. Following this line of reasoning, handwarming FB should be associated with head warming: increased skin temperature at both sites would indicate decreased sympathetic activity. However, concomitant head and hand warming has not been a FB treatment for migraine. Rather, the initial procedure trained handwarming and forehead *cooling* (Sargent et al., 1973).

Other FB programs, typically temporal artery pulse amplitude (Bild, 1976; Feuerstein & Adams, 1977; Feuerstein, Adams, & Beiman, 1976; Friar & Beatty, 1976; Zamani, 1974), have attempted to train vasoconstriction of the external cranial blood flow directly. The procedures used in these studies are physiologically antagonistic to the handwarming procedure. Furthermore, one study demonstrated improvement in migraine with finger vasoconstriction. Friar and Beatty (1976) compared head and finger vasoconstrictive training. They conceptualized the finger constriction as a type of control group. Finger vasoconstrictive training reduced finger pulse amplitude to .67 of baseline, but temporal artery training also reduced finger volume substantially, to .69 of baseline. Major migraine attacks were only decreased with the temporal artery training. The Friar and Beatty (1976) findings show migraine reduction with finger vasoconstriction, although the finger vasoconstriction was incidental to temporal artery vasoconstriction. These results appear clearly to contradict the handwarming, sympathetic-reduction rationale for most FB treatment of migraine.

The physiological basis underlying FB treatments for migraine clearly requires clarification.

While the physiological correlates of various forms of pain are usually considered separately, the distinction is chiefly academic rather than empirical. The separation of migraine from muscle-contraction headache best exemplifies the actual intermingling of pain processes. Bakal and Kaganov (1977) have reported higher EMG levels with migraine than with MC headache. Factor analysis of headache symptoms reported by migraine sufferers does not yield factors congruent with diagnostic opinion (Ziegler, Hassanein, & Hassanein, 1972). The three symptoms most frequently related to the diagnosis of migraine (unilateral onset of pain, warning signs, nausea) may occur together at a rate only 1% greater than chance (Waters, 1973). Pain processes almost certainly involve a mixture of physiological changes, making selection of an appropriate FB parameter more difficult.

In summary, pain phenomena, as treated by FB, include numerous psychological, social, and behavioral features, as well as a complex physiological substrate. The use of EMG feedback for muscle-contraction pain seems moderately supported by existing literature. The relationship of migraine to sympathetic nervous system activity is far from certain. FB training programs that apparently contradict each other have been used to treat migraine. The relationship of alpha EEG to pain also requires further documentation (Melzack & Perry, 1975).

Biofeedback Treatments of Pain: Current Status

The following summary of current findings on FB treatments for pain is based on the 64 studies classified in Table 12-1 according to their target symptom (see also Jessup, Neufeld, & Merskey, in press). If one word can summarize the findings of the entire body of research it is "nonspecific." A large proportion of the studies are poorly controlled. Nonetheless, their findings are similar to the better controlled work. The best controlled studies almost entirely do not support the specific benefit

Table 12-1   **Research on Biofeedback Treatment of Pain**

MUSCLE CONTRACTION HEADACHE	MIGRAINE	MISCELLANEOUS PAIN SYNDROMES
Budzynski, Stoyva, & Adler, 1970	Adler & Adler, 1976	Carlsson, & Gale, 1976
Budzynski, Stoyva, Adler, &		
Mullaney, 1973	Andreychuk & Skriver, 1975	Carlsson, Gale, & Ohman, 1975
Chesney & Shelton, 1976	Beasley, 1976	Cleeland, 1973
Cox, Freundlich, & Meyer, 1975	Bild, 1976	Coger & Werbach, 1975
Ehrisman, 1973	Blanchard, Theobald, Williamson,	
	Silver & Brown, 1978	
	Diamond & Franklin, 1974	Grabel, 1973
Epstein, Hersen, & Hemphill, 1974	Diamond & Franklin, 1975	Gannon & Sternbach, 1971
Haynes, Griffen, Mooney, &		
Parise, 1975	Drury, DeRisi & Liberman, 1975	Jacobs & Felton, 1969
Hutchings & Reinking, 1976	Feuerstein & Adams, 1977	Lipp, 1976
	Feuerstein, Adams, & Beiman,	
Kondo & Canter, 1977	1976	Melzack & Perry, 1975
McKenzie, Ehrisman, Montgomery,		
& Barnes, 1974	Friar & Beatty, 1976	Mulhall & Todd, 1975
Montgomery & Ehrisman, 1976	Graham, 1974	Russ, 1977
		Stenn, Mothersill, & Brooke, in
Peck & Kraft, 1977	Jessup, under review	press
	Kentsmith, Strider, Copenhaver,	
Philips 1977	& Jacques, 1976	Surwit, 1973
Raskin, Johnson, & Rondesvedt,		Uchiyama, Luttarjohann, &
1973	Kewman, 1978	Shah, 1977
	Medina, Diamond, & Franklin,	
Reeves, 1976	1976	Welgan, 1974
	Mitch, McGrady, & Iannone,	Wickramasekera, Truang, Bush,
Reinking, 1976	1976	& Orr, 1976
	Mullinex, Norton, Hack, &	
Russ, Adderton, & Hammer, 1977	Fishman, 1978	
	Pearse, Walters, Sargent, &	
Weiss, 1974	Meers, 1975	
Wickramasekera, 1976	Peper & Grossman, 1974	
	Sargent, Walters, & Green, 1973	
	Solbach & Sargent, 1977	
	Thompson, 1977	
	Turin, 1977	
	Weinstock, 1972	
	Wickramasekera, 1973	
	Zamani, 1974	

of FB. Certainly hundreds of people have experienced reduced pain during and after FB treatment. However, in most cases FB was not likely necessary for the improvement. Consequently, the benefits can legitimately be termed nonspecific, that is, not specifically due to the unique features of the treatment.

The use of EMG FB to treat muscle-contraction headache offers the most encouraging results of any FB procedure for pain. Even these seemingly positive findings, though, are not as optimistic as they first appear when compared to simpler relaxation training. Of the 20 studies examined, only 5 utilized control groups (Budzynski et al., 1973; Chesney & Shelton, 1976; Haynes et al., 1975; Kondo & Canter, 1977;

Philips, 1977). Two of the controlled studies were positive, one had mixed results and two showed benefit in comparison groups that called into question the treatment-specific nature of the other studies' positive findings. One positive study was by Budzynski et al. (1973). They compared EMG FB and concomitant home relaxation practice to pseudofeedback with home relaxation and a no-treatment control group. Reported headache intensity decreased from a mean of .5 to .2 during 8 weeks of true FB compared to a decline from .7 to .6 with pseudo-FB, and no change from .6 in the no-treatment condition. Frontalis EMG levels also declined during the study, from 10μv microvolts to 3.3 with true FB, and from 10 μv to 6.9 with pseudo-FB. These encouraging findings were among the earliest on the control of MC headache by EMG FB. Note, however, that FB is confounded with home-relaxation practice. Interactions of the differential FB instructions and home practice could have contributed to the seemingly positive results of FB.

A second study reporting positive findings compared true to false frontalis EMG FB. True FB decreased EMG more both across and within sessions than false FB. True FB decreased headache frequency from 5.3 per 5 days to 1 per 5 days, while false FB decreased frequency from 5.0 per 5 days to 3.5 per 5 days. This study is probably the strongest existing support for the effectiveness of EMG FB in the reduction of MC headache. It was rigorous in both design and data analysis. Note, however, the 30% placebo effect in the pseudo-FB group.

Philips (1977) offered somewhat equivocal support for the benefit of EMG FB in the treatment of MC headache. He compared FB from the muscle deemed to be the most tense at rest to a taped pseudo-FB sound. Only true FB decreased mean EMG across sessions, from 5.6 μv to 2.9. Rated headache intensity and medication use decreased significantly more in the true FB group only at an 8 week follow-up. Headache frequency decreased 30% in both treatment groups.

The two other controlled studies on EMG FB for headache suggested that FB is no more effective than simpler, less expensive relaxation training. As well, FB did not appear to be a necessary component of mixed FB-relaxation training programs. Chesney and Shelton (1976) compared four treatment groups: EMG FB, relaxation instructions, FB and relaxation combined, and no treatment. The instructions and the combined treatments reduced headache frequency significantly more than no treatment, from 5.5 headaches per week to 1.3. The relaxation instructions and the combined treatments were both significantly superior to FB alone for reducing headache duration. Only the combined condition reduced headache intensity. In the Chesney and Shelton (1976) study, FB alone was not effective in alleviating MC headache, nor was it essential to the combined FB-relaxation treatment.

A fifth controlled study of EMG FB for headache also fails to support the specific benefit of FB. Haynes et al. (1975) compared EMG FB to relaxation instructions and to uninstructed self-relaxation. FB and instructions were equally superior to unaided self-relaxation in reducing headache frequency and weekly headache activity. In two controlled studies, then, relaxation training seems as effective as FB for reducing headache.

The findings of the controlled studies are in keeping with the results of the uncontrolled studies (see Jessup, Neufeld, & Merskey, in press, for a detailed analysis of each study). While FB does offer benefits greater than no treatment or pseudo treatment, these benefits are not greater than relaxation instructions. Two positions seem arguable from this finding: (1) FB is a unique treatment that has specific effects which happen to be equal to those of another treatment, relaxation training; and (2) FB is inadvertently a type of relaxation training and does not have specific effects beyond those of relaxation.

Although resolving these two positions would require more intensive measurement of relaxation parameters, the second position seems more defensible on the basis of the controlled studies. The study of Budzynski et al. (1973) confounded FB with home-relaxation practice and so cannot clarify the specific benefit of FB. The studies comparing true versus false FB (Kondo & Canter, 1977; Philips, 1977), although elegantly designed to test the specific benefit of true FB, do not address the issue of treatment process. The pseudo-FB design would not distinguish whether FB works as a form of more global relaxation training or as a unique process for operantly conditioning frontalis muscle tension. This leaves the findings that relaxation training alone is as effective as FB or FB combined with relaxation training. As a treatment component analysis, these studies at least show that FB is not a necessary part of the combined FB-relaxation treatment. Measurement of the generalization of FB and relaxation instructions to several physiological, behavioral, and self-report (cognitive) measures would help to clarify the process by which EMG FB and relaxation training equivalently reduce MC headache. Finally, on purely practical grounds, relaxation training is a much less expensive and more accessible treatment than FB.

The findings on FB treatments for migraine are even less supportive than those for MC headache. Seven of the 28 studies on migraine used controlled group designs. Three of these examined handwarming FB (Beasley, 1976; Kewman & Roberts, 1978; Mullinix et al., 1978). Four assessed the frequently used combination of handwarming FB and simultaneous autogenic relaxation training, often referred to as autogenic feedback training (AFT) (Beasley, 1976; Blanchard et al., 1978; Jessup, under review; Thompson, 1977). Autogenic relaxation training utilizes six standard suggestions of relaxed physiological states to induce relaxation, "My arm is heavy" (Schultz & Luthe, 1969), for example. Two of the standard phrases, "My arm is warm" and "My forehead is cool," are particularly congruent with handwarming FB training. One controlled study evaluated direct feedback of components of cephalic blood-flow, a measure sometimes referred to as the cephalic vasomotor response (CVMR), to include both pulse amplitude and tissue blood-volume components of photoplythesmographically measured vascular activity at the forehead (Bild, 1976).

Hand-temperature FB alone did not seem to reduce migraine. Beasley (1976) compared four groups: (1) FB alone, (2) relaxation exercises plus autogenic suggestions, (3) treatments 1 and 2, combined AFT, and (4) no treatment. FB alone failed to reduce migraine intensity and frequency, but the combined AFT program was more effective than no treatment. Kewman and Roberts (1978) showed that handwarming, handcooling and no treatment all reduced migraine equally. Similarly, in the study by Mullinix et al. (1978), four of six subjects improved their migraines with handwarming training, and so did three of five subjects using handcooling training. Both Kewman and Roberts and Mullinix et al. discussed their results in terms of nonspecific placebo effects.

AFT—the concurrent use of handwarming training and autogenic suggestion—also does not appear to be a specifically effective treatment for migraine. Blanchard, Theobald, Williamson, Silver, and Brown (1978) compared AFT to progressive relaxation and a no-treatment control group. The no-treatment group was subsequently treated with one of the two experimental procedures. By the end of the training portion of the study, progressive relaxation training was more effective than AFT on five of six measures. Over a three month follow-up, the groups did not differ on any measure.

Jessup (under review) compared 5 experimental conditions: (1) handwarming autogenic phrases; (2) handwarming AFT; (3) handcooling phrases; (4) handcooling AFT; and (5) a weekly lab visit, attention-placebo control condition. All of the groups improved significantly. A 6-month follow-up found that improvement was maintained, even though the original effects were nonspecific. Thompson (1977) compared four treatment groups, consisting of those receiving or not receiving AFT, who were given positive or neutral therapeutic expectancy. All four groups improved, with no apparent specific effect of AFT.

Handwarming FB, without or with autogenic training (AFT) does not appear to be a specific effective treatment for migraine. Nonspecific features of the treatment are as strong as any treatment-specific effects. As with EMG FB for MC headache, simple relaxation training is as beneficial as more complex, temperature-FB procedures.

If any FB treatment proves to benefit migraine, it may be direct vasoconstrictive training of blood flow at the temple—CVMR FB. However, key studies remain to be done in this area, and biofeedback has already seen far too much unwarranted early enthusiasm. In the one controlled study of CVMR FB, Bild (1976) compared CVMR FB to EMG FB and a no-treatment control group. CVMR "seemed" more beneficial than EMG FB, and both were better than no treatment.

Other group comparison studies also offered some support for CVMR FB. Zamani (1974) found CVMR FB significantly superior to relaxation instructions in reducing the frequency, duration, intensity, and need for medication of migraine sufferers. Friar and Beatty (1976) reported that CVMR FB reduced the frequency of major migraine attacks more than finger-pulse-amplitude FB. Feuerstein and his colleagues (Feuerstein & Adams, 1977; Feuerstein, Adams, & Beiman, 1976) report three systematic case studies that also suggest CVMR FB may be specifically beneficial for migraine compared to EMG FB.

The CVMR FB results are somewhat encouraging, but further controlled research is needed to establish clearly treatment-specific effects. The relationship between migraine reduction and changes in vascular processes at the head requires further documentation. Further comparisons to attention-placebo and relaxation training groups would also help to clarify treatment specificity. CVMR procedures are not easily performed reliably (Zamani, 1974), and they are almost impossible to calibrate equally across sessions.

FB Treatment of Miscellaneous Pain Syndromes

Forms of FB have been applied to a variety of pain syndromes other than headache, usually in relatively exploratory studies (see Jessup, Neufeld, & Merskey, in press). Syndromes treated have included low back pain (Grabel, 1973; Melzack & Perry, 1975), menstrual stress (Russ, 1977), neck pain due to torticollis or injury (Cleeland, 1973; Jacobs & Felton, 1969), peptic ulcers (Welgan, 1974), pyelonephritis (Coger & Werbach, 1975), post-traumatic head pain (Gannon & Sternbach, 1971), Raynaud's disease (Lipp, 1976; Surwit, 1973), rheumatoid arthritis (Wickramasekera et al., 1976), temporomandibular joint pain (Carlsson & Gale, 1976; Carlsson, Gale, & Ohman, 1975; Mulhall & Todd, 1975; Stenn, Mothersill, & Brooke, 1979) and writers' cramp (Uchiyama, Lutterjohann, & Shah, 1977).

Much of this literature consists of anecdotal case studies. Among the more extensive work is the group-outcome research of Melzack and Perry (1975). Melzack and Perry compared hypnosis with occipital alpha wave EEG FB to hypnosis alone and EEG FB alone. The combined treatment resulted in significantly larger pain reduction from the no-treatment baseline. However, Melzack and Perry (1975) concluded that the combined treatment was effective due to nonspecific features of treatment, such as the patients' sense of control, attention, and distraction. Application of FB treatments to each of the miscellaneous pain syndromes other than headache is still at the earliest, most tentative level of research. In most instances, the applied work needs to be advanced in conjunction with basic research directed toward linking treatment with a clear understanding of the pain processes involved.

Theoretical and Methodological Issues

The theoretical issue most frequently discussed by biofeedback researchers is whether or not biofeedback represents "pure" operant conditioning of the autonomic nervous system (ANS), free of somatic or cognitive mediation. Kimmel (1967) expressed concern that the reported instances of operant ANS conditioning "may be artifactual consequences of some somatic response" (p. 343). However, he noted that somatic responses that can reduce an autonomic response are unlikely to increase it as well:

It is one thing to assert that an experimental S (subject) may learn to make some somatic response which, incidentally, elicits a GSR or a change in heart rate, but it is quite something else to claim that in the same experiment *S*s learn to *not make* some somatic response and thus emit fewer GSRs. This is particularly cogent in those studies showing both directions of change within the same *S*s. Nevertheless, the more obvious potential somatic mediators should undoubtedly be examined, observed or controlled. (p. 343).

Kimmel (1967) seems to have ignored the possibility that subjects could learn different somatic or cognitive maneuvers to develop spurious ANS control. Nonetheless, Kimmel's (1967) positive evaluations of bidirectional control designs and somatic monitoring seem sound.

Katkin and Murray (1968) discussed the possibility of classical ANS conditioning occurring within operant procedures. Following Skinner (1938), they noted four ways in which apparently operant ANS conditioning could be classically mediated. The ANS changes could be unconditioned or conditioned responses to external or internal stimuli. The situation in which an ANS response is classically conditioned to an internal source of stimulation is particularly pertinent when biofeedback is used for therapy: an individual may engage in subvocal activity (thinking) and this activity may elicit a previously conditioned response pattern (p. 53). However, Katkin and Murray (1968) went on to note:

At a practical level a distinction must be drawn between *conditioning* the ANS and *controlling* it (Black, 1966). For those researchers whose primary goal is to gain control over ANS function . . . it may be unnecessary to demonstrate the pure phenomenon of instrumental conditioning . . . the desired control of autonomic activity might be more efficiently produced by proper reinforcement of both the somatic and the cognitive mediators (p. 66).

Katkin and Murray (1968) offered "minimal criteria for the acceptability of evidence for instrumental conditioning" (p. 53). For applied researchers, Katkin and Murray's (1968) criteria are useful guidelines for evaluating biofeedback processes:

First there should be some demonstration that the response being reinforced shows an increase in frequency or amplitude, or probability of occurrence over the level shown in a free-operant period. Second, the experimental design should allow comparisons between experimental groups and appropriate control groups. Finally, the data should be, within reasonable limits, free of obvious alternative explanations (pp. 53–54).

Crider, Schwartz, and Shnidman (1969) criticized Katkin and Murray's (1968) theoretical remarks and interpretations of the operant ANS conditioning reports. Crider et al. (1968) argued that classical conditioning interpretations of the operant results are weakened by: "findings that the same S^r (reinforcer) can be used either to increase or to decrease the frequency of a given autonomic response" (p. 456). Crider et al's. (1968) argument is in keeping with Kimmel's (1967) earlier remarks, and, again, it emphasizes the utility of the bidirectional research design as a control for classical conditioning effects within the operant paradigm. Crider et al. also questioned the importance of cognitive mediation. They offered two observations that they believed weakened the cognitivists' position: ". . . operant autonomic conditioning seems to be specific to the reinforced response" (p. 457), and " . . . it is a currently debatable question that cognitive activity per se produces any marked autonomic effects at all" (p. 458).

Crider et al's. (1969) observations, although empirical questions are still far from resolved, also underscored the importance of assessing possible somatic and cognitive processes in biofeedback studies. In a rejoinder to Crider et al., Katkin, Murray, and Lachman (1969) urged experimenters to attempt to adequately describe "relationships between verbal reports of mediation and the dependent variables under investigation" (p.465). Schwartz (1973) adopted a similar position and stated that researchers should "analyze carefully what else is simultaneously being 'reinforced'" (p. 668).

The question of mediation is complex, especially at the level of the brain, and one must evaluate (a) relations between responses, (b) the nature of the reinforcement contingency and (c) natural biological environmental and "state" constraints in order to understand and predict exactly what is being learned (pp. 669–670).

Patients may be able to learn certain cognitive or somatic strategies which they can use without feedback (p. 671).

Theoreticians (Crider et al., 1969; Katkin & Murray, 1968; Katkin et al., 1969; Kimmel, 1967; Schwartz, 1973) concur then in the need to control for and evaluate cognitive and classical conditioning factors in biofeedback research.

Another more concrete way of thinking about the problem of experimental control is to try to define "self-regulation" operationally. The operational definition can then be used to evaluate whether or not a particular study is an instance of "self-regulation." Stoyva (1976) "broadly defined" self-regulation as "the endeavor to modify voluntarily one's own physiological activity, behaviour or processes of consciousness" (p. 2). Stoyva (1976) did not further refine or operationalize his definition, but, from his context, he would apparently accept any change that is not obviously an unconditioned response as an instance of voluntary self-regulation. The least stringent definition of physiological self-regulation, then, requires two events to be present: a discriminative stimulus (S^D) and a significant physiological change that occurs when the S^D is present, the physiological change not being an obvious unconditioned response to the S^D. Trivial instances of self-regulation, e.g., holding ice to cause vasoconstriction, are eliminated by this definition. However, it paradoxically admits classically *conditioned* responses as instances of self-regulation, while excluding the processes that led to their classical conditioning in the first place. For example, if the S^D "imagine yourself lying on a warm beach" was followed by vasodilation, the definition would accept the vasodilation as an instance of self-regulation. However, vasodilation actually due to lying on a warm beach would not be accepted.

Incidentally, classical conditioning as a self-regulatory technique has its supporters. Furedy and Paulos (1974), in a study of classically conditioned cardiac deceleration, remarked:

> The lack of attention to the feasibility of using such Pavlovian behavioural control is probably due to a confluence of factors. First, while the power of operant experimental procedures have been recently emphasized (e.g., Miller, 1969), the parallel power of many Pavlovian procedures (e.g., cf. Gormezano, 1966) have failed to be as widely noted. Secondly, the very notion of behavioural "control" implies some kind of *direct* alteration of the target behaviour, while the clinical aspects of the Pavlovian strategy would involve *indirect* control in the sense of pitting an antagonistic response (i.e., a decelerative CR) against the target response (i.e., stress-elicited acceleration). Needless to say, indirectness of this sort does not entail less behavioural control (p. 32).

Reberg (1974) concurred with the potential value of the classical approach, noting: " . . . where practical control is the goal, one should certainly be prepared to consider any working method" (p. 51).

Miller (1969) took particular care to control for classical mediation in his studies of operant ANS conditionning. He used bidirectional groups to insure that any observed physiological changes had not been inadvertently elicited as unconditioned responses by the experimental situation (i.e., the S^D) or by reinforcement (S^r). Miller's (1969) remarks about the bidirectional design offered a more stringent definition of voluntary control than Stoyva's (1976) inasmuch as the possibility of unconditioned classical mediation was more rigorously controlled:

> We used the experimental design of rewarding dogs in one group whenever they showed a burst of spontaneous salivation, so that they would be trained to increase salivation, and rewarding dogs in another group whenever there was a long interval between spontaneous bursts, so that they would be trained to decrease salivation. If the reward had any unconditioned effect, this effect might be classically conditioned to the experimental situation and therefore produce a change in salivation that was not a true instance of instrumental learning. But in classical conditioning the reinforcement must elicit the response that is to be acquired. Therefore, conditioning of a response elicited by the reward could produce either an increase or a decrease in salivation, depending upon the direction of the unconditioned response elicited by the reward, but it could not produce a change in one direction for one group and in the opposite direction for the other group. The same type of logic applies for any unlearned cumulative aftereffects of the reward; they could not be in opposite directions for the two groups. With instrumental learning, however, the reward can reinforce any response that immediately preceeds it; therefore, the same reward can be used to produce either increases or decreases (p. 436–437).

Miller's (1969) bidirectional approach can be used as a criterion for judging the rigour of experiments that attempt to demonstrate self-regulation.

Vanderwolf (1971) also struggled with the problem of defining "voluntary" behaviour. He commented:

> There is no generally accepted objective definition of "volution" or of "voluntary movement" and the difference between it and "automatic movement". Some possibilities are that voluntary acts are those that can be brought under the control of many different drive states and can be performed in a variety of combinations and sequences (pp. 83–84).

In the context of physiological self-regulation, Vanderwolf's (1971) remarks offer another even more rigorous criterion for the demonstration of voluntary physiological self-regulation: the physiological response should at least be able to be turned on and off to more than one reinforcer.

The definitions of voluntary self-regulation provided by Stoyva (1976), Miller (1969), and Vanderwolf (1971) form a hierarchy of increasingly rigorous operational criteria. The minimum criterion is a significant physiological change in the presence of a discriminative stimulus. This criterion can only generate a list of S^Ds that result in physiological change. The appropriate control at this level of description consists of the same stimulus array as the experimental condition, except for the particular S^D under study. A unidirectional response to verbal instructions is an example meeting this criterion. The second criterion requires proof that the change is not an unconditioned response. The bidirectional design (e.g., Miller, 1969) appears to be the most effective technique of controlling for at least overt unconditioned responses. The possibility of classically conditioned mediation in humans—e.g., by cognition—cannot be completely eliminated. Bidirectional change to verbal instructions with different meanings (e.g., "Now warm your hands," "Now cool your hands") mixes classical and operant control in unknown proportions, but it may be of practical convenience in the development of clinical control (see Katkin & Murray, 1968). Rigorous control for classical mediation would require bidirectional control to one stimulus, for example, both handwarming and cooling after appropriate reinforcement to the stimulus "Now warm your hands." Finally, a further dimension of voluntary self-regulation is demonstrated when a physiological response can be turned on and off for different types of reinforcement (Vanderwolf, 1971). The rigour of attempts to demonstrate voluntary self-regulation can be gauged by the level of criteria they meet. Table 12-2 summarizes 19 experiments that attempted to train voluntary self-regulation of peripheral blood flow. Excepting York's (1975) study, the research is equally divided between control group and bidirectional control studies. The basic studies are notably more rigorous than the applied. Unfortunately, only two of the studies utilized migraineurs as subjects (Price & Tursky, 1976; York, 1975), while the others relied on nonclinical populations, usually undergraduates. Neither Price and Tursky (1976) nor York (1975) found a difference between migrainous and non-migrainous subjects in their response to the blood-flow training procedures. Price and Tursky's (1976) study did show a groups by periods interaction in which nonmigrainous subjects exhibited more finger volume dilation than migraineurs. However, for both groups finger dilation was not significantly different under finger volume biofeedback, relaxation, or yoked control, indicating that the changes were not treatment-specific anyway.

Possible thermal reflex abnormalities in migraineurs may limit the clinical generalizability of biofeedback results based on normal subjects (see Downey & Frewin, 1972; Morley, 1977). Consequently, the basic research findings in Table 12-2 may not be entirely pertinent to the question of learned control of peripheral blood flow *in migraineurs*. Nonetheless, their rigour permits an overall conclusion about self-regulation of blood flow, even if the conclusion may only be true for undergraduates and healthy adults. The results in Table 12-2 show that learned control of peripheral blood flow has been demonstrated and independantly replicated. However, the changes are typically of small magnitude, usually no more than 1°C or 1°F in either direction when measured as skin temperature. Furthermore, skin temperature decreases, representing increased arousal, are easier to learn and of larger magnitude than skin temperature increases. And the changes from baseline temperatures are sometimes statistically nonsignificant (e.g., Ohno et al., 1977; Surwit et al., 1976) or only significant in the decrease direction (e.g., Alberstein, 1976). Often statistical significance is only attained when comparing groups trained to change their hand temperature in opposite directions. Such an approach is apt to generate statistical significance more often than the small changes from baseline actually warrant. Given the small absolute changes in temperature, particularly increases, in normal subjects, voluntary control of hand blood flow in migraineurs may not be a very robust phenomen. The relationship between voluntary control of blood flow and alleviation of migraine symptoms is another question that requires further elucidation.

Concluding Remarks

The central conclusion that seems to follow from the current literature on chronic pain and its treatment by FB is that far too much remains unknown. Symptomatic relief during FB appears to be mediated by more potent nonspecific components of the treatment experience rather than any unique features of FB. The relationship between pain reduction and changes in physiological mechanisms related to pain remain equivocal. The role of placebo effects requires elucidation in the FB context. Perhaps the area of FB research would be best served by redirecting its conceptualization. FB could be evaluated in terms of the components of the pain experience affected by treatment, and the role of coping strategies and cognitive processes in mediating pain symptom changes.

Table 12-2 Summary of Basic Research on the Biofeedback Control of Peripheral Blood Flow

AUTHORS	INDEPENDENT VARIABLES	RESEARCH DESIGN	DEPENDENT VARIABLES	SUBJECTS NUMBER, TYPE	FREQUENCY AND DURATION OF TREATMENT	RESULTS	COMMENTS
Alberstein 1977 (*Abstract*)	Finger temp FB increase; finger temp FB decrease; relax only (no treatment); EMG FB decrease	Bidirectional + control group	Finger temp; frontalis EMG	56 male undergraduates	5 sessions: 1 30 min baseline; 4 session consisting of a 10 min wait, 15 min baseline, & 15 min FB	Temp increase not different from baseline & relax; temp decrease significant vs baseline & relax; EMG FB decreased EMG vs baseline & relax	EMG & vasoconstriction learned, but not vasodilation
Bloom, Houston & Burish 1976	Threat vs no threat of shock	Control group	Finger pulse volume (FPV), Heart rate (HR), affect adjective check list (AACL)	192 female undergraduates	1 session, 10 min	Residualized score (base free) higher HR, anxiety, lower FPV under threat. Correlations: $FPVrHR = -.41$; $rAACL = -.24$; $HRrAACL = -.25$	Residual scores; very brief intervention.
Boudewyns 1976 *Study* 1	Sit for 3 min	Baseline only (normative data collection)	Finger temp	57 male & 76 female, normal adult volunteers	3 min	Possible bimodal distribution of initial finger temp	Rare bimodal distribution of finger temp; female fingers cooler; higher baseline in summer
Study 2	Relaxation tape, 4 shocks vs no shock, relaxation	Control group	Finger temp, arousal rating (ALR) gain scores	10 males & 11 females from study 1	1 session, 10 min; relax, 7 min stress vs no stress, 15 min relax	Finger temp increased with both relaxations; decreased with stress, corresponding changes in rated arousal	

Study		Design	Measures	Sessions	Results	Comments
Study 3	Same as study 2	Control group	Finger temp; arousal rating; heart rate (HR) skin conductance (SC) gain scores	1 session; 10 min; relax, 15 min stress, 15 min relax	Decreased temp & increased SC under stress, compared to control group; during second relaxed phase finger temp correlated with arousal − .46	Baseline SC differences between experimental and control groups larger than experimental effect itself; finger temp suitable index of arousal for FB
Carlton, M. 1974 (Abstract)	Control self-relaxation; autogenic; finger temp FB	Control group	Finger temp Eysenek Personality Inventory	3 × 90 second base trials; 20 × 90 second trials, 2/day	FB no different from no FB on finger temp; no effect of personality	Trend for less temp increase in stable introverts; very brief sessions
Carlton, P 1974 (Abstract)	Relaxation-instructed; autogenic; autogenic + finger temp FB	Control group	Finger temp	Same as Carlton, M.	No differences between the 3 groups	Very brief sessions
Gardner & Keefe 1976 (Abstract)	Informed vs uniformed of target response by increase vs decrease forehead skin temp	2 × 2, bidirectional 4 independent groups	Forehead skin temp	12 × 30 min; consisting of: 10 min adaptation, 10 min baseline, 10 min FB	Increase & decrease in correct direction; mean = ± 1.5° − 2.0 F; knowledge of target made acquisition faster but not larger	
Keefe 1975	Increase vs decrease finger temp referenced to head, auditory and visual FB	2 bidirectional groups	Finger temp change referenced to head	12 daily sessions; 5 min rest, 10 min FB	At session 12 mean increase 1.9°F, mean decrease 1.5°F p .01	Small sample; no control at session 4, control appeared at session 8; room temp 21°C; lack of an "instructions only" group noted

Table 12-2 Summary of Basic Research on the Biofeedback Control of Peripheral Blood Flow (*Continued*)

Authors	Independent Variables	Research Design	Dependent Variables	Subjects Number Type	Frequency and Duration of Treatment	Results	Comments
Koppman, McDonald, & Kunzel 1974	Blood volume, pulse (BVP) FB; mental imagery	9 systematic case studies with bidirectional control	Temporal artery pulse amplitude (BVP)	9 migraine	1hr, 2–3/wk, for 4 wks	7/9 learned significant control of constricting vs dilating temporal artery	Includes critical evaluation of instrumentation
Leeb 1974 (*Abstract*)	Positive, neutral or negative instructional set about autogenic FB hand temp training	Control group	Finger temp	15 female normals, age 18–35	12 - ½ hr sessions; 1/day	Main effect of instructional set; need for positive set for hand temp control supported	Instructional not analagous to placebo effect; young normal Ss
Maslach, Marshall, & Zimbardo 1972	10 hrs hypnosis + 10 min hypnotic suggestion vs none; 1 hand warm other cold	Bidirectional (opposite hands) + control	10 sites of hand & forearm temp; temp difference between hands	9 paid undergraduates	10 hrs hypnotic training for hypnosis group; then 2 - 10 min testing sessions	Hypnotic Ss averaged over 3°C difference between hands; no difference for others; temp increase larger	Small sample size; specificity of temp change to hand vs forearm
Ohno, Tanaka, Takeya & Ikemi 1977	Finger temp increase; finger temp decrease; false FB; no FB	Bidirectional + control group	Finger temp; Cornell Medical Index; Manifest Anxiety Scale	40 healthy adults	30 min/day, 3 days; 5 min baseline, 17 min training, 5 min post	Only 3rd session increase vs decrease; changes significantly different; no pre-post changes significant; increase = 1°F decrease = −1.5°F false FB = −1°F	No relation of personality scales to finger temp control; small absolute change
Price & Tursky 1976	Finger blood volume FB; yoked FB; relaxation tape; neutral tape	Control group	Finger blood volume; forehead blood volume	40 migraine; 40 non-migraine female volunteers	1 session, 16 × 2 min periods	No overall effect of groups or treatments; groups and treatments interaction *with periods*	FB no better for finger dilation than yoked control or relaxation tape; *positive hand vs hand*

Study	Treatment	Design	Dependent measure	Subjects	Procedure	Results	Comments	
Roberts, Kewman, & MacDonald 1973	Warming & cooling hands with hot & cold pads; hypnotic training	Bidirectional (opposite hands) single group	Temp difference between hands	4 female, 2 male undergraduates, "selected", age 20–24, "extensive hypnotic training and experience"; high hypnotic susceptibility	5 to 9 × 1 hr training then 9 separate sessions of 10 min trials in 3 hypnosis, 5 min rest & relax, 8 min test trial	3 Ss show more than 1°C difference between hands	Room temp = 22.5°C	correlation between finger and forehead pulse volume change = .67 for migraine & = .7 for non. blood flow correlation contradicts Sargent's et al (1973) rationale
Roberts, Schuler, Bacon, Zimmerman, & Patterson 1975	Warming & cooling opposite hands by audio FB (high vs low susceptibility + absorption)	Bidirectional (opposite hands)	Difference in finger temp of opposite hands	7 high, 7 low on hypnotic susceptibility + absorption paid undergraduates	16 × 1 hr sessions; 10 min relax, then 3 × 8 min trials of temp difference between hands, reverse direction on alternate trials	1°C average difference between hands on sessions 8–16; no effect of hypnotic susceptibility + absorption; 4/14 showed mean overall temp difference 1°C	Small value of absolute temp difference (1°C); 4 response patterns: wrong direction, same direction different rates of change, correct change in 1 finger only finger temps diverged or converged; high positive correlation of absolute temp between hands in poor responders & early sessions	

Table 12-2 Summary of Basic Research on the Biofeedback Control of Peripheral Blood Flow (*Continued*)

Authors	Independent Variables	Research Design	Dependent Variables	Subjects Number Type	Frequency and Duration of Treatment	Results	Comments
Sheridan, Boehm, Ward & Justesen 1976 (*Abstract*)	Control; autogenic phrases; finger temp FB; autogenic phrases + finger temp FB for hand warming	Control group	Hand temp	40 undergraduates	15 min after stabilization, daily for 5 sessions	Autogenic phrases alone effective for both male and female Ss; autogenic + FB effective for female Ss only	"These findings may not generalize to patients"; "simplicity & economy of autogenic phrases makes it worthwhile to assess the effectiveness of mere autogenic phrases"
Snyder & Noble 1968	Reinforcement (light on) for finger vasoconstriction vs vasostability vs no reinforcement instructions	Control group	Number of vasoconstrictions/5 min	27 male & 27 female undergraduates	1 session; 5 min baseline, 25 min conditioning, 10 min extinction	Reinforcement for vasoconstriction caused 5.5 times more vasoconstrictions than vasostability or baseline control which did not change	Controlled for body & finger movement, EMG, HR & respiration; vasoconstriction not mediated by these systems
Surwit, Shapiro & Feld 1976 Study 1	Increase vs decrease finger skin temp	Bidirectional	Finger skin temp (& other blood flow measures for comparison)	8 male & 8 female normal volunteers from newspaper ad, ages 18–30	2 baseline & 5 training days; 20 × 75 second trials/session in 4 blocks of 5 trials	Only decrease significant across trials; no effect of days; warm vs cool differed on trials; mean decrease = −2°C, mean increase = +25°C, first to last trial block	9 days no more effective than 5 days reflectance plethysmograph & strain gauge finger volume & temp all correlate .87 to .96 therefore, increased superficial blood flow

Study	Method	Design	Measure	Subjects	Sessions	Results	Conclusions
Study 2	As in Study 1, but with cooler ambient temp	As in Study 1	As in Study 1	4 males & 4 females	As in Study 1	Lower room temp decreased baseline from 33.3°C to 29.9°C; training to increase finger temp in cool room led to actual decrease	Change in room temp a larger effect than FB training; suggested "arousal" behaviour easier to condition than relaxation
Thompson & Russel 1976 (Abstract)	Finger temp FB; yoked no FB controls; relaxation tape	Control group (yoked)	Finger temp	35 undergraduates	4 sessions; 15 min	Only FB Ss increased finger temp	High reported anxiety related to low initial finger temp; visual imagery of heat scenes best technique
York 1975 (Abstract)	Autogenic classical vs operant finger temp training (+ migraine vs nonmigraine Ss; preferred vs non preferred hand)	Counter balanced repeated measures with 2 populations 2 group outcome	Hand skin temp	10 migraine 10 non-migraine	6 weekly sessions; 3 operant/3 classical	All Ss warmed hand; faster with initial classical conditioning; no differences between migraine vs non migraine Ss; 1 wk cooling enhanced Ss hand-warming ability	Classical conditioning with heating pad potentiated operant conditioning (autoshaping); anecdotal support for migraine relief

Note: Abbreviations: EMG = Electomyograph, FB = feedback, freq = frequency, hr = hour, min = minute, mo = month, *S* = subject, temp = temperature, vs = versus, wk = week

References

Adler, C., & Adler S. Biofeedback-psychotherapy for the treatment of headaches: A 5-year follow-up. *Headache*, 1976, *16*, 189–191.

Alberstein, B. Biofeedback and skin temperature control: A controlled study. *Psychophysiology*, 1977, *14*, 155. (Abstract)

Andreychuk, T., & Skriver, C. Hypnosis and biofeedback in the treatment of migraine headache. *International Journal of Clinical and Experimental Hypnosis*, 1975, *23*, 172–183.

Bakal, D. Headache: A biopsychological perspective. *Psychological Bulletin*, 1975, *82*, 369–382.

Bakal, D. A., & Kaganov, J. A. Muscle contraction and migraine headache: Psychophysiologic comparison. *Headache*, 1977, *17*, 208–215.

Beasley, J. Biofeedback in the treatment of migraine headaches. *Dissertations Abstracts International*, 1976, *36* (11-B), 5850B-5851B. (Abstract)

Beecher, H. K. The measurement of pain. *Pharmacological Reviews*, 1957, *9*, 59–209.

Beecher, H. K. *Measurement of subjective responses. Quantitative effects of drugs.* New York: Oxford University Press, 1959.

Bild, R. Cephalic vasomotor responses biofeedback as a treatment modality for vascular headache of the migraine type. *Dissertations Abstracts International*, 1976, *37* (5-B), 2494B. (Abstract)

Black, A. H. The operant conditioning of heart rate in curarized dogs: Some problems of interpretation. Paper presented at the meeting of the Psychonomic Society, St. Louis, October, 1966.

Blanchard, E. B., Scott, R. W., Young L. D. & Edmundson, E. D. Effect of knowledge of response on the self-control of heart rate. *Psychophysiology*, 1974, *11*, 251–264.

Blanchard, E., Theobald, D., Williamson, D., Silver, B., & Brown, D. Temperature biofeedback in the treatment of migraine headaches. *Archives of General Psychiatry*, 1978, *35*, 581–588.

Bloom, L., Houston, B., & Burish, T. An evaluation of finger pulse volume as a psychophysiological measure of anxiety. *Psychophysiology*, 1976, *13*. 40–42.

Boeckh, S. Paying pain's price. *Financial Post Magazine*, 1979 (June), 25–30.

Boudewyns, P. A comparison of the effects of stress vs. relaxation instruction on the finger temperature response. *Behavior Therapy*, 1976, *7*, 54–67.

Budzynski, T., Stoyva, J., & Adler, C. Feedback-induced muscle relaxation: Application to tension headache. *Journal of Behavior Therapy and Experimental Psychiatry*, 1970, *1*, 205–211.

Budzynski, T., Stoyva, J., Adler, C., & Mullaney, D. EMG biofeedback and tension headache: A controlled outcome study. *Psychosomatic Medicine*, 1973, *35*, 484–496.

Carlsson, S. G., & Gale, E. N. Biofeedback treatment for muscle pain associated with the temporomandibular joint. *Journal of Behavior Therapy and Experimental Psychiatry*, 1976, *7*, 383–385.

Carlsson, S. G., Gale, E. N., & Ohman, A. Treatment of temporomandibular joint syndrome with biofeedback training. *Journal of the American Dental Association (JADA)*, 1975, *91*, 602–605.

Carlton, M. The Eysenck Personality Inventory as a prognostic index for autogenic training and biofeedback procedures. *Dissertation Abstracts International*, 1974, *34* (10-B), 5183B. (Abstract)

Carlton, P. The biofeedback technique as a facilitator in autogenic training. *Dissertation Abstracts International*, 1974, *34* (10-B). 5183B-5184B. (Abstract)

Chesney, M. A., & Shelton, J. L. A comparison of muscle relaxation and electromyogram biofeedback treatments for muscle contraction headache. *Journal of Behavior Therapy and Experimental Psychiatry*, 1976, *7*, 221–225.

Cleeland, C. S. Behavior techniques in the modification of spasmodic torticollis. *Neurology*, 1973, *23*, 1241–1247.

Coger, R., & Werbach, M. Attention, anxiety and the effects of learned enhancement of EEG alpha in chronic pain: a pilot study in biofeedback. In B. L. Crue, (Ed.), *Pain research and treatment.* New York: Academic Press, 1975.

Cox, D. J., Freundlich, A., & Meyer, R. G. Differential effectiveness of electromyograph feedback, verbal relaxation instructions, and medication placebo with tension headaches. *Journal of Consulting and Clinical Psychology*, 1975, *43*, 892–898.

Crider, A., Schwartz, G., & Shnidman, S. On the criteria for instrumental autonomic conditioning: A reply to Katkin and Murray. *Psychological Bulletin,* 1969, *71,* 445–461.

Dalessio, D. *Wolff's Headache and Other Head Pain.* New York: Oxford University Press, 1972.

Dalessio, D. Mechanisms and biochemistry of headache. *Postgraduate Medicine.* 1974, *56*(3), 55–61.

Diamond, S., & Franklin, Mary. *Indications and contraindications for the use of biofeedback therapy in headache patients.* Paper presented at the Biofeedback Research Society Annual Meeting, Colorado Springs, Colorado, 1974.

Diamond, S., & Franklin, Mary. *Intensive biofeedback therapy in the treatment of headache.* Paper presented at the Biofeedback Research Society Annual Meeting, Monterey, California, 1975.

Downey, J., & Frewin, D. Vascular responses in the hands of patients suffering from migraine. *Journal of Neurology, Neurosurgery and Psychiatry,* 1972, *35,* 258–263.

Drury, R., DeRisi, W., & Liberman, R. *Temperature feedback treatment for migraine: a controlled study.* Paper presented at the Biofeedback Research Society Annual Meeting, Monterey, California, 1975.

Ehrisman, W. F. A comparison of the effects of biofeedback training in alpha enhancement and progressive relaxation training on tension headache symptoms, EEG occipital alpha, forehead and neck EMG, and self report measures of anxiety. *Dissertation Abstracts International,* 1973, *34B,* 2301B.

Epstein, L. H., Hersen, M., & Hemphill, D. P. Music feedback in the treatment of tension headache: An experimental case study. *Journal of Behavior Therapy and Experimental Psychiatry,* 1974, *5,* 59–63.

Feuerstein, M., & Adams, H. E. Cephalic vasomotor feedback in the modification of migraine headache. *Biofeedback & Self-Regulation,* 1977, *2,* 241–254.

Feuerstein, M., Adams, H. E., & Beiman, I. Cephalic vasomotor and electromyographic feedback in the treatment of combined muscle contraction and migraine headaches in a geriatric case. *Headache,* 1976, *16,* 232–237.

Fordyce, W., Fowler, R., & DeLateur, B. An application of behavior modification technique to a problem of chronic pain. *Behavior Research and Therapy,* 1968, *6,* 105–107.

Friar, L., & Beatty, J. Migraine: management by trained control of vasoconstriction. *Journal of Consulting and Clinical Psychology,* 1976, *44,* 46–53.

Friedman, A., Finley, L., Graham, J., Kinkle, C., Ostfield, A., & Wolff, H. Classification of headache. *Journal of the American Medical Association,* 1962, *179,* 717–718.

Fuller, G. D. Current status of biofeedback in clinical practice. *American Psychologist,* 1978, *33,* 39–48.

Furedy, J., & Poulos, C. Clinical and theoretical implications of human Pavlovian decelerative cardiac conditioning based on a decelerative unconditioned reflex. In P. Stenn & D. Reberg (Eds.), *Clinical applications and implications of biofeedback.* London, Ontario: University of Western Ontario, Department of Psychology, June, 1974. (Research Bulletin 326).

Gannon, L., & Sternbach, R. Alpha enhancement as a treatment for pain: A case study. *Journal of Behavior Therapy and Experimental Psychiatry,* 1971, *2,* 209–213.

Gardner, E., & Keefe, F. The effects of knowledge of response on temperature biofeedback training. *Biofeedback and Self-Regulation,* 1976, *1,* 314. (Abstract)

Grabel, J. A. Electromyographic study of low back muscle tension in subjects with and without chronic low back pain. *Dissertation Abstracts International,* 1973, *34,* 2929B.

Graham, G. Hypnosis and biofeedback as treatments for migraine headaches. *Dissertation Abstracts International,* 1974, *35* (5-B) 2428B-2429B. (Abstract)

Haynes, S. N., Griffin, P., Mooney, D., & Parise, M. Electromyographic biofeedback and relaxation instructions in the treatment of muscle contraction headaches. *Behavior Therapy,* 1975, *6,* 672–678.

Hutchings, D. F., & Reinking, R. H. Tension headaches: What form of therapy is most effective? *Biofeedback and Self-Regulation,* 1976, *1,* 183–190.

Jacobs, A., & Felton, G. S. Visual feedback of myoelectric output to facilitate muscle relaxation in normal persons and patients with neck injuries. *Archives of Physical Medicine and Rehabilitation,* 1969, *50,* 34–39.

Jessup, B. A. Autogenic feedback for migraine: A placebo effect. (Under review)

Jessup, B. A., Neufeld, R. W. J., & Merskey, H. Biofeedback treatment of headache and other pain: A review: *Pain,* 1980, *9,* 115–116.

Katkin, E., & Murray, E. Instrumental conditioning of autonomically mediated behavior: Theoretical and methodological issues. *Psychological Bulletin,* 1968, *70,* 52–68.

Katkin, E., Murray, E., & Lachman, R. Concerning instrumental autonomic conditioning: A rejoinder. *Psychological Bulletin,* 1969, *71,* 462–466.

Keefe, F. Conditioning changes in differential skin temperature. *Perceptual and Motor Skills,* 1975, *40,* 283–288.

Keefe, F. J., & Gardner, E. T. Learned control of skin temperature: Effects of short- and long-term biofeedback training. *Behavior Therapy,* 1979, *10,* 202–210.

Kentsmith, D., Strider, F., Copenhaver, J., & Jacques, D. Effects of biofeedback upon suppression of migraine symptoms and plasma dopamine $-\beta$-hyroxylose activity. *Headache,* 1976, *16,* 173–177.

Kewman, D. G. Voluntary control of digital skin temperature for treatment of migraine headaches. *Dissertation Abstracts International,* 1978, *38,* 3399B-3400B. See Kewman, D. G., & Roberts, A. H. Skin temperature biofeedback and migraine headaches: A double-blind study. (Under review)

Kewman, D. G., & Roberts, A. H. Skin temperature biofeedback and migraine headaches: A double blind study. (Under review.) See Kewman, D. G. Voluntary control of digital skin temperature for treatment of migraine headaches. *Dissertation Abstracts International,* 1978, *38,* 3399B-3400B.

Kimmel, H. Instrumental conditioning of autonomically mediated behavior. *Psychological Bulletin,* 1967, *67,* 337–345.

Kondo, C., & Canter, A. True and false electromyogram feedback: effect on tension headache. *Journal of Abnormal Psychology,* 1977, *81,* 93–95.

Koppman, J., McDonald, R., & Kunzel, M. Voluntary regulation of temporal artery diameter by migraine patients. *Headache,* 1974, *14,* 133–138.

Lang, P. J., & Twentyman, C. T. Learning to control heart rate: Binary vs. analogue feedback. *Psychophysiology,* 1974, *11,* 616–629.

Lazarus, R. S. A cognitively oriented psychologist looks at biofeedback. *American Psychologist,* 1975, *30,* 553–561.

Leeb, C. The effect of instructional set on autogenic biofeedback and temperature training. *Dissertation Abstracts International,* 1974, *34* (7-A), 3992A. (Abstract)

Liebeskind, J. C., & Paul, L. A. Psychological and physiological mechanisms of pain. *Annual Review of Psychology,* 1977, *28,* 41–60.

Lipp, J. Experimental analysis of biofeedback effects on skin temperature in Raynaud's Syndrome. *Dissertation Abstracts International,* 1976, *36,* 5834B.

Marinacci, A. A., & Horande, M. Electromyogram in neuromuscular reeducation. *Bulletin of the Los Angeles Neurological Society,* 1960, *25,* 57–65.

Maslach, C., Marshall, G., & Zimbardo, P. Hypnotic control of peripheral skin temperature. *Psychophysiology,* 1972, *9,* 600–605.

McKenzie, R. E., Ehrisman, E. J., Montgomery, P. S., & Barnes, R. H. The treatment of headache by means of electroencephalographic biofeedback. *Headache,* 1974, *14,* 164–172.

Medina, J., Diamond, S., & Franklin, Mary. Biofeedback therapy for migraine. *Headache,* 1976, *16,* 115–118.

Melzack, R. *The puzzle of pain.* London: Penguin, 1973.

Melzack, R., & Perry, C. Self-regulation of pain: The use of alpha-feedback and hypnotic training for the control of chronic pain. *Experimental Neurology,* 1975, *46,* 452–463.

Merskey, H. Psychological aspects of pain relief; hypnotherapy; psychotropic drugs. In M. Swerdlow (Ed.), *Relief of Intractable Pain.* New York: Elsevier/North-Holland, 1978.

Miller, N. E. Biofeedback and visceral learning. *Annual Review of Psychology,* 1978, *29,* 373–404.

Miller, N. E. Interactions between learned and physical factors in mental illness. *Seminars in Psychiatry*, 1972, *4*, 14–31.

Miller, N. Learning of visceral and glandular responses. *Science*, 1969, *163*, 434–445.

Miller, N. E., & DiCara, L. V. Instrumental learning of heart-rate changes in curarized rats: Shaping and specificity to discriminative stimulus. *Journal of Comparative Physiology and Psychology*, 1967, *63*, 12–21.

Mitch, P., McGrady, A., & Iannone, A. Autogenic feedback training in migraine: A treatment report. *Headache*, 1976, *15*, 267–274.

Montgomery, P. S., & Ehrisman, W. J. Biofeedback-alleviated headaches: A follow-up. *Headache*, 1976, *16*, 64–65.

Morley, S. Point of view: Migraine: A generalized vasomotor dysfunction? A critical review of evidence. *Headache*, 1977, *17*, 71–74.

Mulhall, D. J., & Todd, R. W. Deconditioning by the use of EMG signals. *Behavior Therapy*, 1975, *6*, 125–127.

Mullinex, J. M., Norton, B. J., Hack, S., & Fishman, M. A. Skin temperature biofeedback and migraine. *Headache*, 1978, *17*, 242–244.

Ohno, Y., Tanaka, Y., Takeya, T., & Ikemi, Y. Modification of skin temperature by biofeedback procedures. *Journal of Behavior Therapy and Experimental Psychiatry*, 1977, *8*, 31–34.

Pearse, B., Walters, E., Sargent, J., & Meers, M. *Exploratory observations of the use of an intensive autogenic biofeedback training (IAFT) procedure in a follow-up study of out-of-town patients having migraine or tension headaches*. Paper presented at the Biofeedback Research Society Annual Meeting, Monterey, California, 1975.

Peck, C. L., & Kraft, G. H. Electromyographic biofeedback for pain related to muscle tension. *Archives of Surgery*, 1977, *112*, 889–895.

Peper, E., & Grossman, E. *Preliminary observation of thermal biofeedback training in children with migraine*. Paper presented at the Biofeedback Research Society Annual Meeting, Colorado Springs, Colorado, 1974.

Philips, C. The modification of tension headache pain using EMG biofeedback. *Behavior Research and Therapy*, 1977, *15*, 119–129.

Pick, J. *The autonomic nervous system: Morphological, comparative, clinical and surgical aspects*. Philadephia: Lippincott, 1970.

Price, K., & Tursky, B. Vascular reactivity of migraineurs and non-migraineurs: A comparison of responses to self-control procedures. *Headache*, 1976, *26*, 210–217.

Raskin, M., Johnson, G., & Rondestredt, J. Chronic anxiety treated by feedback induced muscle relaxation. *Archives of General Psychiatry*, 1973, *28*, 263–267.

Reberg, D. Prospects of application of biofeedback research, in P. Stenn & D. Reberg (Eds.), *Clinical applications and implications of biofeedback*. London, Ontario: University of Western Ontario, Department of Psychology, June, 1974. (Research Bulletin 326).

Reeves, J. L. EMG-biofeedback reduction of tension headache: A cognitive skills-training approach. *Biofeedback and Self-regulation*, 1976, *1*, 217–226. (Abstract)

Reinking, R. Follow-up and extension of "Tension-headaches—what method is most effective?" *Biofeedback and Self-regulation*, 1976, *1*, 350. (Abstract)

Roberts, A., Kewman, D., & MacDonald, H. Voluntary control of skin temperature; unilateral changes using hypnosis and feedback. *Journal of Abnormal Psychology*, 1973, *82*, 163–168.

Roberts, A., Schuler, J., Bacon J., Zimmerman, R., & Patterson, R. Individual differences and autonomic control: Absorption, hypnotic susceptibility, and the unilateral control of skin temperature. *Journal of Abnormal Psychology*, 1975, *84*, 272–279.

Rodbard, S. Pain associated with muscle contraction. *Headache*, 1970, *10*, 105–115.

Russ, C. A. Thermal biofeedback and menstrual distress. *Dissertation Abstracts International*, 1977, *37*, 4702B-4703B.

Russ, K. L., Adderton, M., & Hammer, R. L. Clinical follow-up: Treatment and outcome of functional headache patients treated with biofeedback. *Biofeedback and Self-Regulation,* 1977, *2,* 298. (Abstract)

Sargent, J., Walters, E., & Green, E. Psychosomatic self-regulation of migraine headache. *Seminars in Psychiatry,* 1973, *5,* 415–428.

Schultz, J., & Luthe, W. *Autogenic Therapy.* New York: Grune & Stratton, 1969.

Schwartz, G. Biofeedback as therapy: Some theoretical and practical issues. *American Psychologist,* 1973, *28,* 666–673.

Shapiro, D., Schwartz, G. E., & Tursky, B. Control of diastolic blood pressure in man by feedback and reinforcement. *Psychophysiology,* 1972, *9,* 296–304.

Shapiro, D., Tursky, B., & Schwartz, G. Differentiation of heart rate and systolic blood pressure in man by operant conditioning. *Psychosomatic Medicine,* 1970, *32,* 417–423.

Sheridan, C., Boehm, M., Ward, L., & Justesen, D. Autogenic-biofeedback, autogenic phrases, and biofeedback compared. *Biofeedback and Self-Regulation,* 1976, *1,* 315–316. (Abstract)

Sicuteri, F. Dry and Wet theory in headache. In Friedman, A. (Ed.), *Research and clinical studies in headache* (Vol. 3). Basel: S. Karger, AG, 1972.

Skinner, B. *The behavior of organisms: An experimental analysis.* New York: Appelton-Century, 1938.

Snyder, C., & Noble, M. Operant conditioning of vasoconstriction. *Journal of Experimental Psychology,* 1968, *77,* 263–268.

Solbach, P., & Sargent, J. D. A follow-up of the Menninger pilot migraine study using thermal training. *Headache,* 1977, *17,* 198–202.

Stenn, P. G., Mothersill, K. J., & Brooke, R. I. Biofeedback and a cognitive behavioral approach to treatment of myofascial pain dysfunction syndrome. *Behavior Therapy,* 1979, *10,* 29–36.

Sternbach, R. A. *Pain: A psychophysiological analysis.* New York: Academic Press, 1968.

Sternbach, R. A. *Pain patients: Traits and treatment.* New York: Academic Press, 1974.

Stoyva, J. Self-regulation and the stress-related disorders: A perspective on biofeedback. In D. Mostofsky (Ed.), *Behavioral control and modification of physiological activity.* Englewood Cliffs, N.J.: Prentice-Hall, 1976.

Surwit, R. S. Biofeedback: A possible treatment for Raynaud's disease. *Seminars in Psychiatry,* 1973, *5,* 483–490.

Surwit, R., Shapiro, D., & Feld, J. Digital temperature autoregulation and associated cardiovascular changes. *Psychophysiology,* 1976, *13,* 242–248.

Tarchanoff, J. R. Voluntary acceleration of the heart beat in man. Translated by D. A. Blizard. In D. Shapiro, T. X. Barber, L. V. DiCara, J. Kamiya, N. E. Miller, & J. Stoyva (Eds.), *Biofeedback and Self-Control 1972.* Chicago: Aldine, 1973.

Thompson, C. Autogenic feedback training: The effects of outcome and accessibility of hand temperature biofeedback on the reduction of migraine headaches. *Dissertations Abstracts International,* 1977, *37* (7-B), 3635B-3636B.

Thompson, D., & Russel, H. Learning voluntary control of fingertip skin temperature: Issues, questions and answers. *Biofeedback and Self-Regulation,* 1976, *1,* 316–317. (Abstract)

Turin, A. C. Biofeedback and suggestion in finger temperature training: An effect for the controls but not the "treatments." *Biofeedback and Self-Regulation,* 1977, *2,* 296.

Turin, A., & Johnson, W. Biofeedback therapy for migraine headaches. *Archives of General Psychiatry,* 1976, *33,* 517–519.

Turk, D. C., Meichenbaum, D. H., & Berman, W. H. The application of biofeedback for the regulation of pain: A review. *Psychological Bulletin,* 1979, *86,* 1322–1338.

Uchiyama, K., Lutterjohann, M., & Shah, M. D. Biofeedback-assisted desensitization treatment of writer's cramp. *Journal of Behavior Therapy and Experimental Psychiatry,* 1977, *8,* 169–171.

Vanderwolf, C. Limbic-diencephalic mechanisms of voluntary movement. *Psychological Review,* 1971, *78,* 83–113.

Venables, P. H., & Christie, M. J. (Eds.), *Research in psychophysiology.* New York: Wiley, 1975.

Waters, W. The epidemiological enigma of migraine. *International Journal of Epidemiology*, 1973, *2*, 189–194.

Weinstock, S. A tentative procedure for the control of pain: Migraine and tension headaches. In D. Shapiro, T. Barber, L. DiCara, J. Kamiya, N. Miller, & J. Stoyva (Eds.), *Biofeedback and self-control, 1972*. Chicago: Aldine, 1973.

Weiss, R. M. The relative efficacy of relaxation training and autogenic-feedback training in the modification of cold-pressor pain and headache pain. *Dissertation Abstracts International*, 1974, *35*, 1421B.

Welgan, P. R. Learned control of gastric acid secretions in ulcer patients. *Psychosomatic Medicine*, 1974, *36*, 411–419.

Whatmore, G. B., & Kohli, D. R. Dysponesis: A neurophysiologic factor in functional disorders. *Behavioral Sciences*, 1968, *13*, 102–124.

Wickramasekera, I. Temperature feedback for the control of migraine. *Journal of Behavior Therapy and Experimental Psychiatry*, 1973, *4*, 343–345.

Wickramasekera, I. Electromyographic feedback training and tension headache: Preliminary observations. In I. Wickramasekera (Ed.), *Biofeedback, behavior therapy and hypnosis*. Chicago: Nelson-Hall, 1976, 23–28. (a)

Wickramasekera, I. The applicaton of verbal instructions and EMG feedback training to the management of tension headache: Preliminary observations. In I. Wickramasekera (Eds.), *Biofeedback, behavior therapy and hypnosis*. Chicago: Nelson-Hall, 1976, 29–33. (b)

Wickramasekera, I., Truang, X. T., Bush, M., & Orr, C. The management of rheumatoid arthritic pain: Preliminary observations. In I. Wickramasekera (Ed.), *Biofeedback, behavior therapy and hypnosis*. Chicago: Nelson–Hall, 1976, 47–55. (c)

York, D. Voluntary control of vasodilation (handwarming) by migraine and non-migraine subjects with autogenic feedback training. *Dissertations Abstracts International*, 1975, *35*(8-B), 4206B. (Abstract)

Zamani, R. *Treatment of migraine headache through operant conditioning of vasoconstriction*. Ann Arbor: University Microfilms, 1974.

Zborowski, M. *People in pain*. San Francisco: Jossey-Bass, 1969.

Ziegler, D., Hassanein, R., & Hassanein, K. Headache syndromes suggested by factor analysis of symptom variables on a headache prone population. *Journal of Chronic Diseases*, 1972, *25*, 353–363.

OVERVIEW

RICHARD W. J. NEUFELD

The preceding contributions have presented varying mixtures of original data and have emphasized the contributor's own work or evaluations and reviews of the work of others. Regardless of the approach, each contribution presents some potentially important outstanding issues. Even though initial efforts at a simple taxonomy seemed premature because the number of necessary qualifications for such a taxonomy quickly offset any early promise of parsimony, this chapter enumerates some of the outstanding issues.

Spring has emphasized the distinction between two parameters of periodic occurrences of "florid schizophrenic symptomatology": (1) their collective presence or absence, and (2) their distribution over time in relation to "stressing events." Implicit in this division is that a set of factors closely associated with (1) may be quite different from a set closely associated with (2). Two of the more intractable components of unbiased estimates of relations between stress on the one hand and both "proneness" (1) and "episodic" (2) aspects of symptomatology on the other, include delineating the degree to which the examined stressors occur in an independent fashion rather than resulting from the very behavioral anomalies under study and pinpointing the exact onset of (periods of) symptomatology.

Shean has observed that convergent evidence from work on cognition and emotion in schizophrenia suggests that at least two subclassifications—paranoid versus non-paranoid-process schizophrenia—may differ in their patterns of response to stressing demands associated with emotional experience and expression. As Shean noted, the proposed distinctions are tentative at present; for example, some of the supporting data consists of post-hoc observations secondary to initial experimental purposes. While currently provocative, the formulation requires further systematic investigation for consolidation and/or appropriate modification.

The chapter by Buehring et al. demonstrates a clever use of multivariate path analysis to plot the strength and tentative directions of several types of developmental incidents which may increase the probability of illness among samples already at risk. In their interpretations of this data the authors take care to note the viability of alternate viewpoints. A stimulating line of future study may be the analysis of the seemingly more critical incidents for factors which may feed on the autonomic over-reactivity and quick recovery thought to generate patterns of cognitive avoidance among these patients.

Costello has dealt with the major issues surrounding the concept of "loss as a source of stress in psychopathology." Similar to Spring's treatment of the distinctions between stress as a precipitant versus an agent of vulnerability to schizophrenic symptomatology, Costello has discussed issues surrounding "significant loss" as a provoker versus an agent of susceptibility to both stress and symptoms of depression. His evaluation of relevant studies underscores several factors which tend to limit available inferences in this area of research. Some of the more prominent of these factors include practical constraints in data acquisition (e.g., limits in patient sample sizes necessary for adequate statistical analyses, hurdles in accurately measuring relevant variables among patient samples, and so on), difficulties raised by the viability of multiple interpretations of given data sets, as well as the frequent restrictions on generalizations, even from those portions of results which are relatively less equivocal than others. Despite the intuitive appeal of the concept of "loss as a source of stress and psychopathology," gaps in empirical evidence leave several basic issues outstanding (enumerated at the end of his chapter). Because critical analysis shows data to be overinferred frequently, these gaps tend to be larger than they often appear to be at first blush according to the investigators' claims.

Shaw has mentioned the need to ferret out those aspects of the cognitive framework associated with depression which are unique relative to other disorders and to identify differential correlates among depressive subtypes. As Costello notes in his chapter, when base rates of certain stressing events (i.e., their preponderance among the population at large) are taken into account, less than 10% become clinically depressed. Hence, Shaw underscores, among other issues, the need to examine whether specific types of stressors and/or coping inabilities are linked to clinical depression.

In Miller and Seligman's chapter, data on nonpatient depressed subjects are presented which are compatible with the stance that certain patterns of interpreting personal experiences are predisposing toward depression. However, Miller and Seligman recurrently echo the importance of additional investigations of causality throughout their chapter. Particularly informative in this regard should be future studies of treatment manipulations among depressed patients designed to reverse hypothesized adverse patterns of personal interpretations.

Anisman and Lapierre point out the difficulties in generalizing certain findings across different types of experimental stressors and the inevitable hurdles in applying physiological and cognitive findings from animals to humans. The notion of transference of "load-on coping" from one system—overt behavioral—to another—physiological, involving amine depletion and synthesis—has been put forth. Whether such transference is simply a case in point of "cognizance of available behavioral escapes" lightening the subjective and consequent physiological impact of otherwise potent events, or some other set of mechanisms, may be clarified in future work.

Lazarus, Coyne, and Folkman have applied a somewhat "global" perspective to their analysis of conceptual orientation and research techniques involved in psychopathological aspects of stress. They have noted the frequent conceptual dissociation among cognition, emotion, and motivation perhaps necessary for the facilitation of experimental research. Unfortunately, the other constructs tend to be "ignored" while the investigator is studying one of them. This conceptual isolation is often not mended before generalizing inferences beyond the immediate research context. These authors have underscored the need for some compensating regard to the interrelatedness among those constructs in the individual as "thinker and emotional responder," rather than "passive endurer of the interplay of these constructs."

In Neufeld's formulation of decisional-theoretical components of psychopathology, the semi-independent dimensions of (1) propensity toward counterstress activity and (2) stress arousal await more formal investigation. Empirical relations are apt to be somewhat more complex than those stated. The more promising empirical questions seem to involve the interplay between these two dimensions and the empirical antecedants of the decisional components said to underlie them.

Essman's chapter makes it clear that the multiplicity of variables active in the relationship between psychopharmacological agents and stress response is further complicated by the morphology of these relations which is, as often as not, "exponential" in nature.

The psychological treatment of "stress inoculation" has thus far proven to be clinically appealing and to have promising preliminary data. However, Meichenbaum and Turk underscore the need for considerable further documentation of significant effects; undoubtedly, assessment of this already relatively popular technique will include further considerations of whether its effects are of clinically meaningful magnitude.

Jessup's review of the biofeedback literature on pain leads him to conclude that that area is so fraught with inadequacies in rationale and in methodology that incidental aspects of these procedures (such as various aspects of the treatment milieu) rather than their advertised effects command principal interest.

In conclusion, it can be said that, as in most areas of psychopathology, it is not difficult to find numerous instances where clinically disturbed individuals fare less well than others. As we progress in this research domain, it will become essential to catalogue our findings in terms of the comparative *degrees* of contribution to psychopathology of the examined variables as these variables are considered both in isolation and in interaction with each other.

Name Index

Subject Index